WITHDRAWN

PRINCIPLES
OF ARITHMETIC

PRINCIPLES

OF ARITHMETIC

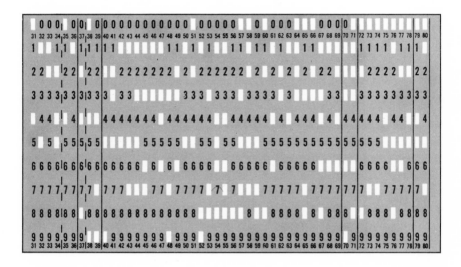

CHARLES F. BRUMFIEL, *The University of Michigan*

ROBERT E. EICHOLZ, *Ball State Teachers College, Burris Laboratory School*

MERRILL E. SHANKS, *Purdue University*

P. G. O'DAFFER, *Ball State Teachers College, Burris Laboratory School*

ADDISON-WESLEY PUBLISHING COMPANY, INC.
READING, MASSACHUSETTS · PALO ALTO · LONDON

Preface

This is primarily a text in arithmetic. It is especially appropriate for students who plan to teach mathematics in elementary schools, but who did not have strong mathematical training in high school. However, it can be used with any students whose mathematical backgrounds are insufficient for a college algebra course and who desire a solid mastery of basic arithmetic concepts.

The fundamental properties of addition and multiplication, the commutative, associative, and distributive laws, are introduced at an early stage and used consistently to present systematic explanations of the algorithms used in computing with whole numbers and rational numbers. No algebraic skill is presupposed, but from the very beginning some of the symbolism of algebra is introduced. Quite a bit of intuitive algebra is developed.

Many of the exercises call for relatively little computation but for a great deal of reasoning. We emphasize that the text is written with the expectation that it be carefully studied by the student. Clear definitions are formulated and used. The chapters on percent and ratio exemplify this fact. The teacher will find that students who read the text with care will be stimulated to raise many questions that will lead to valuable classroom discussion.

The principal objective of the book is to describe concisely the structure of the rational number system and to present many of the important applications of arithmetic. A secondary objective is to convey to the student an appreciation of the cultural significance of mathematics.

A unit on numeration systems in bases other than ten is included. There is a chapter on elementary concepts of logic. This chapter is followed by a careful development of the arithmetic of the integers. Informal proofs are presented, establishing computational techniques for addition, subtraction, multiplication, and division of integers. Two chapters on geometry contrast the characteristics of mathematical geometry with the geometry of the physical world. The treatment is informal, but the process of abstraction

v

by which the axioms of mathematical geometry are drawn from our physical environment is discussed with some care. A chapter on elementary aspects of probability introduces the concept of a sample space for an experiment.

An Appendix is included on the use of the slide rule. In many chapters sections on Recreational Math are included. These contain stimulating puzzle problems, elementary topics of number theory, geometry paradoxes, and interesting number properties.

The student who has experienced frustration in his elementary school and high school mathematics courses because he has approached mathematics as a body of unrelated facts to be memorized will find in this book an opportunity to place his knowledge of arithmetic upon a firm basis. At the same time he should acquire enough mathematical maturity to enable him to continue the study of mathematics if he desires to do so.

C.F.B., R.E.E., M.E.S., P.G.O.

Contents

1 SYMBOLS FOR NUMBERS

  1. Introduction   1
  2. New symbols for old numbers   1
  3. Our own numeration system   4

2 COUNTING

  1. Introduction   9
  2. The use of counting to add and subtract   12
  3. The number line   14
  4. Recreational math   19

3 PROPERTIES OF ADDITION AND SUBTRACTION OF WHOLE NUMBERS

  1. Introduction   20
  2. Using sets in addition and subtraction   22
  3. Properties of zero   24
  4. The commutative property of addition   25
  5. The associative property of addition   26
  6. Relationships between addition and subtraction . . .   29
  7. Using equations to solve problems   31

4 PROPERTIES OF MULTIPLICATION AND DIVISION OF WHOLE NUMBERS

  1. Introduction   33
  2. Using sets in multiplication and division   35
  3. Properties of 0 and 1   39
  4. The commutative property of multiplication   42
  5. The associative property of multiplication   43
  6. The distributive property   46
  7. Relationships between multiplication and division . .   50

8. Multiplication and division on the number line . . . 52
9. Recreational math 53

5   TECHNIQUES OF ADDITION AND SUBTRACTION

1. Introduction 61
2. The basic facts of addition 61
3. Using the properties of addition and subtraction . . . 65
4. Recreational math 71

6   TECHNIQUES OF MULTIPLICATION AND DIVISION

1. Introduction 75
2. The basic facts of multiplication 75
3. Using the properties in multiplication and division . . 80
4. Developing skill in multiplication and division . . . 82
5. Division with a remainder 87
6. Recreational math 89

7   PROBLEM SOLVING

1. Introduction 94
2. Avoiding careless mistakes 96
3. Drawing diagrams in problem solving 97
4. Recognizing needed information 100
5. Using common sense—estimating 101
6. Problem solving 103

8   LOGICAL REASONING

1. Introduction 107
2. Drawing conclusions 108
3. Establishing proofs 111
4. Logic 113
5. Recreational math 119

9   A NEW SET OF NUMBERS

1. Introduction 122
2. The set of integers 123
3. Addition of integers 124
4. Subtraction of integers 127
5. The number line 129
6. Multiplication and division of integers 132
7. Recreational math 137

10   ADDITION AND MULTIPLICATION OF RATIONAL NUMBERS

1. Introduction 139
2. Getting rational numbers from the world 140
3. The rational number line 145
4. Techniques of addition and multiplication 150
5. Reducing fractions and choosing common denominators 163
6. Using the basic properties 172
7. Recreational math 175

11   SUBTRACTION AND DIVISION OF RATIONAL NUMBERS

1. Introduction 180
2. Techniques for subtraction and division 184
3. The numbers 0 and 1 in division 192
4. Picturing division on the number line 194
5. Recreational math 197

12   PROBLEM SOLVING USING RATIONAL NUMBERS 205

13   DECIMAL NOTATION

1. Introduction: the need for decimal notation 211
2. Understanding decimal notation 212
3. Addition and subtraction by means of decimal notation 218
4. Multiplication and division by means of decimal notation 221
5. Converting fractions to decimals 230
6. Scientific notation 233

14   PERCENT NOTATION

1. Introduction 237
2. Using percent notation 238
3. Using percent in estimating 242
4. Relations between fraction, decimal, and percent notations 245
5. Problem solving 248

15   APPLICATIONS OF RATIONAL NUMBERS

1. Introduction 254
2. Measurement of length 254
3. Measurement of time 259
4. Measurement of weights and volumes 259
5. Measurement of temperatures 262

6. Interest 264
7. Taxes 266
8. Arithmetic in business 268
9. Insurance 269
10. Approximate measurement 271

16 INTRODUCTION TO GEOMETRY

1. Introduction 273
2. Imaginary world of geometry 273
3. Plane figures 281
4. Space figures 287
5. Recreational math 292

17 MEASUREMENT

1. Introduction 297
2. Measuring segments 297
3. Measuring the circumference 301
4. Measuring areas of regions 305
5. Measuring volumes of regions in space 316
6. Measuring angles 319
7. Recreational math 327

18 RATIO AND PROPORTION

1. Introduction: ratio in geometry 330
2. Using the language of ratio to compare sets 335
3. Problem solving by means of the language of ratio . . 338
4. Ratio and percent 341
5. Ratio and proportion in science 345
6. How the ideas of ratio and proportion led to the invention of new numbers 348

19 PROBABILITY

1. Introduction 350
2. Sample spaces 352

APPENDIX. THE SLIDE RULE

1. Introduction 361
2. Reading the scale 362
3. Multiplication 363
4. Division 367

INDEX 371

Chapter 1

SYMBOLS
FOR NUMBERS

1. INTRODUCTION

In this chapter we shall study the symbols used for numbers. A mark (or symbol) for a number is called a *numeral*. The special numerals that we use are only a few hundred years old. Today we write the numeral 10 to represent the number of fingers on a man's two hands. The Romans and most people of medieval Europe wrote the numeral X. Egyptian scribes wrote the numeral ∩. In ancient Babylon the symbol ⟨ was used. The Greek mathematicians wrote ι (the letter iota of their alphabet) (Fig. 1–1).

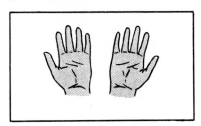

10; *X*; ∩; ⟨; ι

FIGURE 1–1

Of course, men today have the same number of fingers that men had 10,000 years ago. *Numbers* do not change, but we may use many different symbols for one number. After studying this chapter you should realize how much your skill in arithmetic depends upon understanding the symbols that we write for numbers.

2. NEW SYMBOLS FOR OLD NUMBERS

If people are living on planets in solar systems other than our own, it is quite unlikely that the symbols they use for numbers are the same as our symbols. Let us invent an imaginary planet, Nova, upon

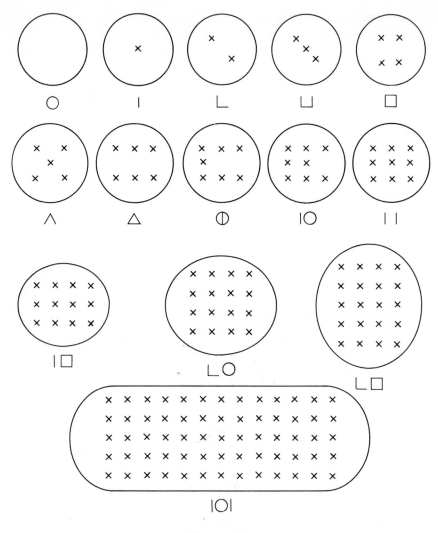

FIGURE 1–2

which an advanced civilization has developed . Figure 1–2 shows some
of the marks that the inhabitants of Nova use to indicate how many
objects are in certain sets.

EXERCISES

1. Work the addition problems.
   (a) □ + L =   (b) □ + □ =   (c) △ + ○ =
   (d) ① + ⊔ =   (e) △ + ⊔ =   (f) |○ + |○ =

(g) $\triangle + \triangle =$ (h) $① + \wedge =$ (i) $|\triangle + \triangle =$
(j) $\triangle + |\triangle =$ (k) $① + \mathsf{L} =$ (l) $\mathsf{L} + ① =$

2. Work the subtraction problems.

(a) $\triangle - \mathsf{L} =$ (b) $|\mathsf{O} - \square =$ (c) $\triangle - \mathsf{O} =$
(d) $|\mathsf{L} - \mathsf{U} =$ (e) $|| - \mathsf{U} =$ (f) $\mathsf{LO} - |\mathsf{O} =$
(g) $|\square - \triangle =$ (h) $|\square - \wedge =$ (i) $\mathsf{L}\square - \triangle =$

3. Multiply.

(a) $\mathsf{L} \times \mathsf{U} =$ (b) $| \times | =$ (c) $\mathsf{O} \times \square =$
(d) $\mathsf{U} \times \square =$ (e) $\square \times \mathsf{U} =$ (f) $\wedge \times \square =$
(g) $\square \times \wedge =$ (h) $\mathsf{L} \times |\mathsf{O} =$ (i) $|\mathsf{O} \times \mathsf{L} =$

4. Divide.

(a) $\triangle \div \mathsf{U} =$ (b) $| \div | =$ (c) $\mathsf{O} \div \square =$
(d) $|\square \div \square =$ (e) $|\square \div \mathsf{U} =$ (f) $\mathsf{L}\square \div \square =$
(g) $\mathsf{L}\square \div \wedge =$ (h) $\mathsf{U}\mathsf{O} \div |\square =$ (i) $\mathsf{U}\mathsf{O} \div \mathsf{L} =$

5. Work the following problems.

(a) $(\square + \triangle) + \mathsf{L}$ (b) $\square + (\triangle + \mathsf{L})$
(c) $(|| + \triangle) + \wedge$ (d) $|| + (\triangle + \wedge)$
(e) $(\mathsf{L} \times \mathsf{U}) \times \square$ (f) $\mathsf{L} \times (\mathsf{U} \times \square)$
(g) $(\square \times \wedge) \div \wedge$ (h) $(\triangle \times \mathsf{L}) \div \mathsf{L}$

6. Work as indicated.

(a) $(\mathsf{L}\mathsf{O} - ①) - \mathsf{U}$ (b) $\mathsf{L}\mathsf{O} - (① - \mathsf{U})$
(c) $(\mathsf{L}\mathsf{O} \div |\mathsf{O}) \div \mathsf{L}$ (d) $\mathsf{L}\mathsf{O} \div (|\mathsf{O} \div \mathsf{L})$

7. In the following addition problems with their solutions, one answer is incorrect. Which one is it?

(a) LO (b) $\mathsf{U}|$ (c) $\square\mathsf{O}$
  $\underline{\mathsf{LO}}$ $\underline{\mathsf{L}\square}$ $\underline{\square\mathsf{O}}$
  $\square\mathsf{O}$ $\wedge\wedge$ $|\mathsf{O}\mathsf{O}$

  (d) $\triangle\mathsf{O}$ (e) $①\mathsf{L}$
    $\underline{\square\mathsf{O}}$ $\underline{\square|}$
    $||\mathsf{O}$ $|\mathsf{U}\mathsf{U}$

8. One of the answers to the subtraction problems below is incorrect. Which one?

(a) $\square\square$ (b) $|\mathsf{O}\mathsf{O}$ (c) $①\mathsf{U}$ (d) $\square\mathsf{O}\mathsf{O}$
  $\underline{|\wedge}$ $\underline{\wedge\wedge}$ $\underline{\square\triangle}$ $\underline{\mathsf{L}\square\square}$
  $\mathsf{L}①$ $\mathsf{L}\mathsf{U}$ $\mathsf{L}①$ $|\mathsf{U}\square$

9. Work the addition problems.

   (a) ∟ | (b) □ □   (c) □ □   (d) △ △
       ∟ □   ∐ ∐   □ □   ∐ ∐

10. Subtract.

   (a) ①□   (b) □ ○   (c) | ○ ○   (d) ∟ ○ ○
       □ ∐   ∐ □   ① ①   □ ①

11. Use the new numerals to write the numbers from (a) fourteen to twenty-nine, (b) sixty to seventy.

12. How many fingers do you think the imaginary people on Nova might have on each hand?

3. OUR OWN NUMERATION SYSTEM*

The strange system of numerals described in the last section has the same important properties that make our own system so convenient. Students on this faraway planet would learn their addition and multiplication tables more easily than students on earth learn their tables. They would work their problems in arithmetic at about the same speed that we work our exercises.

Our numeration system is based upon *ten* and uses the important idea of *place value*. As you will have recognized, the inhabitants of Nova group by *eights* rather than by tens, but they use the same ideas of place value that we use. The charts in Fig. 1–3 compare the two systems.

When we say that our system has ten for its *base*, we mean that we group repeatedly by tens. When we say that a system uses the idea of *place value*, we mean that depending upon its position in a numeral, a digit can represent groups of one, groups the size of the base, groups the size of the base times the base, etc. In our system the numeral

$$2222$$

is an abbreviation for

$$(2 \times 10 \times 10 \times 10) + (2 \times 10 \times 10) + (2 \times 10) + (2 \times 1)$$

These four digits "2" stand for two *thousands*, two *hundreds*, two *tens*, two *ones*.

---

* A numeration system is a set of symbols and the rules for using these symbols to write numbers.

	EARTH'S SYSTEM:									
zero	one	two	three	four	five	six	seven	eight	nine	ten ...
0	1	2	3	4	5	6	7	8	9	10 ...

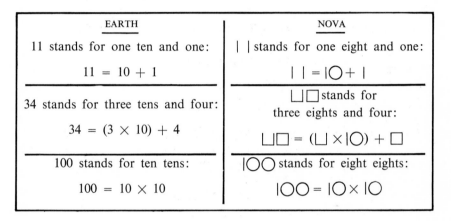

(a)

(b)

FIG. 1–3. Comparison of two numeration systems.   (a) Counting in both systems. (b) Place value in both systems.

EXERCISES

1. Write the usual numeral for each number.

    (a) $300 + 50 + 7$

    (b) $5000 + 400 + 30 + 2$

    (c) $800 + 70 + 9$

    (d) $60{,}000 + 4000 + 300 + 20 + 5$

    (e) $(3 \times 10 \times 10) + (7 \times 10) + 2$

    (f) $(5 \times 10 \times 10) + 9$

    (g) $(1 \times 10 \times 10) + (1 \times 10) + 1$

    (h) $(7 \times 10 \times 10) + (7 \times 10) + 7$

    (i) $(4 \times 10 \times 10 \times 10) + (5 \times 10 \times 10) + (6 \times 10) + (7 \times 1)$

(j) $(9 \times 10 \times 10 \times 10) + (9 \times 10) + 9$
(k) $(6 \times 10 \times 10 \times 10) + (3 \times 10 \times 10) + 1$
(l) $(8 \times 10 \times 10 \times 10) + 8$
(m) $(3 \times 10 \times 10 \times 10 \times 10) + (4 \times 10 \times 10 \times 10) +$
     $(5 \times 10 \times 10) + (6 \times 10) + 7$
(n) $(6 \times 10 \times 10 \times 10 \times 10 \times 10) + (9 \times 10 \times 10) + (4 \times 10)$
(o) $(4 \times 10 \times 10 \times 10 \times 10 \times 10 \times 10) +$
     $(7 \times 10 \times 10 \times 10) + 3$

2. Write expanded numerals, as in Exercise 1, for the following numbers.

(a) 524   (b) 302   (c) 5003
(d) 4070   (e) 5500   (f) 73,000
(g) 90,909   (h) 40,600   (i) 380,004
(j) 500,500   (k) 4,300,001   (l) 5,050,505

3. Read the following numbers in the usual way.

(a) $(4 \times 10 \times 10) + (7 \times 10) + 1$
(b) $(6 \times 10 \times 10) + (9 \times 10)$
(c) $(3 \times 10 \times 10) + 6$
(d) $(2 \times 10 \times 10 \times 10) + (7 \times 10 \times 10) + (6 \times 10) + 2$
(e) $(5 \times 10 \times 10 \times 10) + (6 \times 10 \times 10) + 8$
(f) $(7 \times 10 \times 10 \times 10) + (4 \times 10) + 5$
(g) $(6 \times 10 \times 10 \times 10) + 7$
(h) $(3 \times 10 \times 10 \times 10) + (5 \times 10 \times 10)$
(i) $(8 \times 10 \times 10 \times 10) + (3 \times 10)$
(j) $(3 \times 10 \times 10 \times 10) + (0 \times 10 \times 10) + (0 \times 10) + (0 \times 1)$
(k) $(5 \times 10 \times 10 \times 10 \times 10) + (2 \times 10 \times 10 \times 10) +$
     $(7 \times 10 \times 10) + (6 \times 10) + 3$
(l) $(9 \times 10 \times 10 \times 10 \times 10) + (7 \times 10 \times 10 \times 10) +$
     $(2 \times 10 \times 10) + 7$
(m) $(6 \times 10 \times 10 \times 10 \times 10) + (6 \times 10 \times 10) + (6 \times 10) + 6$
(n) $(3 \times 10 \times 10 \times 10 \times 10) + (5 \times 10 \times 10 \times 10) + 9$
(o) $(5 \times 10 \times 10 \times 10 \times 10) + 7$
(p) $(3 \times 10 \times 10 \times 10 \times 10) + (4 \times 10 \times 10)$
(q) $(2 \times 10 \times 10 \times 10 \times 10) + (6 \times 10 \times 10 \times 10) + (9 \times 10)$
(r) $(8 \times 10 \times 10 \times 10 \times 10) + (5 \times 10 \times 10) + 7$
(s) $(7 \times 10 \times 10 \times 10 \times 10 \times 10) +$
     $(4 \times 10 \times 10 \times 10 \times 10) +$
     $(6 \times 10 \times 10 \times 10) + (3 \times 10 \times 10) + (9 \times 10) + 2$
(t) $5 + (7 \times 10) + (3 \times 10 \times 10)$
(u) $6 + (3 \times 10) + (4 \times 10 \times 10) + (1 \times 10 \times 10 \times 10)$
(v) $(3 \times 10 \times 10) + 5 + (2 \times 10 \times 10 \times 10)$

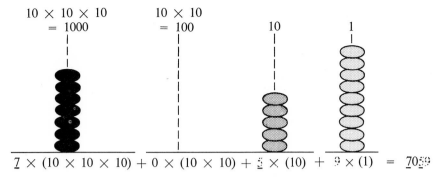

$$\underline{7} \times (10 \times 10 \times 10) + 0 \times (10 \times 10) + \underline{5} \times (10) + 9 \times (1) = \underline{7}0\underline{59}$$

Illustrating *place value* with colored beads

(w) $(6 \times 10 \times 10) + (2 \times 10) + 7 + (1 \times 10 \times 10 \times 10)$

(x) $(3 \times 10 \times 10 \times 10 \times 10 \times 10) +$
     $(5 \times 10 \times 10 \times 10 \times 10) +$
     $(2 \times 10 \times 10 \times 10 \times 10) + (7 \times 10 \times 10 \times 10) +$
     $(2 \times 10 \times 10) + (4 \times 10) + 8$

(y) $(8 \times 10 \times 10 \times 10 \times 10 \times 10 \times 10) +$
     $(4 \times 10 \times 10 \times 10) + 9$

(z) $(3 \times 10) + (7 \times 10 \times 10 \times 10 \times 10) +$
     $(5 \times 10 \times 10 \times 10 \times 10 \times 10 \times 10)$

4. Write the usual symbols for the following sums and differences.

    (a) $(3 \times 10 \times 10) + (5 \times 10 \times 10)$
    (b) $(4 \times 10) + (2 \times 10)$
    (c) $(5 \times 10 \times 10 \times 10) + (3 \times 10 \times 10 \times 10)$
    (d) $(7 \times 10 \times 10) - (4 \times 10 \times 10)$
    (e) $(9 \times 10) - (6 \times 10)$
    (f) $(8 \times 10 \times 10 \times 10) + (2 \times 10 \times 10 \times 10)$
    (g) $(1 \times 10 \times 10 \times 10 \times 10) - (6 \times 10 \times 10 \times 10)$
    (h) $(8 \times 10 \times 10 \times 10) - (8 \times 10 \times 10)$

5. Write simpler expanded numerals for the sums and differences.

    (a) $(7 \times 10) - (3 \times 10)$
    (b) $(9 \times 10 \times 10) - (2 \times 10 \times 10)$
    (c) $(5 \times 10 \times 10) + (3 \times 10 \times 10)$
    (d) $(4 \times 10 \times 10) + (6 \times 10 \times 10)$
    (e) $(10 \times 10) - (3 \times 10)$
    (f) $(10 \times 10 \times 10) - (4 \times 10 \times 10)$
    (g) $(2 \times 10 \times 10) + (6 \times 10) + (4 \times 10)$
    (h) $(3 \times 10 \times 10) + (9 \times 10 \times 10)$

6. Give the products orally.

(a) $3 \times (2 \times 10)$ (b) $4 \times (2 \times 10)$
(c) $5 \times (3 \times 10)$ (d) $(3 \times 10) \times 6$
(e) $5 \times (2 \times 10)$ (f) $(2 \times 10) \times (3 \times 10)$
(g) $(4 \times 10) \times (2 \times 10)$ (h) $(4 \times 10) \times (3 \times 10)$
(i) $(2 \times 10) \times (5 \times 10)$ (j) $3 \times (2 \times 10 \times 10)$
(k) $(4 \times 10 \times 10) \times 2$ (l) $(3 \times 10 \times 10) \times 5$
(m) $(6 \times 10) \times (7 \times 10)$ (n) $(8 \times 10) \times (10 \times 10)$

(o) $(3 \times 10 \times 10) \times (2 \times 10)$
(p) $(5 \times 10) \times (2 \times 10 \times 10)$
(q) $(5 \times 10 \times 10) \times (8 \times 10)$
(r) $(9 \times 10) \times (7 \times 10 \times 10)$
(s) $(2 \times 10 \times 10) \times (4 \times 10 \times 10)$
(t) $(3 \times 10 \times 10) \times (3 \times 10 \times 10)$
(u) $(5 \times 10 \times 10) \times (2 \times 10 \times 10)$
(v) $(9 \times 10 \times 10) \times (9 \times 10 \times 10)$
(w) $(3 \times 10) \times (2 \times 10 \times 10 \times 10)$
(x) $(5 \times 10 \times 10 \times 10) \times (4 \times 10)$
(y) $(6 \times 10 \times 10 \times 10) \times (2 \times 10 \times 10 \times 10)$
(z) $(8 \times 10 \times 10) \times (2 \times 10 \times 10 \times 10 \times 10)$

7. Write the following products.

(a) 4×20 (b) 3×40 (c) 50×4 (d) 30×20
(e) 20×50 (f) 50×80 (g) 3×200 (h) 5×200
(i) 500×8 (j) 200×30 (k) 20×400 (l) 500×20
(m) 600×40 (n) 200×300 (o) 500×200 (p) 400×800
(q) 30×2000 (r) 500×2000

Chapter 2

COUNTING

1. INTRODUCTION

A young child who could "count" had before him five pieces of candy. He counted them, touching each one as he said, "one," "two," "three," "four," "five." Then he picked up two of the pieces and ate them. His father thought he would teach the child a little arithmetic and said, "You had five pieces of candy and ate two. How many are left?"

The child gave his father a puzzled look and answered earnestly, "I didn't eat *two*. I ate *one* and *four*. It's *two*, *three*, and *five* that are left."

How would you try to help a small child understand what it means to count? When were *you* first able to count with understanding? Many students in kindergarten can say "one," "two," ..., "ten," but some of them say this just as they might recite anything they have memorized without really understanding the meaning of the words. In this chapter we will take a fresh look at counting. Our main purpose is to study the relationships between counting and addition and subtraction.

Each number name, as for example the word "ten," stands for an idea that we associate, say, with the set of fingers on our two hands, with a set of basketball players on a playing floor, and with many other sets. Some of these sets are pictured in Fig. 2–1.

When a child learns to count with understanding he has, first of all, learned a great many *definitions*. He has learned that the property common to all sets like those shown in Fig. 2–2 is named by the word "one." When he sees the word "one," he thinks about sets such as these. We say that the child has learned the *definition* of "one."

By placing one more object in each of the sets of one, sets are formed which have in common the property named by the word "two" (Fig. 2–3).

The symbols "one" and "two" are numerals. A number is an *idea*. A numeral is a *name*. We *write* numerals on paper. We *think* about numbers.

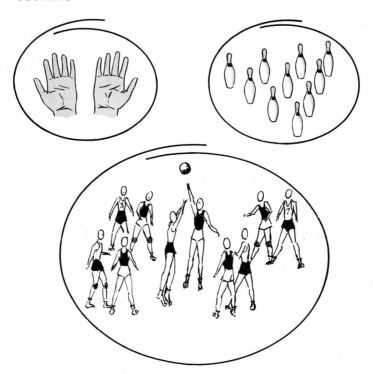

FIGURE 2–1

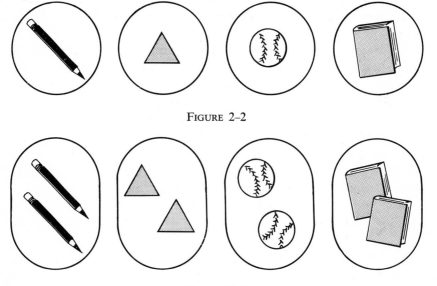

FIGURE 2–2

FIGURE 2–3

The first step in learning to count is to learn each new number name as, one by one, new elements are placed in our sets.

> One and one are *two*
> Two and one are *three*
> Three and one are *four*
> Four and one are *five*
> Five and one are *six*
> Six and one are *seven*
> Seven and one are *eight*
>   etc.

Basic definitions of arithmetic

Once the meaning of the words "one," "two," "three," "four," "five," "six," "seven," "eight," etc., is understood and the order is memorized, then we can count the number of things in the set in Fig. 2–4 by saying, as we touch them in turn, "one," "two," "three," "four."

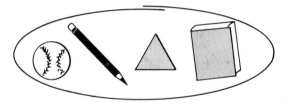

FIGURE 2–4

Since we end with the word "four," we know that the set we are counting belongs with sets like the ones illustrated in Fig. 2–5. The property (number) that these sets have in common is named by the word "four."

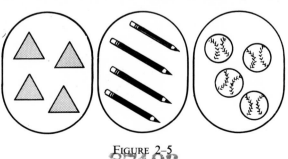

FIGURE 2–5

EXERCISES

Give the number of objects in each set described below if you can determine this number by counting.

1. The set of stars in the Great Dipper.
2. The set of whole numbers larger than 8 and smaller than 23.
3. The set of pages in this chapter.
4. The set of hairs on your head.
5. The set whose members are the even numbers between 10 and 20.
6. The set consisting of the odd numbers less than 30 which are squares of odd numbers.
7. The set of different letters used in writing the word "Mississippi."
8. The set of whole numbers that are divisors of 24.
9. The set of whole numbers that are multiples of 24.
10. The set of blue buffalos which you own.
11. The set of stars in the Milky Way.

The property common to the set of Exercise 10 and the sets shown in Fig. 2–6 is named by the word "zero." When we count the number of objects in sets like these, we use the number 0. *Zero is an important number.* Properties of the number zero are of fundamental importance in the study of mathematics.

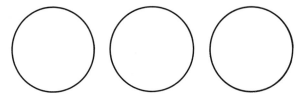

FIGURE 2–6

2. THE USE OF COUNTING TO ADD AND SUBTRACT

We can add 8 and 2 by beginning at 8 and counting forward 2. We can add 50 and 30 by beginning at 50 and counting forward 30 by tens: "sixty, seventy, eighty." We might subtract 34 from 87 by starting with 87, counting backward 30 by tens, and then counting backward 4 by twos: "seventy-seven, sixty-seven, fifty-seven, fifty-five, fifty-three."

In the exercises below, use these ideas of counting to work each problem.

EXERCISES

1. Give the usual word name for
   (a) ninety-nine and one,
   (b) nine hundred ninety-nine and one,
   (c) nine thousand nine hundred ninety-nine and one,
   (d) ninety-nine thousand nine hundred ninety-nine and one,
   (e) nine hundred ninety-nine thousand nine hundred ninety-nine and one.

2. Write the simplest Hindu-Arabic numeral for
   (a) 9 + 1   (b) 99 + 1   (c) 999 + 1
   (d) 9999 + 1   (e) 99,999 + 1   (f) 999,999 + 1
   (g) 9,999,999,999,999 + 1

3. Show how a child who knew very few addition facts, but who could count very well, could get answers quickly to the following problems.
   (a) 9 + 8   (b) 19 + 8   (c) 99 + 7
   (d) 99 + 42   (e) 199 + 8   (f) 199 + 27
   (g) 999 + 8   (h) 999 + 84   (i) 998 + 653

4. Count by tens from 83 to 123.
5. Count by hundreds from 857 to 1157.
6. Count by thousands from 3412 to 7412.
7. Count by fifties from 482 to 932.
8. Count backward by two hundreds from 4200 to 2800.
9. Begin with 285; count by hundreds to 585, then on by tens to 625, and then by ones to 631. Remembering how you counted, tell what must be added to 285 to make 631.
10. Begin with 712; count backward by hundreds to 412, then by tens to 382, and by ones to 377. Remembering how you counted, tell what must be subtracted from 712 to make 377.

As the exercises above point out, skill in counting does make it possible to add and subtract. A student might add 32 and 23 by thinking: "forty-two, fifty-two, fifty-three, fifty-four, fifty-five." He might subtract 31 from 70 by thinking: "sixty, fifty, forty, thirty-nine."

EXERCISES

1. Use counting to get answers to the following addition problems.
   (a) 33 + 21   (b) 42 + 56   (c) 58 + 53
   (d) 230 + 320   (e) 520 + 540   (f) 2300 + 4000
   (g) 142 + 63   (h) 224 + 350   (i) 342 + 230

2. Use counting to work the subtraction problems below.

(a) 57 − 23   (b) 80 − 31   (c) 93 − 56
(d) 100 − 64   (e) 400 − 246 (f) 1000 − 542
(g) 80 − 42   (h) 100 − 31   (i) 342 − 230

3. Explain each of the four methods used to work the addition problem below.

(a)	534	(b)	534	(c)	534	(d)	534
	247		247		247		247
	734		541		747		251
	774		581		777		281
	781		781		781		781

4. Explain each method used below in working the subtraction problem.

(a)	534	(b)	534
	247		247
	334		527
	294		487
	287		287

5. Exercises (3) and (4) show how a student who can count well might write out his work for addition and subtraction problems even though he has not learned about carrying or borrowing. Using one of the methods shown above, write out the solution to each problem below.

(a) 542 + 367   (b) 800 − 256   (c) 3456 + 2644
(d) 3000 − 1359

3. THE NUMBER LINE

It is helpful to think of numbers as points on a ray (Fig. 2–7). We call the set of numbers

$$\{0, 1, 2, 3, 4, \ldots\}$$

the set of *whole numbers*, and we call this set of points the *whole number line* or just *number line*. We imagine that this ray extends on forever to the right, so that there is a point for each whole number. Addition

FIGURE 2–7

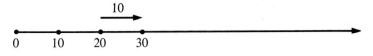

FIGURE 2–8

and subtraction are easily pictured on the number line. Addition may be pictured as "moving to the right," and subtraction as "moving to the left." Figure 2–8 pictures the addition fact, 20 + 10 = 30. Reversing the arrow, we have a picture (Fig. 2–9) of the subtraction statement, 30 − 10 = 20.

FIGURE 2–9

EXERCISES

For each drawing below tell what fact of arithmetic is pictured. Then imagine each arrow pointing in the opposite direction and state a second fact.

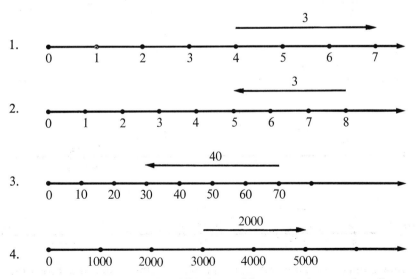

We can represent more difficult problems on the number line. In Fig. 2–10, we represent adding 243 to 536 by adding first the *hundreds*, then the *tens*, and finally the *ones*. If we reverse the arrows, the resulting diagram represents subtracting 243 from 779.

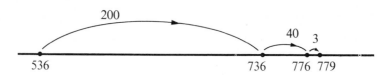

FIGURE 2–10

EXERCISES

1. Tell what addition fact is illustrated in each of the figures below. Then
think of the arrows as reversed and state the matching subtraction fact.

(a)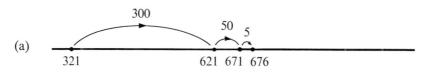

(b)

(c)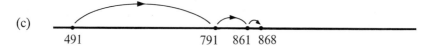

(d)

(e)

(f)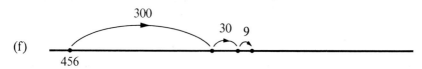

2. Draw number lines illustrating the problems below. Add or subtract the
hundreds, tens, and ones separately.

(a) $413 + 257 = 670$ (b) $670 - 257 = 413$
(c) $542 + 86 = 628$ (d) $628 - 86 = 542$
(e) $821 + 179 = 1000$ (f) $1000 - 179 = 821$

3. Thinking of a number line, decide where you must start so that

    (a) after adding 200 you are at 500;
    (b) after subtracting 300 you are at 400;
    (c) after adding 400 you are at 627;
    (d) after subtracting 300 you are at 655;
    (e) after adding 220 you are at 640;
    (f) after subtracting 330 you are at 420;
    (g) after adding 356 you are at 788;
    (h) after subtracting 239 you are at 475.

4. Think of the number line and decide where you will end if you begin at 50 and make the following additions and subtractions.

    (a) Add 74; subtract 74.   (b) Add 74; subtract 73.
    (c) Add 74; subtract 75.   (d) Add 60; subtract 50.
    (e) Add 60; subtract 70.   (f) Add 231; subtract 230.
    (g) Add 231; subtract 241.
    (h) Add 74; subtract 73; add 92; subtract 91.
    (i) Add 63; add 37; subtract 37; subtract 63.
    (j) Add 142; add 84; subtract 84; subtract 140.
    (k) Add 107; add 65; subtract 64; subtract 108.
    (l) Add 243; add 156; subtract 155; subtract 242.
    (m) Add 132; add 257; subtract 258; subtract 133.

5. Decide for each part of Exercise 3 whether you were working an addition problem or a subtraction problem.

We often must decide whether or not one number is larger than a second. Of course, if we could see the numbers marked on a number line, the decision would be easily made. From Fig. 2–11, we see that 28 is less than 47, and that 55 is greater than 47.

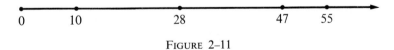

FIGURE 2–11

We use special symbols as abbreviations for "is less than" and "is greater than." These symbols are called symbols of *inequality:*

$$>\quad \text{means}\quad \textit{is greater than,}$$
$$<\quad \text{means}\quad \textit{is less than.}$$

For example, $37 > 15$ is read, "37 is greater than 15," and $0 < 1$ is read, "0 is less than 1."

EXERCISES

1. For each pair of numbers write a true statement, using an inequality symbol and stating that the first number is either greater than or less than the second.

   (a) 73, 75   (b) 39, 93   (c) 452, 442
   (d) 3574, 3534   (e) 8878, 8888   (f) 6491, 6492
   (g) 4672, 4592   (h) 1000, 999   (i) 0, 3

2. Write the symbols that should be placed in the spaces indicated below, to show whether the first sum is greater than, less than, or equal to the second.

   (a) $24 + 37 \bigcirc 25 + 37$ (b) $356 + 428 \bigcirc 355 + 429$
   (c) $62 + 93 \bigcirc 72 + 83$ (d) $249 + 356 \bigcirc 239 + 346$
   (e) $48 + 52 \bigcirc 41 + 62$ (f) $342 + 76 \bigcirc 442 + 66$
   (g) $487 + 352 \bigcirc 497 + 342$
   (h) $326 + 184 \bigcirc 366 + 284$
   (i) $3572 + 2854 \bigcirc 3571 + 2856$
   (j) $6941 + 7213 \bigcirc 6841 + 7513$

3. In each example below decide how much more the first sum is than the second.

   (a) $86 + 79; 76 + 79$ (b) $352 + 295; 352 + 195$
   (c) $342 + 564; 242 + 464$ (d) $85 + 73; 75 + 72$
   (e) $86 + 49; 76 + 39$ (f) $642 + 527; 542 + 517$
   (g) $642 + 527; 542 + 537$ (h) $862 + 415; 872 + 315$
   (i) $845 + 271; 745 + 261$ (j) $864 + 864; 764 + 884$
   (k) $6672 + 3594; 5672 + 3694$
   (l) $7143 + 4195; 7243 + 2195$

4. In each example below tell what must be added to one number to give the second. It may help if you visualize a number line.

   (a) 653; 693   (b) 721; 512   (c) 447; 497
   (d) 812; 662   (e) 703; 502   (f) 704; 505
   (g) 3246; 3846   (h) 5271; 4971   (i) 0; 865
   (j) 4137; 4187   (k) 3942; 5942   (l) 2653; 2763
   (m) 2653; 2743   (n) 4536; 3425   (o) 8000; 6999
   (p) 1000; 888   (q) 2000; 1890   (r) 3000; 2876
   (s) 10,000; 9000   (t) 10,000; 8800   (u) 10,000; 8850
   (v) 10,000; 8854   (w) 8700; 6500   (x) 8700; 6540
   (y) 8700; 6549   (z) 8762; 4358

4. RECREATIONAL MATH

There are many interesting counting games. One can be played with 13 counters laid out in a row:

Two persons play against each other. Each one must, at his turn to play, take one, two, or three counters. The player who is forced to remove the last counter loses the game.

Questions. If there are five counters left and it is your turn to play, will you win or will you lose? If there are seven counters left and it is your turn, how many should you take?

A second game much like this one is played as follows. The first player names a number from one to ten. The second thinks of a number from one to ten and adds it to the first number. He gives this sum. The first player now adds a number from one to ten to the second player's sum, and so on. The player who is forced to say 100, or to go past 100, loses the game. For example, the numbers given might be

$$7, 17, 26, 36, 44, 50, 60, 68, 75, 80, 90, 99, \ldots$$

Now, since it is the first player's turn, he loses.

Question. At the first player's last play he added 10 to 80, getting 90, and then he lost the game. What should he have added to 80 instead of 10 in order to win?

Both of these games can be played with variations. If in the first game two rows of counters are used and each player is permitted to take one, two, or three counters from just one of the two rows, then the game is more complicated.

Chapter 3

PROPERTIES
OF ADDITION
AND SUBTRACTION
OF WHOLE NUMBERS

1. INTRODUCTION

It is natural to think of addition and subtraction as things that we *do* to numbers. In this chapter we shall look upon addition and subtraction as abstract operations. We can think of all the addition facts as listed in a giant table (see Fig. 3–1). This table presents truths that do not depend upon what man has done in the past or will do in the future.

If the time ever comes when life in the universe is extinct, 3 stars and 2 stars will still be 5 stars.

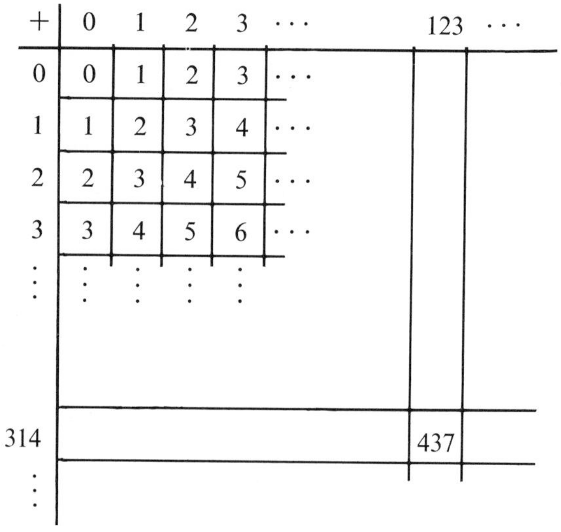

FIGURE 3–1

20

We refer to addition and subtraction of whole numbers as *operations*. In this chapter we shall study the properties of these operations. Some of these properties will seem so simple and obvious that you may wonder why we even bother to mention them. But, as we develop concepts systematically, you will see that knowledge of these properties is very useful.

Addition is an operation that combines a first number and a second number to give one number. We call the two numbers addends. We call the result the sum of the addends, or simply the sum.

When we add we think about two numbers, the *addends*, and de-determine their *sum*. We can think of addition as a machine. We feed into this machine a pair of numbers, a first number and a second number. The machine processes this pair of numbers and turns out one number (Fig. 3–2).

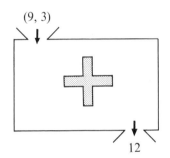
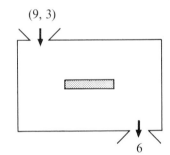

FIG. 3–2.   The addition machine. FIG. 3–3.   The subtraction machine.

Subtraction is an operation that combines a first number and a second number to give one number. The first number is the sum of the other two numbers.

When we subtract we think about two numbers, the first one a *sum* and the second an *addend*, and we determine the missing addend.

We can think of subtraction as a machine. We feed into this machine a pair of numbers, a *first* number and a *second* number. The machine processes this pair of numbers and turns out one number (Fig. 3–3).

You can feed *any* pair of numbers into the addition machine, but only certain pairs into the subtraction machine. If you feed the pair (10, 12) into the subtraction machine, the machine chokes up and refuses to operate (see Table 3–1).

TABLE 3–1

ADDITION AND SUBTRACTION AS OPERATIONS

Number pair	Operation	Result
(8, 4)	Addition	12
(8, 4)	Subtraction	4
(9, 9)	Addition	18
(9, 9)	Subtraction	0
(6, 12)	Addition	18
(6, 12)	Subtraction	The machine breaks down
(a, b)	Addition	$a + b$
(a, b)	Subtraction	$a - b$

EXERCISES

1. On each line in Table 3–1 point out the number that is the sum of the two addends. For each of the first five lines write the usual addition or subtraction statement.

2. Which of the following pairs of numbers are rejected by the subtraction machine?

    (a) (9, 6)   (b) (6, 9)   (c) (7, 0)   (d) (0, 7)
    (e) (10, 10)   (f) (0, 0)

3. If you feed the pair of numbers $(89 + 73, 73)$ into the subtraction machine, what is the result? What is the result if you feed in the pair $(a + b, b)$?

4. If you feed the pair of numbers $(98 - 14, 14)$ into the addition machine, what is the result? What is the result if you feed in the pair $(a - b, b)$?

5. If b is not zero and you feed the pair of numbers $(a - b, a)$ into the subtraction machine, what is the result?

2.   USING SETS IN ADDITION AND SUBTRACTION

The relationships between addition and subtraction are most clearly seen by visualizing sets of objects. In each addition problem, and in each subtraction problem, there are three sets to consider. Two of these sets are combined to form the third. When we know the number of things in each of the first two sets, we *add* to find the number of things in the third set. When we know the number of things in the

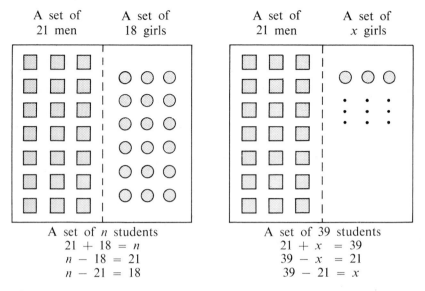

A set of 21 men   A set of 18 girls   A set of 21 men   A set of x girls

A set of n students
$$21 + 18 = n$$
$$n - 18 = 21$$
$$n - 21 = 18$$

A set of 39 students
$$21 + x = 39$$
$$39 - x = 21$$
$$39 - 21 = x$$

FIGURE 3–4

third set and also the number in one of the first two sets, we *subtract* to find the number of things in the other set. Addition facts and subtraction facts go together. Each addition fact gives us subtraction facts. Each subtraction fact gives us an addition fact and a second subtraction fact. When we visualize the sets involved in an addition or subtraction problem (see Fig. 3–4), it is easy to understand these statements.

When we look at an expression like $39 - 21$, we should think: "39 is the *sum*. 21 is *one* of the *addends*. Then the *other addend*, written as $39 - 21$, is 18."

We can write

$$\overset{S}{39} - \overset{A}{21} = \overset{A}{18}$$

to show that 18 and 21 are the addends and 39 is the sum. If we subtract either addend from the sum, we obtain the other addend.

EXERCISES

1. In each problem below, indicate by writing A and S above the proper numerals which number is the sum and which numbers are addends.

  (a) $42 = 28 + 14$ (b) $42 - 30 = 12$ (c) $42 - 12 = 30$
  (d) $250 + 120 = 370$ (e) $7 + 12 = n$ (f) $a - 20 = 30$

(g) $40 - x = 30$ (h) $60 + b = 90$ (i) $80 - r = s$

(j) $x - 40 = y$ (k) $a - b = c$ (l) $a - a = 0$

2. In each number statement below tell whether the missing number is an addend or is the sum of the other two numbers.

(a) $n + 125 = 341$ (b) $46 + x = 124$ (c) $78 + 461 = y$

(d) $64 - x = 22$ (e) $323 - 156 = r$ (f) $r - 481 = 224$

(g) $537 = t - 415$ (h) $537 = t + 415$ (i) $415 = 537 - t$

3. Determine the missing number in each part of Exercise 2.

4. If in an addition problem the sum is twice one of the addends, what can you say about the other addend?

5. What second subtraction fact is given by the fact that $812 - 443 = 369$? that $100 - r = s$? that $a - b = c$?

3. PROPERTIES OF ZERO

The number zero plays a very special role in addition. It is called the *identity element* for addition and subtraction. The chart below explains why it is given this name.

$$\text{For each whole number } a,$$
$$a + 0 = a$$
$$a - 0 = a$$
$$a - a = 0$$

Zero is the identity element for addition

EXERCISES

1. Give answers orally.

(a) $74 + 0$ (b) $0 + 0$ (c) $96 - 0$

(d) $753 - 753$ (e) $x + 0$ (f) $y - y$

(g) $73 + (86 - 86)$ (h) $(84 - 84) + 7$ (i) $17 + (x - x)$

2. Tell what number x is, given that

(a) $67 + x = 67$ (b) $92 - x = 0$

(c) $74 - x = 74$ (d) $x - 43 = 0$

(e) $x - 0 = 99$ (f) $87 + (x - 12) = 87$

(g) $96 - (x + 96) = 0$ (h) $x + x = 0$

3. You are given a subtraction problem for which the answer is zero. Describe the two addends and the sum.

4. THE COMMUTATIVE PROPERTY OF ADDITION

The addition fact $12 + 15 = 27$ shows that if a set of 12 things is combined with a set of 15 other things, then one gets a set of 27 things. The 12 things can be watermelons and the 15 things can be pigs. Of course,

$$12 + 15 = 15 + 12$$

Whether we combine 12 things with 15 or 15 with 12, we obtain the same total. We say that addition has the *commutative* property. In other words, we can add two numbers in either order, and the sums are the same.

> **For each pair of whole numbers *a* and *b*,**
>
> $$a + b = b + a$$

The commutative property of addition

This property of addition is so clear when we think in terms of combining sets that you must wonder why we mention it. However, if we think of addition as *counting*, it is not quite so obvious that addition has the commutative property.

"If we begin with 12 and count forward 15, we get the same result as if we had begun with 15 and counted forward 12."

If you ask a child who adds by counting to solve the problem $8 + 2$, and then a little later give him the problem $2 + 8$, he may work the two problems differently.

When we represent addition on the number line (Fig. 3–5), the commutative property seems more important.

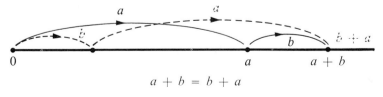

$$a + b = b + a$$

FIGURE 3–5

EXERCISES

1. Thinking of addition as counting forward on the number line, get the sums in (a) through (c). Point out how you are using the commutative property.

   (a) $7 + 99$ (b) $3 + 999$ (c) $11 + 9999$

2. Fill in the blanks so that the resulting number sentences are true.

   (a) $3 + \underline{\quad} = 5 + 3$ (b) $87 + 91 = 91 + \underline{\quad}$
   (c) $8 + (3 + 7) = \underline{\quad} + 8$ (d) $x + 12 = 12 + \underline{\quad}$
   (e) $r + s = s + \underline{\quad}$
   (f) $7 + (4 + x) = (x + \underline{\quad}) + 7$
   (g) $(a + b) + c = c + (b + \underline{\quad})$
   (h) $7 + \underline{\quad} = \underline{\quad} + 7$
   (i) $\underline{\quad} + a = a + \underline{\quad}$
   (j) $(7 + x) + y = \underline{\quad} + (\underline{\quad} + 7)$

3. Does subtraction have the commutative property?

5. THE ASSOCIATIVE PROPERTY OF ADDITION

The commutative property permits us to add *two* numbers in either one of the two possible *orders*. If *three* numbers are to be added, and we do not change their order, there are *two* ways of grouping these numbers as we add. For example, if we are adding 4, 7, and 3, we may compute the sum as

$$(4 + 7) + 3 \quad \text{or} \quad 4 + (7 + 3)$$

This fact is illustrated in Fig. 3–6.

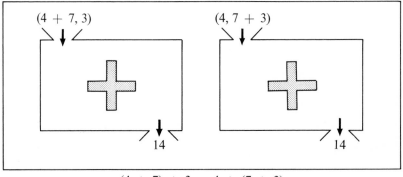

$$(4 + 7) + 3 = 4 + (7 + 3)$$

FIGURE 3–6

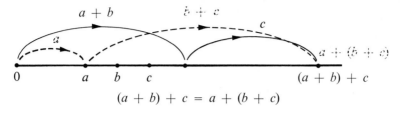

$$(a + b) + c = a + (b + c)$$

FIGURE 3–7

When we think of combining sets, it is quite clear that both ways of grouping the addends give the same sum.

> **For each three whole numbers, *a*, *b*, and *c*,**
>
> $$(a + b) + c = a + (b + c)$$

The associative property of addition

If we think of addition as *counting* (see Fig. 3–7), the associative property is not quite so obvious.

EXERCISES

1. Add the numbers below without pencil and paper, using the indicated grouping.

    (a) $9 + (1 + 7)$ (b) $(9 + 1) + 7$
    (c) $99 + (1 + 23)$ (d) $(99 + 1) + 23$
    (e) $1 + (999 + 463)$ (f) $(1 + 999) + 463$

2. Compute these sums, using the grouping you prefer.

    (a) $90 + 10 + 63$ (b) $23 + 80 + 20$
    (c) $990 + 10 + 79$ (d) $641 + 997 + 3$

3. Use the commutative and associative properties to compute the sums.

    (a) $99 + (47 + 1)$ (b) $999 + (356 + 1)$
    (c) $96 + (79 + 4)$ (d) $990 + (328 + 10)$
    (e) $80 + (65 + 20)$ (f) $(200 + 653) + 800$
    (g) $(50 + 64) + 50$ (h) $(500 + 647) + 500$
    (i) $(75 + 89) + 25$ (j) $(750 + 896) + 250$

4. Fill in the blanks so that the resulting number sentences are true.

  (a) $7 + (9 + 3) = (7 + \underline{\hspace{1cm}}) + 3$
  (b) $8 + (6 + \underline{\hspace{1cm}}) = (8 + 6) + 4$
  (c) $(x + 6) + r = x + (6 + \underline{\hspace{1cm}})$
  (d) $a + (b + c) = (\underline{\hspace{1cm}} + \underline{\hspace{1cm}}) + c$
  (e) $\underline{\hspace{1cm}} + 7 = 8 + (x + 7)$
  (f) $(x + \underline{\hspace{1cm}}) + y = \underline{\hspace{1cm}} + (r + \underline{\hspace{1cm}})$

5. Tell whether each example below illustrates the commutative property, or the associative property, or both properties.

  (a) $8 + 7 = 7 + 8$
  (b) $5 + (6 + 2) = (6 + 2) + 5$
  (c) $(4 + 3) + 1 = 4 + (3 + 1)$
  (d) $(a + 7) + b = a + (b + 7)$
  (e) $(r + s) + t = t + (s + r)$
  (f) $(2 + 2) + 2 = 2 + (2 + 2)$

6. Without adding, use the commutative and associative properties to prove that the following statements are true.

  (a) $30 + 54 = 34 + 50$ (b) $80 + 93 = 83 + 90$
  (c) $27 + 71 = 77 + 21$ (d) $86 + 54 = 84 + 56$
  (e) $270 + 89 = 280 + 79$ (f) $354 + 62 = 364 + 52$
  (g) $888 + 777 = 877 + 788$ (h) $988 + 655 = 955 + 688$
  (i) $746 + 359 = 349 + 756$

7. Compute:

  (a) $20 - (10 - 2)$ (b) $(20 - 10) - 2$
  (c) $12 - (6 - 2)$ (d) $(12 - 6) - 2$
  (e) $(a + 6) - (a - 2)$ (f) $(a + 6) - a - 2$

8. Does subtraction have the associative property? That is, is it true that if the subtractions can be performed, then for all numbers a, b, and c,

$$a - (b - c) = (a - b) - c?$$

9. Use the associative property of addition and rewrite $r + (s + t)$. Now show how you can use the commutative property and write this sum as $t + (r + s)$.

10. Show how you can use the associative property, then the commutative property, and then the associative property again, to write the sum $a + (b + c)$ as $(c + a) + b$.

11. Show how to use the commutative property, then the associative property, and again the commutative property, to write the sum $a + (b + c)$ as $(c + a) + b$.

6. RELATIONSHIPS BETWEEN ADDITION AND SUBTRACTION

It is sometimes said that addition and subtraction are *inverses* of each other.

Consider the following number sentences:

$$(12 - 7) + 7 = 12,$$
$$(89 + 7) - 7 = 89;$$

$$(n + 4) - 4 = n,$$
$$(r - 4) + 4 = r;$$

$$(a + b) - b = a,$$
$$(x - b) + b = x.$$

The two operations *adding seven* and *subtracting seven* "undo" each other. Each operation is called the *inverse* of the other operation. The operations *adding four* and *subtracting four* are also inverses of each other. For each whole number, the operations of *adding* and *subtracting* that number are inverses of each other. Figure 3–8 shows the relationship between the operations of adding 7 and subtracting 7.

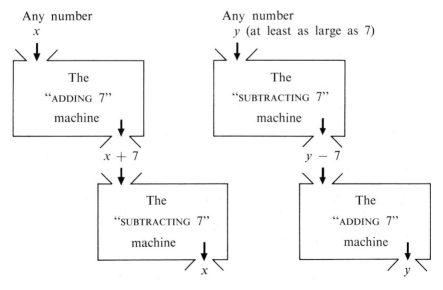

FIG. 3–8. The operations of adding 7 and subtracting 7 are inverses of each other.

EXERCISES

1. Give answers without using pencil and paper.
   (a) $(714 - 86) + 86$ (b) $(952 + 463) - 463$
   (c) $(x + 75) - 75$ (d) $(x - 75) + 75$
   (e) $(415 - y) + y$ (f) $(415 + y) - y$
   (g) $(b + t) - t$ (h) $(b - t) + t$
   (i) $(r + s) - s$ (j) $(r - s) + s$
   (k) $(815 + 461) - 460$ (l) $(815 - 461) + 460$
   (m) $(352 - 174) + 173$ (n) $(352 + 174) - 173$
   (o) $(x - 121) + 122$ (p) $(x + 121) - 122$
   (q) $(743 + x) - 743$ (r) $(743 - x) + (x + 1)$
   (s) $(a - b) + (b + 1)$ (t) $(a + b) - (b + 1)$
   (u) $(x + x) - x$ (v) $(x - x) + x$
   (w) $(r + r) - (r + 1)$ (x) $(r + r) - (r - 1)$
   (y) $(a - b) + (b + b)$ (z) $(a + b) - (b + b)$

2. Determine n given that
   (a) $(n + 84) - 84 = 63$ (b) $(n - 162) + 162 = 214$
   (c) $(n + 84) - 85 = 93$ (d) $(n - 84) + 85 = 93$
   (e) $(n - 162) + 163 = 214$ (f) $(n + 162) - 163 = 214$
   (g) $(84 - n) + 70 = 84$ (h) $(84 + n) - 70 = 84$
   (i) $(263 + n) - 123 = 262$ (j) $(263 - n) + 123 = 262$
   (k) $(84 + n) - 70 = 85$ (l) $(84 - n) + 70 = 85$
   (m) $(87 + 90) - n = 87$ (n) $(87 + 94) - n = 86$
   (o) $(a + n) - a = 56$ (p) $(n + n) - n = 30$
   (q) $(n + n) - (n + 1) = 10$
   (r) $(n + n) - (n - 1) = 10$
   (s) $(a + n) - (a + 1) = 21$
   (t) $(a + n) - (a - 1) = 21$

3. Determine the number x in the number sentences given below.
   (a) $85 - x = 40$ (b) $85 - (x + 1) = 40$
   (c) $(y - x) + 40 = y$ (d) $(a + x) - 30 = a + 1$
   (e) $(a + x) - 50 = a - 1$ (f) $(x + 40) - 35 = 20$
   (g) $20 - (20 - x) = 8$ (h) $a - (a - x) = 10$
   (i) $120 - x = x$ (j) $87 - x = x + 1$
   (k) $31 - x = x - 1$ (l) $20 + (x - 40) = 100$

4. In each exercise below state whether $x = y$, $x > y$, or $x < y$.
   (a) $12 + x = 11 + y$ (b) $12 - x = 11 - y$
   (c) $x - y = 3$ (d) $80 - (x + 10) = 70 - y$
   (e) $x + y = x + x$ (f) $x + y = x + (x + 4)$

(g) $x + (x - 4) = y + y$
(h) $(x + 1) + (x - 2) = (y + 2) + (y - 1)$

5. In each part of Exercise 4, if x is greater than y or less than y, tell how much greater or how much less.

7. USING EQUATIONS TO SOLVE PROBLEMS

When solving verbal problems it is often helpful to write special number sentences called *equations*. We use letters to stand for certain numbers in the verbal problem. For example, we might write the equation

$$356 + 297 = n$$

when working a problem such as

"There are 356 men students and 297 women students in the freshman class of a certain college. How many students are there in all?"

As a second example, we might write the equation

$$257 + x = 493$$

for the problem:

"A family has driven 257 miles on a trip of 493 miles. How much farther have they to drive?"

EXERCISES

For the first five exercises below choose a letter to represent the number that is the answer to the problem and write a number sentence that states that *the sum of two numbers is one number*. Using this number sentence, decide whether to add or subtract to get the answer to the problem. Be sure to write the number sentence. *This is the most important part of each problem.* Work the remaining problems by any method you wish.

1. A school library had 240 books. The librarian purchased 80 new books. How many books are now in the library?
2. A farmer was raising 450 hogs. He sold 270. How many did he have left?
3. On a trip a family drove 942 miles in two days. The first day they drove 422 miles. How far did they drive the second day?
4. A college student spent $2100 his first year in college. His tuition was $880. How much were his other expenses?

5. The pilot of a jet plane announces that you are flying at an elevation of 31,000 feet above sea level. You are over Laramie, Wyoming, and you know that the elevation of Laramie is 8000 feet above sea level. How high is the plane above the ground?

6. A jet plane is flying east at 640 mph and the pilot announces that it has a tail wind of 60 mph.
    (a) What would be the speed of the plane without the tail wind?
    (b) What would be the speed of the plane if it were flying west into the wind?

7. A friend says, "I am thinking of a number. If you add 81 to the number and then subtract 80 from the sum, the result is 52." What is the number?

8. Find a number such that if you add it to itself and then subtract 10, you have 2 more than the number.

9. Find a number such that if you add 10 and then add this sum to the number itself, you will have 50 more than the original number.

10. The sum of two numbers is 80. The difference between the numbers is 12. Find each number.

11. The difference between two whole numbers is equal to their sum. Find two such numbers.

12. The larger of two numbers is 24. The difference between these two numbers is half their sum. Find the smaller number.

13. Find two whole numbers such that each number is a multiple of 5, their difference is a multiple of 6, and their sum is a multiple of 7.

Chapter 4

PROPERTIES OF MULTIPLICATION AND DIVISION OF WHOLE NUMBERS

1. INTRODUCTION

In this chapter we shall study properties of the multiplication and division operations. An understanding of these properties is fully as important as skill in computation.

Multiplication is an operation that combines a first number and a second number to give one number. We call the two numbers factors. We call the result the product of the factors, or simply the product.

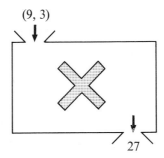

FIG. 4–1. The multiplication machine.

When we multiply we think about two numbers, the factors, and determine their product. We can think of multiplication as a machine (Fig. 4–1). We feed into this machine a pair of numbers, a first number and a second number. The machine processes this pair of numbers and turns out one number.

Division is an operation that combines a first number and a second number to give one number. The first number is the product of the other two numbers.

33

TABLE 4–1

MULTIPLICATION AND DIVISION AS OPERATIONS

Number pair	Operation	Result
(8, 4)	Multiplication	32
(8, 4)	Division	2
(9, 9)	Multiplication	81
(9, 9)	Division	1
(6, 12)	Multiplication	72
(6, 12)	Division	The machine breaks down
(a, b)	Multiplication	$a \times b$
(a, b)	Division	$a \div b$

When we divide we think about two numbers, the first one a product and the other a factor of this product, and we determine the missing factor. We can think of division as a machine (Fig. 4–2).

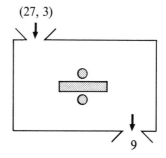

FIG. 4–2. The division machine.

You can feed any pair of numbers into the multiplication machine, but since these are whole number machines, we can feed only *certain* pairs into the division machine. If you try to run the number pair (6, 12) through this machine, it throws the pair out without processing it (Table 4–1).

EXERCISES

1. On each line in Table 4–1 above, point out the number that is the product of the two factors. For each of the first five lines, write the usual multiplication or division statement.

2. Which of the following pairs of numbers are rejected by the division machine?

(a) (12, 2)   (b) (2, 12)   (c) (7, 1)
(d) (1, 7)   (e) (10, 10)   (f) (1, 1)

3. If you feed the pair of numbers ($89 \times 73, 73$) into the division machine, what is the result? What is the result if you feed in the pair ($a \times b, b$)?

4. If you feed the pair of numbers ($98 \div 14, 14$) into the multiplication machine, what is the result? What is the result if you feed in the pair ($a \div b, b$)?

5. If b is not 1 and you feed the pair of numbers ($a \div b, a$) into the division machine, what is the result?

2. USING SETS IN MULTIPLICATION AND DIVISION

We have related addition of whole numbers to the combining of sets. It is also possible to describe multiplication of whole numbers in terms of operations with sets. The example below illustrates this fact.

Consider a set of 5 cups and a set of 4 saucers. No two cups or two saucers are of the same color. How many different cup-saucer color combinations can be formed? It is clear that each cup can be paired with each of the four saucers and that a total of 20 different color combinations can be formed. If we denote the set of cups by $\{a, b, c, d, e\}$ and the set of saucers by $\{1, 2, 3, 4\}$, a convenient way to denote the set of all cup-saucer combinations is by listing the following set of pairs.

$$\{(a, 1), (a, 2), (a, 3), (a, 4), (b, 1), \ldots, (e, 4)\}$$

Note that from a set of 5 objects and a set of 4 objects a set of 20 objects has been constructed. We call each of these pairs an *ordered pair*. In the ordered pair (a, 3) we refer to cup a as the *first* element and to saucer 3 as the *second*.

We can use a rectangular dot array to picture the set of ordered pairs listed above.

```
4  •  •  •  •  •
3  •  •  •  •  •←— This dot represents
2  •  •  •  •  •      the ordered pair (e, 3)
1  •  •  •  •  •
   a  b  c  d  e
```

EXERCISES

1. In the above dot array, used to describe the cup-saucer combinations, what combinations are designated by (a) the top row of dots? (b) the left-hand column? (c) the second column from the right?

2. In traveling from town A to town C it is necessary to pass through town B. There are 3 different roads from A to B and 4 different roads from B to C. Denote the first 3 roads by X, Y, Z and the last 4 by R, S, T, U. List the set of ordered pairs describing all possible routes from A to C. How would you list ordered pairs to describe the routes from C to A?

3. Mark an array of dots picturing the routes of Exercise 2.

4. A first set contains 12 elements and a second 15. How many ordered pairs can be formed by choosing the first element in each ordered pair from the first set and the second element in each ordered pair from the second set?

5. You plan to conduct an experiment. You will roll a die upon which are the numerals 1, 2, 3, 4, 5, 6, and then you will toss a coin which will fall either heads or tails. You will record the result of your experiment by writing down an ordered pair like $(3, H)$ or $(4, T)$. How many elements are there in the set of ordered pairs which presents all possible outcomes of your experiment?

6. If a first set contains a elements and a second set contains b elements, how many elements are there in the set of all ordered pairs that can be formed by selecting the first element in each ordered pair from the first set and the second element in each ordered pair from the second set?

Using arrays we can relate multiplication to addition. The array below calls attention to the fact that we can determine the number 3×4 by deciding how many objects are in one set that is formed by putting together 3 sets with 4 objects in each set.

$$3 \times 4 = 4 + 4 + 4$$

For convenience in drawing diagrams, let us agree that by a 3×5-array we shall mean one with 3 horizontal rows and 5 vertical columns, and by a 5×3-array we shall mean one with 5 rows and 3 columns. In other words, the first number tells you the number of rows, and the second the number of columns.

EXERCISES

In Exercises 1 through 5, give the multiplication fact pictured by each array.

1. • • • •
   • • • •

2. • •
   • •
   • •
   • •

3. • • • •
   • • • •
   • • • •
   • • • •
   • • • •

4. • • • • •
   • • • • •
   • • • • •
   • • • • •

5. • • • • • • • • • •
   • • • • • • • • • •
   • • • • • • • • • •
   • • • • • • • • • •
   • • • • • • • • • •
   • • • • • • • • • •
   • • • • • • • • • •
   • • • • • • • • • •
   • • • • • • • • • •
   • • • • • • • • • •

6. Point out a property of multiplication suggested by Exercises 1 and 2.

7. Draw two arrays representing 3×5 and 3×2. If these are combined to form one array, how would you describe the large array?

8. Draw two arrays illustrating 2×4 and 3×4. Combine these into one array. What multiplication fact is illustrated by this large array?

9. Show by arrays that
   (a) $(3 \times 5) + (4 \times 5) = 7 \times 5$
   (b) $(4 \times 3) + (4 \times 4) = 4 \times 7$

Arrays may be used to illustrate division facts. The array below contains 28 dots. It has 4 rows. How many columns has it?

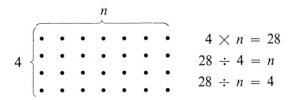

$$4 \times n = 28$$
$$28 \div 4 = n$$
$$28 \div n = 4$$

When we look at the expression 28 ÷ 4 we think: "28 is the *product*. 4 is *one of the factors*. The *other factor*, written 28 ÷ 4, is 7." We write: 28 ÷ 4 = 7.

Division is the most complicated of the four operations. Properties of the division operation are most easily understood by studying the relationships between multiplication and division. Each multiplication problem, and each division problem, has to do with *three* numbers. Two of these numbers are *factors*. The third is the *product*. When we know both factors, we determine the product by multiplying. When we know one factor and the product, we determine the missing factor by *dividing*. In thinking about a multiplication or division problem, it may be helpful to visualize the array that illustrates both of the factors and the product.

EXERCISES

Give the multiplication and division facts suggested by the arrays below.

1.
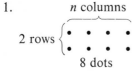

2. 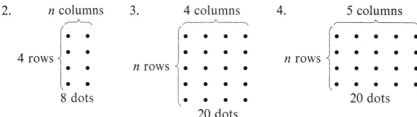 3. 4.

5.
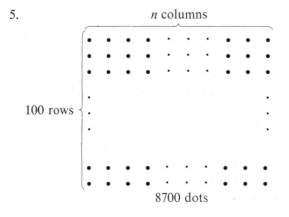

Multiplication facts present related division facts. In each multiplication statement that does not have zero as one of the factors, if the product is divided by one factor, the result is the other factor. When we look at a statement like 24 ÷ 6 = 4, we think: "24 is the *product*. 6 is *one of the factors*. The *other factor*, written 24 ÷ 6, is 4." We can write

$$P \quad F \quad F$$
$$24 \div 6 = 4$$

to show that 6 and 4 are the factors and 24 is the product.

EXERCISES

1. In each problem below, indicate by writing P and F above the proper numbers which number is the product and which numbers are the factors.
   (a) $32 = 8 \times 4$ (b) $32 \div 4 = 8$ (c) $32 \div 8 = 4$
   (d) $200 \div 20 = 10$ (e) $12 \times 15 = n$ (f) $a \div 20 = 30$
   (g) $40 \div x = 10$ (h) $60 \times n = 900$ (i) $80 \div r = s$
   (j) $x \div 40 = y$ (k) $a \div b = c$ (l) $a \div a = 1$

2. In each number statement below, decide whether the missing number is a factor or is the product of the other two numbers.
   (a) $n \times 17 = 221$ (b) $43 \times n = 516$ (c) $78 \times 11 = y$
   (d) $64 \div x = 32$ (e) $324 \div 36 = r$ (f) $r \div 481 = 224$
   (g) $537 = t \div 415$ (h) $1312 = t \times 32$ (i) $100 = 100,000 \div a$

3. Determine the missing number in each part of Exercise 2.
4. What second division fact is given by the fact that $672 \div 32 = 21$? that $100 \div r = s$? that $a \div b = c$?

3. PROPERTIES OF 0 AND 1

The numbers 0 and 1 play a special role in multiplication and division. The number 1 is called the *identity element* for multiplication and division because it has the important properties described below.

For each whole number a,

$a \times 1 = a$

$a \div 1 = a$

$a \div a = 1$ when a is not 0

One is the identity element for multiplication

EXERCISES

1. Give answers orally.

(a) 74×1 (b) 1×1 (c) $96 \div 1$

(d) $753 \div 753$ (e) $n \times 1$ (f) $n \div n$

(g) $73 \times (86 \div 86)$ (h) $(84 \div 84) \times 7$ (i) $17 \times (n \div n)$

2. Tell what number a is, given that

(a) $67 \times a = 67$ (b) $92 \div a = 1$

(c) $74 \div a = 74$ (d) $a \div 43 = 1$

(e) $a \div 1 = 99$ (f) $87 \times (a \div 12) = 87$

(g) $96 \div (a \times 96) = 1$ (h) $a \times a = 1$

(i) $a \times (a + 1) = a$

It is surprisingly difficult to see clearly the part that zero plays in multiplication and division. But if we go back to our definition of the product 6×0 as the numbers of pairs that can be formed by picking a first object from a set of six things and a second object from a set of zero things, we see that $6 \times 0 = 0$. If there are 6 girls willing to dance and if 0 boys will dance, then there are exactly 0 girl-boy partnerships that can be formed. We see that if any whole number is multiplied by zero, the product is zero.

For each whole number a,

$$a \times 0 = 0$$

Multiplying by zero

It is helpful also to think of 6×0 as $0 + 0 + 0 + 0 + 0 + 0$, for this way of thinking shows that $6 \times 0 = 0$.

Division problems involving 0 are not confusing if you remember that to divide is to determine a missing factor. If the product of two numbers is 0 and one factor is 7, certainly you can determine the missing factor. It must be 0.

$$\begin{array}{ccc} P & F & F \\ 0 \div 7 & = & n \end{array}$$

If you are told that the product of two factors is 0 and one of the factors is 0, can you determine the missing factor?

$$\begin{array}{ccc} P & F & F \\ 0 \div 0 & = & n \end{array}$$

It is clear that the missing factor could be *any whole number*. Because there is no way to determine *n*, *we agree not to divide 0 by 0. The symbol* $0 \div 0$ *does not represent a number.*

If you are told that the product of two factors is 3 and that one of the factors is 0, can you determine the missing factor?

$$\overset{P}{3} \overset{F}{\div} \overset{F}{0} = n$$

With a little thought it becomes clear that no whole number *n* has this property. If one factor is 0, the product is certainly not 3. (Why?) We cannot divide 3 by 0.

We can divide zero by every whole number except zero. We do not divide any number by zero.

For every whole number *a* except 0,

$$\overset{P}{0} \overset{F}{\div} \overset{F}{a} = 0$$

The expressions

$$\overset{P}{a} \overset{F}{\div} 0 \qquad \text{and} \qquad \overset{P}{0} \overset{F}{\div} 0$$

do not represent numbers.

Zero in division

EXERCISES

1. Give answers orally.
   (a) 793×0 (b) $0 \div 432$ (c) $75 \times (a - a)$
   (d) $(x - x) \div 17$ (e) $(7 + 7) \times (7 - 7)$ (f) $(16 \times 0) \div 8$

2. In each of these problems, write correctly *P* or *F* above each number. If it is possible to do so, determine *n*.
   (a) $83 \times n = 0$ (b) $n \div 14 = 0$
   (c) $(7 - n) \times 12 = 0$ (d) $(7 - n) \times n = 0$
   (e) $(7 + n) \times n = 0$ (f) $n \div a = 0$
   (g) $n \times 0 = 0$ (h) $n \times 75 = n$
   (i) $n \div 75 = n$

3. Which of the expressions below do not represent numbers?
   (a) $0 \div 6$ (b) $6 \div 0$ (c) $6 \div 6$ (d) $0 \div 0$

4. Tell which of the following exercises indicate dividing by 0 and which indicate dividing 0 by another number. Give answers when you can.

(a) $0 \div 3$ (b) $5 \div 0$ (c) $0\overline{)23}$ (d) $3\overline{)10}$ (e) $0 \div 0$

4. THE COMMUTATIVE PROPERTY OF MULTIPLICATION

Each multiplication fact, and each division fact, gives us information about three sets. The multiplication fact $10 \times 12 = 120$ shows that from a set of 10 things and a set of 12 things we can build a set of 120 pairs. The 10 things can be watermelons and the 12 things can be pigs. Of course,

$$10 \times 12 = 12 \times 10$$

and we say that multiplication has the *commutative* property.

For each pair of whole numbers *a* and *b*,

$$a \times b = b \times a$$

The commutative property of multiplication

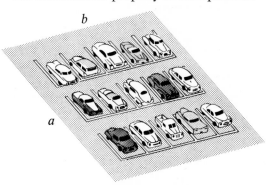

When we think in terms of arrays, the commutative property is quite obvious. But if we think of multiplication as repeated addition, the property is not so obvious.

"If we add ten 12's together, we get the same sum as if we had added twelve 10's."

If a second-grade student is asked to find the sum of four 10's, then a little later to find the sum of ten 4's, he may work the two problems differently.

EXERCISES

1. Thinking of multiplication as repeated addition, work the following problems *without* using the multiplication facts that you know and *without* using the commutative property.

   (a) 5 × 6   (b) 6 × 5   (c) 10 × 8
   (d) 8 × 10   (e) 8 × 13   (f) 13 × 8

2. Work the multiplication problems below by repeated addition. Use the commutative property if you wish.

   (a) 100 × 7   (b) 25 × 9   (c) 1500 × 6

3. Fill in the blanks so that the resulting statements are true.

   (a) 3 × ____ = 5 × 3   (b) 87 × 91 = 91 × ____
   (c) 8 × (3 × 7) = ____ × 8   (d) a × 12 = 12 × ____
   (e) r × s = s × ____
   (f) 7 × (4 × a) = (a × ____) × 7
   (g) (a × b) × c = c × (b × ____)
   (h) ____ × a = a × ____

4. Does division have the commutative property?

5. THE ASSOCIATIVE PROPERTY OF MULTIPLICATION

The commutative property permits us to multiply *two* numbers in either one of the two possible *orders*. If *three* numbers are to be multiplied and we do not change their order, there are *two* different ways to

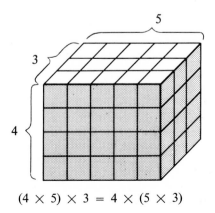

(4 × 5) × 3 = 4 × (5 × 3)

FIGURE 4–3

group these numbers as we multiply. For example, if we are multiplying $4 \times 5 \times 3$, we may compute the product as

$$(4 \times 5) \times 3 \quad \text{or} \quad 4 \times (5 \times 3)$$

Explain how the solid in Fig. 4–3 shows that both ways of multiplying give the same product.

We can make the following statement.

For each three whole numbers

a, b, and c,

$(a \times b) \times c = a \times (b \times c)$

The associative property for multiplication

EXERCISES

1. Multiply, using the indicated grouping.
   (a) $5 \times (2 \times 7)$ (b) $(5 \times 2) \times 7$
   (c) $25 \times (4 \times 8)$ (d) $(25 \times 4) \times 8$
   (e) $125 \times (8 \times 17)$ (f) $(125 \times 8) \times 17$

2. Compute these products, using either grouping you prefer.
   (a) $5 \times 2 \times 17$ (b) $23 \times 25 \times 4$
   (c) $25 \times 4 \times 97$ (d) $581 \times 125 \times 8$

3. Use the commutative and associative properties of multiplication and give the products.
   (a) $5 \times (13 \times 2)$ (b) $25 \times (37 \times 4)$
   (c) $(25 \times 41) \times 4$ (d) $(50 \times 97) \times 2$
   (e) $(25 \times 34) \times 8$ (f) $(125 \times 93) \times 8$

4. Fill in the blanks so that the resulting statements are true.
   (a) $7 \times (9 \times 3) = (7 \times \underline{\quad}) \times 3$
   (b) $8 \times (6 \times \underline{\quad}) = (8 \times 6) \times 4$
   (c) $(n \times 6) \times r = n \times (6 \times \underline{\quad})$
   (d) $a \times (b \times c) = (\underline{\quad} \times \underline{\quad}) \times c$
   (e) $\underline{\quad} \times 7 = 8 \times (n \times 7)$
   (f) $(a \times \underline{\quad}) \times b = \underline{\quad} \times (r \times \underline{\quad})$

5. Tell whether each example below illustrates the commutative property, or the associative property, or both.

(a) $8 \times 7 = 7 \times 8$ (b) $5 \times (6 \times 2) = (6 \times 2) \times 5$

(c) $(4 \times 3) \times 1 = 4 \times (3 \times 1)$

(d) $(a \times 7) \times b = a \times (b \times 7)$

(e) $(r \times s) \times t = t \times (s \times r)$

(f) $(2 \times 2) \times 2 = 2 \times (2 \times 2)$

6. Compute. In (e) and (f), a is not zero.

(a) $20 \div (10 \div 2)$ (b) $(20 \div 10) \div 2$

(c) $12 \div (6 \div 2)$ (d) $(12 \div 6) \div 2$

(e) $(a \times 6) \div (a \div 2)$ (f) $[(a \times 6) \div a] \div 2$

7. Does division have the associative property? That is, is it true that if the divisions can be performed, then for all numbers a, b, and c,

$$a \div (b \div c) = (a \div b) \div c?$$

8. Use the associative property of multiplication and rewrite $r \times (s \times t)$. Now, show how you can use the commutative property to write this product as $t \times (r \times s)$.

9. Show how you can use the associative property, then the commutative property, and then the associative property again, to write the product

$$a \times (b \times c) \qquad \text{as} \qquad (c \times a) \times b.$$

10. Show how to use the commutative property, then the associative property, and again the commutative property, to write the product

$$a \times (b \times c) \qquad \text{as} \qquad (c \times a) \times b.$$

We use the associative property to find products like 30×10, for

$$30 \times 10 = (3 \times 10) \times 10 = 3 \times (10 \times 10) = 300$$

For finding products like 20×30 and 200×300, we use both the associative and commutative properties:

$$20 \times 30 = (2 \times 10) \times (3 \times 10)$$
$$= (2 \times 3) \times (10 \times 10) = 600$$
$$200 \times 300 = (2 \times 10 \times 10) \times (3 \times 10 \times 10)$$
$$= (2 \times 3) \times (10 \times 10 \times 10 \times 10)$$
$$= 60{,}000$$

EXERCISES

Explain your use of the associative and commutative laws, and give the following products.

1. $(2 \times 10) \times 10$ 2. 50×10
3. $(3 \times 10) \times (3 \times 10)$ 4. 40×20
5. $(2 \times 10 \times 10) \times (4 \times 10)$ 6. 300×50
7. 60×90 8. 400×900
9. $(8 \times 10 \times 10 \times 10) \times (3 \times 10 \times 10)$
10. 6000×700

6.   THE DISTRIBUTIVE PROPERTY

Addition and multiplication are related to each other by a property known as the distributive property. If you can find shortcuts to work the problems below, you will have discovered this property. Explain how this shortcut can be related to the visualization of arrays.

EXERCISES

1. $(7 \times 8) + (3 \times 8)$ 2. $(9 \times 7) + (1 \times 7)$
3. $(7 \times 17) + (3 \times 17)$ 4. $(9 \times 23) + (1 \times 23)$
5. $(8 \times 12) + (2 \times 12)$ 6. $(6 \times 59) + (4 \times 59)$
7. $(97 \times 81) + (3 \times 81)$ 8. $(43 \times 97) + (43 \times 3)$
9. $(8 \times 6) + (3 \times 6)$ 10. $(7 \times 7) + (4 \times 7)$
11. $(998 \times 56) + (2 \times 56)$ 12. $(77 \times 998) + (77 \times 2)$
13. $(80 \times 76) + (20 \times 76)$ 14. $(75 \times 85) + (75 \times 15)$
15. $(18 \times 32) + (2 \times 32)$ 16. $(12 \times 17) + (12 \times 3)$
17. $(27 \times 40) + (3 \times 40)$ 18. $(44 \times 19) + (44 \times 1)$
19. $(555 \times 63) + (445 \times 63)$ 20. $(74 \times 888) + (74 \times 112)$

21. Fill in the blanks so that the resulting statements are true.

    (a) $(\underline{\hspace{1cm}} \times 7) + (3 \times 7) = 70$
    (b) $(9 \times 8) + (\underline{\hspace{1cm}} \times 8) = 80$
    (c) $(6 \times 9) + (4 \times \underline{\hspace{1cm}}) = 90$
    (d) $(\underline{\hspace{1cm}} \times 6) + (\underline{\hspace{1cm}} \times 6) = 60$
    (e) $(80 \times 72) + (\underline{\hspace{1cm}} \times 72) = 7200$
    (f) $(89 \times 73) + (\underline{\hspace{1cm}} \times 73) = 7300$
    (g) $(\underline{\hspace{1cm}} \times 19) + (\underline{\hspace{1cm}} \times 19) = 1900$
    (h) $(800 \times 97) + (\underline{\hspace{1cm}} \times 97) = 97,000$
    (i) $(19 \times 23) + (\underline{\hspace{1cm}} \times 23) = 460$
    (j) $(42 \times 17) + (42 \times \underline{\hspace{1cm}}) = 840$

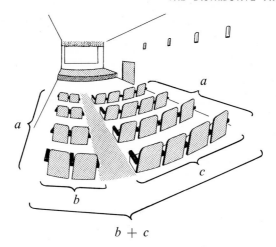

$$b + c$$

The distributive property is used in two-digit multiplication. When you multiply 12 by 3 you may think:

Three 2's are 6,
Three 10's are 30,
The product is 30 + 6 or 36.

We may write this as

$$3 \times (10 + 2) = (3 \times 10) + (3 \times 2)$$

or as

$$(10 + 2) \times 3 = (10 \times 3) + (2 \times 3)$$

or as

$$\begin{array}{r} 10 + 2 \\ 3 \\ \hline (3 \times 10) + (3 \times 2) \end{array}$$

With arrays it is easy to illustrate the distributive property. Looking at the diagram below,

$$5 \times (5 + 2) = (5 \times 5) + (5 \times 2)$$

point out the 5 × 5 array and the 5 × 2 array which together form the 5 × 7 array.

Mathematically, the distributive property can be stated as follows.

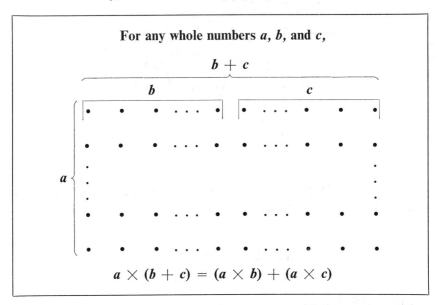

For any whole numbers *a*, *b*, and *c*,

$$a \times (b + c) = (a \times b) + (a \times c)$$

Multiplication is distributive over addition

EXERCISES

1. In the boxed array above, point out the *a* × *b* arrays and the *a* × *c* arrays which together form the *a* × (*b* + *c*) array.

2. Draw a figure picturing the distributive law for the special case *a* = 4, *b* = 5, *c* = 1.

3. Turn your book through an angle of 90° and look at the boxed array above. Point out how it shows that

$$(b + c) \times a = (b \times a) + (c \times a).$$

4. Turn the array you drew in Exercise 2 through an angle of 90° and explain how it shows that (6 × 4) = (5 × 4) + (1 × 4).

5. Each array below illustrates the distributive property. Write a number sentence suggested by the array.

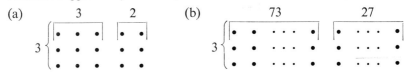

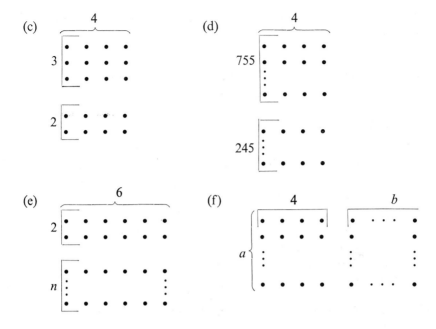

6. Write the number sentences suggested if the arrays of Exercise 5 are rotated 90°.

The distributive property may be employed to explain the method used in working a division problem. Consider the problem $48 \div 4$. Now, by the distributive property,

$$\overset{P}{48} = (10 \times 4) + (2 \times 4) = \overset{\overset{F}{\frown}}{(10 + 2)} \times \overset{F}{4}$$

and hence we see that

$$48 \div 4 = 10 + 2$$

We ordinarily write out the work for a division problem as follows:

$$
\begin{array}{r}
14 \\
12)\overline{168} \\
120 \\
\hline
48 \\
48 \\
\hline
\end{array}
$$

Point out how the 168 has been broken into the two numbers 120 and 48:

$$168 = \overset{P}{(10 \times 12)} + (4 \times 12) = \overset{F}{\overbrace{(10 + 4)}} \times \overset{F}{12}$$

$$168 \div 12 = 10 + 4$$

EXERCISES

Without using pencil or paper give the answers to the following division problems. If you use the distributive property, explain how it is used.

1. $(13 \times 8) \div 8$
2. $[(10 + 3) \times 9] \div 9$
3. $[(10 \times 7) + (3 \times 7)] \div 7$
4. $(80 + 24) \div 8$
5. $(70 + 35) \div 7$
6. $[(20 \times 7) + (6 \times 7)] \div 7$
7. $(120 + 36) \div 12$
8. $(700 + 900) \div 100$
9. $[(20 \times 12) + (7 \times 12)] \div 12$
10. $[(30 \times 100) + (7 \times 100)] \div 100$
11. Work problems 5, 6, 7, and 9 by the usual long division method.

7. RELATIONSHIPS BETWEEN MULTIPLICATION AND DIVISION

Just as the operations *adding seven* and *subtracting seven* "undo" each other, so do the operations *multiplying by seven* and *dividing by seven*. The diagram in Fig. 4–4 shows the relationship between the operations.

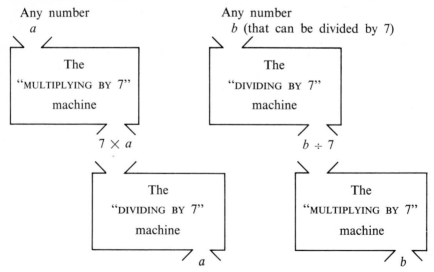

FIG. 4–4. For each whole number except zero, the operations of multiplying and dividing by that number are inverses of each other.

For example,

$$(14 - 7) + 7 = 14, \qquad (14 + 7) - 7 = 14$$
$$(14 \div 7) \times 7 = 14, \qquad (14 \times 7) \div 7 = 14$$

EXERCISES

1. Give answers without using pencil and paper.

   (a) $(189 \div 7) \times 7$ (b) $(28 \times 7) \div 7$
   (c) $(n \times 7) \div 7$ (d) $(n \div 75) \times 75$
   (e) $(640 \div y) \times y$ (f) $(640 \times y) \div y$
   (g) $(b \times t) \div t$ (h) $(b \div t) \times t$
   (i) $(r \times s) \div s$ (j) $(r \div s) \times s$
   (k) $(42 \times 4) \div 8$ (l) $(42 \times 8) \div 4$
   (m) $(567 \times 843) \div 843$ (n) $(567 \div 81) \times 81$
   (o) $(6612 \div 87) \times 87$ (p) $(1024 \div 64) \times 32$
   (q) $(a \div 4) \times 8$ (r) $(a \times 8) \div 4$
   (s) $(a \times a) \div a$ (t) $(10 \times a) \div (2 \times a)$
   (u) $(a \div a) \times a$ (v) $(a \div b) \times (2 \times b)$

2. Determine n in the exercises below.

   (a) $(n \times 7) \div 7 = 29$ (b) $(n \div 8) \times 8 = 72$
   (c) $(n \times 84) \div 84 = 63$ (d) $(n \div 162) \times 162 = 648$
   (e) $(n \times 40) \div 80 = 22$ (f) $(n \div 120) \times 60 = 300$
   (g) $(168 \times n) \div 12 = 168$ (h) $(168 \div n) \times 12 = 84$
   (i) $(168 \times n) \div 12 = 84$ (j) $(168 \times 84) \div n = 168$
   (k) $(720 \div 18) \times n = 720$ (l) $(86 \times 22) \div n = 43$
   (m) $(n \times n) \div n = 135$ (n) $(n \times a) \div a = 57$
   (o) $(n \div a) \times a = 0$ (p) $(n \times 7) \div 8 = 14$

3. Can you determine the whole number n in problems (a) through (j)?

   (a) $(25 \times n) \div n = 25$ (b) $(1 \times n) \div n = 1$
   (c) $(1 \div n) \times n = 1$ (d) $(7 \div n) \times n = 7$
   (e) $(n \times 0) \div n = 0$ (f) $n \times (n + 1) = 0$
   (g) $n \times (n - 1) = 0$ (h) $n \div (n - 1) = 2$
   (i) $n \div (n + 1) = 0$ (j) $n \times n = (5 \times n) - 6$

4. Determine the number a in problems (a) through (j).

   (a) $40 \div (a + 1) = 10$ (b) $80 \div (a - 4) = 8$
   (c) $(y \times a) \div 30 = 2 \times y$ (d) $(y \times a) \div 30 = y \div 2$
   (e) $24 \div (24 \div a) = 8$ (f) $b \div (b \div a) = 10$
   (g) $144 \div a = a$ (h) $156 \div a = a \times 1$
   (i) $(a \times 72) + (68 \times 72) = 7200$
   (j) $(79 \times a) + (21 \times a) = 5600$

5. In each exercise below state whether $a = b$, $a > b$, or $a < b$.

    (a) $240 \times a = 200 \times b$ (b) $240 \div a = 200 \div b$

    (c) $a \div b = 3$ (d) $800 \div (2 \times a) = 400 \div b$

    (e) $800 \div (2 \times a) = 600 \div b$ (f) $a \times b = b \times (b + 4)$

    (g) $a \times (a - 4) = b \times b$ (h) $a \times (a \div 4) = b \times b$

6. In which parts of Exercise 5 is the larger number more than twice the smaller? less than twice the smaller?

8. MULTIPLICATION AND DIVISION ON THE NUMBER LINE

We can use a number line to represent both multiplication and division facts. For example, in Fig. 4–5 we have illustrated the fact that $3 \times 4 = 12$. We look at this figure and see that there are four 3's in 12, so $12 \div 3 = 4$. We also see that if we divide a line 12 units long into 4 parts of equal length, each part has length 3; that is, $12 \div 4 = 3$.

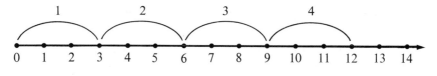

FIGURE 4–5

EXERCISES

1. Give the multiplication and division facts shown by each figure in parts (a) through (e).

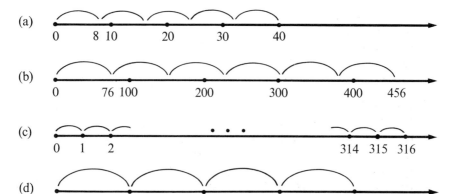

(e)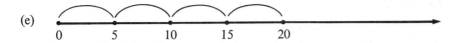

2. Draw a number line for each statement.

(a) $4 \times 6 = 24$ (b) $6 \times 250 = 1500$

(c) $32 \div 8 = 4$ (d) $2800 \div 400 = 7$

9. RECREATIONAL MATH

We have used arrays of dots to show relationships among numbers. For example, there are 24 dots in each array below, and each array calls attention to certain number facts.

· ·

$1 \times 24 = 24, \quad 24 \div 1 = 24, \quad 24 \div 24 = 1$

$2 \times 12 = 24, \quad 24 \div 12 = 2 \qquad 3 \times 8 = 24, \quad 24 \div 8 = 3$

$24 \div 2 = 12 \qquad\qquad\qquad 24 \div 3 = 8$

$4 \times 6 = 24, \quad 24 \div 6 = 4$

$24 \div 4 = 6$

The Greek mathematicians called 24 a rectangular number because it can be represented by rectangular arrays other than a single line of dots. The smallest rectangular number is 4; the next is 6.

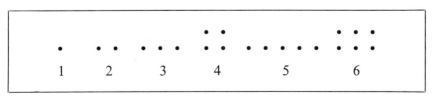

Four is the smallest rectangular number

EXERCISES

1. List the first 10 rectangular numbers.
2. How would you describe the numbers that are not rectangular numbers?
3. The number 24 can be represented as a rectangular number in 3 different ways, 2×12, 3×8, and 4×6. Find a rectangular number smaller than 50 that can be illustrated in more than 3 ways. In how many ways can 100 be represented as a rectangular number? 144?

Some numbers are called *square* numbers. These are the numbers that can be represented by arrays made up of the same number of rows as columns.

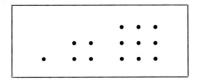

The first three square numbers

EXERCISES

1. List the first ten square numbers.
2. Is every square number a rectangular number?
3. What is the smallest square number that can be pictured by a rectangular array that is not a square?
4. What is the smallest square number that is the sum of two square numbers? Show that 100 is the sum of two square numbers.

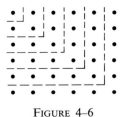

FIGURE 4–6

5. Explain how Fig. 4–6 shows the number facts listed below.

$$1 + 3 = 2 \times 2$$
$$1 + 3 + 5 = 3 \times 3$$
$$1 + 3 + 5 + 7 = 4 \times 4$$
$$1 + 3 + 5 + 7 + 9 = 5 \times 5$$
$$1 + 3 + 5 + 7 + 9 + 11 = 6 \times 6$$

6. Guess the sum of all odd numbers less than 100. Try to find a simple way to check your guess.

7. Every number is either a square number or it is the sum of two, three, or four square numbers. For example,

$$5 = 4 + 1, \qquad 13 = 9 + 4, \qquad 27 = 9 + 9 + 9,$$
$$23 = 9 + 9 + 4 + 1$$

(a) Find all numbers less than 20 which are not square numbers but are the sum of two square numbers; not the sum of two, but the sum of three square numbers.

(b) What numbers less than 32 are the sum of four square numbers but not the sum of fewer than four? Guess what numbers less than 100 have this property.

(c) Show that 625 is a square number and is also the sum of two square numbers, and the sum of three square numbers, and the sum of four square numbers.

Each square number is the sum of two triangular numbers. The figure below shows what is meant.

The dashed line splits the square array into two triangular arrays. Any number that can be represented by such an array is called a triangular number.

EXERCISES

1. Using an array, represent 4 as a square number and show that 1 and 3 are both triangular numbers.

2. List the first 10 triangular numbers.

3. If a number is not a triangular number, it is either the sum of two or of three triangular numbers. Find all numbers between 20 and 30 that are not triangular and are not the sum of two triangular numbers. Express 40 as the sum of 3 triangular numbers in as many different ways as you can.

REVIEW EXERCISES—GROUP I

1. Our symbol 25 stands for two tens and five because we work with a number system which is *based* on *ten*—no doubt because man has ten fingers. If men had six fingers on each hand, what would the symbol 25 probably represent?

2. In exercises (a) through (c), write the usual numeral and read the result.
   (a) $(7 \times 10 \times 10) + (9 \times 10) + 3$
   (b) $(6 \times 10 \times 10 \times 10) + 6$
   (c) $(3 \times 10 \times 10 \times 10 \times 10) + (4 \times 10)$

3. Write expanded numerals for
   (a) 643   (b) 7070   (c) 90,091

4. Write the usual symbol for each product below.
   (a) $5 \times (10 \times 2)$ (b) 40×20
   (c) $(3 \times 10) \times (5 \times 10)$ (d) 5×200

5. Count backward by 50's from 713 to 363.
6. What fact is represented by each number line in Fig. 4–7?

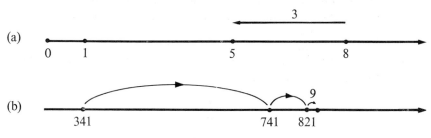

FIGURE 4–7

7. Draw a number line and represent on it the facts given below.
   (a) $312 + 256 = 568$ (b) $1000 - 256 = 744$

8. Where must you start on the number line to be sure that
   (a) after adding 200 you are at 743?
   (b) after subtracting 240 you are at 529?

9. Write an inequality stating whether the first number is greater than or
   less than the second.
   (a) 67, 76   (b) 3574, 3614   (c) 6421, 6381

10. Think of the number line and decide what your stopping point will be
    if you begin at 85 and make the following additions and subtractions.
    (a) Subtract 63; add 64
    (b) Add 70; subtract 60
    (c) Add 50; subtract 49; add 60; subtract 62

11. Tell what must be added to the first number to give the second.
    (a) 412, 472   (b) 356, 426
    (c) 503, 704   (d) 4134, 4184

(e)   88, 100   (f)   888, 1000
(g)   8888, 10,000   (h)   2876, 3000

12. Which of the following pairs of numbers cannot be fed into the "subtraction machine"?

(a)   (3, 7)   (b)   (6, 6)   (c)   (0, 0)   (d)   (0, 7)

13. Tell whether the number x is the sum or an addend.

(a) $42 = 28 + x$ (b) $37 = 91 - x$
(c) $37 = x - 9$ (d) $x = 72 + 50$
(e) $x = 72 - 50$ (f) $80 - 33 = x$

14. Determine x in each part of Exercise 13.

15. What number is x, given that

(a) $43 + x = 43$ (b) $215 - x = 215$
(c) $63 + (x - 10) = 63$ (d) $94 - (x + 94) = 0$

16. Use the commutative and associative properties to compute each sum quickly.

(a) $98 + (57 + 2)$ (b) $890 + (97 + 10)$
(c) $999 + (762 + 1)$ (d) $888 + (764 + 112)$

17. Tell whether each example below illustrates the commutative property, the associative property, or both.

(a) $7 + (9 + 3) = (9 + 3) + 7$
(b) $4 + (3 + 7) = (4 + 3) + 7$
(c) $(a + 6) + b = a + (b + 6)$
(d) $x + (y + z) = (z + y) + x$

18. Give an example showing that subtraction does not have the associative property.

19. Write out answers for exercises (a) through (h).

(a) $(652 + 97) - 97$ (b) $(463 - 215) + 215$
(c) $(68 - 23) + 24$ (d) $(812 - 24) + 23$
(e) $(a + 92) - 92$ (f) $(t - 84) + 84$
(g) $(a + 57) - 56$ (h) $(t - 43) + 42$

20. Write the value of n in the equations below.

(a) $(n + 32) - 32 = 27$ (b) $(n - 18) + 18 = 43$
(c) $(n - 57) + 58 = 70$ (d) $(n + 91) - 92 = 64$
(e) $(84 + n) - 60 = 85$ (f) $(84 - n) + 60 = 85$
(g) $60 - (n + 1) = 20$ (h) $(a - n) + 50 = a$
(i) $(a - n) + 50 = a + 1$ (j) $(a - n) + 50 = a - 1$

21. For each problem write an equation. You need not solve the equation.

 (a) There are 547 students in an elementary school. There are 69 students in the sixth grade. How many are in the other grades?

 (b) On a certain day the lowest temperature was 59 degrees and the highest 81. Find the change in temperature from coldest to warmest.

 (c) The circumference of the earth is about 25,000 miles. A satellite circling the earth at an average height of about 500 miles travels about 28,000 miles in one revolution about the earth. How much more is this than the distance around the earth?

 (d) A family drove to a vacation spot in the mountains in two days. On the first day they drove x miles and on the second 412 miles. It took them two days to drive home by the same route. They drove 500 miles the first day and 463 the second. How far did they drive the day they left home?

 (e) Find a number such that when you add 65 to it and then subtract 63 from the sum, the result is 47.

 (f) Find a number such that if you add it to itself and then add 15 to this sum, you have 25 more than the original number.

22. From a set of cups in 6 different colors and saucers in 4 colors, how many different colors of cup-saucer combinations can be formed?

23. What facts of arithmetic are shown by a 5×8 dot array?

24. In problems (a) through (d), decide whether n is one of the two factors or is the product.

 (a) $432 \div n = 27$ (b) $432 \div 27 = n$

 (c) $n \times 18 = 378$ (d) $n \div 19 = 24$

25. Determine n in each part of Exercise 24.

26. Work the following problems without using pencil and paper.

 (a) $856 \times (73 \div 73)$ (b) $856 \times (73 - 73)$

 (c) $(a \div a) \times 43$ (d) $(a - a) \times 574$

 (e) $(16 \times 0) \div 8$ (f) $(16 + 0) \div 8$

27. Determine the number n, given that

 (a) $43 \times (n - 7) = 43$ (b) $86 + (n - 25) = 86$

 (c) $63 \times (n - 18) = 0$ (d) $n \div 1 = 56$

 (e) $84 \times (n \div 17) = 84$ (f) $(n + 2) \times (b \div b) = 15$

28. Which expressions below do not represent numbers?

 (a) $1 \div 1$ (b) $1 \div 0$ (c) $0 \div 1$ (d) $0 \div 0$

29. Fill in the blanks so that the resulting statements are true by the commutative property for multiplication.

(a) $3 \times \underline{\hspace{1cm}} = 7 \times \underline{\hspace{1cm}}$ (b) $\underline{\hspace{1cm}} \times 9 = 9 \times \underline{\hspace{1cm}}$
(c) $(r + s) \times t = (s + \underline{\hspace{1cm}}) \times \underline{\hspace{1cm}}$
(d) $b \times \underline{\hspace{1cm}} = \underline{\hspace{1cm}} \times b$

30. Use the commutative and associative laws to compute the products without using pencil and paper.

(a) $5 \times 9 \times 2$ (b) $5 \times 3 \times 4$
(c) $25 \times 17 \times 4$ (d) $50 \times 46 \times 2$
(e) $500 \times 37 \times 2$ (f) $8 \times 49 \times 125$

31. Compute mentally:

(a) 5×44 (b) 25×88 (c) 50×48
(d) $500 + 446$ (e) 40×60 (f) 400×20

32. Show by an example that division does not have the associative property.

33. Write answers for problems (a) through (f). Use the distributive property.

(a) $(6 \times 9) + (4 \times 9)$ (b) $(7 \times 8) + (7 \times 2)$
(c) $(97 \times 46) + (3 \times 46)$ (d) $(87 \times 95) + (13 \times 95)$
(e) $(60 \times 57) + (40 \times 57)$ (f) $(75 \times 995) + (75 \times 5)$

34. Fill in the blanks so that each statement is true.

(a) $(\underline{\hspace{1cm}} \times 9) + (7 \times 9) = 90$
(b) $(8 \times 17) + (\underline{\hspace{1cm}} \times 17) = 170$
(c) $(\underline{\hspace{1cm}} \times 14) + (\underline{\hspace{1cm}} \times 14) = 140$
(d) $(23 \times \underline{\hspace{1cm}}) + (23 \times \underline{\hspace{1cm}}) = 230$

35. Find the answers to the division problems given below.

(a) $(70 + 14) \div 7$ (b) $(50 + 15) \div 5$
(c) $(120 + 48) \div 12$ (d) $(250 + 75) \div 25$
(e) $(460 + 46) \div 46$ (f) $(460 + 46) \div 23$

36. Find n for problems (a) through (f).

(a) $(n \times 7) \div 7 = 41$ (b) $(32 \times n) \div 41 = 32$
(c) $(n \div 84) \times 84 = 252$ (d) $(n \times 24) \div 12 = 60$
(e) $(n \times n) \div n = 34$ (f) $(n \times 12) \div 11 = 24$

37. In each exercise decide whether $a = b$, $a > b$, or $a < b$.

(a) $15 + a = 13 + b$ (b) $15 - a = 13 - b$
(c) $15 \times a = 13 \times b$ (d) $120 \div a = 80 \div b$
(e) $a + b = a + (a + 9)$ (f) $a \times b = a \times (a + 9)$

38. Solve each equation.

(a) $3 \times (n + 2) = 18$ (b) $(n \times 4) \div 6 = 4$

(c) $(5 \times r) - 4 = 26$ (d) $(4 \times r) + 8 = 20$

(e) $(18 \times s) = 46 + 8$ (f) $(42 \div s) + 12 = 14$

(g) $500,000 \div q = 100$ (h) $(q \div 32) - 16 = 35 - 28$

(i) $3 \times (a + 4) - 6 = 33$

(j) $4 \times (2 \times a + 3) - 5 = 23$

(k) $25 - 2 \times (a - 3) = 15$ (l) $100 \div (2 \times a - 3) = 20$

(m) $20 \div (8 - a) = 4$ (n) $20 - (24 \div a) = 17$

(o) $2 \times (15 - 2 \times a) + 3 = 13$ (p) $3 \times [8 \div (2a - 5)] = 24$

Chapter 5

TECHNIQUES
OF ADDITION
AND SUBTRACTION

1. INTRODUCTION

This chapter has two main goals. Its chief purpose is to explain the mathematical principles that justify the methods we use as we work addition and subtraction problems. The second purpose is to point out ways to improve speed and accuracy in computation.

Our civilization is becoming more and more complex, and machines are rapidly taking over many of the simple tasks that men have performed in the past. Today most of the computations in business and scientific work are done by machines. But men must build these machines, and men must prepare programs which tell the machines what they are to do. Man's job is to *reason* and *understand*. We turn over to machines those tasks which require no thought.

But all of us need skill in arithmetic. It is not convenient to carry a calculating machine everywhere we go. Man's brain is a finer and more complicated machine than will ever be built. It is important to train it to do the problems of everyday arithmetic.

To lay a foundation of knowledge that enables us to work arithmetic problems rapidly and correctly, we need to train our minds to remember basic facts. It is because of the cleverness of the men who built a system of numeration that uses *place value* and has ten for its *base* that these basic facts are few in number. Knowing these facts and understanding the properties of addition, subtraction, multiplication, and division, we can calculate other facts.

2. THE BASIC FACTS OF ADDITION

We sometimes say that there are 100 basic addition facts. These facts are given in Table 5–1.

The table shows many of the important properties of addition. A dashed line has been drawn from the upper left-hand corner of the

TABLE 5–1

THE BASIC ADDITION FACTS

	0	1	2	3	4	5	6	7	8	9	10	11
0	0	1	2	3	4	5	6	7	8	9		
1	1	2	3	4	5	6	7	8	9	10		
2	2	3	4	5	6	7	8	9	10	11		
3	3	4	5	6	7	8	9	10	11	12		
4	4	5	6	7	8	9	10	11	12	13		
5	5	6	7	8	9	10	11	12	13	14		
6	6	7	8	9	10	11	12	13	14	15		
7	7	8	9	10	11	12	13	14	15	16		
8	8	9	10	11	12	13	14	15	16	17		
9	9	10	11	12	13	14	15	16	17	18		
10												
11												

table to the lower right. This line divides the table into two halves that are alike. If we fold the table over on this line, the squares containing 17 fall upon each other, as do the squares containing 16, etc. Of course, the table of *all* addition facts is endless, as the arrows show. However, we need learn only the facts in this tiny corner of the indefinitely large table. The entry in the row labeled 843 and in the column headed 562 is the number 1405. The properties of this table mentioned in the list of exercises below apply to the whole table, not just to the 10 by 10 section shown.

EXERCISES

1. What property of addition is illustrated by folding the table along the diagonal line?
2. What property of addition is illustrated by the top row and left-hand column of the table?

3. Diagonal rows running from the left margin to the top of the table (as we move to the right) have the same entry in every square. For example, one diagonal from lower left to upper right is 9, 9, 9, . . . Explain why this is so.

4. The entries in a diagonal running from the left margin down as we move to the right increase by two. Explain why this is so.

5. What have the second row and the second column to do with counting?

6. What are the first five entries in the column headed 500?

7. What are the first five entries in the row headed 420?

8. Are the numbers in the column headed 743 the same as those in the row labeled 743?

9. Without looking at the table, imagine starting at a square labeled 4 and then moving down 3 squares and right 2 squares. What number is in the square you reach?

10. Where must you start in order that

    (a) after moving right 3 and down 2 you are at a square labeled 10?

    (b) after moving left 3 and down 3 you are at a square labeled 7?

    (c) after moving diagonally downward and to the left 3 squares you are at 15?

    (d) after moving diagonally up and to the right 2, to the left 3, and diagonally down and to the right 3 you are at 11?

It is interesting to realize that knowledge of counting, the commutative property, and the property of zero makes it unnecessary to memorize the entire table. It is enough to know the sums listed in Table 5–2. Explain why this is true.

A student in first or second grade can learn many of these 36 key facts very easily. Because of the associative property all the facts involving 9 are easy to learn; for example,

$$9 + 9 = 9 + (1 + 8) = (9 + 1) + 8 = 18$$
$$9 + 7 = 9 + (1 + 6) = (9 + 1) + 6 = 16$$

The associative property is also helpful with sums involving 8:

$$8 + 8 = 8 + (2 + 6) = (8 + 2) + 6 = 16$$
$$8 + 7 = 8 + (2 + 5) = (8 + 2) + 5 = 15$$

Learning the doubles,

$$2 + 2 = 4, \quad 3 + 3 = 6, \quad 4 + 4 = 8, \quad 5 + 5 = 10, \quad \text{etc.}$$

TABLE 5–2

THE 36 KEY ADDITION FACTS

	0	1	2	3	4	5	6	7	8	9
0										
1										
2			4	5	6	7	8	9	10	11
3				6	7	8	9	10	11	12
4					8	9	10	11	12	13
5						10	11	12	13	14
6							12	13	14	15
7								14	15	16
8									16	17
9										18

is closely related to counting by twos. Nearly everyone learns these special sums easily. Other sums can be related to these doubles; for example,

$$4 + 5 \quad \text{is one } less \text{ than} \quad 5 + 5$$
$$5 + 6 \quad \text{is one } more \text{ than} \quad 5 + 5$$
$$6 + 7 \quad \text{is one } more \text{ than} \quad 6 + 6$$
$$6 + 7 = (5 + 5) + (1 + 2)$$

The best way to learn the addition combinations is to learn a few key facts and then use the properties of addition to derive other facts from these as they are needed.

This suggestion calls attention to a basic principle that applies not only to elementary mathematics but to all the mathematics that *you* will ever study. Instead of trying to memorize a great many unrelated details, learn a few important basic ideas. Learn how to use these basic ideas to reason out new facts for yourself. All the ideas of mathematics can be derived from just a few basic ideas with the help of logical reasoning. These *ideas* and the ability to *reason* are the important tools you must have.

EXERCISES

1. The key facts in the addition table printed in arithmetic books on the planet Nova are given below. Use the properties of addition, and fill out the table.

+	○	I	L	⊔	□	∧	△	①
○								
I								
L			□	∧	△	①	IO	II
⊔				△	①	IO	II	IL
□					IO	II	IL	I⊔
∧						IL	I⊔	I□
△							I□	I∧
①								I△

2. Show how the associative property may be used to learn easily sums involving ① (seven).

3. USING THE PROPERTIES OF ADDITION AND SUBTRACTION

The usual method of adding a column of numbers is to add "up" or "down." If it is then desirable to check the result, one adds the column in the other direction. The commutative and associative properties of addition guarantee that both sums are the same. Thus one ensures that if a mistake is made, he is not so likely to repeat the same mistake when he checks. For example, adding the column below, we proceed as follows.

```
8
3        Adding up one thinks:
4          8, 13, 20, 24, 27, 35
7
5        Adding down one thinks:
6          11, 15, 22, 27, 33, 35
2
—
```

In accounting it is important to be able to add accurately numbers written in rows. Working additions lined up horizontally requires a little more concentration than adding the usual columns, but with a little practice one can use this method effectively.

EXERCISES

1. Write the sums without copying the exercise. Work each problem from right to left and from left to right.

(a) 37 + 52
(b) 86 + 37
(c) 45 + 21 + 32
(d) 56 + 32 + 25
(e) 534 + 256
(f) 357 + 468
(g) 213 + 321 + 432
(h) 217 + 314 + 253
(i) 57 + 32 + 14 + 91
(j) 46 + 25 + 87 + 64
(k) 312 + 456 + 387 + 564
(l) 328 + 426 + 153 + 867
(m) 23 + 52 + 47 + 36 + 51
(n) 31 + 84 + 23 + 52 + 37 + 41
(o) 231 + 425 + 352 + 143 + 273
(p) 452 + 316 + 537 + 218 + 394 + 52

2. Find the sums by adding up. Check your results by adding down.

(a)	431	(b)	625	(c)	914	(d)	241
	256		814		268		368
	748		792		757		527
	359		346		462		493
	217		817		356		642
	463		523		539		519

(e)	6243	(f)	4736	(g)	4273
	1527		8295		8106
	4639		3784		9574
	7254		2713		8927
	3162		9225		9184

When we work addition problems, we use simple *basic facts* such as 4 + 2 = 6 or 2 + 3 = 5. For example, when we add 32 and 24, we write:

$$\begin{array}{r} 32 \\ \underline{24} \\ 56 \end{array}$$

We think:

$$4 + 2 = 6, \qquad 2 + 3 = 5$$

Certainly this is a very simple problem, and thinking in this way, we arrive at the correct answer. But it is rather difficult to show that *our right to think* in this manner depends upon the *commutative, associative*, and *distributive* properties. Study the example below. We write:

$$32 + 24 = (30 + 2) + (20 + 4)$$
$$= (30 + 20) + (2 + 4)$$
$$= [(3 \times 10) + (2 \times 10)] + 6$$
$$= (3 + 2) \times 10 + 6$$
$$= 5 \times 10 + 6$$
$$= 56$$

We think: "32 plus 24 is 30 plus 20, and 2 plus 4. 30 is three 10's, and 20 is two 10's. Three 10's plus two 10's is five 10's. 2 plus 4 is 6. Five 10's and 6 is 56."

In this example, show where the commutative and associative properties were used; also show where the distributive law was employed.

In subtraction we use the same properties. When we subtract 342 from 976, we write:

$$\begin{array}{r} 976 \\ 342 \\ \hline 634 \end{array}$$

We think:

$$6 - 2 = 4, \qquad 7 - 4 = 3, \qquad 9 - 3 = 6$$

We explain this way of working the problem as follows.

$$976 - 342 = [(9 \times 100) + (7 \times 10) + 6]$$
$$- [(3 \times 100) + (4 \times 10) + 2]$$
$$= [(9 \times 100) - (3 \times 100)]$$
$$+ [(7 \times 10) - (4 \times 10)] + [6 - 2]$$
$$= (6 \times 100) + (3 \times 10) + 4$$
$$= 634$$

In subtractions we must sometimes "borrow." For example, in subtracting 457 from 923, we write:

$$\begin{array}{r} 923 \\ 457 \\ \hline 466 \end{array}$$

We think:

$$13 - 7 = 6, \quad 11 - 5 = 6, \quad 8 - 4 = 4$$

We can explain our procedure by writing the problem, $923 - 457$, in the following form:

$$\begin{array}{r} 800 + 110 + 13 \\ 400 + 50 + 7 \\ \hline 400 + 60 + 6 \end{array}$$

EXERCISES

1. Write out each subtraction problem, breaking up the numbers as shown in the example, 923–457.

(a) $754 - 332$ (b) $754 - 372$ (c) $754 - 337$

(d) $754 - 387$ (e) $1000 - 865$ (f) $4000 - 1999$

2. Work the following subtraction problems.

(a) 867   (b) 917   (c) 836   (d) 340   (e) 500
    432   409   228   127   360

(f) 500   (g) 512   (h) 420   (i) 307   (j) 900
    306   287   129   188   744

(k) 5137   (l) 8721   (m) 9004   (n) 8500   (o) 7000
    4085   3809   2543   4376   4879

When subtracting we usually work from right to left. However, as the problems in the above list of exercises show, this is not necessary. We can work from left to right, or we could begin in the middle and work both ways! When the digit 5 occurs below the digit 7 in a subtraction problem, what digit belongs under the 5?

$$\begin{array}{r} ---7--- \\ ---5--- \\ \hline ---?--- \end{array}$$

Of course, you see that the digit will be either a 2 or 1.

EXERCISES

1. In each subtraction problem below, you will find that some of the digits
are listed. In the answer give those digits that you *know* are correct and
give the two possible choices in the other cases.

(a) $84 - - - 76 -$ (b) $- - 7 - 4 - 6$ (c) $8 - 2$
     $38 - - - 69 -$ $- - 3\ 0\ 1 - 8$ $4\ 9\ 6$

(d) $8\ 9\ 2$ (e) 576 (f) $66 - - 4$
     $4 - 6$ $27 -$ $32 - - 1$

(g) $- - 4 - 5$ (h) $6 - - 5$ (i) $145 - - 1$
     $- - 3 - 9$ $4 - - 2$ $39 - - 5$

(j) $19 - - 9$ (k) $4\ 9\ 1$ (l) $66 - 9 - 4$ (m) $4 - 9$
     $8 - - 5$ $2 - 6$ $27 - 4 - 1$ $3\ 9\ 8$

2. Work the following subtraction problems, writing your answers from
left to *right*.

(a) 83 (b) 241 (c) 812
     46 128 355

(d) 8147 (e) 71482 (f) 800000
     3526 35128 463528

(g) 7234861 (h) 14312 (i) 8020
     2891485 9875 6784

An interesting method of subtraction taught in many countries of
the world is known as the *Austrian* or *additive* method of subtraction.
Since to subtract 185 from 452 is to determine the missing addend n
such that $185 + n = 452$, students are taught to obtain this addend
by *adding* to 185 rather than "taking away" from 452. The long
method below shows how this is done.

$$
\begin{array}{r}
185 \\
\underline{7} \\
192 \\
\mathbf{60} \\
\underline{} \\
252 \\
\mathbf{200} \\
\underline{} \\
452
\end{array}
$$

By adding 7, 60, and 200 to 185 we get 452. Therefore,

$$452 - 185 = 267.$$

The exercises below will help you develop skill in this method of subtraction.

EXERCISES

1. Fill in the omitted numbers.

(a)	32 + (4 + ____) = 76;	76 − 32 = _____
(b)	32 + (____ + 50) = 89;	89 − 32 = _____
(c)	45 + (3 + ____) = 68;	68 − 45 = _____
(d)	45 + (____ + 50) = 96;	96 − 45 = _____
(e)	37 + (4 + ____) = 81;	81 − 37 = _____
(f)	37 + (____ + 20) = 63;	63 − 37 = _____
(g)	86 + (4 + ____) = 130;	130 − 86 = _____
(h)	86 + (____ + 70) = 162;	162 − 86 = _____
(i)	235 + (____ + 40 + 300) = 578;	578 − 235 = _____
(j)	235 + (4 + ____ + 500) = 789;	789 − 235 = _____
(k)	235 + (2 + 60 + ____) = 697;	697 − 235 = _____
(l)	356 + (____ + 30 + 400) = 792;	792 − 356 = _____
(m)	356 + (6 + ____ + 300) = 702;	702 − 356 = _____
(n)	356 + (7 + 80 + ____) = 643;	643 − 356 = _____
(o)	53 + (____ + ____) = 89;	89 − 53 = _____
(p)	256 + (____ + ____ + 400) = 699;	699 − 256 = _____
(q)	512 + (____ + ____ + ____) = 843;	843 − 512 = _____
(r)	147 + (____ + ____ + ____) = 500;	500 − 147 = _____
(s)	324 + (____ + ____ + ____) = 818;	818 − 324 = _____

2. Work the following subtraction problems by the additive method.

(a) 792 461	(b) 997 234	(c) 800 532	(d) 4387 2156	(e) 5000 2643
(f) 4060 2387	(g) 6000 2499	(h) 7654 4567	(i) 8213 4721	(j) 6030 2819

3. Work mentally each subtraction problem below. For some of them think in terms of what you add to the known addend to get the sum.

(a) 87 − 32	(b) 99 − 47	(c) 71 − 45
(d) 100 − 77	(e) 574 − 223	(f) 999 − 547
(g) 651 − 328	(h) 1000 − 753	(i) 724 − 486
(j) 815 − 369	(k) 7384 − 3122	(l) 9999 − 5879
(m) 6412 − 2851	(n) 10,000 − 6853	(o) 8147 − 3528
(p) 9130 − 4876	(q) 6451 − 2386	(r) 6666 − 3777

4. A student who learns the Austrian method for subtraction finally uses a shortcut and thinks in the following way.

$$\begin{array}{r} 452 \\ 185 \\ \hline \mathbf{7} \end{array}$$ 5 and **7** are 12; carry 1;
8 and 1 are 9.

$$\begin{array}{r} 452 \\ 185 \\ \hline \mathbf{6}7 \end{array}$$ 9 and **6** are 15; carry 1;
1 and 1 are 2.

$$\begin{array}{r} 452 \\ 185 \\ \hline \mathbf{2}57 \end{array}$$ 2 and **2** are 4.

He writes down the bold-faced numbers. Explain why this way of thinking leads to the correct answer.

5. Some schools teach the following method for subtraction. Explain the reasoning.

$$\begin{array}{r} 83 \\ 47 \\ \hline 6 \end{array} \quad 13 - 7 = 6; \qquad \begin{array}{r} 83 \\ 47 \\ \hline 36 \end{array} \quad 80 - 50 = 30$$

4. RECREATIONAL MATH

Rapid computers regroup numbers when they add, watching for combinations that make 10. The following example illustrates their method.

$$7 + 4 + 3 + 2 + 6 + 8 = 30$$

Most students can double their speed in addition by watching for such combinations.

EXERCISES

1. Using the associative and commutative properties, group numbers to form tens and give answers as quickly as possible.

(a) $6 + 9 + 4 + 1$ (b) $8 + 7 + 3 + 2$
(c) $4 + 3 + 4 + 7$ (d) $5 + 9 + 5 + 2$
(e) $5 + 2 + 8 + 4 + 6 + 5$ (f) $7 + 1 + 9 + 8 + 3$

(g) 8	(h) 4	(i) 8	(j) 6	(k) 5	(l) 9
3	6	3	6	7	9
7	5	2	8	3	1
2	7	7	2	5	4
9	5	4	4	4	6

(m) 5	(n) 8	(o) 3	(p) 6	(q) 7	(r) 3
3	8	4	3	7	4
7	7	5	4	9	5
5	2	6	4	3	6
4	2	7	6	1	5

(s) 2	(t) 8	(u) 4	(v) 9	(w) 3	(x) 2
9	7	5	9	3	4
1	8	7	7	6	6
8	2	6	1	7	8
7	3	4	1	4	9

2. Work the following addition problems, watching for opportunities to group by tens.

(a) 83	(b) 71	(c) 46	(d) 83	(e) 254
57	36	46	39	637
54	89	34	61	376
36	54	53	77	452
72	57	77	44	783

(f) 614	(g) 864	(h) 683
286	356	527
451	247	436
251	772	752
862	438	384

3. Use the fact that $6 + 7 + 8 + 9 = 30$ to obtain the following sums quickly.

(a) $6 + 7 + 4 + 8 + 9$ (b) $7 + 8 + 7 + 9 + 6$
(c) $6 + 8 + 6 + 9 + 7$ (d) $7 + 9 + 3 + 6 + 8$
(e) $4 + 7 + 9 + 6 + 2 + 8$ (f) $3 + 9 + 7 + 8 + 5 + 6$
(g) $9 + 2 + 6 + 7 + 8 + 5$ (h) $8 + 8 + 9 + 1 + 6 + 7$

4. Use the facts that $8 + 7 + 5 = 20$, $6 + 6 + 8 = 20$, $8 + 8 + 4 = 20$, and $9 + 9 + 2 = 20$ to get answers quickly.

(a) 8	(b) 3	(c) 9	(d) 3	(e) 6
7	8	7	5	8
5	5	1	8	6
4	7	8	6	1
4	3	5	6	5

(f) 6	(g) 8	(h) 5	(i) 7	(j) 3
3	8	5	8	8
8	4	8	4	4
6	7	4	8	7
7	1	8	1	8

(k) 9	(l) 7	(m) 6	(n) 5	(o) 6
9	2	9	6	7
2	9	4	7	8
5	9	9	8	7
4	1	2	9	6

5. In the following addition problems, replace the asterisks by digits so that the answers are correct.

(a) *937	(b) 574*	(c) 5373*	(d) 3*7
8*	2*7	*1059	8524
109	63	*006	1*
4*85	8*28	69	*35
85*7	**174	*31**1	*623

6. Replace the asterisks by digits so that the answers to these subtraction problems are correct.

(a) 9*74*	(b) *6**2	(c) 3*548*	(d) 5583*
6*23	*975	*3*7*5	**2**
*11*5	7948*	126*62	9639

Persons who do rapid mental calculation add from *left* to *right*. For example, in adding 32 + 53 they think first 80, and then 5. When adding 47 + 39, they see that there is one to carry and think 8 and then 6, that is 86. Compute the following sums:

32	51	27	46	73	46	69	85
43	34	53	29	82	57	72	76

With practice, this method will enable you to add a column of several two-digit numbers rapidly. For example, to work the problem below you would think:

Tens Ones	Tens Ones	Tens Ones		$14\binom{31}{24}4$
8 9	11 3	14 4	or 144	$11\binom{24}{53}3$
				$8\binom{53}{36}9$

EXERCISES

Work the problems below.

1. 32	2. 42	3. 34	4. 32	5. 23
21	33	20	46	35
14	25	53	15	68
6. 23	7. 34	8. 41	9. 26	10. 64
34	27	38	43	53
21	45	64	52	27
36	62	55	17	81
11. 42	12. 35	13. 75	14. 91	15. 76
21	23	83	36	87
35	57	46	28	49
46	84	27	47	66
17	32	65	56	75

Chapter 6

TECHNIQUES OF MULTIPLICATION AND DIVISION

1. INTRODUCTION

In this chapter we shall see that our usual methods for working multiplication and division problems depend upon the properties of these operations. Again, if we learn a few basic facts (the multiplication table from 0 × 0 up to 9 × 9), we can use the associative, commutative, and distributive properties to multiply any numbers, no matter how large; we never need more than these basic facts. Of course, we are able to simplify our computation in this way because our system of numeration makes use of *place value*.

2. THE BASIC FACTS OF MULTIPLICATION

We have 100 addition facts from 0 + 0 to 9 + 9. There are also 100 multiplication facts from 0 × 0 to 9 × 9. These are given in Table 6–1. Of course, Table 6–1 shows only the 10 by 10 corner of a multiplication table that extends endlessly in both directions. If we fold this table on the diagonal through the upper left-hand corner, two squares that fall together contain the same number.

EXERCISES

1. What property of multiplication is illustrated by folding the table along the diagonal line?
2. What property is illustrated by the top row and left-hand column? by the second row and the second column?
3. What are the first five entries in the column headed 500? in the row headed 420?
4. What is the entry in the row labeled 432 and the column labeled 526? in the 526 row and the 432 column?

TABLE 6–1

THE BASIC MULTIPLICATION FACTS

	0	1	2	3	4	5	6	7	8	9	10	11
0	0	0	0	0	0	0	0	0	0	0		
1	0	1	2	3	4	5	6	7	8	9		
2	0	2	4	6	8	10	12	14	16	18		
3	0	3	6	9	12	15	18	21	24	27		
4	0	4	8	12	16	20	24	28	32	36		
5	0	5	10	15	20	25	30	35	40	45		
6	0	6	12	18	24	30	36	42	48	54		
7	0	7	14	21	28	35	42	49	56	63		
8	0	8	16	24	32	40	48	56	64	72		
9	0	9	18	27	36	45	54	63	72	81		
10												
11												

5. Are all the entries in the column headed 743 the same as those in the row headed 743?

6. Look at any column. If the first number other than 0 is even, all the numbers in the column are even. If this first number is odd, the numbers alternate: odd, even, odd, even, etc. Explain why this is so.

7. Look at any *row* or *diagonal*. It has the property described in Exercise 6. Can you explain why?

8. Look at the numbers in the diagonal through the upper left-hand corner. They are 0, 1, 4, 9, 16, 25, 36, etc. Note how they increase in size:

$$1 - 0 = 1; \quad 4 - 1 = 3; \quad 9 - 4 = 5; \quad 16 - 9 = 7; \ldots$$

That is, they increase by

$$1, 3, 5, 7, 9, 11, 13, 15, 17, \ldots$$

Do you think that this pattern continues forever? Write what you think are the next ten numbers on this diagonal.

TABLE 6–2

THE 28 KEY MULTIPLICATION FACTS

	0	1	2	3	4	5	6	7	8	9
0										
1										
2										
3				9	12	15	18	21	24	27
4					16	20	24	28	32	36
5						25	30	35	40	45
6							36	42	48	54
7								49	56	63
8									64	72
9										81

9. Study other diagonals, for example, the one just below the diagonal through the upper left-hand corner with the entries 0, 2, 6, 12, 20, 30, . . . Note that these numbers increase by

$$2, 4, 6, 8, 10, \ldots$$

Can you explain why?

10. Study diagonals running down and to the left. What are some of the patterns that you observe?

It is interesting to realize that knowledge of the commutative property and the properties of 0 and 1 makes it unnecessary to memorize the entire table. We already know the facts given by the first two rows and columns. The numbers in the row and column headed 2 are simple addition facts, for example, $2 \times 7 = 7 + 7$. It is enough to learn the products listed in Table 6–2.

Many of the 28 key facts listed in the table are easily learned. For example, the numbers in the row or column headed 5 are easy to remember. (Why?) Hence we may drop these, which leaves us with

TABLE 6–3

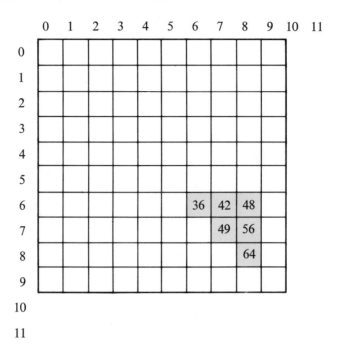

	0	1	2	3	4	5	6	7	8	9	10	11
0												
1												
2												
3												
4												
5												
6							36	42	48			
7								49	56			
8									64			
9												
10												
11												

only 21 facts to master. Next we see that the 9 column is not difficult because

$$9 \times 3 = (10 \times 3) - (1 \times 3); \quad 9 \times 7 = (10 \times 7) - (1 \times 7), \quad \text{etc.}$$

We therefore eliminate the numbers in the 9 column and have only 15 facts left to learn. Using the distributive property, we find that the 4 row is easy to learn:

$$4 \times 7 = (2 + 2) \times 7$$
$$= (2 \times 7) + (2 \times 7) \quad \text{(by the distributive property)}$$
$$= 14 + 14$$
$$= 28$$

Very few students have trouble learning the multiples of 3:

$$3 \times 8 = (2 + 1) \times 8 = (2 \times 8) + (1 \times 8) = 16 \times 8 = 24$$

TABLE 6–4

THE BASIC MULTIPLICATION FACTS ON NOVA

	O	|	L	⊔	□	∧	△	⊕
O								
|								
L			□	△	|O	|L	|□	|△
⊔				||	|□	|⊕	LL	L∧
□					LO	L□	⊔O	⊔□
∧						⊔|	⊔△	□⊔
△							□□	∧L
⊕								△|

Throwing away all entries in the rows and columns labeled 3, 4, and 5 and the entries in the 9 column, we are *left with only six "difficult" basic facts. All others can be calculated very quickly from the addition combinations by means of the associative, commutative, and distributive properties.* Many students become discouraged in their attempts to learn the multiplication facts because they think that all must be memorized. A student who does not know these facts as well as he should might use the method described below.

(1) Memorize the six "difficult" facts.

(2) Compute unknown facts, using the known facts and the associative, commutative, and distributive properties.

Table 6–3 shows the six facts that everybody should memorize.

The problem of learning the basic multiplication facts is the same as the problem that you face when you try to master any body of knowledge. *You must not depend upon your memory alone.* You *must understand basic ideas* so that if you should forget some fact, you can quickly work out what you want to know. By concentrating on the important ideas and using these important ideas to work out many special problems you will learn far more than by depending upon rote memory.

EXERCISES

1. The key facts in the multiplication table printed in arithmetic books on the planet Nova are given in Table 6–4. Use the properties of multiplication to fill out the table.
2. Explain how to use the distributive property to get the products in the ① (seven) column.

3. USING THE PROPERTIES IN MULTIPLICATION AND DIVISION

In working multiplication problems with large numbers, we use the properties in such a way that each calculation depends upon the basic facts. For example, when we multiply 8×24, we write:

$$\begin{array}{r} 24 \\ 8 \\ \hline 192 \end{array}$$

We simply think:

$$8 \times 4 = 32: \quad 3 \text{ to carry};$$
$$8 \times 2 = 16, \quad 16 + 3 = 19$$

We have the *right to think* in this manner because of the *associative*, *commutative*, and *distributive* properties. Let us write out all the steps. We write

$$\begin{aligned} 8 \times 24 &= 8 \times (20 + 4) \\ &= (8 \times 20) + (8 \times 4) \\ &= [(8 \times 2) \times 10] + 32 \\ &= [(10 + 6) \times 10] + (3 \times 10) + 2 \\ &= (10 \times 10) + (6 \times 10) + (3 \times 10) + 2 \\ &= (10 \times 10) + (9 \times 10) + 2 \\ &= 192 \end{aligned}$$

We think: "Eight twenty-fours are eight 20's and eight 4's. Eight times 20 is eight times two 10's, or sixteen 10's; and eight 4's are three 10's and 2. This is 100 and nine 10's and 2, or 192."

In this example, point out how the distributive property was used.

In division we use the same properties. When we divide 288 by 12, we write:

$$
\begin{array}{r}
24 \\
12\overline{)288} \\
24 \\
\hline
48 \\
48 \\
\hline
\end{array}
$$

We think:

$$2 \times 12 = 24; \quad 28 - 24 = 4;$$

$$\text{bring down the } 8; \quad 4 \times 12 = 48$$

We explain this method of working the problem below:

$$
\begin{aligned}
\overset{P}{288} &= (240 + 48) \\
&= (10 \times 24) + 48 \\
&= [(10 \times 2) \times 12] + (4 \times 12) \\
&= (20 \times 12) + (4 \times 12) \\
&= \overset{F}{(20} + 4) \overset{F}{\times} 12
\end{aligned}
$$

Hence we have

$$\overset{P}{288} \div \overset{F}{12} = \overset{F}{20 + 4}$$

EXERCISES

1. Use your understanding of place value to get the answer to each problem. After working each problem write it in the ordinary multiplication form. For example, for (a) you would write 4×21.

   (a) $[4 \times (2 \times 10)] + (4 \times 1)$ [*Hint:* We are multiplying by 4.]
   (b) $[4 \times (2 \times 10)] + (4 \times 3)$
   (c) $[8 \times (5 \times 10)] + (8 + 6)$
   (d) $[3 \times (2 \times 10 \times 10)] + 3 \times (3 \times 10) + (3 \times 2)$
   (e) $[5 \times (4 \times 10 \times 10)] + 5 \times (6 \times 10) + (5 \times 7)$
   (f) $[10 \times (3 \times 10)] + (10 \times 2) + [4 \times (3 \times 10)] + (4 \times 2)$
   (g) $[30 \times (6 \times 10)] + (30 \times 5) + [7 \times (6 \times 10)] + (7 \times 5)$

2. Give the answer to each problem. After working each problem write it in the ordinary division form. For example, for (a) you would write 161 ÷ 7.

(a) [(2 × 10 × 7) + (3 × 7)] ÷ 7
(b) [(3 × 10 × 9) + (6 × 9)] ÷ 9
(c) [(3 × 10 × 12) + (3 × 12)] ÷ 12
(d) [(4 × 10 × 14) + (5 × 14)] ÷ 14
(e) [(2 × 10 × 10 × 8) + (3 × 10 × 8) + (2 × 8)] ÷ 8
(f) [(5 × 10 × 26) + (4 × 26)] ÷ 26
(g) [(6 × 10 × 54) + (3 × 54)] ÷ 54

4. DEVELOPING SKILL IN MULTIPLICATION AND DIVISION

The arrays of dots that we used for multiplication and division are not very helpful when we are working with large numbers. However, if we visualize a 12 × 13 array, we can use the distributive property and obtain the product mentally. Using the distributive law several times, we get

$$(10 + 2) \times (10 + 3) = (10 \times 10) + (2 \times 10) + (10 \times 3) + (2 \times 3)$$

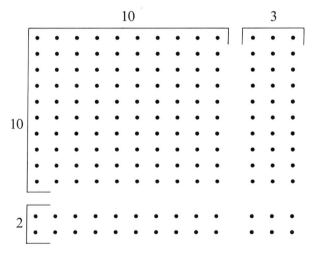

$$12 \times 13 = (10 \times 10) + (2 \times 10) + (10 \times 3) + (2 \times 3)$$

EXERCISES

Think of dot arrays and write answers for as many of the following problems as you can, doing all work mentally.

1. 10×10 2. 10×11 3. 11×10 4. 11×11

5. 12×14 6. 11×13 7. 11×15 8. 13×13

9. 14×14 10. 15×15 11. 12×15 12. 15×13

13. 12×16 14. 16×14 15. 12×17 16. 13×16

17. 15×16 18. 16×16 19. 17×17 20. 18×18

21. 19×19 22. Draw dot arrays for Exercises 5, 12, 15 and 19.

Skill in multiplication and division depends very much upon the ability to multiply any number mentally by 10, 100, 1000, etc. You undoubtedly remember the rules:

To multiply a number by 10, annex one zero.

To multiply a number by 100, annex two zeros.

To multiply a number by 1000, annex three zeros.

There is little value in memorizing rules like these. But it is certainly necessary that you understand the ideas behind these rules. *When you understand, then there is no need to memorize.*

Using the rules above, you would multiply 34 by 10, 100, and 1000 by writing

$$340, \quad 3400, \quad 34{,}000$$

Using the distributive property we can explain why these answers are correct.

$$34 \times 10 = [(3 \times 10) + 4] \times 10 = (3 \times 10 \times 10) + (4 \times 10) = 340$$
$$34 \times 100 = [(3 \times 10) + 4] \times (10 \times 10)$$
$$= (3 \times 10 \times 10 \times 10) + (4 \times 10 \times 10)$$
$$= 3000 + 400 = 3400$$

EXERCISES

1. Use the distributive property as above and show that

$$42 \times 10 = 420 \quad \text{and} \quad 42 \times 1000 = 42{,}000$$

2. Give answers to the following problems.

   (a) $(10 + 5) \times 10$ (b) $(100 + 10 + 2) \times 10$
   (c) $(30 + 7) \times 10$ (d) $(200 + 40 + 5) \times 10$
   (e) $(10 + 6) \times 100$ (f) $(30 + 7) \times 100$
   (g) $(100 + 4) \times 10$ (h) $(300 + 50 + 7) \times 100$
   (i) $(1000 + 10 + 1) \times 10$ (j) $(1000 + 300 + 50 + 4) \times 100$

3. Use the shortcut and give the products.

   (a) 36×10 (b) 45×100
   (c) 246×10 (d) 452×100
   (e) 2534×10 (f) 2156×100
   (g) 2463×1000 (h) 8888×1000

4. Write the products.

   (a) 20×30 (b) 200×30 (c) 200×300
   (d) 20×3000 (e) 30×40 (f) 300×400
   (g) 30×400 (h) 60×50 (i) 80×70
   (j) 60×600 (k) 600×700 (l) 220×20
   (m) 220×30 (n) 220×200 (o) 132×20
   (p) 132×300 (q) 2134×200 (r) 2132×2000

5. Find the missing factor.

   (a) $240 \div 24 = n$ (b) $850 \div 85 = n$
   (c) $670 \div 67 = n$ (d) $3200 \div 32 = n$
   (e) $8900 \div 89 = n$ (f) $430 \div 10 = n$
   (g) $670 \div 10 = n$ (h) $1200 \div 100 = n$
   (i) $3600 \div 36 = n$ (j) $9700 \div 97 = n$
   (k) $47,300 \div 100 = n$ (l) $53,600 \div 536 = n$
   (m) $8000 \div 8 = n$ (n) $17,000 \div 1000 = n$
   (o) $60 \div 20 = n$ (p) $600 \div 20 = n$
   (q) $6000 \div 20 = n$ (r) $600 \div 200 = n$
   (s) $6000 \div 200 = n$ (t) $800 \div 20 = n$
   (u) $6400 \div 200 = n$ (v) $6400 \div 20 = n$
   (w) $8640 \div 20 = n$ (x) $66,000 \div 2000 = n$
   (y) $8800 \div 44 = n$ (z) $66,000 \div 220 = n$

When we multiply 324 by 232, we multiply it by 200, by 30, and by 2 and add these three products:

$$
\begin{array}{ll}
324 & \\
232 & \\
\hline
648 & 2 \times 324 \\
9720 & 30 \times 324 \\
64800 & 200 \times 324 \\
\hline
75168 & 232 \times 324
\end{array}
$$

Of course, the result tells us also that

$$75168 \div 324 = 232 \quad \text{and} \quad 75168 \div 232 = 324$$

EXERCISES

For each problem, give a multiplication fact and two division facts.

1. 2300	2. 2300	3. 4600
230	460	230
23	46	69
2553	2806	4899

4. 3400	5. 4100	6. 7300
340	820	146
68	123	292
3808	5043	7738

7. Find the products. Explain the algorithm you use.

(a) 32	(b) 32	(c) 27	(d) 352
43	54	58	46

(e) 257	(f) 368	(g) 423	(h) 367
84	29	514	425

(i) 378	(j) 3524	(k) 4763	(l) 8732
496	86	584	4658

We can get answers to multiplication problems by repeated addition:

$$5 \times 8 = 8 + 8 + 8 + 8 + 8$$
$$12 \times 8 = (10 \times 8) + 8 + 8$$

We can get answers to division problems by repeated subtraction.

Example 1.

$$
\begin{array}{r}
48 \\
12 \\
\hline
36 \\
12 \\
\hline
24 \\
12 \\
\hline
12 \\
12 \\
\hline
0
\end{array}
$$

This shows that

$$4 \times 12 = 48 \quad \text{or} \quad 48 \div 12 = 4$$

Example 2.

$$
\begin{array}{rl}
276 & \\
240 & 20 \times 12 \\
\hline
36 & \\
36 & 3 \times 12 \\
\hline
0 &
\end{array}
$$

This shows that

$$23 \times 12 = 276 \quad \text{or} \quad 276 \div 12 = 23$$

Example 3.

$$
\begin{array}{rl}
4704 & \\
4200 & 100 \times 42 \\
\hline
504 & \\
420 & 10 \times 42 \\
\hline
84 & \\
84 & 2 \times 42 \\
\hline
0 &
\end{array}
$$

This shows that

$$4704 \div 42 = 112$$

EXERCISES

Give a division fact shown by each of the repeated subtractions below.

1.	2.	3.	4.
129	385	372	533
43	350	360	520
86	35	12	13
43	35	12	13
43	0	0	0
43			
0			

5. 1476	6. 4096	7. 4551	8. 5313
1200	3200	3700	4600
276	896	851	713
240	640	740	690
36	256	111	23
36	256	111	23
0	0	0	0

Our shortcut method of long division is the repeated subtraction method used in the last exercise list. We usually omit some of the zeros. Compare the three examples below.

```
4551                        3
3700      100 × 37         20
 851                      100            123
 740       20 × 37     37)4551       37)4551
 111                      3700           37
 111       3 × 37          851           85
                          740           74
                          111          111
                          111          111
```

EXERCISES

Find the quotients. Explain the algorithm you use.

1. 3808 ÷ 34	2. 4114 ÷ 34	3. 1584 ÷ 12
4. 4704 ÷ 42	5. 2553 ÷ 23	6. 736 ÷ 32
7. 5082 ÷ 22	8. 1548 ÷ 43	9. 2448 ÷ 24
10. 3296 ÷ 32	11. 6072 ÷ 253	12. 30,104 ÷ 142
13. 79,608 ÷ 321	14. 28,304 ÷ 232	15. 53,460 ÷ 243
16. 6794 ÷ 86	17. 35,376 ÷ 67	18. 171,424 ÷ 352
19. 151,351 ÷ 493	20. 6794 ÷ 79	21. 35,376 ÷ 528
22. 308,025 ÷ 555	23. 443,556 ÷ 666	24. 298,224 ÷ 654
25. 778,743 ÷ 987		

5. DIVISION WITH A REMAINDER

Not all division problems "come out even." For example,

$$2415 = (100 \times 24) + 15$$

There is no whole number factor n such that

$$24 \times n = 2415$$

We see that

$$24 \times 100 < 2415, \qquad 24 \times 101 > 2415$$

We say that when 2415 is divided by 24, the *quotient* is 100 and the *remainder* is 15. If a group of 2415 people is separated into groups of 24 each, then there will be 100 such groups, and 15 persons are left—not enough to form another group of 24. When the division problem "comes out even," as, for example, in

$$2448 \div 24 = 102$$

we say that the *remainder is zero.*

In describing division with a remainder, we use the terms *divisor*, *quotient*, *remainder.* The diagram below shows how these terms apply.

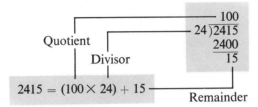

Looking at the statement $2415 = (100 \times 24) + 15$, we can say that the divisor is 24 or we can say that it is 100. There are twenty-four 100's in 2415 and 15 is left over. We agree that the remainder must be *less than* the divisor. Let us now look at

$$2435 = (100 \times 24) + 35$$

If we are dividing 2435 by 24, we subtract another 24 from the 35. In this case, the *quotient* is 101, and the remainder is 11.

EXERCISES

1. Give the quotient and remainder for each problem below.

(a) $814 \div 100$	(b) $814 \div 81$	(c) $900 \div 100$
(d) $824 \div 10$	(e) $824 \div 8$	(f) $3526 \div 1000$
(g) $3526 \div 100$	(h) $3526 \div 10$	(i) $3526 \div 352$
(j) $3526 \div 35$	(k) $934 \div 1000$	(l) $934 \div 100$
(m) $934 \div 10$	(n) $934 \div 1$	(o) $934 \div 934$
(p) $934 \div 93$	(q) $934 \div 9$	(r) $93 \div 10$
(s) $247 \div 10$	(t) $247 \div 24$	(u) $247 \div 2$
(v) $93 \div 1000$	(w) $93 \div 100$	(x) $12,000 \div 1000$
(y) $35,712 \div 35$		

2. *Estimate* the quotient for each of the problems given.

(a) 600 ÷ 99   (b) 8000 ÷ 999   (c) 3600 ÷ 99
(d) 800 ÷ 199   (e) 7999 ÷ 99   (f) 9001 ÷ 99
(g) 4000 ÷ 998   (h) 2400 ÷ 98   (i) 9000 ÷ 101
(j) 4000 ÷ 198   (k) 6101 ÷ 102   (l) 4312 ÷ 99

3. In Exercise 2, give what you think are the exact remainders.

4. Each number sentence below can be used to get the quotient and remainder for two division problems. For example, because $3260 = (101 \times 32) + 28$, we can say that if the divisor is 101, the quotient is 32 and the remainder is 28, and if the divisor is 32, the quotient is 101 and the remainder is 28. Give the two possible sets of divisor, quotient, and remainder for each sentence.

(a) $2715 = (100 \times 27) + 15$ (b) $3681 = (102 \times 36) + 9$
(c) $5374 = (111 \times 48) + 46$ (d) $8375 = (306 \times 27) + 13$
(e) $9645 = (300 \times 32) + 45$ (f) $8674 = (172 \times 50) + 74$
(g) $8729 = (203 \times 43) + 0$ (h) $300,994 = (842 \times 357) + 400$

5. Find the quotient and remainder for each problem below.

(a) 6832 ÷ 32   (b) 6832 ÷ 64   (c) 6832 ÷ 68
(d) 3557 ÷ 32   (e) 8144 ÷ 77   (f) 8888 ÷ 76
(g) 30,000 ÷ 50   (h) 14,421 ÷ 72   (i) 5972 ÷ 94
(j) 8613 ÷ 65   (k) 10,426 ÷ 81   (l) 37,524 ÷ 124
(m) 9882 ÷ 94   (n) 26,763 ÷ 126   (o) 28,743 ÷ 251
(p) 31,487 ÷ 568   (q) 76,438 ÷ 847   (r) 386,254 ÷ 999
(s) 111,111 ÷ 77   (t) 111,111 ÷ 777

6. RECREATIONAL MATH

Since we can mentally multiply any number by 100 or 1000, it is easy to multiply by numbers near 100 or 1000. For example,

$$100 \times 73 = 7300$$

hence

$$101 \times 73 = (100 + 1) \times 73$$
$$= 7300 + 73$$
$$= 7373$$

$$99 \times 73 = (100 - 1) \times 73$$
$$= 7300 - 73$$
$$= 7227$$

In the last example, 99×73, if we subtract mentally from left to right, we can write the answer at once.

EXERCISES

Compute the following products mentally.

1. 101 × 43	2. 99 × 43	3. 101 × 87
4. 99 × 87	5. 102 × 34	6. 98 × 34
7. 102 × 23	8. 98 × 23	9. 1001 × 357
10. 999 × 357	11. 1001 × 886	12. 999 × 886
13. 998 × 423	14. 1002 × 423	15. 99 × 317

16. Determine the missing digits in the following multiplication problems. Each star (*) stands in the place of some digit.

(a)
```
  2*
   4
  --
  92
```

(b)
```
  **
   6
  --
  78
```

(c)
```
  23
  **
 ---
 368
```

(d)
```
   42
   3*
  ---
  2*0
  126
 ----
 1**0
```

(e)
```
   36
   1*
  ---
  1*0
   36
  ---
  **0
```

(f)
```
   37
   2*
  ---
  *4*
   74
  ---
  88*
```

(g)
```
   **
   43
  ---
   **
  ***
 -----
 11*8
```

(h)
```
   **
   42
  ---
   7*
  ***
 -----
 ***0
```

(i)
```
   **
   6*
  ---
  **1
  **2
 -----
 29*1
```

(j)
```
   **
   54
  ---
  ***
  ***
 -----
 3*34
```

(k)
```
   99
   **
  ---
  ***
  ***
 -----
 22**
```

(l)
```
  ***
   77
 ----
 ****
 ****
 ------
 276**
```

(m)
```
   ***
   999
  ----
  ****
  ****
  ****
 ------
 47***4
```

(n)
```
   ***
    78
  ----
  ****
  ****
 ------
 524**
```

17. Determine the missing digits in the division problems. All answers have remainder zero.

```
           34                    2*                  **                  *3*
(a)   12)***       (b)   3*)*2*       (c)   84)***       (d)   **)3**8
        3*                   **                  **                  **
      ─────                ─────               ─────               ─────
        4*                  16*                  **                  8*
        48                  16*                  *4                  *2
      ─────                ─────               ─────              ─────
                                                                   1*8
                                                                   1*8
                                                                  ─────
```

A special shortcut method of multiplication which places a mild strain upon one's mental processes is described below. We omit a detailed explanation, but of course the method can be justified by the basic principles. The product of two 2-digit numbers is found in 3 steps as shown below.

$$
\begin{array}{ccc}
12 \rangle & 1\;2 & \swarrow 12 \\
23 \diagup & 2\!\!\times\!\!3 & \diagdown 23 \\
\hline
6 & 7\;6 & 276
\end{array}
$$

The computation of the product of two 3-digit numbers requires five steps, as shown.

$$
\begin{array}{ccccc}
213 \rangle & 21\!\times\!3 & 2\diagdown\!1\diagup3 & 2\diagup 13 & \swarrow 213 \\
123 \diagup & 12\;3 & 1\diagdown2\;3 & 1\diagup 23 & \diagdown 123 \\
\hline
9 & 9\;9 & 1\;9\;9 & 6\;199 & 26199
\end{array}
$$

(1 to carry)

Without drawing arrows to indicate the proper combinations we give the step by step solutions of two other problems below.

```
            34                34                34
            25                25                25
           ───               ───               ───
             0                50               850
      (2 to carry)     (2 to carry)
```

```
     364           364           364           364           364
     235           235           235           235           235
    ────          ────          ────          ────          ────
       0            40           540          5540         85540
 (2 to carry)  (4 to carry)  (4 to carry)  (2 to carry)
```

EXERCISES

Use the method described above to find the following products.

1. 32	2. 32	3. 32	4. 123
11	12	22	111
5. 214	6. 32	7. 26	8. 71
121	43	53	42
9. 232	10. 315	11. 445	12. 654
143	423	326	738

There is an interesting shortcut for squaring any number whose units digit is five. This shortcut may be explained by the commutative, associative, and distributive principles. Here we only describe the method. The final two digits for such a product will be always "25." Hence, to determine a product like 65×65 we need only determine the first two digits:

$$65 \times 65 = \_\_25.$$

The first two digits are given by the product 6×7. Hence

$$65 \times 65 = \mathbf{42}25$$

As other examples:

$$35 \times 35 = \mathbf{12}25 \qquad (12 = 3 \times 4)$$
$$55 \times 55 = \mathbf{30}25 \qquad (30 = 5 \times 6)$$
$$125 \times 125 = \mathbf{156}25 \qquad (156 = 12 \times 13)$$

EXERCISES

1. Give the products.

   (a) 75×75 (b) 95×95 (c) 25×25
   (d) 105×105 (e) 995×995 (f) 245×245

2. A shortcut has been used in each multiplication problem below. Can you give an explanation?

7436	35274
639	42357
66924	246918
468468	1234590
4751604	14815080
	1494100818

3. There is a shortcut for dividing by 99. This is illustrated by the two examples below. Can you give an explanation?

$$99\,\overline{)\,73\,|\,12}$$
$$73$$
$$\overline{85}$$

The quotient is 73;
the remainder is 85.

$$99\,\overline{)\,416\,|\,72}$$
$$4\,|\,16$$
$$|\,4$$
$$\overline{420\,|\,92}$$

The quotient is 420;
the remainder is 92.

Chapter 7

PROBLEM
SOLVING

1. INTRODUCTION

Mathematics is more than counting, computing, and measuring. Mathematicians have far more interesting things to do than to spend their time adding long columns of numbers. In this chapter we shall give you an opportunity to use your reasoning powers to solve problems involving the four operations we have been studying. In the next chapter we shall see that reasoning is also important for the solution of problems that have nothing to do with the operations of arithmetic. Often scientists and mathematicians use electronic computers to carry out the necessary calculations. But someone has to program (prepare) the machine for this purpose. Programming requires that the problem be analyzed and that the operations needed to complete the calculation be determined so that the machine can be directed to perform these operations. Very careful reasoning is needed to determine the operations required to solve complicated problems.

EXERCISES

In each problem decide which operation or operations you would perform upon the known numbers to arrive at the required answer.

1. If you knew how many marbles each of two boys had, how would you decide how many more one had than the other?
2. If you knew how far a family taking a trip had driven on each of two days, how would you decide how far they had driven in all?

3. If you knew how many hours one had worked and how much he had earned each hour, how would you compute his earnings?

4. If you knew a man's yearly salary, how would you find his average monthly salary?

5. If you know the height of a pile of boards and the number of boards in the pile, and if you know that all boards are of the same thickness, how do you determine the thickness of each board?

6. If you know the number of students in each class of a school, how do you find the total school enrollment?

7. If, for a certain class, you know the number of students absent and also the number present, how do you arrive at the total class enrollment?

8. A girl knows the price of a new bicycle. She counts her money and finds that she does not have enough. How can she find out how much more she needs?

9. You have a collection of nickels and dimes. After counting the nickels and the dimes, how do you decide how much money you have in cents?

10. You know the average speed of a satellite in miles per minute and you know how many hours it has been circling the earth. How do you decide how many miles it has traveled?

11. Two cars enter a toll road at the same time but drive in opposite directions. You know the average speed of each car. How do you find out how far apart they are after a certain number of hours?

12. Work Exercise 11 with the condition that the cars travel in the same direction.

13. Each number expression below represents the answer to a problem programmed for a computer. Make up a word problem for each expression.

(a) $17 + 15$ (b) $30 - 14$
(c) 7×12 (d) $(5 \times 4) + (10 \times 3)$
(e) 53×4 (f) $(40 + 50) \times 3$
(g) 12×550 (h) 52×98
(i) $814 - 427$ (j) $4160 \div 52$

2. AVOIDING CARELESS MISTAKES

Students in a high school class were studying verbal problems. Their teacher gave them the following problem.

A boy had 20 hamsters. All but 7 died. How many were left?

Jill raised her hand and said, "I think he must have had 13 left." How would you analyze Jill's error?

A little later the following problem was given.

One boy can wax a car in 6 hours and another can wax the car in 3 hours. If they work together how long will it take them to wax one car?

Ted, who was an excellent student, answered quickly. "That's easy," he said, "the answer is 9 hours."

Most of the students in the class nodded their heads in agreement, but one disagreed. "I don't know the answer," he said, "but I can prove that 9 hours is wrong." What argument do you think he gave to convince the class?

It is easy to make mistakes. Often we make mistakes just because we fail to use common sense. Frequently, we try to answer too quickly and overlook some important information in the problem. Sometimes the wording of the problem is such that we are tricked into thinking we should add when we really should subtract or vice versa. In order to avoid careless mistakes we should read each problem carefully and think about its meaning before trying to solve it.

EXERCISES

For each problem below, a wrong answer is given. Explain why the given answer is wrong and, using common sense, estimate the correct answer. Explain how one might reason in giving each incorrect answer.

1. A watch and a ring cost $140. The watch cost $40 more than the ring. How much did each cost?

   Answer: Watch $40, ring $100

2. How many inches are there in 48 feet?

   Answer: 4

3. A baseball team played 150 games. It has won 30 more games than it has lost. How many games has it won?

   Answer: 180

4. It is 74 miles from town *A* to town *B*. It is 32 miles from town *B* to town *C* and town *C* is on the road between *A* and *B*. How far is it from *A* to *C*?

Answer: 106 miles

5. One pipe can fill a tank in 15 minutes and another in 12 minutes. How long will it take to fill the tank if both pipes are used?

Answer: 27 minutes

6. Joe had $20. He spent $2 in one store and half of the remainder of his money in a second store. How much money did he have left?

Answer: $8

7. An archery set and a tennis racket together cost $48. The archery set cost 3 times as much as the tennis racket. How much did the tennis racket cost?

Answer: $16

8. The average life of man is about 2,000,000,000 seconds. The giant turtle lives $\frac{1}{2}$ again as long as man. How many seconds is the average life of the giant turtle?

Answer: 1,000,000,000 seconds

9. Six years ago Sam was 6 and Joe was 18. What is the number by which you must multiply Sam's age to get Joe's age?

Answer: 3

10. A tank can be filled in 15 minutes by pumping water through one pipe. A drain pipe makes it possible to empty the tank in 10 minutes. The tank is full of water and the drain pipe is opened at the same moment at which the pump for filling the tank is turned on. How long will it take the tank to empty?

Answer: 5 minutes

3. DRAWING DIAGRAMS IN PROBLEM SOLVING

Diagrams are sometimes helpful in solving problems. What we need, of course, is to form a clear mental picture of each problem situation so we can concentrate on the important ideas. Sometimes a sketch calls our attention to ideas that we might otherwise overlook. There are no rules that can be given for drawing figures to represent problems. Certainly the quality of your art work is not very important. As soon as a sketch shows you how to solve a problem it has served its purpose. Here are some examples of using diagrams.

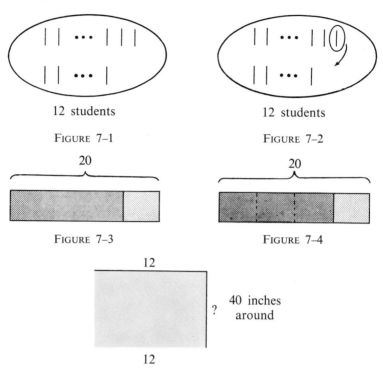

12 students

FIGURE 7–1

12 students

FIGURE 7–2

20

FIGURE 7–3

20

FIGURE 7–4

12

? 40 inches around

12

FIGURE 7–5

Example 1. In a group of 12 students there are two more boys than girls. How many boys and how many girls are there? We make the marks shown in Fig. 7–1. The first row of marks represents the boys, the second the girls. Now, think of moving one of the boys down into the line of girls, as shown in Fig. 7–2. We now have the same number in each row. Since there are 12 students in all, there are now 6 in each row. We see that there are 5 girls and 7 boys.

Example 2. A board 20 feet long is cut into two pieces. One piece is three times as long as the other. How long is each piece? Figure 7–3 shows the two pieces. Now we imagine cutting the longer piece into 3 pieces having the same length as the shorter one (Fig. 7–4). Since the 4 pieces together have length 20, the short one is 5, and hence the long one is 15.

Example 3. The distance around (perimeter of) a rectangle is 40 inches. It is 12 inches long. How wide is it? As we look at Fig. 7–5, it probably will occur to us that *halfway* around the rectangle is 20 inches; hence the width is 8 inches.

EXERCISES

Draw diagrams that might help a student analyze the following problems.

1. A 36-in. board is cut into two pieces. One piece is twice as long as the other. How long is each piece?

2. The perimeter of a rectangle is 50 ft, and its width is 8 ft. How long is the rectangle?

3. A 14-ft board is cut into three pieces. Two of the pieces have the same length and the third is 2 ft longer than each of the others. How long is each piece?

4. A triangle has two sides of equal length. The perimeter of the triangle is 20 in. and the length of one of the two sides of equal length is 8 in. How long is the third side?

5. The perimeter of a triangle having two sides of the same length is 42 in. The third side is 6 in. longer than each of the others. How long is each side?

6. A board is cut into three pieces. The shortest piece is half as long as the next longer piece. The longest piece is 3 ft longer than the middle piece. The board was originally 18 ft long. How long is each piece?

7. There are two stacks of checkers on a table. If you moved 3 checkers from the taller pile to the shorter one, there would be the same number of checkers in each pile. How many more are there in the tall pile than in the short one?

8. There are two rows of cards on a table. One row contains 12 cards. If we moved 5 cards from this row to the second row, the second row would have twice as many cards as the first. How many cards are in the second row?

9. A man fenced his garden so that the fence had the form of a square. When he finished there were 10 fence posts on each side. How many posts did he use?

10. Two cars are 100 miles (mi) apart.

    (a) If they drive toward each other and meet 40 mi from the starting point of the slower car in 2 hours (hr), how fast is each car traveling?

    (b) If they drive in the same direction and the faster car passes the slower one 40 mi from the starting point of the slower car, what is the speed of each car?

11. A bug tries to climb an 8-ft pole. Each day he climbs up 2 ft. Each night while he sleeps he slips down 1 ft. At what time will he reach the top of the pole?

12. If the young nephew of the bug in Exercise 11 brings him his lunch every day at noon, and if the bug climbs steadily so that each day he has climbed 1 ft by noon, how far will the nephew climb up and down the pole?

4. RECOGNIZING NEEDED INFORMATION

When you read the statement of a problem you must recognize what information is important. Sometimes the statement may omit facts that are needed to work the problem. For example, you may need to know the number of feet in one rod and this information may not be given in the problem itself. Sometimes extra information *not needed* to solve the problem is included to test whether you can sort out the important ideas from the unimportant ones.

EXERCISES

1. None of these problems contains enough information to work the problem. What extra facts are needed?

   (a) Strawberries sell for 45¢ a quart. What does a crate of strawberries cost?

   (b) There are 90 students in the seventh grade at Center Junior High. They plan to use buses on a field trip. How many will they need?

   (c) It takes 4 boys and 4 girls to form one set for square dancing. How many sets can be formed from 64 students?

   (d) At $20 a ton, how much will 3000 pounds (lb) of coal cost?

   (e) A farmer had 500 bushels of wheat. He sold a wagon load containing 6900 lb of wheat. How many bushels had he left?

   (f) Students in the seventh-grade class sold 180 tickets for the class play. Adult tickets were $1 and student tickets 50¢. How much did they earn for the class treasury?

2. In each of these problems information that is not needed is given. Pick out unnecessary information.

   (a) A car is traveling at 50 mph. It consumes gasoline at the rate of 25 mi per gallon. How long will it take to travel 150 mi?

   (b) Terry sells newspapers for 5¢ each and gets 1¢ of the sales price for his commission. He is saving what he earns to buy a bike which costs $48. If on the average he earns $12 per week, how many papers must he sell in order to pay for the bicycle?

   (c) A number is multiplied by 5 and to this product 4 is added. The original number is an odd number less than 10 and the final result is 39. Find the original number.

   (d) Mary has three United States coins in her purse which together have a value of 31¢. One of them is a quarter. What are the coins?

   (e) A set of five United States coins has a value of 51¢. There is only one penny in the set. What are the other coins?

(f) A 30-ft board is cut into two pieces. One piece is twice as long as the other. It is also 10 ft longer than the other piece. What is the length of each piece?

5.   USING COMMON SENSE—ESTIMATING

Voltaire once said that we should not call *common sense* "common" because it is really quite *uncommon*. Most of us have a tendency to speak up before we have thought things through carefully. We often make statements without asking ourselves whether what we say is *sensible*. In most problems that we work we could come very close to the correct answers by thinking carefully and making estimates. It is difficult to give rules for estimating answers. Of course we can "round" numbers off. For example, if we are told that a 45-acre field of corn produces 99 bushels per acre, we can reason:

99 is almost 100; therefore the field produces about 45 × 100, or 4500, bushels.

If ten numbers are to be added and every number is between 60 and 100, we might reason:

If each number were 80, the sum would be about the same. Hence, it is about 10 × 80, or 800.

EXERCISES

1. After each problem, we have listed three possible answers. None is correct, but just one of the three will be quite close to the correct result. Use common sense and pick out this answer.

(a) A farmer raised 87 bushels of corn per acre on 102 acres. What was his total crop?

Answers: (1) 900 bushels, (2) 80,000 bushels, (3) 9000 bushels

(b) A baseball team played 182 games. It won 24 more than it lost. How many games did it win?

Answers: (1) 206, (2) 100, (3) 80

(c) For every 4 students at a track meet, there were 3 adults. If there were 124 student tickets sold, how many adult tickets were sold?

Answers: (1) 40, (2) 90, (3) 150

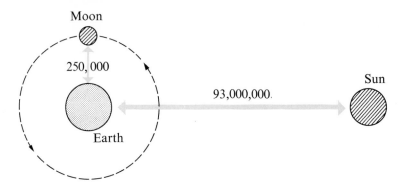

(d) The distance from the earth to the sun is about 93,000,000 mi and that from the earth to the moon is about 250,000 mi. About how many times as far is it from the earth to the sun as from the earth to the moon?

  Answers: (1) 1,000,000, (2) 1000, (3) 400

(e) Find the cost of 98,452 board feet of lumber at $56 per thousand board feet.

  Answers: (1) $5,000,000, (2) $500, (3) $5000

(f) Suppose that a rocket ship can travel from the earth to Mars in 260 days. It takes 45 years and 273 days to reach the planet Pluto. Approximately how many round trips could one rocket ship make between the earth and Mars while a second ship was traveling to Pluto?

  Answers: (1) 30, (2) 6000, (3) 80

2. Estimate answers to the following problems.
   (a) What is the product of 987 and 864?
   (b) What are 3452 bushels of corn worth at $1.50 per bushel?
   (c) A team played 162 baseball games in a season and lost 20 more than it won. How many games did it win?
   (d) A satellite is traveling about 6 miles per second (mi/sec). About how far will it travel in an hour?
   (e) A factory worker earns $132.50 per week. His weekly deductions for taxes, insurance, etc., amount to $13.67. What do you estimate is his take-home pay for a year?
   (f) The conservation department in a state caught 1000 fish in a small lake, marked these fish, and dumped them back into the water. A few months later they caught 1000 more fish from this lake. They found that 22 of these 1000 fish were marked. Estimate the total number of fish in the lake.

3. Make up three problems of your own similar to the ones above. Estimate the answers and give these problems to some of your classmates.

4. Use the following situations to make up problems. After stating each problem, estimate the answer.

   (a) A jet transport can travel 610 mph. It is leaving the airport at Los Angeles to fly to New York.

   (b) There are 93 seventh graders, 81 eighth graders, 80 ninth graders, 75 tenth graders, 68 juniors, and 53 seniors in a junior-senior high school.

   (c) A baseball team has played its schedule of 162 games.

   (d) An archery set and a tennis racket together cost $48.

   (e) Two bicycle riders start in opposite directions from a gasoline station. One rider travels at a speed of 8 mph.

   (f) A certain number is added to 8, and this sum is divided by 6.

6. PROBLEM SOLVING

In working verbal problems it is helpful to be able to compute rapidly and accurately, but it is even more important to be able to decide what to do with the numbers given in a problem. It is impossible to memorize rules that will tell you how to work every problem you may need to solve. You simply must think carefully about the information given and then decide what operations to perform upon the numbers. The following examples show how you might reason in order to solve a couple of difficult problems.

Example 1. A baseball team has played 150 games, winning 30 more than it lost. How many has it won?

Solution 1. *If* the team had played 30 more games and lost them all, then it would have played 180 games and won half of them. Hence, it has won 90 games and lost 60.

Solution 2. We draw a line and think of it as 150 units long, representing the 150 games played (Fig. 7–6). We mark off a part of the "Won"

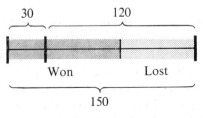

FIGURE 7–6

section to stand for the 30 extra games won. Of the 120 games left we see that 60 were won and 60 lost. Hence, the team has won 90 games.

Example 2. A number is multiplied by 25 and to this product 17 is added. The final result is 2067. Find the original number.

Solution. Before adding 17 we must have had 2067 $-$ 17 or 2050. Let us call the original number n; then $25 \times n = 2050$ and $n = 2050 \div 25 = 82$.

EXERCISES

1. Points A, B, and C are in a straight line. The distance from A to B is 270 ft and that from B to C is 170 ft. How far is it from A to C given that
   (a) B is between A and C?
   (b) B is not between A and C?

2. An airplane averaged 340 mph for 16 hr. How far did it fly?
3. The distance between two cities is 2351 mi. A jet plane has flown 854 mi from one city toward the other. How far is it from the second city?
4. In five days of vacation driving, a family drove 425, 513, 524, 411, and 387 mi. If their speedometer reading was 23,496 when they left home, what was it when they returned?
5. There are 15 red cards in one row and a certain number of black cards in a second row. We move 4 cards from the row of red cards to the other row. Now there are 10 more cards in the second row than in the first. How many black cards are in the second row?
6. There are 1512 trees in a large orchard, with 36 trees in each row. How many rows are there?
7. The sum of the ages of two children is 14 years. What will be the sum of their ages 5 years from now?
8. A board 11 ft long is cut into two pieces. One piece is 3 ft shorter than the other. How long is each piece?
9. A car was driven 352 mi in 8 hr. What was its average speed in miles per hour?
10. A baseball team has lost 61 games. It has won 21 more games than it has lost. How many games has it played?
11. A baseball team has lost 54 games. It lost 5 of these games by only one run. If it had won these 5 games, it would have won and lost the same number of games. How many games has it played?
12. A team has played 154 games and has lost 22 more games than it has won. How many games did the team win?

13. Some children are divided into two groups. There are twice as many children in one group as in the other. Altogether there are 24 children; how many are there in each group?

14. In a certain class there are three girls for every two boys. If there are 18 girls in the class, how many boys are there?

15. At a party there were 3 boys for every 2 girls. There were 5 more boys than girls at the party. How many boys and how many girls were there?

16. A grocery bill of $14.52 was paid with a $20-bill. How much change was received?

17. A house is insured against fire for $15,000. The cost each year for $1000 of fire insurance is $3.52. What is the yearly cost of the insurance on the house?

18. A boy went shopping with $10 in his pocket. He spent half of his money in one store and $1.70 in a second. He spent one-third of the rest of his money in a third store. How much had he left?

19. A boy started shopping with a certain amount of money. He spent half of his money in one store and $2 in a second. If he had $4 left, how much money did he have at the beginning of his shopping trip?

20. I spent $4 in one store and half of the remainder of my money in a second. If I have $10 left, how much had I at first?

21. During one year a city paid total salaries of $189,950 to 29 firemen. What is the average salary for each fireman per year? About what is the average monthly salary?

22. A number is multiplied by 12. To this product 252 is added. The result is 2484. Find the original number.

23. To a number 252 is added. This sum is multiplied by 12. The result is 4836. Find the original number.

24. A watch and ring cost together $140. The watch cost $30 more than the ring. What did each cost?

25. A watch cost three times as much as a ring. Together they cost $140. What did each cost?

26. In driving from town A to town D you pass first through town B and then through town C. It is 10 mi farther from A to B than from B to C and 10 mi farther from B to C than from C to D. If it is 390 mi from A to D, how far is it from A to B?

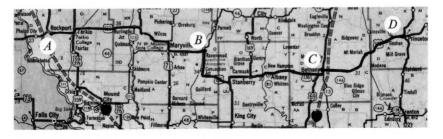

27. A businessman bought 20 suits of clothes, some at $60 each and the rest at $50 each. He paid $1140 for the 20 suits. How may $60-suits did he buy?

28. In an orchard there are 7 peach trees for every 4 cherry trees. There are 60 more peach than cherry trees. How many cherry trees are there in the orchard?

29. Two numbers are multiplied together. The product is 1204. Each of the two numbers is doubled. What will be the product if these two new numbers are multiplied?

30. The sum of seven numbers is 2143. If each number is increased by 50 and the seven resulting numbers are added, what will be the new sum?

31. Find a number between 8400 and 8500 such that, upon dividing it by 73, we have a remainder of 60.

32. Find the largest number between 6900 and 7000 which when divided by 62 will give a remainder of 30.

33. Two cars start out together. The slower car averages 40 mph and the other car, 60. When the slower car has driven 280 mi, how much farther has the other car traveled?

34. A first number is multiplied by a second, and the product is 12,802. When the first number is multiplied by a number one larger than the second, the product is 13,148. Determine the first number and the second one.

35. A first number is divided by a second one. The quotient is 40. When the first number is divided by a number one larger than the second, the quotient is 30. Find the first number.

36. A number is multiplied by 73 and the same number is also multiplied by 125. The smaller product is subtracted from the larger. The remainder is 12,532. Find the number.

37. A man drove 5 hr at an average speed of 40 mph and then 5 hr at an average speed of 60 mph. What was his average speed for the 10 hr?

38. A man drove a distance of 240 mi from his home to a city at an average speed of 40 mph. He returned home averaging 60 mph. What was his average speed for the entire trip?

39. A certain couple had many children. If one of the daughters had been a boy there would have been an equal number of boys and girls. If one of the boys had been a girl there would have been twice as many girls as boys. How many children are in the family?

Chapter 8

LOGICAL

REASONING

1. INTRODUCTION

Not all of mathematics deals with problems of getting numerical answers. If you choose a profession that requires a great deal of mathematics, you will probably find that you will not spend much time solving problems by arithmetic. However, you will spend a great deal of time using the methods of reasoning that you will have learned in your mathematics courses.

The most important task of the mathematician is to develop new ways to solve problems. As we study mathematics, we gather together many facts. These facts lead us to the discovery of new facts. Logical reasoning is the tool that we use to extract new facts out of old knowledge. Our reasoning is of the "if . . . , then . . ." type. Using logical reasoning, we *prove* that *if* certain statements are true, *then* certain other statements are true also. For example, a mathematics student might say:

(1) *If* two whole numbers are odd, *then* their sum is even.

(2) *If* any odd number is multiplied by itself and this product is divided by 8, *then* the remainder is 1.

(3) *If* any odd number is added to the next larger odd number, *then* if we divide this sum by 4, the remainder is zero.

(4) *If* the sum of the digits of a number is divisible by 9, *then* the number is divisible by 9.

(5) *If* A and B are whole numbers less than 10, *then* $A + B$ is less than 19 and $A \times B$ is less than 82.

EXERCISE

Which of the statements above do you think are true? Pick one of these statements. Suppose someone does not believe it. Organize an argument to change his mind.

2. DRAWING CONCLUSIONS

Logical reasoning consists of starting with certain information and figuring out (deducing) other information. We call this kind of reasoning *deductive reasoning*. In each exercise below some information is given, and you are to decide whether anything interesting can be deduced.

EXERCISES

1. On Sunday afternoon you are listening to a ball game. The Detroit Tigers lead the Cleveland Indians 5 to 2 in the fourth inning. You do not listen to the rest of the game. Later a friend tells you that the score was 6 to 4. He does not know who won. But *you* should know.
2. The White Sox are playing the Yankees in New York. In the last half of the ninth inning, with one man out, someone hit a home run and won the game. Which team won? (To answer this question, you need to know some baseball facts that are not given here.)
3. Suppose we know that no one who has green eyes can be trusted. We happen to notice that John Doe has green eyes.
4. Jane says, "We will win our Friday night game *and* our Saturday night game." Monday morning Jane admits that she was mistaken.
5. Joe says, "We will win the ball game this afternoon *or* the track meet tomorrow." After the track meet Joe says, "Well, I was wrong again."
6. Jim says to Pete, "If you beat me this next set of tennis, then I'll eat my hat." Later on Jim admits that he did not tell the truth.
7. Joe tells Kate, "If Sunday is a nice day, I'll come by and take you for a drive." Joe always keeps his promises. Sunday is a nice day.
8. It is announced over the school loudspeaker that 50 tickets are available for a tournament basketball game, but that they will be sold only to seniors. Suzy Gordon buys a ticket. Jim Jackson is a senior.
9. Everyone knows that good health is necessary for happiness. Henry is happy. Joe is miserable.
10. We all know that anyone with large ears is kind and generous. Pete has enormous ears. Jill has very small ears.
11. No one is on the honor roll who did not receive an *A* in mathematics. Sally is on the honor roll. George is not on the honor roll. Kate had an *A* in mathematics.
12. Cats with long tails have curly whiskers. Cats that chase squirrels do not have curly whiskers. Simba is a cat that chases squirrels every day.
13. All six-star generals in the 77th cavalry regiment can waltz beautifully. No groundhog can waltz.
14. All misers are selfish. Misers are the only persons who save eggshells. Jim Jones saves eggshells. Jack Brown does not save eggshells.

15. Every postman has sore feet. Mr. Smith has very sore feet. Mr. Jones is our postman.
16. The sum of any two odd numbers is an even number. A is an odd number. $A + B$ is an odd number.
17. The product of any two odd numbers is an odd number. The product $A \times B$ is an even number.

For the last set of exercises, you may have wondered what could or couldn't be proved in some of the problems. How do we recognize that we *cannot* prove something from given facts? How do we recognize faulty reasoning?

In everyday life we are not so critical of "proofs" as we are in mathematics. Often after we have studied many special cases we feel that something has been proved. For thousands of years men have been throwing rocks. All the rocks that have been thrown have fallen back to the earth. None of them has gone sailing out into space. Does this prove that *if any* rock is thrown, *then* it will fall back to earth? How about the following argument: A fellow student says,

"Every day of my life for the last 18 years the sun has come up in the morning. Therefore, the sun will come up tomorrow morning."

Of course, all of us believe that the sun will come up tomorrow morning. If one of us throws a rock, he expects it to fall back to earth. But, as mathematicians, we would say:

"The fact that the sun has come up every morning for the last trillion mornings is no *proof* that it will come up tomorrow morning."

"The fact that the last trillion stones that men have thrown into the air have fallen back to the earth is no *proof* that the next stone thrown will fall back."

A mathematician who made the statements above would probably be misunderstood by many people. The report might go around that he had said that one of these mornings soon the sun wasn't going to come up. But this is *not* what he is saying. He is saying: *We should look for a better reason for the sun to come up than the fact that it has come up every day of our lives.* And this is exactly what men have done in science. The reason that a scientist will give for a stone falling back to earth has something to do with a basic property of matter called the *law of gravitation.* Many proofs in mathematics depend upon the basic *commutative, associative,* and *distributive* laws that we have studied in these early chapters.

How would you convince a fellow student that the sum of two even numbers is an even number? Would you have him pick two even numbers and add them? Then, if he obtained an even number for the sum would you say, "See, it worked in this case, so it will always work."?

EXERCISES

1. Prime numbers are those whole numbers that have exactly two factors. The number 1 is not a prime number. The numbers 2 and 3 are prime numbers, for 2 has only the factors 1 and 2, while 3 has only the factors 1 and 3. *Prove* that 4 is *not* a prime number. List all prime numbers less than 100.
2. It would be interesting to have a formula for producing prime numbers. Here is one for you to check.

   > Pick any whole number. Multiply it by itself. Subtract the whole number you chose from this product. Add 11.

   Do you get a prime number?
   We could write this formula as

   $$(N \times N) - N + 11$$

   Try out this formula for the whole numbers 0, 1, 2, 3, 4, 5, 6, 7, 8, 9, and 10. Have you proved that this formula gives a prime number for *every* whole number?
3. Check the formula $(N \times N) - N + 41$. Does this formula yield a prime number for every whole number?
4. If we look at the primes in the number series,

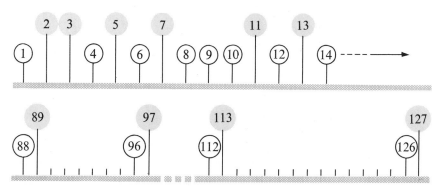

we note that they tend to "thin out," or to get "farther apart." For example, none of the seven numbers between 89 and 97 is a prime number; after 113 there are 13 numbers in a row which are not prime numbers. (Verify these last two statements.)

Mathematicians have proved that if you go out far enough in the set of whole numbers, you will come to a point where *none of the next*

$$1,000,000,000,000,000,000,000,000,000,000,000$$

numbers are prime numbers. Does this prove that from a certain point on there are no more prime numbers?

5. An even number larger than 2 and less than 100 is easily written as the sum of two prime numbers. For example,

$$4 = 2 + 2, \quad 6 = 3 + 3, \quad 8 = 5 + 3, \quad 20 = 13 + 7,$$
$$42 = 19 + 23$$

Express 60, 80, and 98 as sums of two prime numbers.

6. Mathematicians have shown that every even number between 2 and 1,000,000 is the sum of two prime numbers. No mathematician has ever found an even number larger than 2 that *is not* the sum of two prime numbers. Does this *prove* that every even number larger than 2 *is* the sum of two prime numbers?

7. Mathematicians have proved that except for the pair of prime numbers 2 and 5, there is no other pair of prime numbers whose difference is 3. Can you prove this statement?

8. Mathematicians have proved that there is no pair of prime numbers whose difference is 7. Give a proof of this.

3.   ESTABLISHING PROOFS

We have talked about the idea of proving statements to be true, and we have even asked you to try to establish some proofs. But we have not said exactly what it means to prove something in mathematics. In this section we shall briefly consider the idea of proof. In the next few years, if you continue the serious study of mathematics, one of your most important tasks will be to understand how proofs are made.

Let us look at an example. We are sure that *if A* and *B* are *any* two even numbers, *then* the sum $A + B$ is an even number. How might this be proved? We need a *definition*. We call 10 an even number because $10 = 2 \times 5$ and 5 is a whole number. When we say *n* is even, we mean that there is a whole number which when multiplied by 2 gives *n*. Hence we can make the following statement.

---

n is even

means

n = 2 × (a whole number)

Because 2 × 41 = 82, 82 is even. Now we see what we must do if we are to *prove* that some whole number is even. We must find a second whole number such that when we multiply it by 2, we obtain the first whole number.

EXERCISE

Prove that 644 is even.

We now prove that if *A* and *B* are even, then *A* + *B* is even also. The proof consists of the following steps.

(1) Because *A* is an even whole number, there is a whole number *a* such that

$$A = 2 \times a \qquad \text{(Why?)}$$

(2) There is a whole number *b* such that

$$B = 2 \times b \qquad \text{(Why?)}$$

(3) Hence

$$A + B = 2 \times a + 2 \times b.$$

(4) Now, by the *distributive* property,

$$2 \times a + 2 \times b = 2 \times (a + b)$$

so

$$A + B = 2 \times (a + b)$$

(5) This shows that *a* + *b* is a whole number such that when we multiply it by 2, we get the number *A* + *B*.

(6) Therefore, *A* + *B* is even.

The important things to notice about this proof are the following:

(1) We made a definition and used it again and again. We said *exactly* what we meant by the phrase "even number."
(2) We used the distributive property at one point in the proof.

One of the reasons for studying the commutative, associative, and distributive properties is that you will use these properties as you formulate proofs in mathematics. These properties are the main tools that support our logical reasoning in algebra.

EXERCISE

Prove that the product of two even numbers is an even number.

4. LOGIC

The formal study of logic is a systematic analysis of the methods used to draw conclusions from given information. In this section we introduce only a few basic logical concepts.

We shall refer to a sentence that is either true or false as a *statement*. The sentence, $5 + 4 = 9$, is a *true statement*; $7 + 3 = 11$ is a *false* statement. The imperative sentence, "Shut the door," is not a statement, since it is not considered to be either true or false. However, the declarative sentence, "The door is shut," if it refers to a particular door at a particular time, is a statement.

Often a statement is a combination of several statements. For example, we might say, "We will go to the game tonight and we will invite Jim or John to go with us." This single statement is a combination of three simple statements. Denoting these statements by α, β, and γ (the Greek letters alpha, beta, and gamma), we have

α: We will go to the game.

β: We will invite Jim to go with us.

γ: We will invite John to go with us.

We may abbreviate this compound statement by writing

$$\alpha \quad \text{and} \quad (\beta \text{ or } \gamma).$$

EXERCISES

1. In the example given above, suppose it is known that the statement α is *true*, that β is *false* and γ is *true*. Would you consider the compound statement α and $(\beta$ or $\gamma)$ true or false?

2. Judge the truth of the compound statement above in each of the following cases.

   (a) α true, β false, γ false.
   (b) α false, β true, γ false.
   (c) α true, β true, γ true.

The examples above illustrate that the conjunctions *and* and *or* play a fundamental role in the study of logic. If α, β are any two statements, we can combine them by the logical connective *and* to form the single statement, α *and* β. The easiest way to explain how the word *and* is used in logic is by means of the *truth table* shown below.

α	β	α and β
T	T	T
T	F	F
F	T	F
F	F	F

As this truth table shows, the single statement, α *and* β, is true when both of the statements α, β are true and is false in the other three cases. A special logical terminology is used in referring to the single statement, α *and* β. This statement is called the *conjunction* of the two statements α and β.

The truth table below explains how the logical connective *or* is used. Any statement of the form, α *or* β, is referred to as the *disjunction* of the two statements α and β.

α	β	α or β
T	T	T
T	F	T
F	T	T
F	F	F

Note that while the statement, α *and* β, is true in only one of the 4 possible cases, the statement, α *or* β, is true in 3 out of the 4 cases. If a student says, "I will receive an A in English or an A in French," his statement is considered false only if he does not receive an A in either course. If he gets A's in both courses his statement is considered true.

The mathematical usage of the logical connective *or* differs in some ways from everyday usage. Everyday usage of "or" may be ambiguous.

In legal terminology one encounters such expressions as, "... six months in jail *or* $5000 fine." Here the *or* is used in a sense different from the mathematical usage. The judge may invoke one penalty, but not both. In mathematics the connective *or* is always used in the manner described by the truth table above.

EXERCISES

1. Let α be the statement, "There are 31 days in March" and β the statement, "There are 8 days in one week."
   (a) Is the statement, α *and* β, true?
   (b) Is the statement, α *or* β, true?

2. Construct what you consider to be the correct truth table for statements of the form, α *but* β.

Sometimes we wish to say that a certain statement is false. Of course, if α is any statement, we *can* say simply, "α is false." In actual practice we usually formulate such a statement in other ways. For example, if α is the statement, "It will rain tomorrow," we say, "It will not rain tomorrow." The assertion that a statement, α, is false is referred to as the *negation* of α, and we denote it symbolically by *not* α. The truth table is simple.

α	*not* α
T	F
F	T

Examples are given below.

1. α: $3 + 4 = 6$
   not α: $3 + 4 \neq 6$

2. α: 113 is not a multiple of 7.
   not α: 113 is a multiple of 7.

3. α: Some men play golf.
   not α: No man plays golf.

It is especially important to be able to construct correct negations of statements containing such terms as *some, all, every, at least one,* etc. In everyday usage *some* usually means *more than one*. In mathematical usage *some* always means *at least one*. The examples below illustrate how negations are formed for statements which contain these terms.

1. α: All members of the basketball team are more than 6 feet tall.

not α: Some members of the basketball team are not more than 6 feet tall.

2. α: It will rain some day this week.

not α: It will not rain any day this week.

3. α: Some cats are black.

not α: No cats are black.

EXERCISES

1. Explain why the statement, "Some cats are not black," is not the negation of, " Some cats are black."

2. Give the negation of each statement.
    (a)   Every student made a grade of B or better on the examination.
    (b)   All of the regulars on the football team are seniors.
    (c)   All of the regulars on the football team are seniors or juniors.
    (d)   Some of the students in this class hate mathematics.
    (e)   There is at least one real number x such that $x^2 = 2$.
    (f)   Some people always work hard.

Often it is necessary to construct the negation of a conjunction, α *and* β, or a disjunction, α *or* β. It is quite clear that the truth tables for these negations, *not* (α and β) and *not* (α or β), must be as described below.

α	β	α and β	not (α and β)	α or β	not (α or β)
T	T	T	F	T	F
T	F	F	T	T	F
F	T	F	T	T	F
F	F	F	T	F	T

Suppose that the statement, α and β, is the statement, "Smith is a dentist and Jones is a teacher." To say that this statement is false is to say that α is false or β is false. The negation is:

Smith is not a dentist *or* Jones is not a teacher.

The negation of the statement, α and β, is the statement, not α *or* not β. With a little thought you should see that the negation of the disjunction, α or β, is the statement not α *and* not β.

We summarize these rules for forming negations below.

> *Not* (α and β) means the same thing as (not α) or (not β).
>
> *Not* (α or β) means the same thing as (not α) and (not β).

EXERCISES

1. Give negations for the statements below.
   - (a) Today is Tuesday and the weather is cold.
   - (b) $x = 2$ and $y = 5$.
   - (c) Today is Tuesday or the weather is cold.
   - (d) $x = 2$ or $y = 5$.
   - (e) All cats are treacherous and all dogs have fleas.
   - (f) All cats are treacherous or all dogs have fleas.
   - (g) Some will work or all will starve.
   - (h) All roses are red and some violets are blue.

2. Show that the truth table for (not α) or (not β) is the same as the truth table for not (α and β).

3. Show that the truth table for (not α) and (not β) is the same as the truth table for not (α or β).

4. Show that the truth table for (α and β) or γ is different from the truth table for α and (β or γ).

5. Give negations for both (α and β) or γ and the statement α and (β or γ).

Now let us use some of the logical machinery we have developed to analyze some of the logical reasoning we use as we draw conclusions. Suppose that we know that a statement, α or β, is true. Suppose that we know also that the statement, not α, is true. It is clear that the statement β must be true. We can present this basic principle of logical reasoning in the following way:

$$[(\alpha \text{ or } \beta) \text{ and } (\text{not } \alpha)] \rightarrow \beta.$$

We shall read this as:

> If the two statements, α *or* β and *not* α, are both true, then β is a true statement.

We call the given statements whose truth we accept our *hypothesis*.

We call the statement whose truth we deduce from the hypothesis our *conclusion*. Another way to symbolize this reasoning is shown below.

$$\text{Hypothesis:} \quad (1)\ \alpha \text{ or } \beta \qquad\qquad \text{Conclusion:} \quad \beta$$
$$(2)\ \text{not } \alpha$$

EXERCISES

1. In each example draw one or more conclusions from the hypothesis.
   (a) Hypothesis: (1) not (α and β)
                      (2) α
   (b) Hypothesis: (1) α or (not β)
                      (2) β
   (c) Hypothesis: (1) α and (β or γ)
                      (2) not β
   (d) Hypothesis: (1) not (α and *not* β)
                      (2) α or β
   (e) Hypothesis: (1) α or β or γ
                      (2) (not α) or β
                      (3) (not β) or γ

2. In each example decide whether or not any interesting conclusion can be drawn from the given information.
   (a) Every postman has sore feet. Mr. Smith is a postman.
   (b) Every postman has sore feet. Mr. Jones has sore feet.
   (c) Every sophomore was given a ticket. George was given a ticket.
   (d) Every sophomore was given a ticket. Joe is a sophomore.
   (e) Every sophomore was given a ticket. June bought a ticket.
   (f) If a customer was not satisfied then his money was refunded. Mr. Brown was a dissatisfied customer.
   (g) If a customer was not satisfied then his money was refunded. Mr. Smith's money was refunded.
   (h) When it rains it pours. It is raining.
   (i) When it rains it pours. It is pouring.
   (j) When I sleep I breathe. I am sleeping.
   (k) When I sleep I breathe. I am breathing.
   (l) We won Friday's game or Saturday's game. We lost Friday's game.
   (m) All sweet food has honey in it. This food is sweet.
   (n) All sweet food has honey in it. This food has honey in it.
   (o) John always tells the truth. Jim said, "If Joe beats me this set of tennis, then I'll eat my hat." After they had played John said, "Jim's statement was false."

5. RECREATIONAL MATH

In this section we list some problems whose solutions require careful logical reasoning. Of course, you may get the correct answers to some of these problems by making lucky guesses, but others will require more than luck. Good thinking!

EXERCISES

1. You have 3 coins and a pan balance scale. The coins are alike in appearance, but you know that just one of them is counterfeit and is lighter than the other two. How do you find the counterfeit coin in *one* weighing?

2. You have 3 coins and know that just one is counterfeit. The bad coin is either heavier or lighter than the other two, but you do not know which. Can you be sure of finding the counterfeit coin in just one weighing on the pan balance scale? Explain how to locate the bad coin and how to decide whether it is lighter or heavier in two weighings.
3. You have 6 coins, and one is lighter than the others. Find the bad coin in two weighings.
4. You have 8 coins, and one is lighter than the others. Find it in two weighings.
5. You have 9 coins, and one is heavier than the others. Find it in two weighings.
6. You have 9 coins. One is heavier or lighter than the others, but you do not know which. In three weighings, find the bad coin and determine whether it is heavy or light.
7. In Exercise 6 replace 9 by 12 and solve the resulting problem.
8. There are 12 dentists in a town. In one class of 26 students each student goes to one of these dentists. Prove that at least 3 students go to the same dentist.
9. A man needs to take a fox, a goose, and a sack of corn across a river. He has a boat in which he cannot take more than one across at a time. He cannot leave the fox and the goose together or the goose and the corn, for one will eat the other. How can he get all three across the river, taking one at a time with him in the boat?

10. Invent a shortcut for finding the sum of all numbers 1, 2, 3, ..., 100.

11. You have two pails, one that will hold 4 quarts and one that will hold 9. There are no markings on either pail to indicate smaller quantities. How can you measure out 6 quarts of water, using these two pails?

12. A traveler wishes to stay at an inn for several days. He has no money but he has a valuable gold chain. The innkeeper agrees to let him stay, on the condition that each day he pay one link of his chain. The traveler must pay every day; that is, at the end of one day the innkeeper must have one link, at the end of two days, two links, etc. The traveler must cut his chain in order to make these payments. If the chain has 7 links and the traveler stays for 7 days, show how by cutting only one link he can pay for his lodging every day.

13. If, in Problem 12, the chain had 23 links and the traveler stayed for 23 days, what is the smallest number of links that he could cut and still pay his bill each day?

14. The game Nim is played by two persons using three rows of counters, 3 in the first row, 5 in the second, and 7 in the third. Each player in turn takes one or more counters from just one row. The player who is forced to remove the last of the 15 counters loses the game.

For example, the first player might take all 7 counters in the third row and the second might remove 2 from the second row. This leaves two rows of 3.

Show that now the second player can win.

15. In Nim show that if you can play and leave a 1, 2, 3 combination (that is, 1 counter in one row, 2 in another, and 3 in the third), you can win.

16. Show that if you can leave a 1, 4, 5 combination in Nim, you can win.

17. Who can win at Nim, the first player or the second?

18. A man has 5 metal blocks. The weight of each block is a whole number of ounces. Any 4 of these blocks have the property that they can be placed on a pan balance scale, two in one pan and two in the other so that they balance. Prove that all 5 blocks weigh exactly the same.

19. A checkerboard has 64 squares. Suppose that you have 32 rectangular pieces of cardboard, each of which will cover two squares. You cut one piece in two and cover two diagonally opposite corner squares with these pieces. You now have left 31 rectangular cardboard pieces and 62 uncovered squares. Is it possible, without cutting any more of the rectangular pieces, to lay them on the checkerboard so that the remaining 62 squares are covered? Prove your assertion.

20. On a chessboard is it possible to place a knight on one of the corner squares and move him in 63 moves to the diagonally opposite corner square so that he lights on each square of the board exactly once? Prove your assertion.

Chapter 9

A NEW SET OF NUMBERS

1. INTRODUCTION

We have been studying the operations of addition, subtraction, multiplication, and division in the set of whole numbers. We have used properties of these operations to solve equations such as

$$7 \times (a + 2) = 35, \quad [12 \div (a - 3)] \times 4 = 16,$$
$$x + 1 = 4, \quad x + 1 = 3, \quad x + 1 = 2, \quad x + 1 = 1$$

But there are many equations which look simple, and yet, at the moment, we cannot solve them. Examples of such equations are

$$x + 1 = 0, \quad x + 2 = 0, \quad x + 3 = 0, \ldots$$

In the set of whole numbers, there is no number that can be added to 1 to give 0, no number that can be added to 2 to give 0, etc.

In this chapter we shall invent new numbers for the above equations and we shall learn their arithmetic. If you have studied algebra, you realize how important these new numbers are. From the time men first invented the whole numbers until they invented the new numbers of this chapter, a period of more than 10,000 years must have passed. It is a fascinating fact that today a student can learn in a few months ideas that it took the human race thousands of years to develop.

2. THE SET OF INTEGERS

It is difficult to realize that mathematics is a creation of mans' mind. We do not *discover* numbers by turning over rocks and looking underneath. Man invents numbers as a writer invents characters in a play. And when we invent new numbers, it is our right to *say what properties* they shall have. We have the right to *choose names* for these numbers and to choose the *marks* that we shall use to represent them.

Each whole number satisfies one and only one of the following equations:

$$x - 0 = 0, \quad x - 1 = 0, \quad x - 2 = 0, \quad x - 3 = 0, \ldots$$

It will be useful to have numbers that satisfy the equations

$$x + 0 = 0, \quad x + 1 = 0, \quad x + 2 = 0, \quad x + 3 = 0, \ldots$$

We already have a whole number that satisfies the first of these equations. What is this number? But for the other equations we need new numbers. *And so we invent them. And now these new numbers exist because our minds have created them.*

Now, if someone asks you whether there is a number that added to 4 gives 0 you can say *yes*. One thing is slightly embarrassing, however. If someone asks us, "What is this number that added to 4 gives 0?," we have to admit that we haven't named it yet. The new number is like a new-born baby that has not yet been given a name. However, we *know* the number just as you might know a little baby brother before he has been named.

Names are not so important as the things to which they are attached, but it is very difficult to talk about nameless things. Let us agree to call the new numbers that add to 1 to give 0, add to 2 to give 0, add to 3 to give 0, . . . , respectively, *the negative of* 1, *the negative of* 2, *the negative of* 3, etc. We shall write these names in abbreviated form as $-1, -2, -3, -4, -5, -6, \ldots$ *We have agreed on both how to pronounce and how to write names for our new numbers.*

These new numbers, together with the whole numbers, form a set which we call the set of *integers:*

$$\{0, 1, -1, 2, -2, 3, -3, 4, -4, \ldots\}$$

We call the new numbers $-1, -2, -3, \ldots$ *negative integers*, and we call the whole numbers $1, 2, 3, \ldots$ *positive integers*. Zero is just called an *integer*. Zero is neither *positive* nor *negative*. We agree that $-0 = 0$;

that is, *the negative of* zero is zero. The equations for the integers are
shown below.

$$0 \qquad 1 \qquad 2 \qquad 3 \qquad \cdots$$
$$x - 0 = 0, \quad x - 1 = 0, \quad x - 2 = 0, \quad x - 3 = 0, \ldots$$

$$x + 0 = 0, \quad x + 1 = 0, \quad x + 2 = 0, \quad x + 3 = 0, \ldots$$
$$0 \qquad -1 \qquad -2 \qquad -3 \qquad \cdots$$

The equations for the integers

EXERCISES

1. Write equations that are satisfied by the following integers:
   (a) -7 (b) 11   (c) -41

2. What do we call the number that adds to 131 to give 0? the number that
   adds to -17 to give 0?

3. Write the integers from the negative of 10 to the negative of 20.

4. What is n if
   (a) $n + 7 = 0$ (b) $n + (-9) = 0$ (c) $(n + 3) + (-8) = 0$

3. ADDITION OF INTEGERS

We agree that in our new set of numbers addition has the old familiar
commutative and associative properties. We agree also that if A is
any integer, $A + 0 = A$. These properties enable us to decide how
to add and subtract integers.

The basic properties of addition of integers can be stated as follows.

If a, b, and c are any integers, then

$$a + b = b + a$$
$$(a + b) + c = a + (b + c)$$
$$a + 0 = a$$

The basic properties of addition of integers

As an example of how we use these properties, consider the sum $6 + (-4)$. We know that -4 adds to 4 to give 0. We may think of 6 as $2 + 4$. Hence, $6 + (-4) = (2 + 4) + (-4)$. By the associative property, this is $2 + [4 + (-4)]$, or 2.

EXERCISES

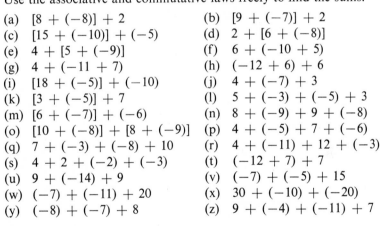

1. Give the sums.

(a) $3 + (-3)$ (b) $9 + (-9)$ (c) $-17 + 0$
(d) $5 + (-3)$ (e) $10 + (-7)$ (f) $8 + (-6)$
(g) $10 + (-4)$ (h) $-7 + 9$ (i) $12 + (-6)$
(j) $8 + (-7)$ (k) $7 + (-0)$ (l) $21 + (-11)$
(m) $12 + (-4)$ (n) $-14 + 15$ (o) $32 + (-23)$
(p) $100 + (-73)$ (q) $7 + (-1)$ (r) $55 + (-44)$
(s) $1000 + (-712)$ (t) $85 + (-37)$ (u) $0 + (-0)$
(v) $61 + (-48)$ (w) $71 + (-49)$ (x) $82 + (-75)$
(y) $16 + (-9)$ (z) $-43 + 131$

2. Use the associative and commutative laws freely to find the sums.

(a) $[8 + (-8)] + 2$ (b) $[9 + (-7)] + 2$
(c) $[15 + (-10)] + (-5)$ (d) $2 + [6 + (-8)]$
(e) $4 + [5 + (-9)]$ (f) $6 + (-10 + 5)$
(g) $4 + (-11 + 7)$ (h) $(-12 + 6) + 6$
(i) $[18 + (-5)] + (-10)$ (j) $4 + (-7) + 3$
(k) $[3 + (-5)] + 7$ (l) $5 + (-3) + (-5) + 3$
(m) $[6 + (-7)] + (-6)$ (n) $8 + (-9) + 9 + (-8)$
(o) $[10 + (-8)] + [8 + (-9)]$ (p) $4 + (-5) + 7 + (-6)$
(q) $7 + (-3) + (-8) + 10$ (r) $4 + (-11) + 12 + (-3)$
(s) $4 + 2 + (-2) + (-3)$ (t) $(-12 + 7) + 7$
(u) $9 + (-14) + 9$ (v) $(-7) + (-5) + 15$
(w) $(-7) + (-11) + 20$ (x) $30 + (-10) + (-20)$
(y) $(-8) + (-7) + 8$ (z) $9 + (-4) + (-11) + 7$

3. Solve the following equations.

(a) $-4 + x = 0$ (b) $3 + x = 0$
(c) $3 + x = 2$ (d) $x + (-5) = 5$
(e) $x + 7 = 2$ (f) $x + (-7) = 2$
(g) $x + (-6) = 1$ (h) $x + (-2) + (-4) = 0$
(i) $x + (-2) + (-4) = 3$ (j) $6 + x + (-5) = 0$
(k) $12 + (x + 2) = 5$ (l) $-4 + x + (-7) = 10$
(m) $-4 + (x + 17) = 10$ (n) $x + (-4) + x = x$
(o) $2 \times [x + (-3)] = 10$ (p) $3 + x + (-5) = 0$
(q) $3 \times [x + (-5)] = 0$ (r) $3 \div [x + (-5)] = 3$

(s) $x + (-1) + x = x + 5$ (t) $-3 + [x + (-4)] = 2$
(u) $x + (-5) = 9 + (-6)$ (v) $7 + (x + 5) = 7$
(w) $-11 + x + (-2) = 0$ (x) $-9 + [x + (-3)] = -9$
(y) $3 \times [x + (-3)] = 15$
(z) $(-3 + x) + (-5 + x) = -3 + x$

4. Find the sums.

(a) $x + (-x)$ (b) $(1 + a) + (-a)$
(c) $(2 + r) + (-r)$ (d) $(a + b) + (-b)$
(e) $[r + (-s)] + (-r)$ (f) $(-s + 9) + s$
(g) $[a + (-b)] + [b + (-a)]$ (h) $(-r + 4) + [r + (-3)]$
(i) $(a + 4) + [-(a + 4)]$ (j) $(x + y) + [-(x + y)]$
(k) $(b + 1) + (-b)$ (l) $(b + 2) + [-(b + 1)]$
(m) $(b + 4) + [-(b + 3)]$ (n) $(a + 7) + [-(a + 3)]$
(o) $-(a + 3) + (a + 10)$

We have not considered problems such as $-3 + (-4)$, but it is possible that in the last exercise list you taught yourself how to compute such sums. What do you think this sum is?

We need to use logical reasoning in order to compute the sum of -3 and -4 and *be certain that our answer is correct.* We know that

$$7 + [(-3) + (-4)] = 0 \qquad \text{(Why?)}$$

What is x if $7 + x = 0$? Because $-3 + (-4)$ added to 7 gives zero, $-3 + (-4)$ *is* -7. Now if we wish to do so, we can break up negative integers, such as $-12, -7, -4, -6$, into sums of two negative integers; for example, into $-2 + (-10), -5 + (-2), -3 + (-1), -4 + (-2)$. We use this idea in working a problem like $-12 + 10$:

$$-12 + 10 = (-2) + (-10) + 10$$

Clearly, this sum is -2.

EXERCISES

1. Give the sums. Be able to prove that your answers are correct.

(a) $-1 + (-1)$ (b) $-2 + (-3)$
(c) $-2 + (-2)$ (d) $-4 + (-4)$
(e) $-10 + (-5)$ (f) $-10 + (-10)$
(g) $-6 + (-4)$ (h) $-7 + (-3)$
(i) $-8 + (-7)$ (j) $-9 + (-9) + (-2)$
(k) $-8 + (-5) + (-7)$ (l) $-8 + (-8) + (-4)$

(m) $-6 + (-6) + (-8)$ (n) $-7 + (-6) + (-7)$
(o) $-6 + (-7) + (-8) + (-9)$ (p) $-2 + 1$
(q) $-4 + 2$ (r) $-7 + 5$
(s) $7 + (-8)$ (t) $10 + (-17)$
(u) $5 + (-8) + (-2)$ (v) $-6 + 1 + 4$
(w) $-8 + 2 + (-3)$ (x) $-4 + (-6) + 7$
(y) $6 + (-3) + (-10)$ (z) $-8 + (-9) + 7 + 8$

2. For what integers are the number sentences below true?

(a) $x + 4 = -3$ (b) $x + 0 = -7$
(c) $x + x = -10$ (d) $a + (-6) = -9$
(e) $a + (-9) = -6$ (f) $b + 7 = -3$
(g) $b + (-3) = -7$ (h) $4 + c = -3$
(i) $c + 4 = -3$ (j) $c + (-3) = 4$
(k) $4 + (-3) = c$ (l) $r + (-8) = -10$
(m) $r + (-3) = -0$ (n) $r + (-3) = 0$
(o) $s + (-3) + 4 = -7$ (p) $(-5 + s) + (-1) = 2$
(q) $(s + 5) + (-1) = 2$ (r) $[t + (-7)] + (-7) = 0$
(s) $(t + 8) + (-10) = -7$ (t) $(t + 10) + (-8) = -7$
(u) $(t + 7) + (-8) = 10$ (v) $t + (-8) + (-7) = 10$
(w) $[t + (-8)] + (-7) = -10$ (x) $(y + 0) + 0 = -4$
(y) $[y + (-7)] + 7 = -9$ (z) $(y + 9) + (-9) = -13$

3. Find the sums for the problems given below.

(a) $(-a + 4) + (-4)$ (b) $a + (-6) + 7$
(c) $[a + (-6)] + 5$ (d) $(-a) + (-b) + b$
(e) $4 + (-a) + (-7) + a$
(f) $3 + (-a) + b + (-3) + (-b)$
(g) $a + (-1) + (-a)$ (h) $[a + (-2)] + (-a)$
(i) $[a + (-3)] + (-a)$ (j) $(-5 + a) + (-a)$
(k) $a + [-(a + 1)]$ (l) $a + [-(a + 2)]$
(m) $a + [-(a + 3)]$ (n) $a + [-(a + 5)]$
(o) $a + (-b) + (-a)$ (p) $a + [-(a + b)]$
(q) $a + (-b) + (-a) + b$
(r) $a + [-(b + 2)] + 2 + (-a)$
(s) $(x + 4) + [-(x + 3)]$ (t) $(x + 4) + [-(x + 5)]$

4. SUBTRACTION OF INTEGERS

Addition of integers is an operation which combines *two* integers called *addends* to give *one* integer, their *sum*.

Subtraction of integers is an operation which combines *two* integers, one the *sum* and the other an *addend*, to give *one* integer, the other *addend*.

Each addition fact gives us subtraction facts. The integer 2 is the sum of the addends 7 and −5.

$$\overset{S}{2} = \overset{A}{7} + \overset{A}{(-5)}$$

Now we have the two subtraction facts:

$$\overset{S}{2} - \overset{A}{7} = \overset{A}{-5}, \qquad \overset{S}{2} - \overset{A}{(-5)} = \overset{A}{7}$$

Just as we did in the set of whole numbers, we subtract one integer from another to find a missing addend. To subtract 4 from 10 is to find what must be added to 4 to give 10. Since

$$4 + 6 = 10$$

it follows that

$$10 - 4 = 6$$

To subtract −4 from 10 is to find what number must be added to −4 to give 10. Since

$$-4 + 14 = 10$$

if follows that

$$10 - (-4) = 14$$

Each subtraction problem, and each addition problem, deals with *three* integers. *One* of these integers is the sum of the other *two*. When we know the addends, we *add* to find the sum. When we know the sum and one addend, we subtract to determine the missing addend.

EXERCISES

1. The sum is 7. One addend is −2. What is the other addend?
   What is 7 − (−2)?
2. One addend is 3, the other addend is −9. What is the sum?
   What is 3 + (−9)?
3. What must be added to −3 to give −5?
   What is −5 − (−3)?
4. What must be added to −5 to give −3?
   What is −3 − (−5)?

5. In each exercise below tell whether a is the sum or an addend.

(a) $a - 3 = -1$ (b) $3 - a = -1$
(c) $3 - (-1) = a$ (d) $a - b = -4$
(e) $-4 - b = a$ (f) $-4 - a = b$
(g) $a - b = c$ (h) $b - a = c$
(i) $a - c = b$ (j) $c - a = b$

6. Write the two subtraction facts that go with each addition fact below.

(a) $4 + (-3) = 1$ (b) $4 + (-4) = 0$
(c) $-2 + (-3) = -5$ (d) $-4 + 1 = -3$
(e) $(a + 1) + (-a) = 1$ (f) $(a + b) + (-b) = a$

7. In each exercise below, determine x. Then write the subtraction problem you have worked.

(a) $-4 + x = 5$ (b) $-4 + x = -4$ (c) $-4 + x = 0$
(d) $3 + x = 2$ (e) $3 + x = 0$ (f) $3 + x = -5$

8. Work the subtraction problems below.   Find the missing addends. Write the addition facts that show that your answers are correct.

(a) $7 - 2$ (b) $7 - (-2)$ (c) $-7 - 2$
(d) $-7 - (-2)$ (e) $4 - 0$ (f) $0 - 4$
(g) $6 - 9$ (h) $9 - 6$ (i) $-6 - 9$
(j) $9 - (-6)$ (k) $-9 - (-6)$ (l) $-6 - (-9)$

9. What must be added to each of the numbers below to give 0?

(a) -7 (b) -3 (c) -11 (d) -5 (e) 8   (f) 10

10. What must be added to each number in Exercise 9 to give 1? to give -1? to give 5? to give -5?

11. Solve the equations below.

(a) $x - 3 = -5$ (b) $x - (-3) = -5$ (c) $3 - x = -5$
(d) $3 - x = 5$ (e) $y + 3 = -10$ (f) $y - 3 = -10$
(g) $3 + y = -10$ (h) $3 - y = -10$ (i) $5 - x = 10$
(j) $y + y = -8$ (k) $-8 - y = y$ (l) $-10 - y = y$

5. THE NUMBER LINE

It is interesting and useful to visualize all the integers as points on a line. For example, we can think of the number line shown in Fig. 9–1.

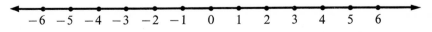

$$-6 \quad -5 \quad -4 \quad -3 \quad -2 \quad -1 \quad 0 \quad 1 \quad 2 \quad 3 \quad 4 \quad 5 \quad 6$$

FIGURE 9–1

We can associate *arrows* with the integers. Any arrow 3 units long and *pointed to the right* can be used to represent the number 3 (Fig. 9–2).

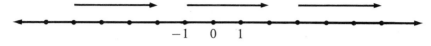

FIGURE 9–2

Any arrow 3 units long and pointed to the left can be used to represent the number −3 (Fig. 9–3).

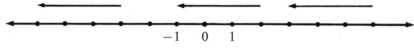

FIGURE 9–3

It is easy to represent addition and subtraction of integers on the number line. Figure 9–4 shows both that $(-3) + 5 = 2$ and that $2 - (-3) = 5$.

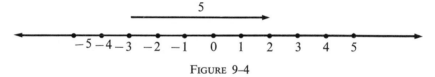

FIGURE 9–4

Figure 9–5 presents the addition problem $(-5) + 3 = n$. The illustration shows that −5 is one addend and 3 is the other addend. What is the sum?

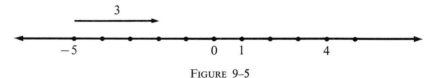

FIGURE 9–5

Figure 9–6 presents the subtraction problem $(-5) - (-3) = n$. The illustration shows that −3 is one addend and −5 is the sum. What is the missing addend?

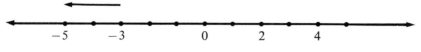

FIGURE 9–6

EXERCISES

1. Each figure below presents an addition problem. Write an equation and find the sum.

(a)
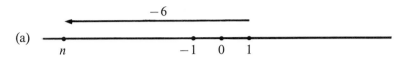

(b)
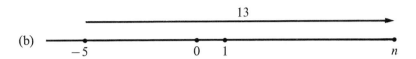

(c)
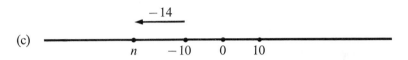

2. Each figure below presents a subtraction problem. Write an equation and determine the missing addend.

(a)
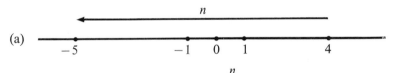

(b)
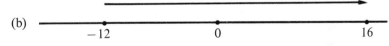

(c)

(d)

(e)

3. Draw number lines to represent the problems below.

(a) $(-3) + (-5) = n$ (b) $(-1) + 7 = n$
(c) $3 - 8 = n$ (d) $(-3) - (-10) = n$
(e) $3 - (-8) = n$ (f) $(-8) - 3 = n$

4. Looking at the number line in Fig. 9–7, answer the following questions.

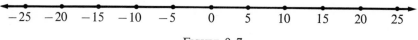

FIGURE 9–7

(a) What must be added to 10 to give 25?
     What is 25 − 10?
(b) What must be added to −10 to yield −25?
     What is (−25) − (−10)?
(c) What must be added to −10 to give 15?
     What is 15 − (−10)?
(d) What must be added to 10 to give −15?
     What is (−15) − 10?
(e) What is (−10) + 15?
(f) What is (−10) − 15?
(g) What is (−10) + (−15)?
(h) What is (−10) − (−15)?

6. MULTIPLICATION AND DIVISION OF INTEGERS

To understand multiplication and division of integers we must make use of the properties of 0 and 1. The properties we will need are described by the sentences below. Complete these sentences.

(a) The product of any integer and zero is _____.
(b) The product of any integer and one is _____.
(c) If the product of two integers is zero and one integer is not zero, then _____.

We can make the following statement concerning the properties of 1 and 0.

> **For every integer N**
>
> $N \times 0 = 0$ and $N \times 1 = N$.
>
> *If A and N are integers and*
>
> $A \times N = 0$ and $A \neq 0$
>
> *then*
>
> $N = 0$

EXERCISES

1. An integer added to 6 gives 0. Which integer is this?
2. When an integer is multiplied by 6, the product is 0. Which integer is this?
3. When an integer is multiplied by 1, the product is -5. Which integer is this?
4. Determine N, given that

   (a) $N + (-3) = 0$ (b) $N + 12 = 0$
   (c) $N \times (-6) = 0$ (d) $3 + (-6 + N) = 3$
   (e) $3 \times (-4 + N) = 0$ (f) $N \times 1 = -8$
   (g) $(-4) \times (-3 + N) = -4$
   (h) $(-4) + (-3 + N) = -4$
   (i) $N + (3 \times 4) = 0$

5. *If* you knew that $(-3) \times (-2)$ added to -6 gives zero, what would you know the product $(-3) \times (-2)$ to be?
6. *If* you knew that $[3 \times (-2)] + 6 = 0$, what would you know the product $3 \times (-2)$ to be?
7. Suppose that you knew that

$$[3 \times (-4)] + (3 \times 4) = 0$$

What could you say about the product $3 \times (-4)$?
8. Solve the following equations.

   (a) $(-3) \times n = 0$ (b) $3 \times (2 + a) = 0$
   (c) $4 \times (5 + b) = 0$ (d) $(4 \times 5) + (4 \times y) = 0$
   (e) $6 \times (7 + y) = 0$ (f) $(6 \times 7) + (6 \times y) = 0$

9. By the distributive property,

$$3 \times (4 + p) = (3 \times 4) + (3 \times p)$$

   (a) If $3 \times (4 + p) = 0$, what number is p?
   (b) If $3 \times (4 + p) = 0$, what number is $3 \times p$?

10. What number is $6 \times r$ if $6 \times (5 + r) = 0$?
11. Consider the product $3 \times (5 \times t) = (3 \times 5) + (3 \times t)$.   If this product is zero, what number is t? What number is $3 \times t$?
12. Consider the product $-5 \times (3 + s) = (-5 \times 3) + (-5 \times s)$.   If this product is zero, what number is s? What number is $(-5) \times s$? [*Hint:* Use Problem 11.]

What do you think is the product of 4 and -5? Perhaps, after working the problems in the last list, you *think* that this product is -20, but can you *prove* it? *The number* −20 *has one special property that no other number has. When we add it to* 20 *we obtain zero.* We shall know that the number 4 × (−5) is −20 if we can show that 4 × (−5) added to 20 gives zero.

Is 4 × (−5) the number −20?

We will know that it is

if

we can show that

[4 × (−5)] + 20 = 0

Using logical reasoning in mathematics

The distributive law and the properties of zero help us settle this question:

$$[4 \times (-5)] + 20 = [4 \times (-5)] + (4 \times 5)$$

But, by using the distributive law, we have

$$[4 \times (-5)] + (4 \times 5) = 4 \times (-5 + 5)$$

Thus [4 × (−5)] + 20 is the same number as the product 4 × (−5 + 5). Certainly this product is zero. (Why?) And we have proved that 4 × (−5) = −20.

We can use the same kind of argument to prove that

$$(-4) \times (-5) = 20$$

The ideas behind these proofs are very interesting. Each number is unique in that it has a property that no other number has. To find out whether (−4) × (−5) is 20, we think of some property that 20 has, but that no other number has. *We then find out whether* (−4) × (−5) *has this property.*

Now 20 added to −20 gives zero. No number other than 20 will do this. We add (−4) × (−5) to −20:

$$[(-4) \times (-5)] + (-20) = \ ?$$

We know that -20 is $4 \times (-5)$; so we can replace -20 by $4 \times (-5)$ and write

$$[(-4) \times (-5)] + [4 \times (-5)]$$

If we can use the distributive law to show that this last number is 0, then we will know that $(-4) \times (-5) = 20$. Do this.

Thus, using logical reasoning and the basic properties, we proceed as shown below to *prove* that $(-4) \times (-5) = 20$.

We know that *if*

$$x + (-20) = 0$$

***then x* must be 20.**

We know that

$$[(-4) \times (-5)] + (-20) = (-4 + 4) \times (-5).$$

Since the above is zero, it follows that

$$(-4) \times (-5) = 20$$

EXERCISES

1. Form the following products. Be ready to *prove* that each answer is correct.

   (a) $2 \times (-4)$ (b) $(-4) \times 3$ (c) $(-4) \times (-3)$
   (d) $(-1) \times 1$ (e) $(-1) \times (-1)$ (f) $(-2) \times (-4)$
   (g) $(-8) \times 0$ (h) $12 \times (-3)$ (i) $(-3) \times 12$
   (j) $(-3) \times (-12)$ (k) $(-4) \times 8$ (l) $(-4) \times (-8)$
   (m) $5 \times (-5)$ (n) $(-5) \times (-5)$ (o) $(-5) \times 0$
   (p) $(-7) \times 6$ (q) $(-7) \times (-6)$ (r) $(-12) \times 13$
   (s) $(-12) \times (-13)$ (t) $14 \times (-12)$ (u) $13 \times (-13)$
   (v) $(-13) \times (-13)$ (w) $10 \times (-27)$ (x) $(-100) \times 38$
   (y) $(-100) \times (-38)$ (z) $486 \times (-1000)$

2. Give the special products below.

   (a) $0 \times (-1)$ (b) $1 \times (-1)$ (c) $2 \times (-1)$
   (d) $3 \times (-1)$ (e) $4 \times (-1)$ (f) $10 \times (-1)$
   (g) Complete the statement,
        "If N is any whole number, then $N \times (-1) = $ _____."

3. Can you prove the statement you made in Exercise 2(g)?

4. Find the missing factor or product.

(a) $-3 = q \times (-1)$ (b) $-18 = 18 \times p$
(c) $q \times 14 = -14$ (d) $(-1) \times 40 = r$
(e) $31 \times (-1) = t$ (f) $1 = (-1) \times s$

5. Determine N so that each number sentence is true.

(a) $(-1) \times N = 9$ (b) $(-1) \times N = -9$
(c) $(-1) \times (N + 3) = 0$ (d) $(-1) \times (N + 3) = 1$
(e) $(-3) \times N = 12$ (f) $(-3) \times N = -12$
(g) $N \times N = 25$ (h) $(-2) \times (N - 3) = 10$

Division of integers is an operation that combines two integers, one a product and the other a factor, to yield one integer, the missing factor. Because

$$\overset{F}{(-3)} \times \overset{F}{(-4)} = \overset{P}{12}$$

we have

$$\overset{P}{12} \div \overset{F}{(-3)} = \overset{F}{-4} \quad \text{and} \quad \overset{P}{12} \div \overset{F}{(-4)} = \overset{F}{-3}$$

EXERCISES

1. Determine the missing factor in each problem below. In each case write out the division problem you have worked.

(a) $2 \times y = -10$ (b) $3 \times n = -18$
(c) $r \times (-2) = -8$ (d) $s \times 5 = -30$
(e) $N \times (-3) = 12$ (f) $N \times 20 = 80$
(g) $N \times 20 = -80$ (h) $N \times (-20) = 80$

2. Work each division problem below. Determine the missing factor by thinking of the number by which you should multiply the given factor to obtain the product.

(a) $12 \div 4$ (b) $12 \div (-4)$ (c) $(-12) \div 4$
(d) $-12 \div (-4)$ (e) $8 \div (-8)$ (f) $-8 \div (-8)$
(g) $0 \div (-6)$ (h) $(-2448) \div (-16)$

3. Work the following division problems.

(a) $20 \div (-5)$ (b) $-45 \div 15$ (c) $-45 \div (-15)$
(d) $28 \div (-7)$ (e) $-28 \div 7$ (f) $-28 \div (-7)$
(g) $-16 \div (-1)$ (h) $-16 \div 1$ (i) $[(-8) \times 7] \div (-8)$
(j) $(a \times b) \div (-a)$

4. Solve the equations listed below. In each case tell whether you are determining the product or a missing factor.

(a) $x \div (-4) = 5$ (b) $30 \div x = (-10)$ (c) $30 \div (-6) = x$
(d) $r \div (-1) = 11$ (e) $r \div 11 = -1$ (f) $11 \div r = -1$
(g) $11 \div (-1) = r$ (h) $r \div (-7) = -3$ (i) $-21 \div r = 3$
(j) $(-80) \div r = -5$

7. RECREATIONAL MATH

Interesting operations can be performed on the number line. Each operation involves a rule which tells us how to move from a starting point to another point on the number line. For example, consider the following rule.

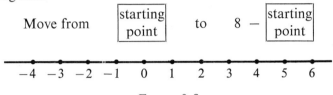

FIGURE 9–8

If we start at 3, we move from

$$3 \quad \text{to} \quad 8 - 3 \quad \text{or} \quad 5$$

From 5 we would move to $8 - 5$ or back to 3.

If we had started at -4 we would have moved first from -4 to $8 - (-4)$ or 12. Our next move brings us back to -4.

We can describe this rule more simply by saying:

$$\text{Move from} \quad N \quad \text{to} \quad 8 - N$$

EXERCISES

1. Using the move from N to $8 - N$, choose 10, 0, and -12 as your starting points and in each case move twice (Fig. 9-9). Does your second move bring you back each time to your starting point? Try three other starting points.

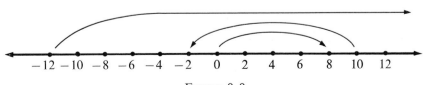

FIGURE 9–9

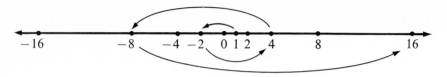

FIGURE 9–10

2. Start from 1 (Fig. 9–10) and move according to the rule:

$$\text{From} \quad N \quad \text{to} \quad (-2) \times N$$

Where are you on your sixth move?

3. Move according to the rule:

$$\text{From} \quad N \quad \text{to} \quad (2 \times N) - 3$$

(a) Start at 1. Where are you after 3 moves?
(b) Start at 2. Where are you after 3 moves?
(c) Start at 4. Where are you after 3 moves?
(d) Where must you start to end up where you started?
(e) Where must you start in order to reach 11 in one move?
(f) Where must you start to reach 11 in two moves?
(g) Where must you start to reach −13 in two moves?

4. Use the rule:

$$\text{Move from} \quad N \quad \text{to} \quad (N - 7) \div (N - 1)$$

(a) Start at 2 and move 3 times
(b) Start at 3 and move 4 times
(c) Start at −1 and move 2 times
(d) Start at −2 and move 3 times
(e) Start at −4 and move 2 times

Chapter 10

ADDITION AND MULTIPLICATION OF RATIONAL NUMBERS

1. INTRODUCTION

Whole numbers suffice for counting and for solving many problems, but the solution of some problems requires other numbers. Men invented whole numbers to describe sets of things. They looked at collections of objects and extracted number ideas from these collections. When we think about *one* set, a set of people at a ball game or a set of geese in a flock, we are very likely to think of the whole number that is matched with this set. Men invented *rational numbers* (you probably call these numbers *fractions*) to describe situations where we are interested in *two* sets. If a piece of candy were broken into 4 pieces of the same size and you were given on piece, you would naturally be interested in the original set of 4 pieces and the set of one piece that you acquired. If you wished to tell someone else what happened, you could say, "There were 4 pieces of candy, all the same size, and I was given one piece." Describe this situation more simply, using rational numbers.

Surely in the beginning men invented rational numbers just to have a convenient way to talk about the physical world. But after they had invented these new numbers, they realized that sometimes when they thought about two of these numbers they found a *third* number. This led to the definitions of addition and multiplication of rational numbers.

In this chapter we shall examine very carefully how these new number ideas are derived from the physical world. Although you undoubtedly can add and multiply rational numbers quite well, it is far more important that you *understand why* we use our special rules for computing with rational numbers. You will see that the associative, commutative, and distributive laws are also basic properties for the rational numbers. These basic laws and the properties of 0 and 1 give us our methods for adding, subtracting, multiplying, and dividing rational numbers.

2. GETTING RATIONAL NUMBERS FROM THE WORLD

In some of the exercises below you are shown figures. Each figure suggests rational number ideas. Think about the sets shown by the figure and answer the questions asked.

EXERCISES

1. In each of problems (a) through (d), tell what portion of each figure is shaded? what portion is not shaded?

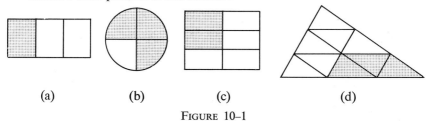

(a)   (b)   (c)   (d)

FIGURE 10–1

2. In exercises (a) and (b), tell what portion of the pole broke off? what portion is standing?

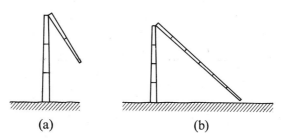

(a)   (b)

FIGURE 10–2

3. In parts (a) through (c), what portion of the pie is left? what part has been eaten?

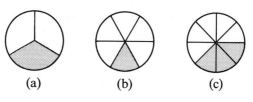

(a)   (b)   (c)

FIGURE 10–3

4. What fractional part of the squares in Fig. 10–4 is labeled "one"? "two"? "three"? "one or two"? "one or three"? "two or three"?

1	1	1	1	1	2
2	2	2	2	2	2
2	2	3	3	3	3
3	3	3	3	3	3

FIGURE 10–4

5. What fractional part of the dots shown in Fig. 10–5 is inside the triangle? the rectangle? the circle? both the rectangle and the circle?

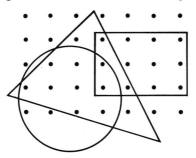

FIGURE 10–5

6. (a) What part of the students scored 100% on their math test (Fig. 10–6)?
   (b) If there were 8 students who scored 100%, how many are there in the class?

All students

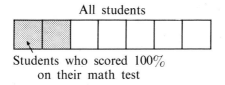

Students who scored 100%
on their math test

FIGURE 10–6

7. About what part of the population of the United States lives either in New York or in California (Fig. 10–7)?

'All United States citizens

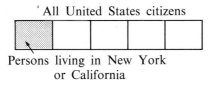

Persons living in New York
or California

FIGURE 10–7

8. (a) According to the diagram in Fig. 10–8, what part of the way has the family driven on its trip?

   (b) If they have driven 140 miles, how much farther have they to travel?

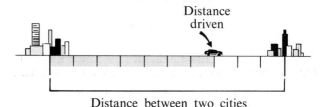

Distance
driven

Distance between two cities

FIGURE 10–8

9. The area of the United States is about six times the area of Alaska. Draw a figure to show what part the area of Alaska is of the entire area of the United States.

10. A certain city spends about 20¢ out of each tax dollar on fire and police protection. Draw a figure to show what part of the taxes is earmarked for this protection.

11. Figure 10–9 compares a length of 1 inch with a length of 1 centimeter. About what part of 1 inch is 1 centimeter?

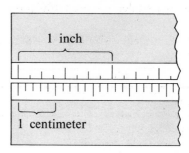

1 inch

1 centimeter

FIGURE 10–9

12. The shaded region in Fig. 10–10 compares a distance of one mile with a distance of one kilometer. Approximately what part of a mile is a kilometer?

1 mile

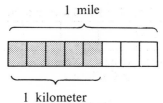

1 kilometer

FIGURE 10–10

13. The shaded region in Fig. 10–11 shows what fractional part the weight of a cubic yard of dirt is of the weight of a cubic meter of dirt. What is this fraction?

Weight of one cubic meter of dirt

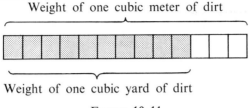

Weight of one cubic yard of dirt

FIGURE 10–11

14. The average weight of the earth in pounds per cubic foot is greater than that of the moon. We say that the density of the moon is less than the density of the earth. In Fig. 10–12 we compare these densities. Express the average density of the moon as a fraction of the average density of the earth.

Average density of earth

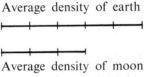

Average density of moon

FIGURE 10–12

15. Gold is quite a bit heavier than iron. Figure 10–13 compares the densities of these metals. Express the density of iron as a fraction of the density of gold.

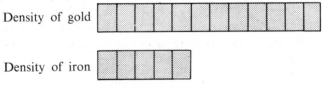

Density of gold

Density of iron

FIGURE 10–13

16. If a cube of iron 1 ft on an edge weighs about 305 lb, about what will a cube of gold of the same size weigh?

17. In Fig. 10–14, the speed of an artificial satellite orbiting about the earth is compared with the speed that a rocket must attain to escape from the earth and never return. Compare these speeds.

Escape speed of a rocket

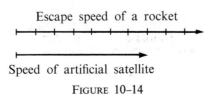

Speed of artificial satellite

FIGURE 10–14

Eagle

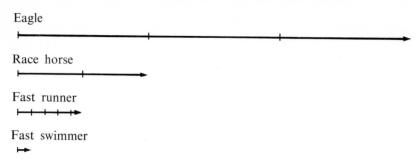

Race horse

Fast runner

Fast swimmer

FIGURE 10–15

18. Figure 10–15 compares certain speeds.
   (a)   Express the speed of each of the last three as a fraction of the speed of the eagle.
   (b)   Given that a race horse can run about 40 mph, what are the other speeds?

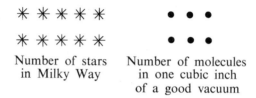

Number of stars   Number of molecules
in Milky Way   in one cubic inch
of a good vacuum

FIGURE 10–16

19. Figure 10–16 compares the number of molecules of air in a cubic inch of the best vacuum we can obtain with the number of stars in the Milky Way. If there are about 1,000,000,000,000 stars in the Milky Way, about how many molecules are there in one cubic inch of the best vacuum we can form?

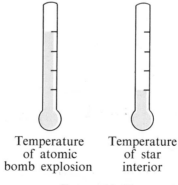

Temperature   Temperature
of atomic   of star
bomb explosion   interior

FIGURE 10–17

20. In Fig. 10–17 the temperature at the interior of a hot star is compared with the temperature at the center of an atomic bomb explosion. Compare these temperatures.

3. THE RATIONAL NUMBER LINE

Many properties of rational numbers are easy to understand when we match these numbers with some of the points of a line. We start with the whole number line shown in Fig. 10–18. We think of all the points that divide the distance between any two whole number points into equal parts. This gives us a number scale of halves (Fig. 10–19).

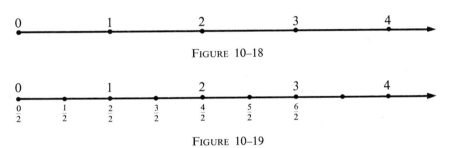

FIGURE 10–18

FIGURE 10–19

We now think of all the points that divide the distance between any two whole number points into thirds (Fig. 10–20).

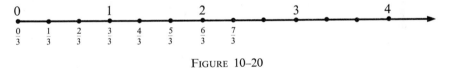

FIGURE 10–20

In the same way we could think of our number line as scaled in fourths, fifths, sixths, sevenths, etc. We imagine all these points paired with the rational numbers. The result is our rational number line. Note that many fractions may be used to name each point. The point 2 can be called $\frac{2}{1}$, $\frac{4}{2}$, $\frac{6}{3}$, $\frac{8}{4}$, $\frac{10}{5}$, etc.

Remark: Just as the symbols "2" and "1 + 1" are numerals for the whole number two, the fractions "$\frac{1}{2}$" and "$\frac{2}{4}$" are numerals for the rational number one-half. We *write* fractions. We *think about* rational numbers.

EXERCISES

1. The number line in Fig. 10–21 is scaled in fifths. Give fraction names for the marked points.

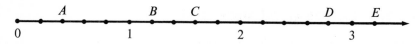

FIGURE 10–21

2. Draw a number line and scale it in fourths. Mark the points $\frac{3}{4}$, $\frac{7}{4}$, $\frac{9}{4}$, and $\frac{12}{4}$ as A, B, C, D respectively.
3. Scale the number line you used in Exercise 2 in eighths and give the fraction names for the points A, B, C, and D in eighths.
4. One of the five numbers, $2\frac{1}{3}$, $\frac{4}{5}$, $\frac{9}{7}$, $3\frac{1}{2}$, $\frac{11}{3}$, is matched with each point on the number line in Fig. 10–22. Match each of the numbers with a point.

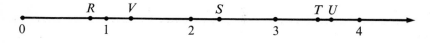

FIGURE 10–22

5. In Exercise 4, which is the largest of the five rational numbers? the smallest? Which of the numbers is larger than 1 and smaller than 2? larger than 2 and smaller than 3?
6. Using the symbols for greater than and less than, write all the inequalities involving the numbers $\frac{9}{7}$, $\frac{4}{5}$, $\frac{11}{3}$.
7. Draw a number line and scale it in halves. Now mark points dividing the distance between each pair of points into three equal parts. How is the resulting line scaled?

It is easy to represent addition on the number line. Figure 10–23 illustrates the addition fact $\frac{3}{5} + \frac{4}{5} = \frac{7}{5}$.

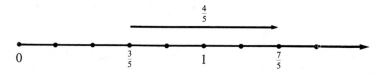

FIGURE 10–23

EXERCISES

1. Give the addition fact represented by each of the number lines (a) through (c).

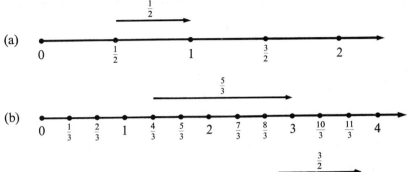

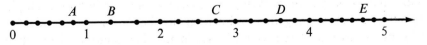

FIGURE 10–24

2. Draw three number lines and show each of the facts given below.

(a) $\frac{2}{3} + \frac{2}{3} = 1\frac{1}{3}$ (b) $\frac{3}{4} + \frac{5}{4} = 2$ (c) $\frac{3}{2} + 3 = 4\frac{1}{2}$

3. Give the addition fact shown by the number line in Fig. 10–25, assuming that it is scaled (a) in halves, (b) in thirds, (c) in sevenths, (d) in tenths, (e) in twentieths, and (f) in units.

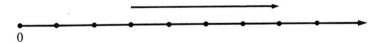

FIGURE 10–25

4. What subtraction facts are shown in Exercises 1 and 2?

5. Give the number that goes with each of the points A, B, C, D, and E shown on the number line in Fig. 10–26.

FIGURE 10–26

6. In Exercise 5 we can say that the distance from point A to point B is $\frac{1}{6} + \frac{1}{3}$. Express in this way the distance

   (a) from B to C (b) from C to D (c) from D to E
   (d) from A to C (e) from B to D (f) from C to E

7. Draw a number line and mark the points 0, 1, 2, 3, 4, and 5. Mark approximately on the line points for

   (a) $\frac{3}{2}$ (b) $2\frac{2}{5}$ (c) $\frac{10}{3}$ (d) $4\frac{5}{6}$ (e) $\frac{11}{2}$

   (f) $\frac{1}{10}$ (g) $\frac{11}{10}$ (h) $\frac{21}{10}$

8. Think of the number line and determine n, given that

   (a) $\frac{2}{3} + n = 1$ (b) $\frac{3}{5} + n = 1$ (c) $\frac{4}{7} + n = 1$

   (d) $\frac{2}{3} + n = \frac{4}{3}$ (e) $1\frac{1}{2} + n = 2$ (f) $\frac{5}{6} + n = \frac{12}{6}$

9. What subtraction problems did you work in Exercise 8?

   Thinking of multiplication as repeated addition we can multiply a rational number by any whole number. Figure 10–27 shows the product $4 \times \frac{2}{3}$.

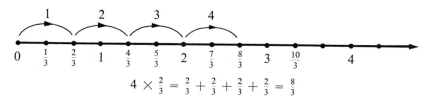

$$4 \times \frac{2}{3} = \frac{2}{3} + \frac{2}{3} + \frac{2}{3} + \frac{2}{3} = \frac{8}{3}$$

FIGURE 10–27

   Because we agree that multiplication of rational numbers is commutative, we also have the result:

$$\frac{2}{3} \times 4 = \frac{8}{3}$$

Note that $4 \times \frac{2}{3}$ is *more than* $\frac{2}{3}$ but is *less than* 4. When we multiply two whole numbers together and neither number is zero, the product is always at least as large as both whole number factors. But when rational numbers are multiplied, the product may be *smaller* than one of the factors.

EXERCISES

1. Give the multiplication facts illustrated in Fig. 10–28 (a) through (c).

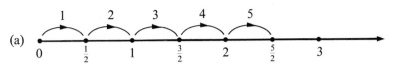

(a)

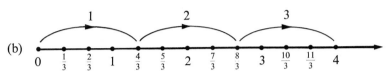

(b)

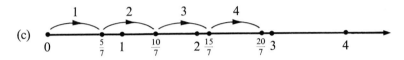

(c)

FIGURE 10–28

2. When the commutative property is used, what other multiplication facts are given by the figures above?

3. Draw a number line to represent each fact.

(a) $4 \times \frac{1}{2} = 2$ (b) $3 \times \frac{3}{2} = \frac{9}{2}$

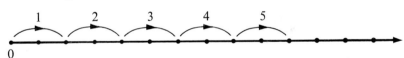

FIGURE 10–29

4. Give the multiplication fact shown by the number line in Fig. 10–29, assuming that it is scaled.

(a) in halves   (b) in thirds   (c) in sevenths
(d) in tenths   (e) in twentieths   (f) in units

5. What division facts are shown in Exercises 1 and 3?

6. Think of the number line and determine n, given that

(a) $n \times \frac{3}{5} = \frac{12}{5}$ (b) $n \times \frac{2}{9} = \frac{10}{9}$

(c) $\frac{4}{3} \times n = \frac{20}{3}$ (d) $\frac{3}{7} \times n = \frac{18}{7}$

7. What division problems did you work in Exercise 6?

4. TECHNIQUES OF ADDITION AND MULTIPLICATION

We have studied addition and multiplication of rational numbers on the number line, but this is not enough for a complete understanding of addition and multiplication.   For example, we have multiplied rational numbers by whole numbers, but we have not considered problems such as $\frac{3}{2} \times \frac{4}{5}$. Our main purpose in this section is to show that a few ideas from the physical world taken together with our basic properties give us our techniques for adding and multiplying rational numbers.

Figure 10–30 below illustrates the addition fact,

$$\frac{2}{7} + \frac{3}{7} = \frac{5}{7}$$

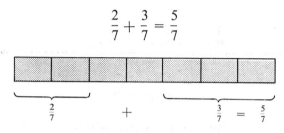

FIGURE 10–30

From Fig. 10–31 we see that the rational numbers $\frac{2}{6}$ and $\frac{1}{3}$ are the same.

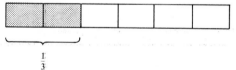

FIGURE 10–31

The drawings in Fig. 10–32 show that

$$\frac{1}{2} + \frac{1}{4} = \frac{3}{4}$$

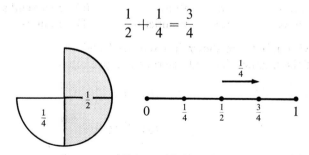

FIGURE 10–32

EXERCISES

1. Give an addition fact shown by each of the sketches (a) through (d) in Fig. 10–33.

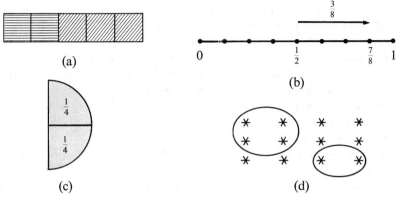

(a)

(b)

(c)

(d)

FIGURE 10–33

2. Explain how each diagram in Fig. 10–34 shows that $\frac{3}{6} = \frac{1}{2}$.

(a)

(b)

(c)

(d)

FIGURE 10–34

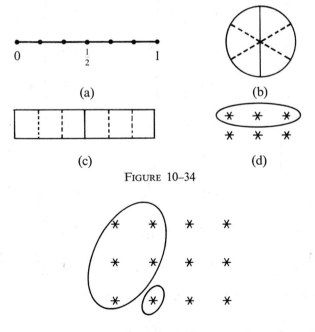

FIGURE 10–35

3. Explain how Fig. 10–35 shows that $\frac{5}{12} + \frac{1}{12} = \frac{1}{2}$.

4. In a group of 80 persons, men, women, boys, and girls, there are 17 boys and 23 girls. Give two fractions and one addition fact suggested by this physical situation.

5. It is 24 mi from town *A* to town *B*. We drive 7 mi and stop for gas. We drive 5 more and stop to fix a flat tire. Give two fractions and one addition fact suggested by this description.

6. A man had 12 children. Five of them went to the movies, four went to a neighbor's and two went to sleep. Then the father was able to read the newspaper. Suppose that each child makes the same amount of noise. Write the fractions (for each group) suggested by this information. Add these numbers to show what part of the noise was removed from the household.

7. Draw a figure to show that $\frac{3}{8} + \frac{1}{8} = \frac{1}{2}$.

8. Make a rectangular 3 by 8 array of dots and use it to show that $\frac{2}{3}$ of 24 is 16.

9. Use a number line to show that $1\frac{3}{4} + \frac{3}{4} = 2\frac{1}{2}$; that $1\frac{2}{3} = \frac{5}{3}$; that $3\frac{1}{4} = \frac{13}{4}$.

10. For problems (a) through (x), give correct answers in any form that you please.

(a) $\frac{1}{3} + \frac{2}{3}$ (b) $\frac{3}{5} + \frac{2}{5}$ (c) $\frac{4}{7} + \frac{3}{7}$

(d) $\frac{3}{4} + \frac{2}{4}$ (e) $\frac{5}{8} + \frac{4}{8}$ (f) $\frac{3}{6} + \frac{4}{6}$

(g) $\frac{1}{2} + \frac{3}{2}$ (h) $\frac{1}{4} + \frac{5}{4}$ (i) $\frac{2}{7} + \frac{9}{7}$

(j) $1\frac{1}{3} + \frac{2}{3}$ (k) $2\frac{1}{4} + \frac{1}{4}$ (l) $3\frac{1}{2} + 1$

(m) $3\frac{3}{4} + \frac{2}{4}$ (n) $1\frac{3}{8} + \frac{5}{8}$ (o) $2\frac{1}{6} + \frac{5}{6}$

(p) $\frac{5}{11} + \frac{7}{11}$ (q) $\frac{7}{12} + \frac{5}{12}$ (r) $\frac{5}{12} + \frac{1}{12}$

(s) $\frac{7}{15} + \frac{4}{15}$ (t) $\frac{3}{10} + \frac{7}{10}$ (u) $\frac{6}{10} + \frac{7}{10}$

(v) $\frac{13}{10} + \frac{7}{10}$ (w) $2\frac{3}{10} + \frac{9}{10}$ (x) $\frac{17}{100} + \frac{22}{100}$

11. Draw an array of 12 dots and use it to show that

(a) $\frac{4}{12} = \frac{1}{3}$ (b) $\frac{6}{12} = \frac{1}{2}$

(c) $\frac{5}{12} + \frac{3}{12} = \frac{2}{3}$ (d) $\frac{3}{4}$ of 12 = 9

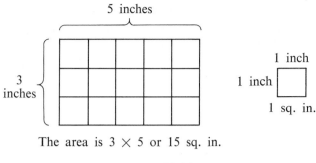

The area is 3 × 5 or 15 sq. in.

FIGURE 10–36

The rule which we use to multiply rational numbers is quite easy to remember. We simply multiply numerators together and denominators together:

$$\frac{7}{5} \times \frac{4}{3} = \frac{7 \times 4}{5 \times 3} = \frac{28}{15}$$

Perhaps the best way to understand why this method has been chosen is to consider the problem of finding areas of rectangles. If Fig. 10–36 represents a rectangle 5 inches long and 3 inches wide, it is clear that the area of the rectangle is 3 × 5, or 15, square inches.

The length and width of a rectangle may not be whole numbers. Nonetheless we would like to be able to compute the area of the rectangle by multiplying the length by the width. *The product $\frac{1}{3} \times \frac{1}{2}$ should give us the area of a rectangle $\frac{1}{3}$ inch wide by $\frac{1}{2}$ inch long.* Let us see what this area is. Figure 10–37 represents a one-inch square whose

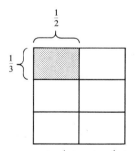

A rectangle $\frac{1}{3}$ in. by $\frac{1}{2}$ in. has
an area of $\frac{1}{6}$ sq. in.

FIGURE 10–37

area is 1 × 1 or 1 square inch. In the upper left-hand corner, we have marked off a rectangle $\frac{1}{3}$ inch by $\frac{1}{2}$ inch. Looking at the figure, we clearly see that the area of the $\frac{1}{3}$ by $\frac{1}{2}$ rectangle is one sixth of the area of the inch square, that is, $\frac{1}{6}$ square inch;

$$\frac{1}{3} \times \frac{1}{2} = \frac{1 \times 1}{3 \times 2} = \frac{1}{6}$$

We note that in this case the rule for multiplying fractions does give the area of the rectangle.

EXERCISES

1. Each part of Fig. 10–38 (a) through (c) shows a rectangle as part of a one-inch square. Find the area of the rectangle by counting and then write out the multiplication problem that yields this area.

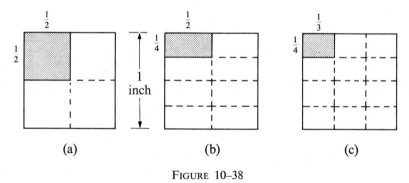

FIGURE 10–38

2. By counting determine the area of each rectangle shown in Fig. 10–39. Write the multiplication problem that gives the area.

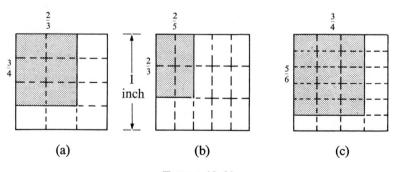

FIGURE 10–39

3. Draw a large square on a sheet of paper or at the blackboard. Use this square to illustrate the rectangles whose dimensions are given below and find their areas.

(a) $\frac{1}{5}$ by $\frac{1}{8}$ (b) $\frac{3}{5}$ by $\frac{5}{8}$

4. Think of a unit square and give the area of each rectangle whose dimensions are given below.

(a) $\frac{1}{4}$ in. by $\frac{1}{7}$ in.   (b) $\frac{1}{8}$ in. by $\frac{1}{8}$ in.

(c) $\frac{1}{3}$ ft by $\frac{1}{5}$ ft   (d) $\frac{1}{4}$ yd by $\frac{1}{10}$ yd

5. Write the following products.

(a) $\frac{1}{2} \times \frac{1}{3}$ (b) $\frac{1}{4} \times \frac{1}{5}$ (c) $\frac{1}{3} \times \frac{1}{3}$

(d) $\frac{1}{5} \times \frac{1}{3}$ (e) $\frac{1}{5} \times \frac{1}{5}$ (f) $\frac{1}{2} \times \frac{1}{4}$

(g) $\frac{1}{6} \times \frac{1}{7}$ (h) $\frac{1}{6} \times \frac{1}{6}$ (i) $\frac{1}{3} \times \frac{1}{6}$

(j) $\frac{1}{5} \times \frac{1}{4}$ (k) $\frac{1}{6} \times \frac{1}{5}$ (l) $\frac{1}{8} \times \frac{1}{5}$

We can use the commutative and associative laws to explain our rule for finding a product like $\frac{4}{3} \times \frac{5}{7}$. We have agreed that $\frac{4}{3} = 4 \times \frac{1}{3}$ and that $\frac{5}{7} = 5 \times \frac{1}{7}$. Hence, using the commutative and associative properties, we have

$$\frac{4}{3} \times \frac{5}{7} = \left(4 \times \frac{1}{3}\right) \times \left(5 \times \frac{1}{7}\right) = (4 \times 5) \times \left(\frac{1}{3} \times \frac{1}{7}\right)$$

Since we have agreed that $\frac{1}{3} \times \frac{1}{7} = \frac{1}{21}$, the total product is $20 \times \frac{1}{21}$, or $\frac{20}{21}$.

EXERCISES

1. Complete the following problems.

(a) $3 \times \frac{2}{5} = 3 \times 2 \times \frac{1}{5} =$

(b) $4 \times \frac{3}{7} = 4 \times 3 \times \frac{1}{7} =$

(c) $4 \times \dfrac{3}{12} = 4 \times 3 \times \dfrac{1}{12} =$

(d) $7 \times \dfrac{9}{13} = 7 \times 9 \times \dfrac{1}{13} =$

(e) $\dfrac{2}{5} \times \dfrac{3}{4} = (2 \times 3) \times \left(\dfrac{1}{5} \times \dfrac{1}{4} \right) =$

(f) $\dfrac{4}{7} \times \dfrac{5}{8} = (4 \times 5) \times \left(\dfrac{1}{7} \times \dfrac{1}{8} \right) =$

(g) $\dfrac{12}{17} \times \dfrac{7}{11} = (12 \times 7) \times \left(\dfrac{1}{17} \times \dfrac{1}{11} \right) =$

(h) $\dfrac{9}{10} \times \dfrac{13}{10} = (9 \times 13) \times \left(\dfrac{1}{10} \times \dfrac{1}{10} \right) =$

(i) $\dfrac{7}{10} \times \dfrac{13}{100} = (7 \times 13) \times \left(\dfrac{1}{10} \times \dfrac{1}{100} \right) =$

(j) $\dfrac{47}{100} \times \dfrac{3}{10} = (47 \times 3) \times \left(\dfrac{1}{100} \times \dfrac{1}{10} \right) =$

2. Write each of the following as the product of one whole number and one fraction whose numerator is 1. For example,

$$\dfrac{3}{5} \times \dfrac{2}{4} = 6 \times \dfrac{1}{20}$$

(a) $\dfrac{2}{3} \times \dfrac{1}{5}$ (b) $\dfrac{3}{7} \times \dfrac{2}{3}$ (c) $\dfrac{4}{7} \times \dfrac{5}{6}$

(d) $\dfrac{7}{3} \times \dfrac{9}{8}$ (e) $\dfrac{7}{10} \times \dfrac{6}{10}$ (f) $\dfrac{11}{100} \times \dfrac{9}{10}$

3. Give the products.

(a) $\dfrac{3}{4} \times \dfrac{3}{5}$ (b) $\dfrac{2}{3} \times \dfrac{4}{5}$ (c) $\dfrac{3}{7} \times \dfrac{5}{6}$

(d) $\dfrac{6}{5} \times \dfrac{4}{3}$ (e) $\dfrac{7}{2} \times \dfrac{5}{3}$ (f) $\dfrac{7}{4} \times \dfrac{5}{2}$

(g) $\dfrac{5}{6} \times \dfrac{3}{8}$ (h) $\dfrac{3}{11} \times \dfrac{5}{13}$ (i) $\dfrac{53}{17} \times \dfrac{21}{34}$

(j) $\dfrac{3}{7} \times \dfrac{4}{19}$ (k) $\dfrac{4}{19} \times \dfrac{3}{7}$ (l) $\dfrac{13}{19} \times \dfrac{7}{7}$

(m) $\dfrac{43}{16} \times \dfrac{7}{16}$ (n) $\dfrac{7}{8} \times \dfrac{5}{6}$ (o) $\dfrac{16}{24} \times \dfrac{27}{36}$

(p) $\dfrac{10}{15} \times \dfrac{50}{100}$ (q) $\dfrac{17}{10} \times \dfrac{7}{10}$ (r) $\dfrac{23}{100} \times \dfrac{47}{100}$

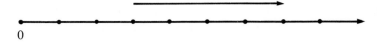

FIGURE 10–40

Addition is easy when the fractions to be added have equal denominators. To add $\frac{3}{5} + \frac{4}{5}$ we can think of a number line scaled in fifths (Fig. 10–40). We could use this same figure to represent adding $\frac{3}{7} + \frac{4}{7}$ or $\frac{3}{23} + \frac{4}{23}$, etc. We would only have to think of our number line as scaled in sevenths or twenty-thirds. We can also use the distributive law to explain the method for adding fractions whose denominators are equal. Since

$$\frac{3}{5} = 3 \times \frac{1}{5} \quad \text{and} \quad \frac{4}{5} = 4 \times \frac{1}{5}$$

we have

$$\frac{3}{5} + \frac{4}{5} = \left(3 \times \frac{1}{5}\right) + \left(4 \times \frac{1}{5}\right)$$

Now, by the distributive law,

$$\left(3 \times \frac{1}{5}\right) + \left(4 \times \frac{1}{5}\right) = (3 + 4) \times \frac{1}{5} = \frac{7}{5}$$

EXERCISES

1. Use the distributive law to complete the following problems.

(a) $\dfrac{2}{3} + \dfrac{5}{3} = \left(2 \times \dfrac{1}{3}\right) + \left(5 \times \dfrac{1}{3}\right) = (\underline{\quad} + \underline{\quad}) \times \underline{\quad}$

(b) $\dfrac{17}{49} + \dfrac{31}{49} = \left(17 \times \dfrac{1}{49}\right) + \left(31 \times \dfrac{1}{49}\right) = (\underline{\quad} + \underline{\quad}) \times \underline{\quad}$

(c) $\dfrac{53}{86} + \dfrac{47}{86} = (\underline{\quad} + \underline{\quad}) \times \underline{\quad}$

(d) $\dfrac{19}{97} + \dfrac{63}{97} = (\underline{\quad} + \underline{\quad}) \times \underline{\quad}$

2. What is n given that

(a) $\dfrac{3}{5} + \dfrac{n}{5} = \dfrac{12}{5}$ (b) $\dfrac{4}{3} + \dfrac{n}{3} = \dfrac{9}{3}$ (c) $\dfrac{7}{11} + \dfrac{n}{11} = \dfrac{16}{11}$

(d) $\dfrac{6}{19} + \dfrac{n}{19} = 1$ (e) $\dfrac{a}{6} + \dfrac{n}{6} = \dfrac{a+7}{6}$ (f) $\dfrac{a}{73} + \dfrac{n}{73} = \dfrac{a+41}{73}$

One thing that makes working with rational numbers difficult is that there are so many different fraction symbols for each rational number. For example,

$$1 = \frac{2}{2} = \frac{3}{3} = \frac{4}{4} = \cdots$$

$$\frac{1}{2} = \frac{2}{4} = \frac{3}{6} = \frac{4}{8} = \cdots$$

However, our method for adding fractions really depends upon this fact. If two fractions have the same denominator, they are easily added. We simply add the numerators:

$$\frac{8}{87} + \frac{6}{87} = \frac{8+6}{87},$$

$$\frac{a}{59} + \frac{b}{59} = \frac{a+b}{59}$$

We can make the following statement.

For all whole numbers a and b,

$$\frac{a}{c} + \frac{b}{c} = \frac{a+b}{c}$$

Adding fractions with equal denominators

To find the sum of the two rational numbers $\frac{1}{2}$ and $\frac{1}{3}$ we exchange these fractions for two fractions with the same denominator. Since

$$\frac{1}{2} = \frac{3}{6} \quad \text{and} \quad \frac{1}{3} = \frac{2}{6}$$

it follows that

$$\frac{1}{2} + \frac{1}{3} = \frac{3}{6} + \frac{2}{6} = \frac{5}{6}$$

The difficult part about adding rational numbers is choosing replacement fractions that have equal denominators. In choosing these replacement fractions we use the following *rule for multiplying fractions and the property of* 1.

For every pair of rational numbers

$$\frac{a}{b} \quad \text{and} \quad \frac{c}{d},$$

$$\frac{a}{b} \times \frac{c}{d} = \frac{a \times c}{b \times d} \quad \text{and} \quad \frac{a}{b} \times 1 = \frac{a}{b}$$

Properties we use in adding rational numbers

As an example, in adding $\frac{3}{5}$ and $\frac{2}{3}$ we use the facts that

$$\frac{3}{5} = \frac{3}{5} \times 1 = \frac{3}{5} \times \frac{3}{3} = \frac{9}{15}$$

$$\frac{2}{3} = \frac{2}{3} \times 1 = \frac{2}{3} \times \frac{5}{5} = \frac{10}{15}$$

Since

$$\frac{3}{5} = \frac{9}{15} \quad \text{and} \quad \frac{2}{3} = \frac{10}{15}$$

we have

$$\frac{3}{5} + \frac{2}{3} = \frac{9}{15} + \frac{10}{15} = \frac{19}{15}$$

EXERCISES

1. In each problem use the hint given to find the sum of the two rational numbers.

(a) $\frac{3}{4} + \frac{2}{3}$; $\quad \frac{3}{4} = \frac{3}{4} \times \frac{3}{3}, \frac{2}{3} = \frac{2}{3} \times \frac{4}{4}$

(b) $\frac{5}{7} + \frac{1}{2}$; $\quad \frac{5}{7} = \frac{5}{7} \times \frac{2}{2}, \frac{1}{2} = \frac{1}{2} \times \frac{7}{7}$

(c) $\frac{3}{8} + \frac{3}{4}$; $\quad \frac{3}{4} = \frac{3}{4} \times \frac{2}{2}$

(d) $\frac{5}{6} + \frac{5}{12}$; $\quad \frac{5}{6} = \frac{5}{6} \times \frac{2}{2}$

(e) $\frac{2}{3} + \frac{1}{5}$; $\quad \frac{2}{3} = \frac{2}{3} \times \frac{5}{5}, \frac{1}{5} = \frac{1}{5} \times \frac{3}{3}$

(f) $\dfrac{3}{8} + \dfrac{1}{12}$; $\dfrac{3}{8} = \dfrac{3}{8} \times \dfrac{3}{3}$, $\dfrac{1}{12} = \dfrac{1}{12} \times \dfrac{2}{2}$

(g) $\dfrac{1}{4} + \dfrac{7}{16}$; $\dfrac{1}{4} = \dfrac{1}{4} \times \dfrac{4}{4}$

(h) $\dfrac{2}{5} + \dfrac{3}{7}$; $\dfrac{2}{5} = \dfrac{2}{5} \times \dfrac{7}{7}$, $\dfrac{3}{7} = \dfrac{3}{7} \times \dfrac{5}{5}$

(i) $\dfrac{1}{6} + \dfrac{2}{7}$; $\dfrac{1}{6} = \dfrac{1}{6} \times \dfrac{7}{7}$, $\dfrac{2}{7} = \dfrac{2}{7} \times \dfrac{6}{6}$

(j) $\dfrac{3}{10} + \dfrac{4}{15}$; $\dfrac{3}{10} = \dfrac{3}{10} \times \dfrac{3}{3}$, $\dfrac{4}{15} = \dfrac{4}{15} \times \dfrac{2}{2}$

(k) $\dfrac{11}{21} + \dfrac{3}{14}$; $\dfrac{11}{21} = \dfrac{11}{21} \times \dfrac{2}{2}$, $\dfrac{3}{14} = \dfrac{3}{14} \times \dfrac{3}{3}$

(l) $\dfrac{7}{9} + \dfrac{4}{15}$; $\dfrac{7}{9} = \dfrac{7}{9} \times \dfrac{5}{5}$, $\dfrac{4}{15} = \dfrac{4}{15} \times \dfrac{3}{3}$

(m) $\dfrac{5}{6} + \dfrac{4}{15}$; $\dfrac{5}{6} = \dfrac{5}{6} \times \dfrac{5}{5}$, $\dfrac{4}{15} = \dfrac{4}{15} \times \dfrac{2}{2}$

(n) $\dfrac{2}{7} + \dfrac{3}{8}$; $\dfrac{2}{7} = \dfrac{2}{7} \times \dfrac{8}{8}$, $\dfrac{3}{8} = \dfrac{3}{8} \times \dfrac{7}{7}$

(o) $\dfrac{7}{9} + \dfrac{3}{10}$; $\dfrac{7}{9} = \dfrac{7}{9} \times \dfrac{10}{10}$, $\dfrac{3}{10} = \dfrac{3}{10} \times \dfrac{9}{9}$

(p) $\dfrac{3}{10} + \dfrac{7}{11}$; $\dfrac{3}{10} = \dfrac{3}{10} \times \dfrac{11}{11}$, $\dfrac{7}{11} = \dfrac{7}{11} \times \dfrac{10}{10}$

(q) $\dfrac{5}{11} + \dfrac{7}{12}$; $\dfrac{5}{11} = \dfrac{5}{11} \times \dfrac{12}{12}$, $\dfrac{7}{12} = \dfrac{7}{12} \times \dfrac{11}{11}$

(r) $\dfrac{7}{12} + \dfrac{5}{13}$; $\dfrac{7}{12} = \dfrac{7}{12} \times \dfrac{13}{13}$, $\dfrac{5}{13} = \dfrac{5}{13} \times \dfrac{12}{12}$

(s) $\dfrac{1}{12} + \dfrac{5}{18}$; $\dfrac{1}{12} = \dfrac{1}{12} \times \dfrac{3}{3}$, $\dfrac{5}{18} = \dfrac{5}{18} \times \dfrac{2}{2}$

(t) $\dfrac{4}{27} + \dfrac{7}{18}$; $\dfrac{4}{27} = \dfrac{4}{27} \times \dfrac{2}{2}$, $\dfrac{7}{18} = \dfrac{7}{18} \times \dfrac{3}{3}$

(u) $\dfrac{5}{57} + \dfrac{7}{95}$; $\dfrac{5}{57} = \dfrac{5}{57} \times \dfrac{5}{5}$, $\dfrac{7}{95} = \dfrac{7}{95} \times \dfrac{3}{3}$

(v) $\dfrac{25}{143} + \dfrac{8}{77}$; $\dfrac{25}{143} = \dfrac{25}{143} \times \dfrac{7}{7}$, $\dfrac{8}{77} = \dfrac{8}{77} \times \dfrac{13}{13}$

(w) $\dfrac{13}{105} + \dfrac{9}{385}$; $\dfrac{13}{105} = \dfrac{13}{105} \times \dfrac{11}{11}$, $\dfrac{9}{385} = \dfrac{9}{385} \times \dfrac{3}{3}$

(x) $\dfrac{5}{23} + \dfrac{3}{41}$; $\dfrac{5}{23} = \dfrac{5}{23} \times \dfrac{41}{41}$, $\dfrac{3}{41} = \dfrac{3}{41} \times \dfrac{23}{23}$

(y) $\dfrac{11}{85} + \dfrac{4}{51}$; $\dfrac{11}{85} = \dfrac{11}{85} \times \dfrac{3}{3}$, $\dfrac{4}{51} = \dfrac{4}{51} \times \dfrac{5}{5}$

(z) $\dfrac{22}{525} + \dfrac{14}{165}$; $\dfrac{22}{525} = \dfrac{22}{525} \times \dfrac{11}{11}$, $\dfrac{14}{165} = \dfrac{14}{165} \times \dfrac{35}{35}$

2. For each pair of fractions below rename the *first* rational number *only* and add.

(a) $\dfrac{1}{2} + \dfrac{1}{4}$

(b) $\dfrac{1}{4} + \dfrac{3}{8}$

(c) $\dfrac{3}{8} + \dfrac{5}{16}$

(d) $\dfrac{3}{2} + \dfrac{3}{4}$

(e) $\dfrac{3}{4} + \dfrac{1}{16}$

(f) $\dfrac{3}{8} + \dfrac{11}{16}$

(g) $\dfrac{2}{3} + \dfrac{5}{6}$

(h) $\dfrac{1}{3} + \dfrac{7}{12}$

(i) $\dfrac{2}{3} + \dfrac{5}{9}$

(j) $\dfrac{3}{5} + \dfrac{7}{20}$

(k) $\dfrac{7}{10} + \dfrac{3}{50}$

(l) $\dfrac{5}{8} + \dfrac{11}{24}$

(m) $\dfrac{4}{9} + \dfrac{1}{45}$

(n) $\dfrac{6}{11} + \dfrac{5}{77}$

(o) $\dfrac{7}{15} + \dfrac{11}{90}$

(p) $\dfrac{3}{82} + \dfrac{3}{410}$

(q) $\dfrac{5}{217} + \dfrac{3}{868}$

(r) $\dfrac{135}{74} + \dfrac{219}{444}$

3. For each problem below rename two of the three rational numbers so that the fractions have the same denominators, and find the sum of the three numbers.

(a) $\dfrac{1}{2} , \dfrac{1}{4} , \dfrac{1}{8}$

(b) $\dfrac{1}{4} , \dfrac{3}{8} , \dfrac{5}{16}$

(c) $\dfrac{1}{2} , \dfrac{3}{4} , \dfrac{5}{16}$

(d) $\dfrac{3}{2} , \dfrac{2}{3} , \dfrac{5}{6}$

(e) $\dfrac{7}{2} , \dfrac{6}{5} , \dfrac{3}{10}$

(f) $\dfrac{1}{3} , \dfrac{4}{5} , \dfrac{7}{15}$

(g) $\dfrac{3}{5} , \dfrac{1}{6} , \dfrac{7}{30}$

(h) $\dfrac{5}{8} , \dfrac{6}{7} , \dfrac{3}{56}$

(i) $\dfrac{4}{7} , \dfrac{7}{10} , \dfrac{11}{70}$

(j) $\dfrac{5}{4} , \dfrac{11}{25} , \dfrac{71}{100}$

4. Choose new names for the rational numbers below and add.

(a) $\dfrac{3}{4} + \dfrac{5}{2}$

(b) $\dfrac{5}{8} + \dfrac{3}{16}$

(c) $\dfrac{2}{3} + \dfrac{1}{6}$

(d) $\dfrac{4}{5} + \dfrac{5}{6}$

(e) $\dfrac{3}{10} + \dfrac{4}{7}$

(f) $\dfrac{1}{3} + \dfrac{1}{5}$

(g) $\dfrac{3}{8} + \dfrac{4}{7}$

(h) $\dfrac{5}{4} + \dfrac{7}{16}$

(i) $\dfrac{3}{8} + \dfrac{11}{24}$

(j) $\dfrac{3}{4} + \dfrac{2}{5}$

(k) $\dfrac{3}{4} + \dfrac{2}{25}$

(l) $\dfrac{7}{11} + \dfrac{7}{12}$

Let us review the most important ideas of this section. First we studied multiplication of rational numbers. We agreed upon the definition for multiplication of "unit" fractions:

$$\frac{1}{3} \times \frac{1}{4} = \frac{1}{3 \times 4}; \qquad \frac{1}{a} \times \frac{1}{b} = \frac{1}{a \times b}$$

We used the associative and commutative laws to get other products. For example,

$$\frac{3}{4} \times \frac{2}{5} = (3 \times 2) \times \left(\frac{1}{4} \times \frac{1}{5}\right)$$

$$\frac{a}{b} \times \frac{c}{d} = (a \times c) \times \left(\frac{1}{b} \times \frac{1}{d}\right)$$

The distributive law helps explain addition:

$$\frac{3}{7} + \frac{2}{7} = \left(3 \times \frac{1}{7}\right) + \left(2 \times \frac{1}{7}\right) = (3 + 2) \times \frac{1}{7} = \frac{5}{7}$$

$$\frac{a}{c} + \frac{b}{c} = \left(a \times \frac{1}{c}\right) + \left(b \times \frac{1}{c}\right) = (a + b) \times \frac{1}{c} = \frac{a + b}{c}$$

To add fractions whose denominators are not equal we use the property of 1 to replace them by fractions having equal denominators. For example, to add $\frac{3}{5}$ and $\frac{2}{3}$, we choose fractions for these rational numbers having denominator 15. We say that we choose the *common denominator* 15.

$$\frac{3}{5} = \frac{3}{5} \times \frac{3}{3} = \frac{9}{15}, \qquad \frac{2}{3} = \frac{2}{3} \times \frac{5}{5} = \frac{10}{15}$$

If we multiply the numerator and denominator of a fraction by any whole number except zero, we obtain a fraction that stands for the same rational number. In other words,

---

If *n* is a whole number

different from zero, then

$$\frac{a}{b} = \frac{a \times n}{b \times n}$$

When we are adding fractions with large denominators, it is often not clear what common denominator should be chosen. In the next section we shall study this problem.

5. REDUCING FRACTIONS AND CHOOSING COMMON DENOMINATORS

The fractions $\frac{1}{2}$, $\frac{2}{3}$, and $\frac{3}{4}$ are in *lowest terms*. The fractions $\frac{2}{4}$, $\frac{6}{9}$, and $\frac{15}{20}$ are not. If we can divide the numerator and denominator of a fraction by a whole number larger than 1, we get a "simpler" fraction for the same rational number. If there is no such whole number, we say that the fraction is in lowest terms. The fraction $\frac{10}{15}$ is not in lowest terms because we can divide both numerator and denominator by 5:

$$\frac{10}{15} = \frac{2 \times 5}{3 \times 5} = \frac{2}{3} \times \frac{5}{5} = \frac{2}{3}$$

$$\frac{10}{15} = \frac{10 \div 5}{15 \div 5} = \frac{2}{3}$$

The fraction $\frac{2}{3}$, however, *is* in lowest terms. When we replace $\frac{10}{15}$ by $\frac{2}{3}$ we say that we have reduced the fraction to lowest terms.

EXERCISES

1. Use the facts given in exercises (a) through (l) to write the first fraction in lowest terms.

(a) $\frac{2}{4} = \frac{1 \times 2}{2 \times 2}$ (b) $\frac{4}{6} = \frac{2 \times 2}{3 \times 2}$

(c) $\frac{6}{8} = \frac{3 \times 2}{4 \times 2}$ (d) $\frac{12}{16} = \frac{3 \times 4}{4 \times 4}$

(e) $\frac{12}{18} = \frac{2 \times 6}{3 \times 6}$ (f) $\frac{20}{25} = \frac{4 \times 5}{5 \times 5}$

(g) $\frac{24}{56} = \frac{3 \times 8}{7 \times 8}$ (h) $\frac{32}{64} = \frac{1 \times 32}{2 \times 32}$

(i) $\frac{68}{119} = \frac{4 \times 17}{7 \times 17}$ (j) $\frac{414}{391} = \frac{18 \times 23}{17 \times 23}$

(k) $\frac{1106}{1738} = \frac{7 \times 158}{11 \times 158}$ (l) $\frac{70597}{25813} = \frac{227 \times 311}{83 \times 311}$

2. Determine a and b and reduce to lowest terms.

(a) $\dfrac{3}{9} = \dfrac{a \times 3}{b \times 3}$ (b) $\dfrac{15}{25} = \dfrac{a \times 5}{b \times 5}$ (c) $\dfrac{12}{30} = \dfrac{a \times 6}{b \times 6}$

(d) $\dfrac{84}{60} = \dfrac{a \times 12}{b \times 12}$ (e) $\dfrac{100}{175} = \dfrac{a \times 25}{b \times 25}$ (f) $\dfrac{64}{72} = \dfrac{a \times 8}{b \times 8}$

(g) $\dfrac{12}{16} = \dfrac{a \times 4}{b \times 4}$ (h) $\dfrac{45}{135} = \dfrac{a \times 45}{b \times 45}$ (i) $\dfrac{0}{8} = \dfrac{a \times 8}{b \times 8}$

(j) $\dfrac{0}{527} = \dfrac{a \times 527}{b \times 527}$ (k) $\dfrac{4}{4} = \dfrac{a \times 4}{b \times 4}$ (l) $\dfrac{672}{672} = \dfrac{a \times 672}{b \times 672}$

3. Determine a and b and reduce to lowest terms.

(a) $\dfrac{14}{28} = \dfrac{a \times 7}{b \times 7}$ (b) $\dfrac{55}{165} = \dfrac{a \times 11}{b \times 11}$ (c) $\dfrac{42}{63} = \dfrac{a \times 7}{b \times 7}$

(d) $\dfrac{156}{234} = \dfrac{a \times 13}{b \times 13}$ (e) $\dfrac{204}{255} = \dfrac{a \times 17}{b \times 17}$ (f) $\dfrac{904}{2260} = \dfrac{a \times 113}{b \times 113}$

(g) $\dfrac{3288}{4384} = \dfrac{a \times 137}{b \times 137}$ (h) $\dfrac{1482}{2223} = \dfrac{a \times 57}{b \times 57}$

4. Reduce the following fractions to lowest terms.

(a) $\dfrac{18}{24}$ (b) $\dfrac{6}{15}$ (c) $\dfrac{18}{12}$ (d) $\dfrac{75}{100}$

(e) $\dfrac{24}{36}$ (f) $\dfrac{70}{90}$ (g) $\dfrac{700}{900}$ (h) $\dfrac{4000}{5000}$

(i) $\dfrac{65}{52}$ (j) $\dfrac{77}{99}$ (k) $\dfrac{34}{51}$ (l) $\dfrac{19}{57}$

(m) $\dfrac{46}{50}$ (n) $\dfrac{46}{92}$ (o) $\dfrac{527}{713}$ (p) $\dfrac{4897}{4189}$

As the exercises above suggest, in reducing a fraction to lowest terms we may find it helpful to write the numerator and denominator each as a product of two factors. For example, since

$$51 = 3 \times 17$$

and

$$85 = 5 \times 17$$

we have

$$\frac{51}{85} = \frac{3}{5}$$

We say that 17 is the *greatest common factor* of 51 and 85, and we reduce $\frac{51}{85}$ to lowest terms by dividing the numerator and denominator by this greatest common factor.

As another example, since

$$70 = 2 \times 5 \times 7$$

and

$$105 = 3 \times 5 \times 7$$

we obtain

$$\frac{70}{105} = \frac{2}{3}$$

The number 5×7 is the greatest common factor of 70 and 105.

When we write 70 as $2 \times 5 \times 7$, we say that we have *completely factored* the whole number 70. Writing 70 as 10×7 would *not* factor it completely, for $10 = 2 \times 5$. If we can factor the numerator and denominator of a fraction completely, it is easy to reduce the fraction to lowest terms. For example,

$$\frac{182}{455} = \frac{2 \times 7 \times 13}{5 \times 7 \times 13} = \frac{2}{5}$$

We see that both numerator and denominator can be divided by the number 7×13.

To discuss factoring it is helpful to speak of *prime* whole numbers. The whole numbers 2 and 3 are prime numbers, while 1 and 4 are not. The whole numbers 5, 7, 11, and 13 are prime numbers. The numbers 6, 8, 9, 10, 12, 14, 15, and 16 are not.

EXERCISES

1. The whole numbers from 1 through 17 are listed below, and those numbers that are not prime numbers are crossed off.

$$\not{1}, 2, 3, \not{4}, 5, \not{6}, 7, \not{8}, \not{9}, \not{10}, 11, \not{12}, 13, \not{14}, \not{15}, \not{16}, 17$$

Pick out the prime numbers from 18 to 50.

2. What reason would you give for saying that 39 is not a prime number? that 37 is a prime number?

0	1	2	3	4	5	6	7	8	9	10	11	12	13
14	15	16	17	18	19	20	21	22	23	24	25	26	27
28	29	30	31	32	33	34	35	36	37	38	39	40	41
42	43	44	45	46	47	48	49	50	51	52	53	54	55
56	57	58	59	60	61	62	63	64	65	66	67	68	69
70	71	72	73	74	75	76	77	78	79	80	81	82	83
84	85	86	87	88	89	90	91	92	93	94	95	96	97
98	99	100	101	102	103	104	105	106	107	108	109	110	111
112	113	114	115	116	117	118	119	120	121	122	123	124	125
126	127	128	129	130									

FIGURE 10–41

In Fig. 10–41, we have listed all the whole numbers from 0 to 130. Those whole numbers which are not prime numbers are crossed off so that only the primes remain.

The statement below presents a definition of prime numbers.

Every whole number can be divided by 1 and by itself. A whole number is a prime number if it has exactly two whole-number divisors.

The prime numbers are important because they are the building blocks for other whole numbers. Each whole number larger than 1 that is not a prime number is the product of just one collection of prime numbers. For example, $48 = 2 \times 24 = 3 \times 16 = 4 \times 12 = 6 \times 8$, but none of these products has only prime number factors. When we factor 48 completely as a product of prime numbers, we have

$$48 = 2 \times 2 \times 2 \times 2 \times 3$$

EXERCISES

1. Write each of the following numbers that is not a prime number as a product of prime numbers.

(a) 9   (b) 30   (c) 46   (d) 57

(e) 111   (f) 131   (g) 105   (h) 345

(i) 279	(j) 180	(k) 211	(l) 1833
(m) 5239	(n) 1331	(o) 1728	(p) 11,663

2. How many prime numbers are there between 1 and 100?

3. Why are 2 and 3 the only pair of prime numbers whose difference is 1?

4. Find two prime numbers larger than 130 whose difference is 2. How many pairs of prime numbers can you find whose difference is 3?

5. Since $10 = 2 \times 5$, we can see that the number 10 has the four factors 1, 2, 5, and 10. Give all factors of

(a) 15 or 3×5 (b) 21 or 3×7
(c) 77 or 7×11 (d) 221 or 13×17
(e) 4 or 2×2 (f) 9 or 3×3
(g) 49 or 7×7 (h) 30 or $2 \times 3 \times 5$
(i) 42 or $2 \times 3 \times 7$ (j) 105 or $3 \times 5 \times 7$
(k) 1001 or $7 \times 11 \times 13$ (l) 3619 or $11 \times 13 \times 23$

6. Determine n given that

(a) $3 \times 5 \times n = 3 \times 5 \times 7$
(b) $2 \times 7 \times n = 2 \times 7 \times 37$
(c) $2 \times 3 \times n = 2 \times 3 \times 7 \times 7$
(d) $11 \times 13 \times n = 11 \times 13 \times 17 \times 19$
(e) $2 \times 5 \times n = 2 \times 2 \times 5 \times 7$
(f) $3 \times 7 \times n = 3 \times 3 \times 5 \times 7 \times 11$

7. Determine prime numbers r and s such that

(a) $3 \times r = s \times 5$ (b) $11 \times r = 7 \times s$
(c) $2 \times r = 19 \times s$ (d) $3 \times 5 \times r = 3 \times s \times 7$
(e) $2 \times 7 \times r = 7 \times 11 \times s$ (f) $13 \times 17 \times r = s \times 13 \times 7$

8. Choose r and s such that r is a prime number and s is the product of two prime numbers, given that

(a) $2 \times 2 \times 3 \times r = 2 \times 5 \times s$
(b) $2 \times 3 \times r \times 7 = 2 \times 11 \times s$
(c) $3 \times 7 \times 7 \times r = 7 \times 13 \times s$
(d) $7 \times 11 \times 13 \times r = 7 \times 19 \times s$

9. Find the smallest pair of numbers r and s such that

(a) $3 \times r = 7 \times s$ (b) $5 \times r = 3 \times 7 \times s$
(c) $2 \times 3 \times r = 11 \times s$ (d) $2 \times 3 \times r = 5 \times 7 \times s$
(e) $2 \times 2 \times r = 2 \times 3 \times s$ (f) $5 \times 5 \times r = 5 \times 7 \times s$
(g) $5 \times 5 \times 3 \times r = 5 \times 3 \times 3 \times s$
(h) $5 \times 5 \times r = 3 \times 11 \times s$

10. What is the greatest common factor of

(a) 7×11 and 7×13
(b) 17×19 and 11×23
(c) $2 \times 3 \times 5$ and $7 \times 11 \times 11$
(d) $3 \times 5 \times 11$ and $2 \times 3 \times 5$
(e) $2 \times 2 \times 3$ and $2 \times 3 \times 11$
(f) $5 \times 5 \times 7$ and 17×19
(g) $3 \times 3 \times 5 \times 7$ and $3 \times 5 \times 13$
(h) $7 \times 11 \times 13$ and $13 \times 17 \times 19$
(i) $2 \times 2 \times 2 \times 7$ and $2 \times 2 \times 5 \times 7$
(j) $5 \times 7 \times 11 \times 19$ and $7 \times 19 \times 31$
(k) $17 \times 17 \times 23$ and $17 \times 23 \times 37$
(l) $31 \times 37 \times 37 \times 43$ and $37 \times 43 \times 59$

If we factor the numerator and denominator of a fraction completely, it is easy to reduce the fraction to lowest terms. For example,

$$\frac{36}{56} = \frac{2 \times 2 \times 3 \times 3}{2 \times 2 \times 2 \times 7}$$

We see that 2×2 is the greatest common factor of 36 and 56, and hence in lowest terms the fraction is

$$\frac{36}{56} = \frac{3 \times 3}{2 \times 7}$$

EXERCISES

1. Reduce the given fractions to lowest terms.

(a) $\dfrac{2 \times 3}{2 \times 5}$

(b) $\dfrac{2 \times 3}{3 \times 5}$

(c) $\dfrac{7 \times 11}{11 \times 13}$

(d) $\dfrac{19 \times 23}{19 \times 31}$

(e) $\dfrac{2 \times 3 \times 5}{2 \times 3 \times 7}$

(f) $\dfrac{5 \times 7 \times 11}{2 \times 5 \times 7}$

(g) $\dfrac{7 \times 11 \times 19}{11 \times 13 \times 19}$

(h) $\dfrac{3 \times 3 \times 7}{3 \times 5 \times 7}$

(i) $\dfrac{11 \times 11 \times 13}{11 \times 13 \times 31}$

(j) $\dfrac{3 \times 5 \times 5 \times 7}{3 \times 5 \times 7 \times 13}$

(k) $\dfrac{2 \times 7 \times 11 \times 11}{7 \times 11 \times 13}$

(l) $\dfrac{3 \times 3 \times 19 \times 31}{7 \times 3 \times 19}$

(m) $\dfrac{2 \times 2 \times 2 \times 11}{2 \times 2 \times 5}$

(n) $\dfrac{7 \times 7 \times 7 \times 17}{7 \times 7 \times 17}$

(o) $\dfrac{3 \times 5 \times 19 \times 23}{5 \times 19 \times 37}$

2. Reduce the fractions below to lowest terms. Not all numerators and denominators are completely factored.

(a) $\dfrac{6 \times 7}{15 \times 7}$ (b) $\dfrac{9 \times 11}{3 \times 5 \times 11}$ (c) $\dfrac{10 \times 7 \times 13}{15 \times 13}$

(d) $\dfrac{5 \times 11 \times 13}{22 \times 13}$ (e) $\dfrac{39 \times 17}{15 \times 13}$ (f) $\dfrac{21 \times 15}{9 \times 7}$

3. Factor numerators and denominators completely and reduce the fractions to lowest terms.

(a) $\dfrac{12}{10}$ (b) $\dfrac{30}{42}$ (c) $\dfrac{63}{105}$ (d) $\dfrac{18}{81}$

(e) $\dfrac{50}{35}$ (f) $\dfrac{40}{36}$ (g) $\dfrac{175}{105}$ (h) $\dfrac{98}{77}$

(i) $\dfrac{57}{95}$ (j) $\dfrac{180}{66}$ (k) $\dfrac{231}{84}$ (l) $\dfrac{455}{156}$

(m) $\dfrac{245}{147}$ (n) $\dfrac{169}{260}$ (o) $\dfrac{1001}{385}$ (p) $\dfrac{429}{330}$

When we add two fractions having different denominators, we must replace them by fractions which have equal denominators. We wish to choose the smallest common denominator possible. It is easier to choose this *least common denominator* if we first completely factor the denominators of our given fractions. We *could* add $\frac{3}{10} + \frac{4}{15}$ by choosing 10×15 as the common denominator:

$$\frac{3}{10} = \frac{3}{10} \times \frac{15}{15} \quad \text{and} \quad \frac{4}{15} = \frac{4}{15} \times \frac{1}{10}$$

hence

$$\frac{3}{10} + \frac{4}{15} = \frac{3 \times 15}{150} + \frac{4 \times 10}{150} = \frac{85}{150}$$

Now, this answer is not in lowest terms. Since

$$\frac{85}{150} = \frac{5 \times 17}{2 \times 3 \times 5 \times 5}$$

the sum in lowest terms is

$$\frac{17}{2 \times 3 \times 5}$$

If we factor our denominators first, we have

$$\frac{3}{10} = \frac{3}{2 \times 5} \quad \text{and} \quad \frac{4}{15} = \frac{4}{3 \times 5}$$

Now we see that we can use

$$2 \times 3 \times 5 \quad \text{or} \quad 30$$

for the common denominator. We have

$$\frac{3}{2 \times 5} = \frac{3}{2 \times 5} \times \frac{3}{3} \quad \text{and} \quad \frac{4}{3 \times 5} = \frac{4}{3 \times 5} \times \frac{2}{2}$$

Then

$$\frac{3}{10} + \frac{4}{15} = \left(\frac{3}{10} \times \frac{3}{3}\right) + \left(\frac{4}{15} \times \frac{2}{2}\right) = \frac{9}{30} + \frac{8}{30} = \frac{17}{30}$$

If we wish to add $\frac{9}{77} + \frac{15}{143}$, we may write these fractions as

$$\frac{9}{7 \times 11} + \frac{15}{11 \times 13}$$

To determine the *least* common denominator we must find the *smallest* possible numbers r and s such that $7 \times 11 \times r = 11 \times 13 \times s$. We see that $r = 13$ and $s = 7$. The least common denominator is $7 \times 11 \times 13$:

$$\left(\frac{9}{7 \times 11} \times \frac{13}{13}\right) + \left(\frac{15}{11 \times 13} \times \frac{7}{7}\right) = \frac{117}{7 \times 11 \times 13} + \frac{105}{7 \times 11 \times 13}$$

$$= \frac{222}{1001}$$

EXERCISES

1. Add $\frac{1}{2} + \frac{1}{3}$ and reduce the result to lowest terms, using as common denominator (a) 18, (b) 12, (c) 6.
2. Add $\frac{3}{4} + \frac{1}{6}$ and reduce the sum to lowest terms, using as common denominator (a) 36, (b) 24, (c) 12.
3. Add $\frac{3}{10} + \frac{2}{15}$ and reduce to lowest terms, using as common denominator (a) 150, (b) 60, (c) 30.
4. Add $\frac{5}{21} + \frac{1}{14}$ and reduce to lowest terms, using as denominator (a) 21×14, (b) 84, (c) 42.

5. Add $\frac{7}{15} + \frac{4}{21}$ and reduce to lowest terms, using as denominator (a) 5×21, (b) 10×21, (c) 15×21.

6. Add $\frac{7}{80} + \frac{3}{50}$ and reduce to lowest terms, using as denominator (a) 8×50, (b) 80×50.

7. In the exercises below, choose least common denominators, add, and reduce your answers to lowest terms.

(a) $\frac{2}{3} + \frac{5}{6}$

(b) $\frac{3}{4} + \frac{1}{6}$

(c) $\frac{1}{2} + \frac{3}{5}$

(d) $\frac{3}{4} + \frac{3}{16}$

(e) $\frac{2}{3} + \frac{3}{5}$

(f) $\frac{5}{6} + \frac{1}{9}$

(g) $\frac{5}{4} + \frac{1}{10}$

(h) $\frac{3}{7} + \frac{2}{11}$

(i) $\frac{2}{5} + \frac{4}{13}$

(j) $\frac{1}{17} + \frac{1}{19}$

(k) $\frac{1}{31} + \frac{1}{29}$

(l) $\frac{1}{3 \times 5} + \frac{1}{3 \times 7}$

(m) $\frac{2}{3 \times 7} + \frac{3}{2 \times 11}$

(n) $\frac{3}{5 \times 5} + \frac{1}{3 \times 5}$

(o) $\frac{1}{7 \times 7} + \frac{1}{7 \times 11}$

(p) $\frac{1}{3 \times 5 \times 7} + \frac{1}{2 \times 3 \times 5}$

(q) $\frac{1}{5 \times 7 \times 11} + \frac{4}{7 \times 11 \times 13}$

(r) $\frac{3}{5 \times 5 \times 7} + \frac{3}{2 \times 5 \times 7}$

(s) $\frac{3}{11 \times 11 \times 13} + \frac{1}{7 \times 11 \times 13}$

(t) $\frac{3}{23 \times 23 \times 31} + \frac{1}{19 \times 23 \times 31}$

(u) $\frac{2}{3 \times 5 \times 31} + \frac{3}{5 \times 11 \times 31}$

(v) $\frac{1}{3 \times 5 \times 7} + \frac{2}{3 \times 7 \times 11}$

(w) $\frac{5}{19 \times 31} + \frac{1}{2 \times 3 \times 19 \times 31}$

(x) $\frac{2}{3 \times 29 \times 47} + \frac{3}{19 \times 29 \times 47}$

(y) $\frac{3}{5 \times 7 \times 11 \times 17} + \frac{4}{7 \times 11 \times 17 \times 19}$

(z) $\frac{3}{2 \times 2 \times 13} + \frac{1}{2 \times 2 \times 5}$

8. Add and give answers in lowest terms.

(a) $\dfrac{5}{12} + \dfrac{7}{16}$ (b) $\dfrac{4}{9} + \dfrac{8}{15}$ (c) $\dfrac{7}{12} + \dfrac{13}{20}$

(d) $\dfrac{5}{6} + \dfrac{2}{9}$ (e) $\dfrac{7}{250} + \dfrac{13}{200}$ (f) $\dfrac{3}{35} + \dfrac{11}{21}$

(g) $\dfrac{11}{18} + \dfrac{4}{27}$ (h) $\dfrac{4}{15} + \dfrac{6}{35}$ (i) $\dfrac{7}{16} + \dfrac{2}{25}$

(j) $\dfrac{3}{40} + \dfrac{7}{16}$ (k) $\dfrac{21}{40} + \dfrac{7}{24}$ (l) $\dfrac{21}{60} + \dfrac{5}{24}$

(m) $\dfrac{7}{25} + \dfrac{8}{30}$ (n) $\dfrac{11}{42} + \dfrac{14}{60}$ (o) $\dfrac{5}{182} + \dfrac{6}{210}$

(p) $\dfrac{11}{147} + \dfrac{2}{105}$ (q) $\dfrac{3}{133} + \dfrac{4}{95}$ (r) $\dfrac{2}{217} + \dfrac{3}{155}$

(s) $\dfrac{1}{338} + \dfrac{1}{130}$ (t) $\dfrac{2}{297} + \dfrac{4}{495}$ (u) $\dfrac{2}{1001} + \dfrac{5}{462}$

9. Add and give answers in any form you wish.

(a) $1\frac{1}{2} + \frac{1}{2}$ (b) $2\frac{1}{3} + \frac{2}{3}$ (c) $2\frac{3}{4} + \frac{3}{4}$

(d) $1\frac{1}{3} + 1\frac{1}{3}$ (e) $2\frac{1}{2} + 3\frac{3}{4}$ (f) $5\frac{3}{5} + 4\frac{3}{5}$

(g) $2\frac{1}{2} + 3\frac{2}{3}$ (h) $4\frac{5}{6} + 3\frac{1}{2}$ (i) $2\frac{7}{10} + 3\frac{2}{5}$

(j) $4\frac{9}{10} + 6\frac{1}{2}$ (k) $3\frac{3}{4} + 2\frac{5}{6}$ (l) $3\frac{17}{50} + 1\frac{14}{100}$

(m) $3\frac{2}{5} + 4\frac{2}{3}$ (n) $5\frac{3}{7} + 2\frac{7}{8}$

10. Multiply and give answers in any form you wish.

(a) $1\frac{1}{2} \times \frac{1}{2}$ (b) $2\frac{2}{3} \times \frac{1}{12}$ (c) $1\frac{3}{4} \times 1\frac{1}{3}$

(d) $2\frac{1}{3} \times 2\frac{1}{2}$ (e) $5\frac{1}{2} \times 2\frac{2}{3}$ (f) $3\frac{1}{2} \times 4$

(g) $6 \times 2\frac{2}{3}$ (h) $3\frac{1}{6} \times 1\frac{1}{5}$ (i) $2\frac{2}{3} \times 3\frac{1}{4}$

(j) $5\frac{2}{3} \times 4\frac{3}{5}$ (k) $2\frac{1}{6} \times 3\frac{1}{5}$ (l) $5\frac{3}{10} \times 2\frac{7}{10}$

6.   USING THE BASIC PROPERTIES

We have seen how the basic properties are used in the addition and multiplication of rational numbers. In this section we shall see that in some problems a knowledge of the basic properties can save much computation. Besides the associative, commutative, and distributive laws we shall use the following three important properties of 0 and 1.

$$\text{For every rational number } \frac{a}{b},$$

$$\frac{a}{b} + 0 = \frac{a}{b}, \qquad \frac{a}{b} \times 0 = 0$$

$$\frac{a}{b} \times 1 = \frac{a}{b}$$

Properties of 0 and 1

Of course, you must understand that

$$0 = \frac{0}{1} = \frac{0}{2} = \frac{0}{3} = \frac{0}{4} = \cdots$$

$$1 = \frac{1}{1} = \frac{2}{2} = \frac{3}{3} = \frac{4}{4} = \cdots$$

Thus

$$\frac{3}{5} + \frac{0}{1} = \frac{3}{5}, \qquad \frac{3}{5} + \frac{0}{11} = \frac{3}{5}, \qquad \frac{3}{5} \times \frac{0}{13} = 0$$

$$\frac{3}{5} \times \frac{0}{43} = 0, \qquad \frac{3}{5} \times \frac{13}{13} = \frac{3}{5}, \qquad \frac{3}{5} \times \frac{493}{493} = \frac{3}{5}$$

EXERCISES

1. Apply the associative and commutative laws and compute mentally.

(a) $\left(\frac{1}{2} + \frac{3}{7}\right) + \frac{1}{2}$

(b) $\left(\frac{5}{6} + \frac{9}{10}\right) + \frac{1}{10}$

(c) $\left(\frac{7}{11} + \frac{5}{9}\right) + \frac{4}{11}$

(d) $(1\frac{1}{3} + 3\frac{5}{8}) + 1\frac{2}{3}$

(e) $(2\frac{3}{4} + 5\frac{7}{8}) + 3\frac{1}{4}$

(f) $(6\frac{4}{7} + 2\frac{11}{12}) + 3\frac{3}{7}$

2. Give the products orally.

(a) $\frac{5}{7} \times \frac{9}{9}$

(b) $\frac{13}{25} \times \frac{47}{47}$

(c) $\frac{73}{42} \times \frac{0}{61}$

(d) $\left(\frac{7}{11} \times \frac{5}{9}\right) \times \frac{0}{23}$

(e) $\frac{31}{31} \times \frac{0}{25}$

(f) $\frac{67}{67} \times \frac{99}{99}$

3. Find the products without using pencil and paper.

(a) $\frac{2}{3} \times \frac{3}{2}$ (b) $\frac{7}{4} \times \frac{4}{7}$

(c) $\frac{11}{21} \times \frac{21}{11}$ (d) $\frac{15}{19} \times \frac{19}{15}$

(e) $\frac{76}{43} \times \frac{43}{76}$ (f) $\frac{69}{95} \times \frac{95}{69}$

4. Use the associative and commutative laws to obtain answers easily.

(a) $\left(\frac{3}{5} \times \frac{7}{11}\right) \times \frac{11}{7}$ (b) $\left(\frac{4}{9} \times \frac{5}{3}\right) \times \frac{9}{4}$

(c) $\left(\frac{7}{9} \times \frac{13}{21}\right) \times \frac{9}{7}$ (d) $\left(\frac{15}{29} \times \frac{23}{31}\right) \times \frac{29}{15}$

5. Compute mentally.

(a) $\frac{3}{5} \times \left(\frac{3}{4} + \frac{1}{4}\right)$ (b) $\frac{6}{7} \times \left(\frac{5}{8} + \frac{3}{8}\right)$

(c) $\left(\frac{15}{19} + \frac{4}{19}\right) \times \frac{17}{23}$ (d) $\left(\frac{23}{39} + \frac{16}{39}\right) \times \frac{37}{45}$

6. Use the distributive law to arrive at your answers easily. For example,

$$\left(\frac{3}{5} \times \frac{4}{7}\right) + \left(\frac{2}{5} \times \frac{4}{7}\right) = \left(\frac{3}{5} + \frac{2}{5}\right) \times \frac{4}{7} = \frac{4}{7}$$

(a) $\left(\frac{2}{3} \times \frac{5}{9}\right) + \left(\frac{1}{3} \times \frac{5}{9}\right)$ (b) $\left(\frac{7}{10} \times \frac{5}{12}\right) + \left(\frac{3}{10} \times \frac{5}{12}\right)$

(c) $\left(\frac{2}{3} \times \frac{5}{9}\right) + \left(\frac{2}{3} \times \frac{4}{9}\right)$ (d) $\left(\frac{7}{10} \times \frac{5}{12}\right) + \left(\frac{7}{10} \times \frac{7}{12}\right)$

(e) $\left(\frac{5}{6} \times \frac{7}{11}\right) + \left(\frac{1}{6} \times \frac{7}{11}\right)$ (f) $\left(\frac{5}{6} \times \frac{7}{11}\right) + \left(\frac{5}{6} \times \frac{4}{11}\right)$

(g) $\left(\frac{11}{13} \times \frac{15}{19}\right) + \left(\frac{2}{13} \times \frac{15}{19}\right)$ (h) $\left(\frac{11}{13} \times \frac{15}{19}\right) + \left(\frac{11}{13} \times \frac{4}{19}\right)$

Fractions such as $\frac{3}{5}$ whose numerator is smaller than the denominator are often called *proper fractions*. Fractions like $\frac{5}{5}$ or $\frac{8}{5}$ are called *improper fractions*. Improper fractions are often written in *mixed-number* form, for example,

$$\frac{8}{5} = 1\tfrac{3}{5}, \qquad \frac{7}{2} = 3\tfrac{1}{2}$$

When we are multiplying fractions in mixed-number form, we can sometimes use the distributive law to make our work easier. As an example, consider the problem

$$4\tfrac{1}{2} \times 2\tfrac{1}{4}$$

We can write this as

$$\frac{9}{2} \times \frac{9}{4} = \frac{81}{8} = 10\tfrac{1}{8}$$

Another method using the distributive law is to write

$$\left(4 + \frac{1}{2}\right) \times \left(2 + \frac{1}{4}\right)$$

or

$$4 \times \left(2 + \frac{1}{4}\right) + \frac{1}{2} \times \left(2 + \frac{1}{4}\right)$$

We see that we must multiply both numbers, 2 and $\tfrac{1}{4}$, by 4 and by $\tfrac{1}{2}$ and then add these four products. We can do all these multiplications mentally and obtain

$$8 + 1 + 1 + \tfrac{1}{8} \qquad \text{or} \qquad 10\tfrac{1}{8}$$

Now use this method to multiply $6\tfrac{1}{2}$ by $2\tfrac{1}{3}$. You must multiply both numbers, 2 and $\tfrac{1}{3}$, by 6 and by $\tfrac{1}{2}$ and add the four products. You should get $15\tfrac{1}{6}$.

EXERCISES

Use the distributive law to obtain the required products with very little pencil and paper work.

1. $2\tfrac{1}{2} \times 4\tfrac{1}{2}$ 2. $2\tfrac{1}{3} \times 3\tfrac{1}{2}$ 3. $3\tfrac{1}{8} \times 8\tfrac{1}{3}$
4. $2\tfrac{1}{5} \times 5\tfrac{1}{2}$ 5. $5\tfrac{1}{6} \times 6\tfrac{1}{5}$ 6. $3\tfrac{1}{4} \times 12\tfrac{1}{3}$
7. $2\tfrac{2}{3} \times 3\tfrac{1}{2}$ 8. $6\tfrac{3}{4} \times 4\tfrac{1}{3}$ 9. $3\tfrac{2}{5} \times 5\tfrac{2}{3}$
10. $8\tfrac{5}{6} \times 12\tfrac{3}{4}$

7. RECREATIONAL MATH

More than 2000 years ago the Greek mathematicians discovered a beautiful method for reducing any fraction to lowest terms. With their method a fraction like

$$\frac{1483417}{897801}$$

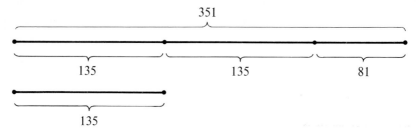

FIGURE 10–42

can be reduced to lowest terms in a few minutes. A student who did not know this method might spend hours on this problem without being able to reduce the fraction. This Greek invention is best understood by geometrical reasoning. Let us look at an example, simpler than the one above.

Suppose that we wish to reduce $\frac{351}{135}$ to lowest terms. We are looking for a number that is a factor of (or is a divisor of) both 351 and 135. Think of two line segments, one 351 and the other 135 units long. We need to find a line segment that is contained a whole number of times in both segments, as shown in Fig. 10–42.

We lay off the 135-unit segment on the longer one. It is contained two times in the 351-unit segment, and an 81-unit segment is left:

$$351 = 2 \times 135 + 81; \quad 135)\overline{351}^{\,2}$$
$$\underline{270}$$
$$81$$

Now, any segment that is contained a whole number of times in both the 351- and 135-unit segments must be contained a whole number of times in the 81-unit segment. (Why?)

We lay off the 81-unit segment on the 135-unit segment, looking for a segment contained a whole number of times in both of these. We get a remainder segment of 54 units as shown in Fig. 10–43. Any segment that is contained a whole number of times in both the 81- and 135-unit segment must be contained a whole number of times in the 54-unit

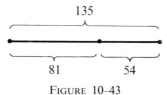

FIGURE 10–43

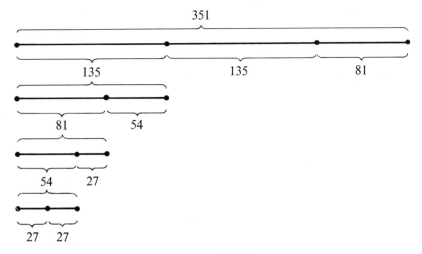

FIGURE 10–44

segment. We lay the 54-unit segment off on the 81-unit segment and get a remainder of 27 (Fig. 10–44). Now, we see that since the 27-unit segment is contained twice in the 54-unit segment, it is contained 3 times in the 81-unit segment, and 5 times in the 135-unit segment, and 13 times in the 351-unit segment. We have found the greatest common factor of 351 and 135 by repeated division. It is 27.

$$
\begin{array}{cccc}
\overset{2}{135\overline{)351}} & \overset{1}{81\overline{)135}} & \overset{1}{54\overline{)81}} & \overset{2}{27\overline{)54}} \\
\underline{270} & \underline{81} & \underline{54} & \underline{54} \\
81 & 54 & 27 & 0
\end{array}
$$

EXERCISES

Use the method described above to reduce each of the following fractions to lowest terms. For problems 1 and 2, draw diagrams as shown in the text, to explain each step, but for the others use division.

1. $\dfrac{115}{391}$ 2. $\dfrac{259}{888}$ 3. $\dfrac{475}{1501}$

4. $\dfrac{2599}{2825}$ 5. $\dfrac{38127}{31737}$ 6. $\dfrac{1483417}{897801}$

The study of prime numbers belongs to an area of mathematics known as *Number Theory*. We list a few interesting facts concerning primes.

One simple way to locate prime numbers is called the *sieve of Eratosthenes*. Eratosthenes was a Greek mathematician who is credited with being the first person to compute the circumference of the earth with reasonable accuracy. His *sieve* is the following procedure.

Imagine the whole numbers listed in order, beginning with 2.

$$2, 3, 4, 5, 6, \ldots$$

Now 2 is a prime, but no other multiple of 2 is a prime. Imagine striking out these other multiples.

$$2, 3, \cancel{4}, 5, \cancel{6}, 7, \cancel{8}, 9, \cancel{10}, 11, \cancel{12}, \ldots$$

Note that the next number beyond 2 which is not stricken out, namely 3, is a prime. No other multiple of 3 is a prime. Strike out these multiples.

$$2, 3, \cancel{4}, 5, \cancel{6}, 7, \cancel{8}, \cancel{9}, \cancel{10}, 11, \cancel{12}, 13,$$

$$\cancel{14}, \cancel{15}, \cancel{16}, 17, \cancel{18}, 19, \cancel{20}, \cancel{21}, \cancel{22}, 23, \cancel{24}, 25, \cancel{26}$$

Note that the first new number that we strike out that is a multiple of 3 and is not a multiple of 2 is the number 9, that is, 3×3.

The next number larger than 3 which is not stricken out must be a prime, for if it were not a prime it would be divisible by a prime smaller than itself, that is by 3 or by 2. This next prime is 5. We proceed to strike out all multiples of 5 which are greater than 5 itself. Note that the multiples, $10 = 2 \times 5$, $15 = 3 \times 5$, and $20 = 4 \times 5$, have already been struck out. (Why?) What is the first multiple of 5 that we must strike out?

Let us summarize these results. After striking out the multiples of 2 we had left

$$2, 3, 5, 7, 9, 11, 13, 15, \ldots$$

The first number in this sequence that is not a prime is 9, or 3^2.

After striking out all multiples of 3 we had left

$$2, 3, 5, 7, 11, 13, 17, 19, 25, 29, 31, 35, \ldots$$

The first number not a prime is 25, or 5^2.

After striking out multiples of 5 we have left

$$2, 3, 5, 7, 11, 13, 17, 19, 23, 29, 31, 37, 41, 43, 47, 49, 53, 61, \ldots$$

The first number not a prime is 49, or 7^2.

A continuation of this process *sifts* out the primes from the set of whole numbers.

EXERCISES

1. After striking out multiples of 7 what will be the first number left that will not be a prime?
2. Multiples of what number must be struck out after having struck out multiples of 7? After these multiples have been eliminated describe the set of primes that will have been sifted out of the set of whole numbers.

As we go out in the whole number sequence the prime numbers are scattered more and more thinly. There are places in the number sequence where there are more than a decillion numbers in a row, none of which is a prime. This fact suggests the possibility that from some point on there might be no more prime numbers. However, it is not too difficult to prove that this is *not* the case. Thousands of years ago the Greek mathematicians proved that the sequence of prime numbers is endless. They did this by showing that no matter how large a prime number might be discovered *there is always a larger prime.* We sketch the proof below.

Let P be any prime number. We shall prove that there is a prime number larger than P. Consider all primes less than P:

$$2, 3, 5, 7, 11, \ldots$$

Form the *product* of all these primes and P.

$$2 \times 3 \times 5 \times 7 \times 11 \times \cdots \times P.$$

Add 1 to this product and call the sum N.

$$N = (2 \times 3 \times 5 \times 7 \times 11 \times \cdots \times P) + 1.$$

Consider the smallest number other than 1 that is a factor of N. Call this number K. Now, K must be a prime number (why?). $K \neq 2$ (why?). $K \neq 3$ (why?). Similarly, K is not any prime number that is *less than or equal to P.* (Why?)

Hence, K is a prime number greater than P, and so the sequence of primes is endless.

Chapter 11

SUBTRACTION AND DIVISION OF RATIONAL NUMBERS

1. INTRODUCTION

The rational number $\frac{3}{4}$ is the *sum* of the *addends* $\frac{1}{2}$ and $\frac{1}{4}$. The rational number $\frac{8}{15}$ is the *product* of the *factors* $\frac{2}{3}$ and $\frac{4}{5}$. Addition of rational numbers is an operation performed on *two* numbers to get *one* number. Multiplication of rational numbers is an operation performed on *two* numbers to get *one* number.

In subtraction of rational numbers we think about two numbers, a sum and an addend. We determine the *missing addend*. In division of rational numbers we think about two numbers, a product and a factor. We determine the *missing factor*. Subtraction and division of rational numbers are related to addition and multiplication of rational numbers in the same way that subtraction and division of whole numbers are related to addition and multiplication of whole numbers. The *ideas* are no more complicated.

Remember that in every addition and subtraction problem three numbers are involved. The *sum* of two of these is the third. And in each multiplication and division problem three numbers are involved.

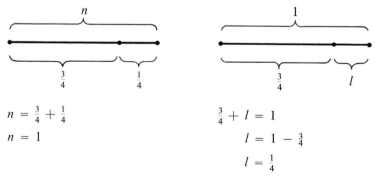

$$n = \frac{3}{4} + \frac{1}{4}$$
$$n = 1$$

$$\frac{3}{4} + l = 1$$
$$l = 1 - \frac{3}{4}$$
$$l = \frac{1}{4}$$

Figure 11–1

180

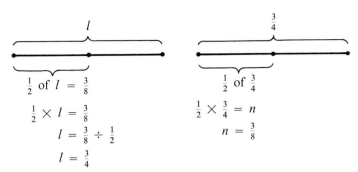

FIGURE 11–2

The *product* of two of these is the third. Figures 11–1 and 11–2 illustrate these ideas.

It is easy to understand subtraction and division of rational numbers if you remember that subtraction is an operation that determines what you must *add* to one number to get a second number; division is an operation that determines by what you must *multiply* one number to get a second number.

Remember the definitions of subtraction and division:

$\dfrac{1}{2} - \dfrac{1}{3}$ **is the number that added to the addend** $\dfrac{1}{3}$ **gives the sum** $\dfrac{1}{2}$.

$\dfrac{1}{2} \div \dfrac{1}{3}$ **is the number that multiplied by the factor** $\dfrac{1}{3}$ **gives the product** $\dfrac{1}{2}$.

That is, using mathematical language, we can say the following.

The addend $\left(\dfrac{a}{b} - \dfrac{c}{d}\right)$ **added to** $\dfrac{c}{d}$ **gives the sum** $\dfrac{a}{b}$.

The factor $\left(\dfrac{a}{b} \div \dfrac{c}{d}\right)$ **multiplied by** $\dfrac{c}{d}$ **gives the product** $\dfrac{a}{b}$.

EXERCISES

1. What must be added to each fraction below to give 1?

(a) $\dfrac{3}{5}$ (b) $\dfrac{2}{4}$ (c) $\dfrac{4}{7}$ (d) $\dfrac{11}{19}$ (e) $\dfrac{41}{52}$

(f) $\dfrac{73}{100}$ (g) $\dfrac{532}{600}$ (h) $\dfrac{723}{1000}$ (i) $\dfrac{13}{17}$ (j) $\dfrac{6}{10}$

2. Use the definition of subtraction as you work these problems.

(a) $1 - \dfrac{3}{5}$ (b) $1 - \dfrac{2}{4}$ (c) $1 - \dfrac{4}{7}$ (d) $1 - \dfrac{11}{19}$

(e) $1 - \dfrac{41}{52}$ (f) $1 - \dfrac{73}{100}$ (g) $1 - \dfrac{532}{600}$ (h) $1 - \dfrac{723}{1000}$

(i) $1 - \dfrac{13}{17}$ (j) $1 - \dfrac{6}{10}$

3. Can you work the problems below?

(a) $\dfrac{2}{3} - 1$ (b) $\dfrac{4}{5} - 1$

4. By what must you multiply each number to get 1?

(a) $\dfrac{2}{3}$ (b) $\dfrac{4}{5}$ (c) $\dfrac{11}{7}$ (d) $\dfrac{17}{23}$ (e) $\dfrac{31}{49}$

(f) 2 (g) $\dfrac{5}{5}$ (h) $\dfrac{3}{4}$ (i) $\dfrac{1}{5}$ (j) $\dfrac{3}{8}$

5. Use the definition of multiplication as you work these problems.

(a) $1 \div \dfrac{2}{3}$ (b) $1 \div \dfrac{4}{5}$ (c) $1 \div \dfrac{11}{7}$ (d) $1 \div \dfrac{17}{23}$

(e) $1 \div \dfrac{31}{49}$ (f) $1 \div 2$ (g) $1 \div \dfrac{5}{5}$ (h) $1 \div \dfrac{3}{4}$

(i) $1 \div \dfrac{1}{5}$ (j) $1 \div \dfrac{3}{8}$

6. Can you work the problems below?

(a) $\dfrac{2}{3} \div 1$ (b) $\dfrac{4}{5} \div 1$

7. In each problem below, what must you add to the first number to obtain the second (if there is such a number)?

(a) $\dfrac{7}{5}, 2$ (b) $\dfrac{12}{5}, 3$ (c) $\dfrac{3}{4}, \dfrac{7}{4}$

(d) $\dfrac{7}{4}, \dfrac{5}{4}$ (e) $\dfrac{3}{2}, \dfrac{9}{2}$ (f) $\dfrac{3}{7}, \dfrac{11}{7}$

8. Write the problems you worked in Exercise 7, using the subtraction symbol, "$-$." For example, when you computed what must be added to $\frac{7}{5}$ to give 2, you computed the number $2 - \frac{7}{5}$.

9. In each problem below, determine what the first number must be multiplied by to give the second number. First think of the number by which you must multiply the given number to get 1.

(a) $\dfrac{7}{5}$, 2   (b) $\dfrac{12}{5}$, 3   (c) $\dfrac{3}{4}$, 2

(d) $\dfrac{2}{3}$, 4   (e) $\dfrac{3}{5}$, 2   (f) $\dfrac{3}{7}$, 5

10. Write problems (a), (b), (c) of Exercise 9, using the division symbol.
11. Point B is between points A and C. Line segment AB is $\frac{1}{2}$ in. long. Line segment AC is $\frac{5}{4}$ in. long. How long is BC?
12. A rectangle has an area of 1 sq. in. It is $\frac{2}{3}$ in. wide. How long is it?
13. A line segment $\frac{7}{2}$ in. long is divided into 4 pieces of equal length. How long is each piece?
14. In a certain schoolroom $\frac{2}{3}$ of the children scored more than 90 on an arithmetic test. Of those who made these high grades in arithmetic, $\frac{3}{4}$ scored over 90 on a spelling test. What fraction of the students had grades over 90 on both tests?
15. One boy lives $\frac{7}{12}$ of a mile from a pool; another lives $\frac{3}{8}$ of a mile from the pool. Which boy lives farther from the pool? how much farther?
16. A measuring can is filled to the $\frac{5}{8}$-mark with oil; enough oil is added to fill the can to the $\frac{3}{4}$-mark. How much oil was added?
17. The school record for the 100-yd dash was $10\frac{2}{5}$ sec. Dave ran 100 yd in $10\frac{3}{10}$ sec. Did he break the record? by how much?
18. A farmer wishes to place a fence post $7\frac{1}{4}$ ft long into the ground. While digging the hole, he hits a large tree root $\frac{7}{4}$ ft below the ground. If he digs no farther, how much of the post will be above the ground?
19. A girl went to the store to get a piece of cloth for her mother. When the clerk asked, "how long and how wide?," she looked for the picture her mother had drawn. But the ink had blotted out part of the information so that the sketch looked like the one in Fig. 11–3. What fraction had been blotted out?
20. Fill in the empty spaces in Fig. 11–4 so that each row, each column, and the two diagonals add up to the same rational number. Such an array is called a magic square.
21. Repeat what you did in Exercise 20 for the array shown in Fig. 11–5.

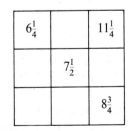

$\frac{3}{4}$ ft

ft

Area $\frac{6}{12}$ sq. ft.

$\frac{1}{2}$	$\frac{7}{12}$	$\frac{1}{6}$
$\frac{1}{12}$	$\frac{5}{12}$	
$\frac{2}{3}$		$\frac{1}{3}$

$6\frac{1}{4}$		$11\frac{1}{4}$
	$7\frac{1}{2}$	
		$8\frac{3}{4}$

FIGURE 11–3   FIGURE 11–4   FIGURE 11–5

22. Make up a magic square, using fractions of your own choice.

23. How must the whole numbers a and b compare in order that we can subtract a/b from 1? Complete the sentence:

$$1 - \frac{a}{b} = \underline{\quad} .$$

24. Complete these sentences:

(a) $1 \div \frac{a}{b} =$ (b) $\frac{a}{b} \div 1 =$

2. TECHNIQUES FOR SUBTRACTION AND DIVISION

We can work any subtraction or division problem by thinking about addition and multiplication.

Subtraction examples

(a) $\dfrac{6}{5} - \dfrac{2}{5} = \dfrac{4}{5}$ because $\dfrac{4}{5} + \dfrac{2}{5} = \dfrac{6}{5}$

(b) $\dfrac{1}{2} - \dfrac{1}{3} = \dfrac{3}{6} - \dfrac{2}{6} = \dfrac{1}{6}$ because $\dfrac{1}{6} + \dfrac{2}{6} = \dfrac{3}{6}$

Note that if we replace our fractions by fractions having the same denominator, the problem is easy:

$$\frac{7}{5} - \frac{4}{3} = \frac{21}{15} - \frac{20}{15} = \frac{1}{15}$$

Division examples

(a) $1 \div \dfrac{3}{5} = \dfrac{5}{3}$ because $\dfrac{5}{3} \times \dfrac{3}{5} = 1$

(b) $\dfrac{1}{4} \div \dfrac{1}{2} = \dfrac{1}{2}$ because $\dfrac{1}{2} \times \dfrac{1}{2} = \dfrac{1}{4}$

(c) $\dfrac{1}{15} \div \dfrac{1}{3} = \dfrac{1}{5}$ because $\dfrac{1}{5} \times \dfrac{1}{3} = \dfrac{1}{15}$

(d) $\dfrac{6}{15} \div \dfrac{2}{3} = \dfrac{3}{5}$ because $\dfrac{3}{5} \times \dfrac{2}{3} = \dfrac{6}{15}$

We can describe our method for subtraction very simply. We replace our two fractions by fractions which have equal denominators. The computation is then easy.

Later on in this section we shall develop a rule for division. However, you will not need any special rule to work the division problems in the following exercise list. In each case you will be able to determine the answer by using the definition of division.

EXERCISES

1. Compute the factor a/b in each example below and tell what division problem you have worked.

   (a) $\dfrac{7}{5} \times \dfrac{a}{b} = \dfrac{21}{20}$

   (b) $\dfrac{3}{4} \times \dfrac{a}{b} = \dfrac{6}{28}$

   (c) $\dfrac{6}{7} \times \dfrac{a}{b} = \dfrac{24}{42}$

   (d) $\dfrac{4}{5} \times \dfrac{a}{b} = \dfrac{16}{15}$

   (e) $\dfrac{2}{3} \times \dfrac{a}{b} = \dfrac{4}{3}$

   (f) $\dfrac{3}{7} \times \dfrac{a}{b} = \dfrac{12}{28}$

   (g) $\dfrac{a}{b} \times \dfrac{5}{11} = \dfrac{15}{77}$

   (h) $\dfrac{a}{b} \times \dfrac{7}{13} = \dfrac{105}{39}$

   (i) $\dfrac{1}{2} \times \dfrac{a}{b} = \dfrac{1}{3}$ [*Hint:* Write $\frac{1}{3}$ as $\frac{2}{6}$.]

   (j) $\dfrac{a}{b} \times \dfrac{2}{3} = \dfrac{3}{4}$ [*Hint:* Write $\frac{3}{4}$ as $\frac{18}{24}$.]

2. Work the following problems.

   (a) $\dfrac{24}{35} \div \dfrac{6}{7}$

   (b) $\dfrac{4}{6} \div \dfrac{2}{3}$

   (c) $\dfrac{10}{4} \div \dfrac{5}{1}$

   (d) $\dfrac{32}{21} \div \dfrac{8}{7}$

   (e) $\dfrac{16}{34} \div \dfrac{16}{2}$

   (f) $\dfrac{21}{25} \div \dfrac{3}{5}$

   (g) $\dfrac{7 \times 11}{5 \times 13} \div \dfrac{7}{5}$

   (h) $\dfrac{3 \times 3 \times 5}{7 \times 11} \div \dfrac{3 \times 5}{11}$

   (i) $\dfrac{7 \times 11 \times 13 \times 19}{3 \times 5 \times 23} \div \dfrac{7 \times 13}{3 \times 5}$

   (j) $\dfrac{5 \times 19 \times 31 \times 31}{3 \times 7 \times 11 \times 43} \div \dfrac{19 \times 31}{7 \times 43}$

   (k) $\dfrac{2}{3} \div \dfrac{1}{5}$ [*Hint:* Write $\frac{2}{3}$ as $\frac{10}{15}$.]

   (l) $\dfrac{6}{7} \div \dfrac{3}{4}$ [*Hint:* Write $\frac{6}{7}$ as $\frac{24}{28}$.]

3. Replace the fraction $\frac{1}{2}$ by another fraction so that you can easily obtain the quotient $\frac{1}{2} \div \frac{3}{4}$.

4. Replace the fraction $\frac{3}{5}$ and compute the quotient $\frac{3}{5} \div \frac{4}{3}$.

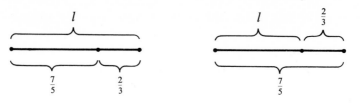

FIGURE 11-6

5. Work the addition and subtraction problems suggested by the two sketches in Fig. 11-6. Write a number sentence in each case.
6. Work the multiplication and division problems suggested by Fig. 11-7 (a) through (d). Write number sentences.

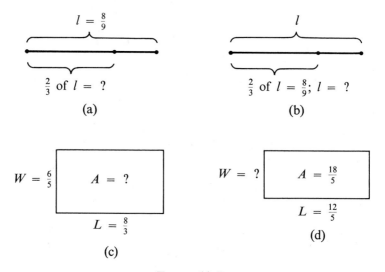

FIGURE 11-7

7. Point T is between points R and S on a line. The lengths of RT and RS are $\frac{3}{10}$ in. and $\frac{7}{5}$ in. How long is ST?
8. The length of a rectangle is $\frac{8}{3}$, and its width is $\frac{6}{4}$. What is its area?
9. The area of a rectangle is $\frac{8}{3}$, and its width is $\frac{6}{4}$. What is its length?
10. The length of a rectangle is $\frac{6}{5}$, and its width is $\frac{4}{5}$. Find its perimeter.
11. The perimeter of a rectangle is $\frac{28}{5}$, and its length is $\frac{8}{5}$. What is its width?
12. There are 800 students in an elementary school. One day $\frac{3}{100}$ of these students were absent. How many were absent?
13. One day 14 students were absent from school. *Exactly* $\frac{2}{100}$ of all the students were absent. How many students are there in the school?
14. Fifteen rows of trees are planted in an orchard with the same number of trees in each row. There are 315 trees altogether. Seven of the rows

are cherry trees and the rest are peach trees. How many of the trees are cherry trees?

15. There are 15 rows of trees in an orchard with the same number of trees in each row. Seven of the rows are cherry trees and the rest are peach trees. If there are 105 cherry trees, how many trees are there in the entire orchard?

16. In an orchard $\frac{3}{5}$ of the trees are apple trees. There are 120 trees in the orchard. How many of these are not apple trees?

17. In an orchard $\frac{3}{5}$ of the trees are apple trees. If 90 trees in the orchard are not apple trees, how many trees are there in the entire orchard?

18. Mr. Smith earns a monthly salary of $640. Mr. Jones earns $\frac{3}{4}$ as much as Mr. Smith, and Mr. Brown earns $\frac{6}{5}$ as much as Mr. Jones. How much does Mr. Brown earn each month?

It is easier to discuss division if we introduce a new term for an idea that is already familiar to you. If the product of two rational numbers is 1, we call each rational number the *reciprocal* of the other. Of course, the number 0 has no reciprocal, for no rational number multiplied by 0 gives 1; but every other rational number has a reciprocal.

For example, $\frac{3}{7}$ and $\frac{7}{3}$ are reciprocals of each other; $\frac{17}{93}$ and $\frac{93}{17}$ are reciprocals of each other; $\frac{2}{3}$ and $\frac{6}{4}$ are reciprocals of each other; 8 and $\frac{1}{8}$ are reciprocals of each other.

We can therefore say the following.

$$\text{If } \frac{a}{b} \text{ is not zero,}$$

$$\frac{a}{b} \text{ is the reciprocal of } \frac{b}{a}$$

$$\text{and}$$

$$\frac{b}{a} \text{ is the reciprocal of } \frac{a}{b}$$

$$\text{since}$$

$$\frac{a}{b} \times \frac{b}{a} = 1$$

Every rational number except 0 has a reciprocal

EXERCISES

1. Give the reciprocal of each of the following numbers.

(a) $\dfrac{1}{2}$ (b) 4 (c) $\dfrac{3}{6}$ (d) $\dfrac{2}{5}$ (e) $\dfrac{4}{10}$

(f) $\dfrac{1}{3} + \dfrac{1}{3}$ (g) $\dfrac{1}{2} + \dfrac{1}{2}$ (h) $\dfrac{1}{2} \times \dfrac{5}{6}$ (i) $\dfrac{817}{943}$

2. The product of two rational numbers is 1. One of these numbers is four times as large as the other. Determine both numbers.

3. Are there two rational numbers larger than 1 such that their product is 1? If two rational numbers are reciprocals of each other and neither one is equal to 1, what can you say about the numbers?

4. What can you say about the reciprocal of a number if you know that the number is

   (a) larger than 2?   (b) larger than 10?

   (c) larger than 4 and less than 5?

   (d) larger than $\frac{2}{3}$?   (e) less than $\frac{5}{7}$?

5. Which pairs of numbers are reciprocals of each other?

   (a) $\dfrac{3}{5}, \dfrac{30}{18}$ (b) $\dfrac{2}{3}, \dfrac{9}{4}$ (c) $\dfrac{27}{18}, \dfrac{2}{3}$

   (d) $5, \dfrac{4}{20}$ (e) $\dfrac{34}{26}, \dfrac{13}{17}$ (f) $\dfrac{34}{75}, \dfrac{5}{3}$

   (g) $\dfrac{32}{58}, \dfrac{232}{124}$ (h) $\dfrac{247}{359}, \dfrac{2154}{1482}$ (i) $\dfrac{123}{358}, \dfrac{1075}{369}$

6. One number is its own reciprocal. What number is this? What number has no reciprocal?

7. Prove, with almost no computation, that

$$\frac{7462}{7435} \quad \text{and} \quad \frac{8635}{8562}$$

   are not reciprocals of each other.

8. Prove with a little mental calculation that

$$\frac{71463}{58247} \quad \text{and} \quad \frac{77872}{93564}$$

   are not reciprocals of each other.

Using the idea of the *reciprocal of a rational number*, we can get the answer to a division problem in two steps. Suppose that we wish to work the division problem

$$\frac{3}{5} \div \frac{2}{3} = n$$

That is, we must determine the missing factor n which when multiplied by $\frac{2}{3}$ gives $\frac{3}{5}$:

$$\frac{2}{3} \times n = \frac{3}{5}$$

We know that $\frac{2}{3} \times \frac{3}{2} = 1$, and by the property of 1, we have

A complicated mark for 1

$$\overbrace{\left(\frac{2}{3} \times \frac{3}{2}\right)} \times \frac{3}{5} = \frac{3}{5}$$

Now, using the associative law, we see that

This is the missing factor

$$\frac{2}{3} \times \overbrace{\left(\frac{3}{2} \times \frac{3}{5}\right)} = \frac{3}{5}$$

and so the missing factor n is $\frac{3}{2} \times \frac{3}{5}$.

We can illustrate this way of working the problem as follows:

$$\frac{2}{3} \xrightarrow{\times \frac{3}{2}} 1 \xrightarrow{\times \frac{3}{5}} \frac{3}{5}$$

Since the diagram shows that the factor $\frac{2}{3}$ multiplied by the factor $(\frac{3}{2} \times \frac{3}{5})$ gives the product $\frac{3}{5}$, we have

$$\overset{P}{\frac{3}{5}} \div \overset{F}{\frac{2}{3}} = \overset{F}{\left(\frac{3}{2} \times \frac{3}{5}\right)}$$

EXERCISES

1. Give the missing number a/b in each of the following equations.

(a) $\dfrac{1}{2} \times \left(\dfrac{2}{1} \times \dfrac{a}{b}\right) = \dfrac{3}{7}$ (b) $\dfrac{3}{7} \times \left(\dfrac{7}{3} \times \dfrac{a}{b}\right) = \dfrac{1}{2}$

(c) $\dfrac{2}{5} \times \left(\dfrac{5}{2} \times \dfrac{a}{b}\right) = \dfrac{2}{3}$ (d) $\dfrac{1}{3} \times \left(\dfrac{3}{1} \times \dfrac{a}{b}\right) = \dfrac{3}{4}$

(e) $\frac{3}{8} \times \left(\frac{a}{b} \times \frac{6}{7}\right) = \frac{6}{7}$ (f) $\frac{2}{7} \times \left(\frac{a}{b} \times \frac{4}{5}\right) = \frac{4}{5}$

(g) $\frac{3}{4} \times \left(\frac{a}{b} \times \frac{1}{3}\right) = \frac{1}{3}$ (h) $\frac{7}{9} \times \left(\frac{a}{b} \times \frac{3}{5}\right) = \frac{3}{5}$

2. Use your work for Exercise 1 and give answers to the following division problems.

(a) $\frac{3}{7} \div \frac{1}{2}$ (b) $\frac{1}{2} \div \frac{3}{7}$ (c) $\frac{2}{3} \div \frac{2}{5}$ (d) $\frac{3}{4} \div \frac{1}{3}$

(e) $\frac{6}{7} \div \frac{3}{8}$ (f) $\frac{4}{5} \div \frac{2}{7}$ (g) $\frac{1}{3} \div \frac{3}{4}$ (h) $\frac{3}{5} \div \frac{7}{9}$

3. Determine the missing number a/b as a product of two numbers. For example, in (a) if

$$\frac{1}{2} \times \frac{a}{b} = \frac{3}{7}, \qquad \text{then} \qquad \frac{a}{b} = \frac{2}{1} \times \frac{3}{7}$$

(a) $\frac{1}{2} \times \frac{a}{b} = \frac{3}{7}$ (b) $\frac{3}{7} \times \frac{a}{b} = \frac{1}{2}$

(c) $\frac{2}{5} \times \frac{a}{b} = \frac{2}{3}$ (d) $\frac{3}{8} \times \frac{a}{b} = \frac{3}{4}$

(e) $\frac{2}{7} \times \frac{a}{b} = \frac{4}{11}$ (f) $\frac{3}{5} \times \frac{a}{b} = \frac{1}{6}$

(g) $\frac{6}{7} \times \frac{a}{b} = \frac{5}{13}$ (h) $\frac{2}{3} \times \frac{a}{b} = \frac{4}{5}$

4. For each problem, write as a product of two numbers what the first number must be multiplied by to give the second.

(a) $\frac{4}{3}, \frac{2}{5}$ (b) $\frac{11}{5}, \frac{4}{3}$ (c) $\frac{17}{23}, \frac{21}{43}$ (d) $\frac{81}{11}, \frac{19}{37}$

5. Write out the division problems that you were working as you determined the missing factors in Exercise 4.

6. Check the answers to the following division problems by multiplying the two factors together to get the product.

(a) $\frac{3}{5} \div \frac{2}{3} = \left(\frac{3}{5} \times \frac{3}{2}\right)$ (b) $\frac{4}{7} \div \frac{5}{9} = \left(\frac{4}{7} \times \frac{9}{5}\right)$

(c) $8 \div \frac{1}{3} = \left(8 \times \frac{3}{1}\right)$ (d) $\frac{91}{79} \div \frac{17}{23} = \left(\frac{91}{79} \times \frac{23}{17}\right)$

We can give a simple rule for division of rational numbers. Note that

$$\overset{F}{\frac{3}{5}} \times \left(\overset{\overbrace{\quad F \quad}}{\frac{5}{3} \times \frac{9}{7}}\right) = \overset{P}{\frac{9}{7}}; \quad \text{so} \quad \overset{P}{\frac{9}{7}} \div \overset{F}{\frac{3}{5}} = \overset{P}{\frac{9}{7}} \times \overset{\overbrace{\quad F \quad}}{\frac{5}{3}}$$

$$\overset{F}{\frac{17}{91}} \times \left(\overset{\overbrace{\quad F \quad}}{\frac{91}{17} \times \frac{4}{31}}\right) = \overset{P}{\frac{4}{31}}; \quad \text{so} \quad \overset{P}{\frac{4}{31}} \div \overset{F}{\frac{17}{91}} = \overset{P}{\frac{4}{31}} \times \overset{\overbrace{\quad F \quad}}{\frac{91}{17}}$$

$$\overset{F}{\frac{c}{d}} \times \left(\overset{\overbrace{\quad F \quad}}{\frac{d}{c} \times \frac{a}{b}}\right) = \overset{P}{\frac{a}{b}}; \quad \text{so} \quad \overset{P}{\frac{a}{b}} \div \overset{F}{\frac{c}{d}} = \overset{P}{\frac{a}{b}} \times \overset{\overbrace{\quad F \quad}}{\frac{d}{c}}$$

Thus we can state the following general rule.

To divide

$$\frac{a}{b} \text{ by } \frac{c}{d},$$

we multiply

$$\frac{a}{b} \text{ by the reciprocal of } \frac{c}{d}$$

The rule for division of rational numbers

EXERCISES

1. Give the reciprocal of

   (a) $\dfrac{3}{5}$ (b) 1   (c) $\dfrac{11}{19}$ (d) $\dfrac{1}{8}$

   (e) 7   (f) $2\frac{1}{2}$ (g) $3\frac{3}{4}$ (h) $4\frac{2}{3}$

2. Write each answer as the product of one number multiplied by the reciprocal of the other.

   (a) $\dfrac{3}{5} \div \dfrac{3}{4}$ (b) $\dfrac{5}{7} \div \dfrac{3}{8}$ (c) $\dfrac{11}{7} \div \dfrac{5}{2}$

   (d) $\dfrac{4}{9} \div \dfrac{7}{8}$ (e) $\dfrac{11}{13} \div \dfrac{7}{12}$ (f) $\dfrac{15}{23} \div \dfrac{7}{11}$

(g) $\dfrac{5}{2} \div \dfrac{4}{7}$ (h) $\dfrac{7}{3} \div \dfrac{5}{6}$ (i) $\dfrac{4}{19} \div \dfrac{19}{7}$

(j) $\dfrac{11}{23} \div \dfrac{13}{31}$ (k) $\dfrac{14}{41} \div \dfrac{23}{19}$ (l) $\dfrac{83}{71} \div \dfrac{49}{62}$

3. Give your answers in lowest terms.

(a) $\dfrac{3}{5} \div \dfrac{3}{8}$ (b) $\dfrac{3}{7} \div \dfrac{6}{5}$ (c) $\dfrac{3}{7} \div \dfrac{5}{14}$

(d) $\dfrac{5}{6} \div \dfrac{10}{9}$ (e) $\dfrac{4}{11} \div \dfrac{8}{11}$ (f) $\dfrac{2}{3} \div \dfrac{5}{6}$

(g) $\dfrac{5}{7} \div \dfrac{15}{14}$ (h) $\dfrac{2}{9} \div \dfrac{4}{3}$ (i) $\dfrac{7}{12} \div \dfrac{5}{9}$

(j) $\dfrac{11}{13} \div \dfrac{22}{17}$ (k) $\dfrac{7}{15} \div \dfrac{14}{5}$ (l) $\dfrac{24}{17} \div \dfrac{12}{7}$

(m) $3\tfrac{1}{2} \div 1\tfrac{2}{5}$ (n) $2\tfrac{3}{4} \div 4\tfrac{1}{2}$ (o) $3\tfrac{1}{5} \div 1\tfrac{1}{7}$

(p) $4\tfrac{2}{3} \div 1\tfrac{3}{4}$ (q) $5\tfrac{3}{5} \div 4\tfrac{2}{3}$ (r) $2\tfrac{1}{3} \div 5\tfrac{1}{4}$

3. THE NUMBERS 0 AND 1 IN DIVISION

Give answers to the following problems.

(a) $\dfrac{3}{5} \div 1$ (b) $1 \div \dfrac{3}{5}$ (c) $0 \div \dfrac{3}{5}$ (d) $\dfrac{3}{5} \div 0$

If you thought carefully and used the properties of 0 and 1 and the definition of division, you should not have missed any of these four problems. If you were careless, you probably missed problem (d). Let us think carefully about each one.

(a) $\tfrac{3}{5} \div 1$. You should have thought: $\tfrac{3}{5}$ *is the product;* 1 *is one factor; clearly* $\tfrac{3}{5}$ *is the missing factor, so*

$$\frac{3}{5} \div 1 = \frac{3}{5}$$

(b) $1 \div \tfrac{3}{5}$. You should have thought: 1 *is the product;* $\tfrac{3}{5}$ *is one factor; the missing factor is* $\tfrac{5}{3}$, *the reciprocal of* $\tfrac{3}{5}$.

$$1 \div \frac{3}{5} = \frac{5}{3}$$

(c) **$0 \div \frac{3}{5}$.** You should have thought: *0 is the product; $\frac{3}{5}$ is one factor; the missing factor is 0, since this is the only number which when multiplied by $\frac{3}{5}$ gives 0:*

$$0 \div \frac{3}{5} = 0$$

(d) **$\frac{3}{5} \div 0$.** You should have thought: *$\frac{3}{5}$ is the product; one factor is 0; no number multiplied by zero gives $\frac{3}{5}$, since every number multiplied by zero is 0. The problem $\frac{3}{5} \div 0$ has no answer.*

These properties of zero and 1 in division are listed below.

$$\frac{a}{b} \div 1 = \frac{a}{b},$$

and if $\dfrac{a}{b}$ is not zero, then

$$1 \div \frac{a}{b} = \frac{b}{a} \quad \text{and} \quad 0 \div \frac{a}{b} = 0$$

We never divide by zero.

The numbers 1 and 0 in division

EXERCISES

1. Explain why the statements (a) $\frac{4}{5} \div 0 = \frac{4}{5}$ and (b) $\frac{4}{5} \div 0 = 0$ are both false.

2. Explain why there is no number $\dfrac{a}{b}$ such that $\dfrac{2}{3} \div 0 = \dfrac{a}{b}$.

3. For each number sentence below decide whether it is true or false.

   (a) $\dfrac{0}{1} \times \dfrac{4}{3} = 0$ (b) $\dfrac{0}{2} \times \dfrac{0}{1} = 0$ (c) $0 \times \dfrac{4}{3} = 0$

   (d) $\dfrac{5}{6} \times 0 = \dfrac{5}{6}$ (e) $\dfrac{5}{6} \div 0 = \dfrac{5}{6}$ (f) $0 \div \dfrac{5}{6} = 0$

   (g) $\dfrac{5}{6} \times 1 = \dfrac{5}{6}$ (h) $\dfrac{5}{6} \div 1 = \dfrac{5}{6}$ (i) $1 \div \dfrac{5}{6} = \dfrac{5}{6}$

   (j) $0 \div \dfrac{4}{3} = 0$ (k) $\dfrac{4}{3} \div 0 = 0$ (l) $0 \div \dfrac{7}{11} = \dfrac{7}{11}$

   (m) $0 \div 0 = 0$ (n) $0 \div 0 = 1$

4. Give answers when you can. Which symbols are meaningless?

(a) $0 \div \frac{7}{8}$ (b) $0\overline{)3}$ (c) $\frac{7}{13} \div 0$

(d) $7\overline{)0}$ (e) $0 \div \frac{3}{11}$ (f) $0 \div 0$

4. PICTURING DIVISION ON THE NUMBER LINE

In Chapter 10, dealing with addition and multiplication, we developed our rules for adding and multiplying rational numbers by studying problems in the physical world and by using the number line. We could have studied division in the same way, but it was much easier to use instead the relationships between multiplication and division. In this section we shall work a few division problems by studying examples from the physical world and by using the number line.

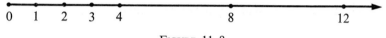

$$0 \quad 1 \quad 2 \quad 3 \quad 4 \qquad\qquad 8 \qquad\qquad 12$$

FIGURE 11–8

Looking at the number line in Fig. 11–8, we can say:

12 ÷ 4 = 3 because it takes 3 copies of the line segment 4 units long from 0 to 4 to cover the line segment 12 units long from 0 to 12.

4 ÷ 12 = $\frac{1}{3}$ because one-third of the 12-unit segment will cover the 4-unit segment.

1 ÷ 8 = $\frac{1}{8}$ because one-eighth of the 8-unit segment covers the 1-unit segment.

3 ÷ 4 = $\frac{3}{4}$ because three-fourths of the 4-unit segment covers the 3-unit segment.

4 ÷ 3 = 1$\frac{1}{3}$ because it takes one 3-unit segment and one-third of another to cover the 4-unit segment.

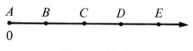

FIGURE 11–9

Study Fig. 11–9. You see that it takes 3 copies of segment AB to cover segment AD. If our number line were scaled in units, the figure would show that $3 \div 1 = 3$. If the number line were scaled in fourths, the figure would show that $\frac{3}{4} \div \frac{1}{4} = 3$.

EXERCISES

1. What part of AD is needed to cover AC (Fig. 11–9)? Write the division fact given by the figure, assuming that the number line is scaled in

    (a) units   (b) halves   (c) thirds

    (d) sevenths   (e) twelfths   (f) twenty-thirds

    (g) tenths   (h) hundredths   (i) thousandths

2. How many copies of AC are needed to cover AD (Fig. 11–9)? Write the division fact indicated by the figure, given that the number line is scaled in

    (a) tenths   (b) hundredths   (c) units

    (d) halves   (e) fifths   (f) thirty-fifths

3. How many copies of AD are needed to cover AE? Write the division fact suggested, assuming that the line is scaled in

    (a) fiftieths   (b) units   (c) fourths

    (d) ninths   (e) hundredths   (f) fifty-sevenths

4. Explain how Fig. 11–10 shows that

    (a) $3 \div 2 = 1\frac{1}{2}$

    (b) $1 \div \frac{2}{3} = 1\frac{1}{2}$

    (c) $30 \div 20 = 1\frac{1}{2}$

    (d) $\frac{3}{7} \div \frac{2}{7} = 1\frac{1}{2}$

    (e) $2 \div 3 = \frac{2}{3}$

    (f) $\frac{2}{3} \div 1 = \frac{2}{3}$

    (g) $20 \div 30 = \frac{2}{3}$

    (h) $\frac{2}{7} \div \frac{3}{7} = \frac{2}{3}$

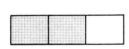

FIGURE 11–10   FIGURE 11–11

5. Explain how Fig. 11–11 shows that

    (a) $4 \div 3 = 1\frac{1}{3}$

    (b) $1 \div \frac{3}{4} = 1\frac{1}{3}$

    (c) $100 \div 75 = 1\frac{1}{3}$

    (d) $\frac{4}{9} \div \frac{3}{9} = 1\frac{1}{3}$

The problems

$$1 \div 8 = \frac{1}{8} \quad \text{and} \quad 3 \div 4 = \frac{3}{4}$$

suggest a new way of thinking about rational numbers. *We may think of each rational number as the quotient of one whole number divided by another.* This way of thinking makes some of our arithmetic a little easier.

Since $\quad \overset{P}{7} \div \overset{F}{8} = \dfrac{\overset{F}{7}}{8},\quad$ it follows that $\quad \overset{F}{8} \times \dfrac{\overset{F}{7}}{8} = \overset{P}{7}$

Since $\quad 31 \div 25 = \dfrac{31}{25},\quad$ it follows that $\quad 25 \times \dfrac{31}{25} = 31$

Since $\quad a \div b = \dfrac{a}{b},\quad$ it follows that $\quad b \times \dfrac{a}{b} = a$

For all pairs of whole numbers a, b, if b is not zero, then

$$a \div b = \frac{a}{b}$$

and

$$b \times \frac{a}{b} = a$$

Each rational number is the quotient of two whole numbers

EXERCISES

1. Write the quotients as fractions.

(a) $3 \div 5$ (b) $5 \div 3$ (c) $11 \div 17$
(d) $21 \div 39$ (e) $73 \div 114$ (f) $0 \div 7$
(g) $1 \div 5$ (h) $7 \div 1$ (i) $13 \div 13$
(j) $r \div s$ (k) $s \div r$ (l) $7 \div s$

2. Write a fraction for f, given that

(a) $3 \times f = 7$ (b) $7 \times f = 3$ (c) $11 \times f = 21$
(d) $21 \times f = 11$ (e) $6 \times f = 1$ (f) $13 \times f = 0$
(g) $39 \times f = 28$ (h) $61 \times f = 93$ (i) $a \times f = 15$
(j) $11 \times f = a$ (k) $a \times f = b$ (l) $r \times f = r$

3. Complete each sentence.

   (a) If $n = \dfrac{11}{3}$, then $3 \times n =$ _____.

   (b) If $F = \dfrac{12}{5}$, then _____ $\times F = 12$.

   (c) If $h = \dfrac{5}{97}$ and $q = \dfrac{97}{104}$ and $r \times q = h$, then $r =$ _____.

4. Give two different names for the rational number which when multiplied by 31 yields 21.
5. Give five different fraction names for the missing factor in the sentence $7 \times n = 2$.
6. If $r \times 18 = s \times 12$, give a fraction in lowest terms for the rational number r/s.
7. Write each fraction as one whole number divided by another.

   (a) $\dfrac{3}{5}$ (b) $\dfrac{7}{12}$ (c) $\dfrac{11}{31}$ (d) $\dfrac{43}{17}$ (e) $\dfrac{17}{28}$

5. RECREATIONAL MATH

Some interesting number relationships are given below.   Satisfy yourself that all these statements are true and try to find some more of this type.

   (a) $1\frac{1}{2} \times 3 = 1\frac{1}{2} + 3$ (b) $1 \times \frac{1}{2} = 1 - \frac{1}{2}$

   $1\frac{1}{3} \times 4 = 1\frac{1}{3} + 4$ $2 \times \frac{2}{3} = 2 - \frac{2}{3}$

   $1\frac{1}{4} \times 5 = 1\frac{1}{4} + 5$ $3 \times \frac{3}{4} = 3 - \frac{3}{4}$

   (c) $1\frac{1}{3} \div \frac{2}{3} = 1\frac{1}{3} + \frac{2}{3}$ (d) $4\frac{1}{2} \div 3 = 4\frac{1}{2} - 3$

   $2\frac{1}{4} \div \frac{3}{4} = 2\frac{1}{4} + \frac{3}{4}$ $5\frac{1}{3} \div 4 = 5\frac{1}{3} - 4$

   $3\frac{1}{5} \div \frac{4}{5} = 3\frac{1}{5} + \frac{4}{5}$ $6\frac{1}{4} \div 5 = 6\frac{1}{4} - 5$

   $7\frac{1}{5} \div 6 = 7\frac{1}{5} - 6$

EXERCISES

1. Find n for each problem below.

   (a) $\dfrac{1}{1 \times 2} + \dfrac{1}{2 \times 3} = n$

   (b) $\dfrac{1}{1 \times 2} + \dfrac{1}{2 \times 3} + \dfrac{1}{3 \times 4} = n$

   (c) $\dfrac{1}{1 \times 2} + \dfrac{1}{2 \times 3} + \dfrac{1}{3 \times 4} + \dfrac{1}{4 \times 5} = n$

(d) $\dfrac{1}{1 \times 2} + \dfrac{1}{2 \times 3} + \dfrac{1}{3 \times 4} + \dfrac{1}{4 \times 5} + \dfrac{1}{5 \times 6} = n$

(e) $\dfrac{1}{1 \times 2} + \dfrac{1}{2 \times 3} + \dfrac{1}{3 \times 4} + \cdots + \dfrac{1}{99 \times 100} = n$

2. Start adding the rational numbers listed below.

$$1 + \frac{1}{2} + \frac{1}{4} + \frac{1}{8} + \frac{1}{16} + \frac{1}{32} + \cdots$$

How many of these numbers must be added together to give a sum greater than 2?

3. A special rubber ball is dropped from a height 2 feet above the sidewalk. Let us pretend that this ball always rebounds *exactly half* as high as it falls. Will the ball ever come to rest? How far will the ball travel as it bounces up and down?

4. Find three whole numbers a, b, and c so that the sum of their reciprocals,

$$\frac{1}{a} + \frac{1}{b} + \frac{1}{c}$$

is 1.

5. Find several pairs of whole numbers x and y such that

$$\frac{1}{x} + \frac{1}{y} = \frac{1}{14}$$

[*Hint:* $\frac{1}{14} = \frac{2}{28} = \frac{3}{42} = \cdots$]

6. Prove that the sum of the rational numbers

$$\frac{1}{101} + \frac{1}{102} + \frac{1}{103} + \cdots + \frac{1}{200}$$

is more than $\frac{1}{2}$. [*Hint:* Which is the smallest of these numbers? How many numbers are there altogether?]

7. Find a fraction such that if you add 6 to both the numerator and the denominator, the new fraction is twice as large as the original fraction.

8. Is there any rational number such that when it is added to its reciprocal, the sum is less than 2?

REVIEW EXERCISES—GROUP II

1. Write answers to the following subtraction problems, working from *left* to *right*.

(a)	58	(b)	91	(c)	857	(d)	962
	23		46		423		457

(e)	713	(f)	900	(g)	1000	(h)	7000
	574		357		532		3563

2. Compute mentally the following subtraction problems.

(a) 86 − 35   (b) 91 − 24   (c) 746 − 323
(d) 651 − 328   (e) 914 − 256   (f) 3000 − 1432
(g) 6204 − 3851   (h) 8321 − 1234   (i) 6513 − 3749

3. Think of dot arrays and find the products mentally.

(a) 10 × 12   (b) 11 × 12   (c) 12 × 12
(d) 10 × 13   (e) 11 × 14   (f) 11 × 16
(g) 12 × 15   (h) 14 × 13   (i) 15 × 15
(j) 16 × 16   (k) 14 × 14   (l) 21 × 21

4. Give the products.

(a) 10 × (30 + 4)   (b) 10 × (200 + 40 + 5)
(c) 100 × (70 + 3)   (d) 100 × (40 + 6)
(e) 20 × 40   (f) 30 × 30
(g) 60 × 70   (h) 40 × 90
(i) 10 × 10 × 10   (j) 10 × 20 × 30
(k) 100 × 27   (l) 100 × 352   (m) 1000 × 86
(n) 473 × 1000   (o) 30 × 300   (p) 400 × 60

5. Find the missing factor.

(a) 350 ÷ 35 = n   (b) 490 ÷ 49 = n
(c) 630 ÷ 63 = n   (d) 820 ÷ 10 = n
(e) 740 ÷ 10 = n   (f) 1000 ÷ 10 = n
(g) 3400 ÷ 34 = n   (h) 8200 ÷ 100 = n
(i) 8700 ÷ 87 = n   (j) 6900 ÷ 100 = n
(k) 42,000 ÷ 42 = n   (l) 63,000 ÷ 1000 = n
(m) 41,000 ÷ 100 = n   (n) 800 ÷ 20 = n
(o) 1000 ÷ 50 = n   (p) 3500 ÷ 50 = n

6. Work the division problems by any method you wish.

(a) 3434 ÷ 34   (b) 3468 ÷ 34   (c) 6834 ÷ 34
(d) 3740 ÷ 34   (e) 9632 ÷ 32   (f) 3264 ÷ 32
(g) 3520 ÷ 32   (h) 4386 ÷ 43   (i) 1248 ÷ 12
(j) 2436 ÷ 12   (k) 1320 ÷ 12   (l) 2640 ÷ 12

7. Give quotient and remainder for each problem below.

(a) 352 ÷ 100   (b) 352 ÷ 99   (c) 352 ÷ 101
(d) 3521 ÷ 100   (e) 3521 ÷ 99   (f) 3521 ÷ 101
(g) 867 ÷ 86   (h) 4817 ÷ 48   (i) 7500 ÷ 75
(j) 96 ÷ 100

8. Write an equation that each of the integers given below satisfies.

(a) −2   (b) 7   (c) −91

9. Find n, given that

    (a) $n + 11 = 0$ (b) $n - 17 = 0$ (c) $n + 43 = 0$

10. Use the associative and commutative laws and find the sums.

    (a) $7 + (-3) + (-7)$ (b) $9 + 3 + (-9)$
    (c) $19 + (-18) + 3$ (d) $7 + (-6) + (-7) + 6$

11. Solve the following equations.

    (a) $-5 + x = 0$ (b) $x + 8 = 2$
    (c) $x + (-8) = 2$ (d) $3 + x + (-4) = 5$
    (e) $13 + (x + 3) = 10$ (f) $-3 + x + (-2) = 5$

12. Give the sums in problems (a) through (j).

    (a) $-2 + (-2)$ (b) $-4 + (-6)$
    (c) $-7 + (-8)$ (d) $-5 + (-10)$
    (e) $-3 + 8 + (-9)$ (f) $-7 + (-4) + 11$
    (g) $a + (-5) + (-a)$ (h) $(a + 1) + (-a)$
    (i) $-(a + 1) + a$ (j) $-1 + (-2) + (-3) + (-4)$

13. For each equation below, tell which number is the sum and which numbers are the addends.

    (a) $(-3) + 5 = 2$ (b) $7 - (-3) = 10$
    (c) $5 - 8 = -3$ (d) $(-1) - (-4) = 3$
    (e) $4 + (-6) = -2$ (f) $-6 - 7 = -13$

14. Find the missing addends.

    (a) $8 - 3$ (b) $3 - 8$ (c) $8 - (-3)$
    (d) $-3 - 8$ (e) $0 - 4$ (f) $4 - 0$
    (g) $0 - (-4)$ (h) $(-4) - 0$ (i) $-2 - (-5)$
    (j) $-5 - (-2)$ (k) $7 - 12$ (l) $7 - (-12)$

15. Solve the equations below.

    (a) $x - 2 = -3$ (b) $x - (-2) = -3$
    (c) $5 - x = -2$ (d) $5 - x = 7$
    (e) $y - 2 = -9$ (f) $y + 2 = -7$
    (g) $6 - y = -7$ (h) $7 - y = 13$

16. What integer is associated with each arrow in Fig. 11–12? Each arrow suggests an addition fact and two subtraction facts. Write out these facts.

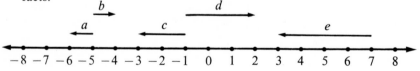

FIGURE 11–12

17. Work the addition problems suggested by the number-line diagrams in Fig. 11–13 (a) and (b).

(a)
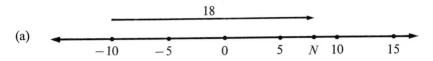

(b)
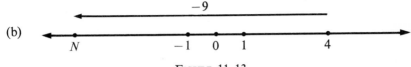

FIGURE 11–13

18. Work the subtraction problems suggested by the diagrams in Fig. 11–14 (a) and (b).

(a)
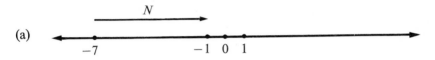

(b)
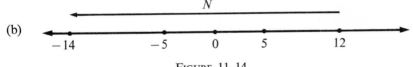

FIGURE 11–14

19. Mark an array of 12 dots. Draw a rectangle that contains two-thirds of these dots. Draw a circle that contains one-half of these dots and draw it so that one-third of the 12 dots are inside both the circle and the rectangle.

20. What addition fact is shown by the number line in Fig. 11–15, given that (a) it is scaled in units? (b) it is scaled in halves? (c) it is scaled in ninths? (d) it is scaled in twenty-fourths?

FIGURE 11–15

21. Determine n in problems (a) through (r).

(a) $\dfrac{3}{5} + n = 1$ (b) $\dfrac{4}{7} + n = 1$ (c) $\dfrac{5}{7} + n = 1\dfrac{3}{7}$

(d) $1\frac{1}{3} + n = 2$ (e) $2\frac{1}{4} + n = 3\frac{1}{2}$ (f) $\frac{5}{6} + n = \frac{13}{6}$

(g) $\frac{7}{9} - n = \frac{4}{9}$ (h) $4\frac{1}{3} - n = 3\frac{2}{3}$ (i) $\frac{11}{7} - n = \frac{5}{7}$

(j) $n - \frac{3}{4} = \frac{5}{4}$ (k) $n - 2\frac{1}{3} = 3\frac{1}{3}$ (l) $n - \frac{11}{7} = \frac{12}{7}$

(m) $n \times \frac{3}{5} = \frac{12}{5}$ (n) $\frac{4}{3} \times n = \frac{28}{3}$ (o) $\frac{3}{7} \times n = \frac{15}{7}$

(p) $\frac{3}{7} + \frac{n}{7} = \frac{11}{7}$ (q) $\frac{a}{5} + \frac{n}{5} = \frac{a + 3}{5}$ (r) $\frac{n}{7} + \frac{b}{7} = \frac{b + 19}{7}$

22. Find the products in problems (a) through (i).

(a) $\frac{1}{4} \times \frac{1}{3}$ (b) $\frac{1}{5} \times \frac{1}{7}$ (c) $\frac{1}{7} \times \frac{1}{11}$

(d) $\frac{2}{3} \times \frac{4}{5}$ (e) $\frac{3}{7} \times \frac{5}{2}$ (f) $\frac{7}{4} \times \frac{5}{11}$

(g) $\frac{3}{4} \times 1$ (h) $\frac{3}{4} \times \frac{5}{5}$ (i) $\frac{3}{4} \times \frac{r}{r}$

23. Add the rational numbers given below.

(a) $\frac{1}{2} + \frac{1}{4}$ (b) $\frac{1}{4} + \frac{1}{8}$ (c) $\frac{1}{8} + \frac{1}{16}$

(d) $\frac{1}{2} + \frac{1}{3}$ (e) $\frac{1}{3} + \frac{1}{5}$ (f) $\frac{1}{5} + \frac{1}{7}$

(g) $\frac{3}{2} + \frac{5}{4}$ (h) $\frac{5}{8} + \frac{7}{16}$ (i) $\frac{2}{5} + \frac{11}{20}$

(j) $\frac{2}{3} + \frac{3}{4}$ (k) $\frac{3}{5} + \frac{5}{9}$ (l) $\frac{3}{11} + \frac{7}{13}$

24. Reduce to lowest terms.

(a) $\frac{3 \times 5}{3 \times 7}$ (b) $\frac{2 \times 5 \times 7}{2 \times 7 \times 13}$ (c) $\frac{3 \times 5 \times 11 \times 13}{3 \times 11 \times 13 \times 19}$

(d) $\frac{2 \times 2 \times 3 \times 7}{2 \times 7 \times 11}$ (e) $\frac{2 \times 3 \times 5 \times 5 \times 7}{5 \times 7 \times 17}$

(f) $\frac{3 \times 7 \times 19 \times 23}{7 \times 19 \times 37}$ (g) $\frac{15 \times 7 \times 11}{3 \times 7 \times 17}$

(h) $\frac{21 \times 5 \times 11}{33 \times 7 \times 13}$ (i) $\frac{28 \times 7 \times 5}{98 \times 3 \times 2}$

25. Write as a product of prime numbers:

(a) 10   (b) 56   (c) 210   (d) 693   (e) 7350

26. Factor numerator and denominator completely and reduce to lowest terms.

(a) $\dfrac{24}{56}$ (b) $\dfrac{90}{66}$ (c) $\dfrac{140}{42}$ (d) $\dfrac{825}{231}$

27. Add and reduce to lowest terms.

(a) $\dfrac{1}{6} + \dfrac{1}{10}$ (b) $\dfrac{1}{6} + \dfrac{1}{14}$ (c) $\dfrac{1}{15} + \dfrac{3}{10}$

(d) $\dfrac{2}{15} + \dfrac{2}{21}$ (e) $\dfrac{1}{30} + \dfrac{1}{42}$ (f) $\dfrac{1}{35} + \dfrac{2}{55}$

(g) $\dfrac{8}{105} + \dfrac{5}{63}$ (h) $\dfrac{1}{210} + \dfrac{1}{330}$ (i) $\dfrac{4}{231} + \dfrac{2}{429}$

28. Use the associative and commutative laws to obtain the sums easily.

(a) $2\frac{1}{2} + \frac{3}{5} + 1\frac{1}{2}$ (b) $\frac{7}{9} + 3\frac{2}{5} + \frac{2}{9}$

(c) $\dfrac{7}{13} + \dfrac{5}{11} + \dfrac{6}{13}$ (d) $2\frac{3}{5} + 3\frac{4}{7} + 5\frac{2}{5}$

29. Use the distributive law to obtain the answers quickly.

(a) $\left(\dfrac{3}{5} \times \dfrac{7}{9}\right) + \left(\dfrac{2}{5} \times \dfrac{7}{9}\right)$ (b) $\left(\dfrac{7}{11} \times \dfrac{5}{12}\right) + \left(\dfrac{7}{11} \times \dfrac{7}{12}\right)$

(c) $\left(\dfrac{5}{3} \times \dfrac{4}{11}\right) + \left(\dfrac{7}{11} \times \dfrac{5}{3}\right)$ (d) $\left(\dfrac{11}{17} \times \dfrac{12}{19}\right) + \left(\dfrac{6}{17} \times \dfrac{12}{19}\right)$

(e) $3 \times 2\frac{2}{3}$ (f) $8 \times 5\frac{1}{4}$ (g) $1\frac{1}{2} \times 6$ (h) $2\frac{1}{3} \times 3\frac{1}{2}$

30. Give the reciprocal of:

(a) $\dfrac{11}{13}$ (b) $3\frac{1}{2}$ (c) $\dfrac{1}{3} + \dfrac{1}{4}$

(d) $\dfrac{2}{3} \times \dfrac{5}{7}$ (e) $\dfrac{615}{499}$ (f) $\dfrac{3}{5} - \dfrac{1}{2}$

31. Find the missing factor in the problems below.

(a) $\dfrac{3}{4} \times \dfrac{a}{b} = \dfrac{15}{28}$ (b) $\dfrac{20}{21} \div \dfrac{a}{b} = \dfrac{4}{7}$

(c) $\dfrac{a}{b} \times \dfrac{2}{11} = \dfrac{10}{66}$ (d) $\dfrac{35}{24} \div \dfrac{7}{12} = \dfrac{a}{b}$

32. Determine the rational number n.

(a) $\left(\dfrac{4}{3} \times n\right) \times \dfrac{5}{7} = \dfrac{5}{7}$ (b) $\left(\dfrac{2}{5} \times n\right) \times \dfrac{4}{9} = \dfrac{2}{5}$

(c) $\dfrac{3}{5} \times \dfrac{2}{7} \times n = 1$ (d) $\left(n + \dfrac{3}{4}\right) \times \dfrac{4}{5} = 1$

33. Express your answers in lowest terms.

(a) $\dfrac{3}{5} \div \dfrac{3}{7}$ (b) $\dfrac{3}{7} \div \dfrac{3}{5}$ (c) $\dfrac{11}{7} \div \dfrac{5}{7}$

(d) $\dfrac{11}{15} \div \dfrac{3}{10}$ (e) $2\frac{2}{3} \div 4\frac{1}{3}$ (f) $36 \div 24$

(g) $124 \div 93$ (h) $\dfrac{3 \times 7 \times 11}{5 \times 13} \div \dfrac{3 \times 7}{2 \times 13}$

34. Decide whether each sentence is true or false.

(a) $\dfrac{3}{7} + \dfrac{5}{5} = \dfrac{3}{7}$ (b) $\dfrac{3}{7} \times \dfrac{5}{5} = \dfrac{3}{7}$

(c) $\dfrac{3}{7} + \dfrac{0}{5} = \dfrac{3}{7}$ (d) $\dfrac{3}{7} \times \dfrac{0}{5} = \dfrac{3}{7}$

(e) $\dfrac{3}{7} \times \dfrac{0}{11} = 0$ (f) $0 \div \dfrac{3}{4} = 0$

(g) $\dfrac{3}{4} \div 0 = 0$ (h) $\dfrac{3}{4} \div 0 = \dfrac{3}{4}$

35. Determine the rational number n.

(a) $n \times 23 = 35$ (b) $23 \div n = 35$

(c) $7 \times n = 2$ (d) $7 \div n = 2$

Chapter 12

PROBLEM SOLVING
USING RATIONAL
NUMBERS

The problems in this chapter require for their solution skill in addition, subtraction, multiplication, and division of rational numbers. Nearly all the problems we shall consider will deal with three numbers. Usually, one of these numbers will be the sum of the other two, or one of the three numbers will be the product of the other two. You will ordinarily know (or be able to calculate quite easily) two of the three numbers in each problem. Then you must decide whether an addition operation, subtraction operation, multiplication operation, or division operation is required. In a complicated problem, you may have to make several decisions of this kind. If you know the sum and one addend, you will *subtract* to find the missing addend. If you know the product and one factor, you will *divide* to determine the missing factor.

In working these problems you will sometimes find that diagrams can be of great assistance. Often it will be helpful to write number sentences which show how the numbers in the problem are related. Let us look at some examples.

Example 1. An airplane flew at $\frac{8}{5}$ of the speed of sound. Since the speed of sound is approximately 800 miles per hour, about how fast was the plane flying?

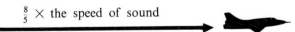

$\frac{8}{5} \times$ the speed of sound

The three numbers in this problem are $\frac{8}{5}$, 800, and the speed of the plane in miles per hour. We need to determine the plane's speed. Thinking carefully about the statement of the problem, we see that the speed of the plane is $\frac{8}{5} \times 800$ miles per hour.

Example 2. The difference between two numbers is $\frac{3}{5}$. The larger number is $\frac{3}{2}$. Find the smaller number.

Let us use a number sentence. Call the smaller number t. Then

$$\frac{3}{2} - t = \frac{3}{5}$$

We see that $\frac{3}{2}$ is the *sum* of t and $\frac{3}{5}$, so

$$t = \frac{3}{2} - \frac{3}{5} \quad \text{(Why?)}$$

Example 3. The difference between two numbers is $\frac{5}{2}$ and the smaller number is $\frac{5}{3}$. Find the other number.

Let l stand for the larger number. Then we can write the number sentence

$$l - \frac{5}{3} = \frac{5}{2}$$

It is clear that l is the sum of $\frac{5}{3}$ and $\frac{5}{2}$.

Example 4. The perimeter of a rectangle is $11\frac{1}{2}$ inches and the length is $4\frac{1}{4}$ inches. What is its width?

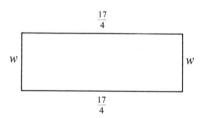

FIGURE 12–1

Let us draw a diagram (Fig. 12–1). Call the width, in inches, w. From the drawing, we can see that $\frac{17}{4} + w$ is *half* of $11\frac{1}{2}$. Now,

$$\frac{1}{2} \times \frac{23}{2} = \frac{23}{4}$$

Hence

$$\frac{17}{4} + w = \frac{23}{4}$$

and hence we have

$$w = \frac{23}{4} - \frac{17}{4} = \frac{6}{4}$$

EXERCISES

1. What is the sum of $\frac{3}{8}$ and $\frac{2}{5}$?
2. What is the difference between $\frac{5}{6}$ and $\frac{3}{5}$?
3. The sum of two numbers is $\frac{11}{4}$. One is $\frac{3}{2}$. Find the other.
4. The difference between two numbers is $\frac{4}{3}$. The larger number is $\frac{7}{2}$. Find the other.
5. Find the product of $\frac{3}{8}$ and $\frac{2}{5}$.
6. Find the quotient of $\frac{5}{6}$ divided by $\frac{3}{2}$.
7. The product of two numbers is $\frac{11}{4}$. One is $\frac{3}{2}$. Find the other.
8. The quotient of two numbers is $\frac{4}{3}$. The larger number is $\frac{7}{2}$. Find the other.
9. The quotient of two numbers is $\frac{4}{3}$. The smaller number is $\frac{7}{2}$. Find the other.
10. The width of a rectangle is $\frac{7}{8}$ in. Find the perimeter, given that the length is $\frac{1}{2}$ in. more than the width.
11. The perimeter of a rectangle is 7 in. and the width is $1\frac{1}{4}$ in. Find the length.
12. Two sides of a triangle are $\frac{5}{3}$ and $\frac{7}{4}$ in. long. The perimeter is 5 in. Find the length of the third side.
13. The base of an isosceles triangle is $\frac{3}{4}$ in. long. If the perimeter is $3\frac{1}{2}$ in., how long is each of the other two sides?
14. A man spent $\frac{3}{5}$ of his money for a watch. If the watch cost $60, how much money had he originally?
15. One person held $\frac{1}{3}$ of the stock of a certain company. A second person held $\frac{2}{3}$ as much as the first one. What part of the stock was held by other people?
16. A carpenter saws $2\frac{3}{8}$ in. from one end of a board $21\frac{1}{2}$ in. long. How long is the remaining piece?
17. A carpenter has a board 3 ft $5\frac{1}{2}$ in. long. He needs to shorten it so that it will be $29\frac{3}{8}$ in. long. How much must be cut off?
18. How many books $1\frac{3}{4}$ in. thick can be placed on a shelf 21 in. wide? on a shelf 22 in. wide?
19. Express 45 min as a fraction of 1 hr.

20. A car drove 60 mph for 1 hr 45 min. How far did it go?

21. A car drove 50 mph for 1 hr 45 min. How far did it go?

22. A dealer paid $2400 for a car. He added on $\frac{1}{5}$ of this cost in order to determine his selling price. What was his selling price?

23. Show that the dealer's selling price in problem 22 is $\frac{6}{5}$ times his cost.

24. Show that if $\frac{1}{3}$ of 14 is added to 14, the sum is the same as the product obtained by multiplying 14 by $\frac{4}{3}$.

25. Two circles are drawn on a sheet of paper. The distance between their centers is $4\frac{1}{2}$ in. One circle has a diameter of $1\frac{1}{2}$ in. and the other has a diameter of $\frac{3}{4}$ in. Find the distance between the two points, one on each circle, which are closer together than any other such pair of points.

26. One number is twice as large as another. The smaller number is $\frac{3}{4}$. What is the product of the two numbers? the difference of the two numbers?

27. Two-thirds of a number is $\frac{16}{3}$. Find the number.

28. A man spent $40 in a store. This was $\frac{2}{3}$ of all the money he had. How much had he left?

29. Jim said, "Three-fourths of my age is 12." If Jim is correct, how old is he?

30. A watch cost $\frac{3}{5}$ as much as a ring. The ring cost $60. What did the watch cost?

31. A watch cost $\frac{3}{5}$ as much as a ring. The watch cost $60. What did the ring cost?

32. A watch cost $\frac{3}{5}$ as much as a ring. The watch and ring together cost $60. How much did each cost?

33. A line segment one centimeter (1 cm) long is *about* $\frac{2}{5}$ as long as a segment one inch long. We shall pretend in the following problems that one centimeter is exactly $\frac{2}{5}$ of an inch.

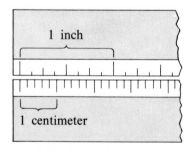

(a) How many inches long is a line segment 1 cm long?

(b) How many inches long is a segment 100 cm long?

(c) How many centimeters long is a line segment 1 in. long?

(d) How many centimeters long is a segment 36 in. long?

(e) A book has a thickness of $\frac{5}{4}$ in. What is its thickness in centimeters?

(f) A desk has a width of 52 cm. What is its width in inches?

(g) A rectangle is 4 in. long and 3 in. wide. What is its area in square centimeters?

(h) A rectangle has an area of 35 sq. cm. Its width is $\frac{7}{3}$ in. Give the dimensions of the rectangle in centimeters.

(i) A centimeter is $\frac{1}{100}$ of a meter. What part of a meter is an inch?

34. On Mars two units of measure are the ogg and the ak. A line segment 15 oggs long has a length of 8 aks.

(a) Which is the greater unit of measure, the ogg or the ak?

(b) What is the length, in oggs, of a segment 1 ak long? in aks, of a segment 1 ogg long?

(c) A segment is $\frac{7}{3}$ oggs long. What is its length in aks?

(d) A segment measures $\frac{7}{3}$ aks. What does it measure in oggs?

(e) Which is the greater length, $\frac{5}{4}$ of an ogg or $\frac{4}{5}$ of an ak?

(f) Find the perimeter, in aks, of a rectangle $\frac{2}{3}$ oggs long and $\frac{2}{3}$ oggs wide.

(g) The area of a rectangle is $\frac{21}{5}$ square aks. The rectangle has a width of $\frac{7}{2}$ oggs. What is the length of the rectangle in oggs?

35. Each of the 64 squares of a checkerboard is $1\frac{7}{8}$ in. on a side, and there is a 1-in. border around the board. What is the area of the checkerboard?

36. One day there was a change in temperature, from lowest to highest temperatures, of 25° centigrade (C). Expressed in degrees fahrenheit (F), this change amounts to 45°.

(a) Which is the greater unit of measure for temperature, the centigrade degree or the fahrenheit degree?

(b) What part of 1°C is 1°F?

(c) What part of 1°F is 1°C?

(d) When the temperature is 15°C, it is 59°F. What is the temperature, in degrees F, when it is 25°C?

37. Show that the sum of $\frac{2}{3}$ and $\frac{2}{5}$ is 4 times as large as their difference.

38. Find a number smaller than $\frac{3}{2}$ such that the sum of these two numbers is

(a) exactly three times their difference;

(b) exactly twice their difference;

(c) exactly equal to their difference.

39. Find a rational number which when added to $\frac{1}{2}$ yields exactly 3 times as much as when you subtract it from $\frac{1}{2}$.

40. One number is twice as large as a second. It is also $\frac{1}{3}$ more than the second. What are the two numbers?

41. A man left $\frac{1}{2}$ of his estate to his wife and $\frac{1}{3}$ to his children. The balance, $50,000, was given to charities. What was his total estate?

42. A man left $\frac{1}{2}$ of his estate to his wife and $\frac{2}{3}$ of the remainder to his son. The rest went to charities. The son received $10,000 more than was given to charities. What was the total estate?

43. If 6 is $\frac{2}{5}$ of a certain number, what part of the number is 3?

44. Two-thirds is $\frac{2}{5}$ of a certain number. What part of the number is $\frac{1}{3}$?

45. Two-thirds of a certain number is 1. Determine the number.

46. Two-thirds of a number is $\frac{3}{4}$. Find $\frac{3}{2}$ of the number.

47. What is the smallest whole number other than zero which when multiplied by $\frac{12}{7}$ gives a whole number as the product?

48. What is the smallest rational number other than zero which when multiplied by $\frac{12}{7}$ yields a product that is a whole number?

49. One number divided by a second is $\frac{3}{8}$. The smaller number is $\frac{3}{4}$. Find the larger number.

50. One number divided by a second is $\frac{3}{8}$. What is the second number divided by the first?

51. Decide whether the following problem has a solution. One number divided by a second is $\frac{3}{8}$. The larger of the two numbers is $\frac{3}{4}$. What is the other number?

52. Is there a number N such that

(a) $1 \times N = 1 + N$? (b) $\frac{1}{2} + N = \frac{1}{2} \times N$?

(c) $2 + N = 2 \times N$? (d) $10 + N = 10 \times N$?

53. In a city where 12 blocks make a mile, a boy lives $7\frac{1}{2}$ blocks from school. What part of a mile is this?

54. An estate was divided among three people. The first received $\frac{2}{5}$ of the estate and the second $\frac{1}{3}$. If the second person received $4,000 more than the third, how much did each receive?

55. One man working alone can do a piece of work in 2 days. A second man alone can do it in 3 days. If they work together for one day,

(a) what part of the work will they have done?
(b) what part of the work will remain to be done?
(c) what part of a day will it take the first man to finish the work alone?

56. A board 30 in. long was cut into two pieces. Find the length of each piece given that

(a) $\frac{1}{2}$ of the longer piece is equal in length to the shorter one;
(b) $\frac{2}{3}$ of the longer piece is equal in length to the shorter one;
(c) $\frac{1}{2}$ of the longer piece is $\frac{3}{4}$ of the shorter piece;
(d) $\frac{1}{2}$ of the longer piece is $\frac{3}{2}$ of the shorter one.

Chapter 13

DECIMAL
NOTATION

1. INTRODUCTION: THE NEED FOR DECIMAL NOTATION

The fractions which we use for rational numbers are not always the most convenient names for these numbers. For example, let us suppose that you see the story below on the sports page of your newspaper.

"Sam Slugger and Bill Belter have completed this season's battle for the league batting championship. Sam has made 177 hits in 529 times at bat. His batting average is $\frac{177}{529}$. Bill has made 169 hits in 521 times at bat. His average is $\frac{169}{521}$."

Fractions like $\frac{177}{529}$ and $\frac{169}{521}$ are not very useful when a quick glance at the paper is to tell us who the batting champion is. These fractions do not give us any feeling for the sizes of the numbers. The batting records could be compared more easily if we used the *decimal* names, 0.335 and 0.324, to present this information.

Suppose that the Air Force is allocated $2,661,525,300 to spend on missile projects during a certain fiscal year. If the sum of $27,621,298 is spent to build and test 10 Atlas missiles, then the Air Force has spent

$$\frac{27{,}621{,}298}{2{,}661{,}525{,}300}$$

of its money on Atlas missiles. Fractions of this type are not very informative. They are difficult to print, hard to read, and not easy to use in computations. One can give information of this kind more easily by using *decimals* than by using complicated fractions. In this chapter we shall consider decimal notation and some of its important uses.

2. UNDERSTANDING DECIMAL NOTATION

Decimal notation is encountered first in working with money. We represent the value of our United States coins, the half-dollar, quarter, dime, nickel, and penny, by the symbols

$$\$.50 \quad \$.25 \quad \$.10 \quad \$.05 \quad \$.01$$

These decimal symbols are just *abbreviations* (Fig. 13–1).

$$\$.50 \quad \text{means} \quad \frac{50}{100} \text{ of one dollar}$$

$$\$.25 \quad \text{means} \quad \frac{25}{100} \text{ of one dollar}$$

$$\$.10 \quad \text{means} \quad \frac{10}{100} \text{ of one dollar}$$

$$\$.05 \quad \text{means} \quad \frac{5}{100} \text{ of one dollar}$$

$$\$.01 \quad \text{means} \quad \frac{1}{100} \text{ of one dollar}$$

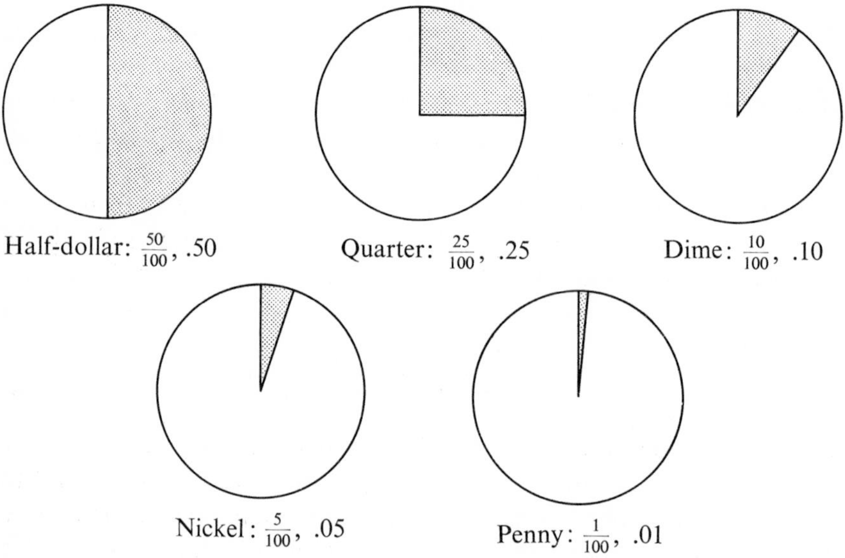

Half-dollar: $\frac{50}{100}$, .50   Quarter: $\frac{25}{100}$, .25   Dime: $\frac{10}{100}$, .10

Nickel: $\frac{5}{100}$, .05   Penny: $\frac{1}{100}$, .01

FIGURE 13–1

We think of the dollar as divided into 100 equal parts. Each of our coins has a buying power that is a certain number of hundredths of the buying power of one dollar.

We use the symbol $.20 to mean $\frac{20}{100}$ of a dollar (or 20¢) just as we use the symbol $.25 to represent the value of our quarter. We use the mark $.45 to mean $\frac{45}{100}$ of a dollar (or 45¢) because it is easy to write and to use in computation. When we deal with money, we use decimal symbols as abbreviations for fractions with 100 as denominator. For example, a symbol like $2.47 is an abbreviation for 2 dollars and $\frac{47}{100}$ of a dollar. Since $2 + \frac{47}{100}$ is $\frac{247}{100}$, we say that $2.47 is an abbreviation for $\frac{247}{100}$ *of a dollar.* Explain why $23.51 is a symbol for $\frac{2351}{100}$ *of a dollar.* Which of the symbols $23.51 and $\frac{2351}{100}$ *of one dollar* is easier to use?

EXERCISES

1. Write decimal symbols for the following amounts of money.

(a) $\frac{137}{100}$ of one dollar

(b) $\frac{2469}{100}$ of one dollar

(c) $\frac{3}{100}$ of one dollar

(d) $\frac{75}{100}$ of one dollar

(e) $\frac{53624}{100}$ of one dollar

(f) $\frac{100}{100}$ of one dollar

(g) $\frac{200}{100}$ of one dollar

(h) $\frac{1000}{100}$ of one dollar

(i) $\frac{1730}{100}$ of one dollar

(j) $\frac{0}{100}$ of one dollar

2. Write the fraction symbols for

(a) $.12   (b) $.23   (c) $35.74   (d) $3.00   (e) $5.36

Decimal notation is very convenient in computations involving amounts of money. When you add two amounts of money, say $23.15 and $46.23, you might think:

15 cents and 23 cents make a total of 38 cents.
23 dollars and 46 dollars make a total of 69 dollars.
The sum is 69 dollars *and* 38 cents or $69.38.

The arithmetic can be done easily by writing

$$
\begin{array}{r}
23.15 \\
46.23 \\
\hline
69.38
\end{array}
$$

Decimal notation makes it possible to arrange work with money in such a way that it is not necessary to think about the *denominators* of the fractions that are used. The invention of decimal notation simplified bookkeeping a great deal. It is difficult to imagine business and science getting along without decimals.

EXERCISES

Work each problem below, using fraction or decimal notation depending upon how the problem is stated.

1. A girl spent $\frac{87}{100}$ of a dollar for milk, $\frac{137}{100}$ of a dollar for a chicken, and $\frac{10}{100}$ of a dollar for bubble gum. The sales tax amounted to $\frac{7}{100}$ of a dollar. What was her grocery bill?

2. If a housewife spends $1.42 for meat, $.91 for milk, and $.15 for candy and the sales tax is $.07, what is her grocery bill?

3. A woman buys 12 pairs of socks for $\frac{69}{100}$ of a dollar per pair. What is the total cost?

4. Find the cost of 15 undershirts at $.89 each.

5. If a grocery clerk is given $\frac{500}{100}$ of one dollar to pay a grocery bill of $\frac{357}{100}$ of one dollar, how much change should he give back?

6. What change does one get back from a $10 bill is he pays a $7.41 grocery bill?

Of course, *decimal* notation is used for many things besides money. When working with money, we use the decimal names as abbreviations for rational numbers that can be written as fractions with denominator 100. In other situations, decimals are used as names for rational numbers that can be represented as fractions with denominators of 10, 1000, 10,000, etc., as well as 100. For example, the decimal 0.4 is used to represent the rational number $\frac{4}{10}$. The decimal 0.323 is used to represent the rational number $\frac{323}{1000}$, and the decimal 0.4624 is used to represent the rational number $\frac{4624}{10000}$. A diagram such as that presented in Fig. 13–2, which shows the decimal representation for the sum

$$
2000 + 400 + 60 + 8 + \frac{7}{10} + \frac{5}{100} + \frac{3}{1000}
$$

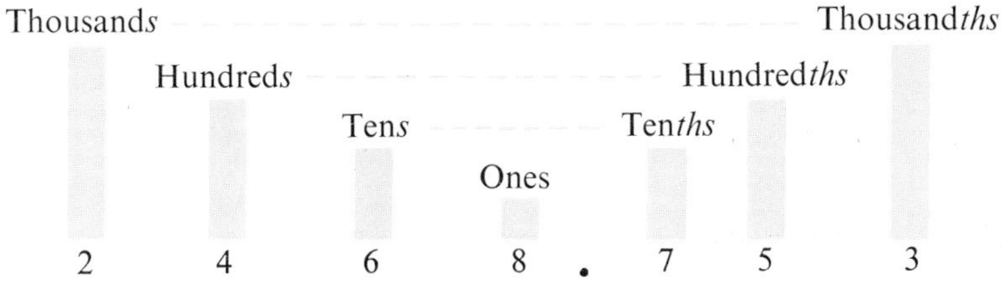

Thousands							Thousandths
	Hundreds					Hundredths	
		Tens			Tenths		
			Ones				
2	4	6	8	.	7	5	3

FIGURE 13–2

is helpful in explaining how decimal notation is used.   The decimal
2468.753 represents

$$(2 \times 1000) + (4 \times 100) + (6 \times 10) + (8 \times 1)$$
$$+ \left(7 \times \frac{1}{10}\right) + \left(5 \times \frac{1}{100}\right) + \left(3 \times \frac{1}{1000}\right)$$

A simple way to read such a symbol would be:

Two thousands plus four hundreds plus six tens plus
eight ones plus seven-tenths plus five-hundredths plus three-
thousandths.

However, since

$$\frac{7}{10} + \frac{5}{100} + \frac{3}{1000} = \frac{700}{1000} + \frac{50}{1000} + \frac{3}{1000} = \frac{753}{1000}$$

we agree to read the given decimal as

Two thousand, four hundred sixty-eight *and* seven hundred
fifty-three *thousandths.*

That is, we think of the number 2468.753 as

$$2468 + \frac{753}{1000}$$

EXERCISES

1. Give the decimal representation for these sums.

(a) $7 + \frac{3}{10}$

(b) $(6 \times 10) + (4 \times 1) + \left(3 \times \frac{1}{10}\right)$

(c) $(5 \times 1) + \left(3 \times \frac{1}{10}\right) + \left(7 \times \frac{1}{100}\right)$

(d) $5000 + 200 + 30 + 6 + \frac{3}{10} + \frac{7}{100} + \frac{5}{1000}$

*(e) $8(100) + 5(10) + 3(1) + 2\left(\frac{1}{10}\right) + 7\left(\frac{1}{100}\right)$

(f) $7(10{,}000) + 5(1000) + 8(100) + 3(10) + 5(1)$
$$+ 4\left(\frac{1}{10}\right) + 6\left(\frac{1}{100}\right) + 2\left(\frac{1}{1000}\right)$$

(g) $8(100{,}000) + 3(100) + 7\left(\frac{1}{100}\right) + 5\left(\frac{1}{1000}\right)$

(h) $3(1{,}000{,}000) + 4(100{,}000) + 8(1) + 7\left(\frac{1}{10}\right) + 4\left(\frac{1}{10{,}000}\right)$

(i) $800 + 30 + 7 + \frac{2}{10} + \frac{3}{100} + \frac{5}{1000}$

(j) $1(10{,}000) + 1\left(\frac{1}{10{,}000}\right)$

2. Write each of the following as the sum of ten thousands, thousands, hundreds, tens, ones, tenths, hundredths, thousandths, etc. (These directions are sometimes given as "Write, using *expanded notation* . . .")

(a)   35.42   (b)   1.254   (c)   562.34   (d)   0.002

(e)   0.0201   (f)   400.04   (g)   504.34007   (h)   56,321.0005

(i)   30.3003

3. Write each of the following as the sum of tenths, hundredths, thousandths, etc., and add the rational numbers, getting an ordinary fraction for the sum. The first problem is worked as an example.

(a) $0.32 = \frac{3}{10} + \frac{2}{100} = \frac{30}{100} + \frac{2}{100} = \frac{32}{100}$

(b)   0.52   (c)   0.364   (d)   0.2763   (e)   0.32546

4. Write the sum of each pair of numbers given below as a decimal.

(a) $8 + \frac{4}{10}$ (b) $21 + \frac{23}{100}$ (c) $4 + \frac{2}{100}$

(d) $0 + \frac{23}{100}$ (e) $1 + \frac{1}{1000}$ (f) $29 + \frac{472}{1000}$

---

* We have written 8(100) for 8×100.

(g) $614 + \dfrac{2152}{10,000}$ (h) $50 + \dfrac{47}{1000}$ (i) $50 + \dfrac{471}{10,000}$

(j) $0 + \dfrac{37,019}{100,000}$ (k) $4 + \dfrac{612}{1,000,000}$

5. Write each decimal as the sum of two numbers (see Exercise 4).

   (a) 6.4   (b) 17.31   (c) 5.03   (d) 0.15
   (e) 2.003   (f) 81.426   (g) 919.7154   (h) 40.0352
   (i) 0.21746 (j) 3.000123

6. Read each number below by reading the number represented by each individual digit.

   (a) 42.351 (b) 104.032   (c) 7123.12345   (d) 42,031.010203

7. Read each number in Exercise 6 in the usual way.

8. In a decimal symbol, the *ones'* place is always just to the left of the decimal point. This is the usual agreement. Suppose, however, that we had adopted the convention of writing the decimal point *below* the ones' place. Answer the questions below using this convention.

   (a) Read the decimal 532643
   (b) Give the decimal representation for the sum

$$5(1000) + 2(100) + 8(10) + 7 + 8(\tfrac{1}{10}) + 2(\tfrac{1}{100}) + 5(\tfrac{1}{1000})$$

   (c) Write $\tfrac{1}{1000}$ as a decimal.
   (d) Write $\tfrac{1}{10}$, $\tfrac{1}{10,000}$, $\tfrac{1}{100}$ as decimals.
   (e) Write $1000 + \tfrac{1}{1000}$ as a decimal.
   (f) Write $100 + \tfrac{1}{100}$ as a decimal.
   (g) With the new agreement, in what way is the decimal for *one-thousandth* like the numeral for *one thousand?*

9. Use a zero in the ones' place and write the decimals for Exercises 8 (c) through (f) in the usual way.

10. Decimal names can be used as abbreviations for fractions with denominators 10, 100, 1000, etc. Can every rational number be represented by a fraction having these special denominators?

We began the discussion of decimal notation by considering its use in work with money. We then pointed out that we use decimal notation for many things other than money. Decimal notation shows exactly how much money is involved. When we give a clerk a nickel we are giving him exactly 0.05 of one dollar. But if someone says that 0.05 of the students were absent from school Friday, you can be reasonably certain that he does not mean exactly $\tfrac{5}{100}$ of the students. If there are 470 students in school, then $\frac{5}{100}$ of 470 is $23\frac{1}{2}$. We can be sure that if one half of a student misses school, then the other half will be absent also. The chances are that between 20 and 25 students were absent from school. If *exact* answers were required for every arithmetic problem in everyday life, decimals would not be nearly so useful. The decimals we use every day in arithmetic (except those for money) are usually approximations.

3. ADDITION AND SUBTRACTION BY MEANS OF DECIMAL NOTATION

Problems in addition and subtraction of decimals can be worked by changing the decimals to fraction symbols. For example,

$$0.4 + 0.5 = \frac{4}{10} + \frac{5}{10} = \frac{9}{10} = 0.9$$

$$0.23 + 0.41 = \frac{23}{100} + \frac{41}{100} = \frac{64}{100} = 0.64$$

$$0.734 - 0.658 = \frac{734}{1000} - \frac{658}{1000} = \frac{76}{1000} = 0.076$$

EXERCISES

1. Write the numbers 0.3 and 4.7 as fractions with denominators 10; denominators 100; denominators 1000.

2. Do not compute any of the sums or differences below. Just tell whether the answer will be given naturally as tenths, hundredths, or thousandths. *Think of each number as it would be written in fraction form.*

   (a) $0.7 + 0.4$ (b) $0.11 + 0.32$ (c) $0.31 - 0.01$

   (d) $3.14 - 1.23$ (e) $5.2 - 4.1$ (f) $0.3 + 0.24$

   (g) $0.5 - 0.42$ (h) $2 - 0.53$ (i) $0.524 + 0.221$

   (j) $0.528 + 0.24$ (k) $4.7 + 3.24$ (l) $22.3 + 3.564$

3. Write problems (a) through (h) of Exercise 2 in fraction form and add or subtract. Give each answer in decimal notation.

If we know how to add and subtract whole numbers, and if we understand decimal notation, computing with decimals presents no new problems.

Explain what the student who adds 23.42 and 32.5 as shown below does not understand.

$$\begin{array}{r} 23.4\,2 \\ 3\,2.5 \\ \hline 26.6\,7 \end{array}$$

The expanded notation below helps to explain his error.

$$\begin{array}{r} 20 + 3 + \dfrac{4}{10} + \dfrac{2}{100} \\ 30 + 2 + \dfrac{5}{10} \\ \hline 50 + 5 + \dfrac{9}{10} + \dfrac{2}{100} \end{array}$$

This example shows that in addition, using decimal notation, we do well to keep decimal points in line.

When we add decimals, keeping the decimal points in line, we are really making use of the associative and commutative properties of addition to regroup the addends. We regroup

$$\left(20 + 3 + \frac{4}{10} + \frac{2}{100}\right) + \left(30 + 2 + \frac{5}{10}\right)$$

into

$$(20 + 30) + (3 + 2) + \left(\frac{4}{10} + \frac{5}{10}\right) + \frac{2}{100}$$

that is, we obtain

$$\begin{array}{r} 23.42 \\ 32.5 \\ \hline 55.92 \end{array}$$

EXERCISES

1. Fill in the blanks to make true statements.

   (a) ____hundredths = 1 tenth

   (b) ____tenths = 1

   (c) 10 thousandths = ____ hundredths

   (d) ____thousands = 1 ten thousand

   (e) ____ ten thousandths = 1 thousandth

2. Compute the following sums and differences.

(a) 0.48 + 0.31   (b) 3.2 + 4.7
(c) 0.321 + 0.245 + 0.223   (d) 0.5 + 3 + 0.02
(e) 2.54 + 37.3   (f)   4.763
                                           −0.321
                                           ‾‾‾‾‾‾

(g)   6.563   (h) 13.354 + 423.4568
       0.278
      37.937
      ‾‾‾‾‾‾

(i) 6 − 0.2   (j) 0.01 − 0.001
(k) 146.2 − 21.462   (l) (3.1416 + 1.4142) − 2.8
(m) 1.002 + 0.0102   (n) 1.05 + 0.75 + 21.5
(o) 1.005 − 0.0005   (p) (0.306 − 0.21) + 0.067
(q) 56 − 12.6582   (r) 0.02 + 0.1 + 0.0004 + 0.003
(s) 457 − 65.37   (t)   5.346
                                          35.27
                                         161.2
                                           4.387
                                          ‾‾‾‾‾‾

(u) 7 + 0.12 + 0.4   (v) 0.35 + 2 + 0.7
(w) 10.2 + 0.34 + 4   (x) 100 − 12.3
(y) 100 − 0.01   (z) 90 + 9 + 0.9 + 0.09

3. Give the missing number in each of the following problems.

(a) $\left(32 \times \frac{1}{100}\right) + \left(68 \times \frac{1}{100}\right) = n$

(b) (72 hundredths) $+ \left(h \times \frac{1}{100}\right) = 0.80$

(c) $\left(54 \times \frac{1}{100}\right) + \frac{n}{100} = 0.59$ (d) $\frac{3}{t} + \frac{54}{t} = 0.57$

(e) $0.635 + (230 \times r) = \frac{865}{1000}$

(f) $\left(q \times \frac{1}{10}\right) + \left(q \times \frac{1}{10}\right) = 1$

(g) $\frac{r}{100} - \left(83 \times \frac{1}{100}\right) = 0.70$

(h) 600 thousandths − s thousandths = 0.200

(i) $\left(128 \times \frac{1}{100}\right) - \frac{y}{100} = 1$

(j) 5 tenths + q hundredths $= \frac{87}{100}$

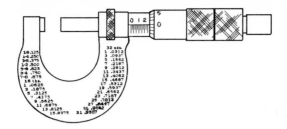

4. MULTIPLICATION AND DIVISION BY MEANS OF DECIMAL NOTATION

We use decimal notation as an abbreviation for fractions with denominators of 10, 100, 1000, etc. If we understand how to multiply fractions with these denominators, then it is not difficult to understand multiplication of decimals.

EXERCISES

1. Give the products below as fractions and as decimals.

(a) $\dfrac{1}{10} \times \dfrac{1}{10}$; 0.1×0.1

(b) $\dfrac{1}{10} \times \dfrac{1}{100}$; 0.1×0.01

(c) $\dfrac{1}{100} \times \dfrac{1}{100}$; 0.01×0.01

(d) $\dfrac{1}{10} \times \dfrac{1}{1000}$; 0.1×0.001

(e) $\dfrac{1}{100} \times \dfrac{1}{1000}$; 0.01×0.001

(f) $\dfrac{1}{1000} \times \dfrac{1}{1000}$; 0.001×0.001

(g) $\dfrac{1}{10} \times \dfrac{1}{10,000}$; 0.1×0.0001

(h) $\dfrac{1}{10,000} \times \dfrac{1}{100}$; 0.0001×0.01

(i) $\dfrac{1}{100,000} \times \dfrac{1}{1000}$; 0.00001×0.001

(j) $\dfrac{1}{100} \times \dfrac{1}{1,000,000}$; 0.01×0.000001

2. Complete the following.
    (a) Tenths × tenths give_____
    (b) Tenths × _____ give thousandths
    (c) Hundredths × _____ give hundred thousandths
    (d) Tenths × _____ give ten thousandths
    (e) Hundredths × hundredths give _____

3. *Do not* compute any of the products below. Just tell whether the answer is given naturally as tenths, hundredths, or thousandths, etc. Think of each number as it would appear in fraction form.
    (a) 0.6 × 0.7   (b) 0.31 × 0.4   (c) 5.2 × 4.1
    (d) 0.3 × 0.24   (e) 0.05 × 0.04   (f) 0.5 × 0.003
    (g) 0.3 × 0.0006   (h) 0.04 × 0.003   (i) 0.25 × 0.35
    (j) 0.321 × 0.25

4. Give products for problems (a) through (h) in Exercise 2; (a) as fractions, (b) as decimals.

5. The commutative and associative laws allow us to regroup our factors in any way we wish when we are multiplying several numbers together. For example,

$$\left(3 \times \frac{1}{10}\right) \times \left(5 \times \frac{1}{100}\right), \qquad \left(3 \times \frac{1}{100}\right) \times \left(5 \times \frac{1}{10}\right)$$

$$3 \times \left(\frac{1}{10} \times \frac{1}{100}\right) \times 5, \qquad (3 \times 5) \times \left(\frac{1}{10} \times \frac{1}{100}\right)$$

all represent the *same product*, $\frac{15}{1000}$.

Change the *order* and *grouping* in any way you choose and give the products as fractions with denominators 10, 100, 1000, etc.

(a) $\left(3 \times \frac{1}{10}\right) \times \left(4 \times \frac{1}{10}\right)$ (b) $\left(7 \times \frac{1}{10}\right) \times \left(11 \times \frac{1}{100}\right)$

(c) $\left(5 \times \frac{1}{10}\right) \times \left(120 \times \frac{1}{1000}\right)$

(d) $\left(12 \times \frac{1}{100}\right) \times \left(13 \times \frac{1}{100}\right)$

(e) $\left(15 \times \frac{1}{1000}\right) \times \left(21 \times \frac{1}{100}\right)$

(f) $\left(32 \times \frac{1}{10}\right) \times \left(27 \times \frac{1}{10}\right)$

(g) $\left(5 \times \dfrac{1}{10}\right) \times \left(230 \times \dfrac{1}{10,000}\right)$

(h) $\left(4 \times \dfrac{1}{100}\right) \times \left(6 \times \dfrac{1}{1000}\right)$

(i) $\left(7 \times \dfrac{1}{10,000}\right) \times \left(4 \times \dfrac{1}{1000}\right)$

(j) $\left(32 \times \dfrac{1}{100}\right) \times \left(14 \times \dfrac{1}{1000}\right)$

6. Write the problems in (5) and give products, using *decimal notation;* for example,

$$(a)\quad 0.3 \times 0.4 = 0.12$$

Let us agree to call decimals like 0.21, 0.54, 3.20, 0.05, etc. (all *hundredths*) *two-place decimals;* decimals like 0.015, 14.342, 0.680, etc. (all *thousandths*), *three-place decimals;* decimals like 0.1204, *four-place decimals*, etc. This language is useful for describing multiplication of decimals. We see that the product of a two-place decimal and a three-place decimal can be written as a five-place decimal. For example,

$$3.24 = \frac{324}{100} \quad \text{and} \quad 0.014 = \frac{14}{1000}$$

If we multiply 3.24 × 0.014, we have

$$\frac{324}{100} \times \frac{14}{1000} = \frac{4536}{100,000} = 0.04536$$

Our product is given as a five-place decimal.

Since multiplying any two-place decimal by any three-place decimal is a problem of multiplying *hundredths* by *thousandths*, it follows that any two-place decimal multiplied by any three-place decimal gives *hundred thousandths*, that is, a five-place product.

If we think about other products in this way, the usual rule for locating decimal points in multiplications should be easy to understand and to remember. Of course, no rule is necessary. In a problem like 4.3 × 2.47 we can reason as follows:

We have to multiply 43 tenths and 247 hundredths. The product will be thousandths. Since 43 × 247 = 10621, the answer is 10.621.

EXERCISES

1. After each pair of numbers below, the correct digits are given for the product. If you locate the decimal point correctly, you will have the product of the two numbers. Give each product.

(a) 35×0.01;   35
(b) 35×0.001;   35
(c) 2.1×3.4;   714
(d) 3.12×2.5;   7800
(e) 0.04×5.6;   224
(f) 1.34×2.01;   26934
(g) 0.012×0.016; 192
(h) 1.35×0.0021; 2835
(i) 0.001×0.001; 1
(j) 71.23×6.51; 4637073
(k) 593×0.057; 33801
(l) 0.03×0.004; 12

2. Work the following problems.

(a) 1.5×3.4
(b) 2.3×0.01
(c) 0.002×0.03
(d) 0.001×0.0001
(e) 0.031×0.020
(f) 0.125×0.8
(g) 0.08×0.07
(h) 2500×0.025
(i) $1,000,000 \times 0.00032$
(j) 43.1×0.06
(k) 2.02×1.6
(l) 0.003×400
(m) 2.75×0.8
(n) 2.5×3.1416
(o) 0.25×0.25
(p) 2.323×0.42
(q) 200×0.126
(r) 0.54×0.45
(s) 1.3×13.13
(t) 0.005×0.005
(u) 10×34.2
(v) 100×34.2
(w) 1000×34.2
(x) 0.1×34.2
(y) 0.01×34.2
(z) 0.001×34.2

There is no *simple*, easily explained rule for locating decimal points in *division*. Some special problems are easy. Since

$$0.25 \times 0.5 = 0.125$$

(a two-place decimal multiplied by a one-place decimal is a three-place decimal), it follows that

$$0.125 \div 0.5 = 0.25$$

(A three-place decimal divided by a one-place decimal is a two-place decimal.) Consider a second example. Since

$$3.12 \times 4.301 = 13.41912$$

(a two-place decimal multiplied by a three-place decimal is a five-place decimal), we have

$$13.41912 \div 4.301 = 3.12$$

(The five-place decimal divided by the three-place decimal is a two-place decimal.)

If all our division problems "came out even," everything would be simple. We could locate the decimal point as we did in the examples above.

EXERCISES

The correct digits are given for each quotient. Locate the decimal point correctly and check your answer by multiplication.

1. $9.43 \div 4.1$;	23	2. $16.544 \div 3.52$;	47
3. $8.0698 \div 2.57$;	314	4. $0.002856 \div 0.714$;	4
5. $0.153126 \div 0.047$;	3258	6. $0.969 \div 0.323$;	3
7. $1.333 \div 0.031$;	43	8. $0.01517 \div 4.1$;	37
9. $30.25 \div 55$;	55	10. $30.25 \div 0.055$;	55

Division problems involving decimals usually do not come out even. For example, suppose that you used a calculating machine to divide 47.325 by 0.00428. The answer would be given on a strip of paper by the following string of digits:

$$110572429 \ldots$$

You will notice that the machine has left it up to us to locate the decimal point correctly. Is the answer

$$11.057249 \ldots ? \quad 1105.72429 \ldots ? \quad 1.10572429 \ldots ?$$

One method of locating the decimal point is by *estimating* and then checking by multiplication. This method is based on common sense. We follow no rules; we simply think and then check. If you estimated the answer to the division problem above to be

$$110.57 \ldots$$

you would be claiming that

$$47.325 \div 0.00428 = 110.57 \ldots$$

that is,

$$47.325 = 0.00428 \times 110.57 \ldots$$

The given factor 0.00428 and the *suggested* missing factor 110.57 . . . are approximately 0.004 and 100. But 100×0.004 is only 0.4. It is far less than 47. We see that the answer 110.57 cannot possibly be correct.

The missing factor is not close to 1000, for the product 1000×0.004 is 4, which also is much less than 47. Since $10,000 \times 0.004 = 40$, our answer (missing factor) must be near 10,000 and indeed is

$$11,057.2429 \ldots$$

A good rule for locating decimal points in division is the following: *Put the point where you think it belongs and then check the answer by multiplication.* To perform this check quickly and accurately requires quite a bit of practice. The main skill you must have is the ability to multiply any number in decimal notation by 10, 100, 1000, etc., and also by 0.1, 0.01, 0.001, etc.

Consider the problem of multiplying 4.372 by 10. This may be written as

$$10 \times \left(4 + \frac{3}{10} + \frac{7}{100} + \frac{2}{1000}\right)$$

Using our basic properties, especially the distributive law, we find that the product is

$$40 + 3 + \frac{7}{10} + \frac{2}{100} \quad \text{or} \quad 43.72$$

Note that

$$10 \times 4.372 = 43.720,$$
$$100 \times 4.372 = 437.20,$$
$$1000 \times 4.372 = 4372.0,$$
$$10,000 \times 4.372 = 43,720$$

We can multiply by 10, 100, 1000, etc., by simply shifting the decimal point to the right. Explain why this is so. It is very important that you understand why this shortcut method leads to the correct answer.

Now consider the problem of multiplying 4.372 by 0.1. We may write this problem as

$$\frac{1}{10} \times \left(4 + \frac{3}{10} + \frac{7}{100} + \frac{2}{1000}\right) = \frac{4}{10} + \frac{3}{100} + \frac{7}{1000} + \frac{2}{10,000}$$

or

$$0.4372$$

Note that

$$0.1 \times 4.372 = 0.4372$$
$$0.01 \times 4.372 = 0.04372$$
$$0.001 \times 4.372 = 0.004372$$
$$0.0001 \times 4.372 = 0.0004372$$

We can multiply by 0.1, 0.01, 0.001, etc., by simply shifting the decimal point to the left. You must understand why this shortcut method gives the correct answer.

EXERCISES

1. For each number below, write (1) the number which is 10 times as large; (2) the number which is 100 times as large; (3) the number which is 1000 times as large.

   (a) 3.71   (b) 42.193   (c) 0.04   (d) 0.0032
   (e) 596.34   (f) 4007.03   (g) 10,010.0110

2. For each number in Exercise 1, write (1) the number 0.1 as large; (2) the number 0.01 as large; (3) the number 0.001 as large.

3. Give a *whole-number* estimate for each of the products below. Do the calculation without writing.

   Examples
   $$101.23 \times 53.89$$

   The product must be about the same as 100×54 or 5400.

   $$0.098 \times 39.21$$

   The product is about 0.1×40 or 4.

   (a) 10.001×54.39 (b) 10.1×99.98
   (c) 10.113×153.71 (d) 0.512×10.0037
   (e) 100.11×0.5032 (f) 102×0.0305
   (g) 45.21×98.532 (h) 5.324×1004.376
   (i) 45.113×20.0974 [*Hint:* To multiply by 20, first multiply by 2 and then by 10.]
   (j) 3.5432×9998.879 (k) 0.1×59.91
   (l) 0.101×59.91 (m) 0.201×59.91
   (n) 0.021×48.04 (o) 0.021×486.31
   (p) 501.54×0.006 [*Hint:* $1000 \times 0.006 = 6$; 500×0.006 would be half as much.]

(q)   19.95 × 0.251   [*Hint:* 10 × 0.25 = 2.5; 20 × 0.25 would be twice as much.]

(r)   298.75 × 0.0332   [*Hint:* 100 × 0.033 = 3.3; 300 × 0.033 is three times as much.]

(s)   52.29 × 64.26   [*Hint:* 100 × 64.26 = 6426; 50 × 64.26 would be half as much.]

(t)   25.37 × 84.48   (u)   33.34 × 963.69

4. Locate the decimal point in 54542 so that the number will be very close to the product 1001.2 × 5.3914.

5. Locate the decimal point in 45154 so that the number will be very close to 107.3 × 42.19.

6. Which of the numbers below is the best approximation to 13.74 × 0.0101 ?

   (a)   13.88   (b)   1.388   (c)   0.1388   (d)   0.01388

7. Which of the numbers below is the best approximation to 13.74 × 0.0211 ?

   (a)   28.991   (b)   2.8991   (c)   0.028991   (d)   0.28991

8. Which of the numbers below is the best approximation to 13.74 × 0.06219 ?

   (a)   85.214   (b)   0.85214   (c)   8.5214   (d)   0.085214

9. Which of the numbers below is the best approximation to 0.00217 × 0.3596 ?

   (a)   0.7812   (b)   0.07812   (c)   0.007812   (d)   0.0007812

10. Which of the numbers below is the best approximation to 4.52 ÷ 0.423 ?

   (a)   1.068   (b)   10.68   (c)   106.8
   (d)   0.01068   (e)   1068

   [*Hint:* If the product is 4.52 and one factor is 0.423, would the missing factor be close to 0.01, 0.1, 1, 10, 100, or 1000 ?]

11. Which of the numbers below is the best approximation to 3.251 ÷ 0.0234 ?

   (a)   1.3893   (b)   13.893   (c)   138.93
   (d)   1389.3   (e)   0.013893

12. Estimate each of the following.

   (a)   0.034 × 18.19   (b)   31.2 × 1.457
   (c)   46.37 × 0.0319   (d)   87.64 ÷ 0.7819
   (e)   423.1 ÷ 21.614   (f)   0.007163 ÷ 0.0625

We shall describe a second method for locating decimal points in division problems. Consider the three problems below.

(a) $4.31 \overline{)31.032}$ (b) $43.1 \overline{)310.32}$ (c) $431 \overline{)3103.2}$

Can you explain why all three quotients are the same?

In problem (c) the divisor is a *whole number*, and hence it is not so difficult to locate the decimal point correctly:

$$
\begin{array}{r}
7.2 \\
431 \overline{)3103.2} \\
3017 \\
\hline
862 \\
862 \\
\hline
\end{array}
$$

The idea underlying this method is to replace the division problem to be worked by one which has the same answer and has a whole-number divisor. Three examples are given below. Explain why in each case the answers are the same and find each quotient.

(a) $3.4 \overline{)13.94}$ $34 \overline{)139.4}$ (b) $.021 \overline{)0.0735}$ $21 \overline{)73.5}$

(c) $3.02 \overline{)483.2}$ $302 \overline{)48320}$

EXERCISES

For each division problem below, digits are given so that if you locate the decimal point correctly, you will have a good estimate of the quotient. Do this and check by estimating the products.

1. $64.53 \div 6.12$;   1054 [*Hint:* $10 \times 6.12 = 61.2$.]
2. $818.93 \div 7.42$;   1104 [*Hint:* $100 \times 7.42 = 742$.]
3. $78.421 \div 9.3$;   843   4. $0.4352 \div 0.023$;   1892
5. $32.54 \div 86.3$;   376   6. $3.165 \div 0.0062$;   5105
7. $4257.3 \div 68.24$;   6238   8. $0.00057 \div 0.0025$;   228
9. $32.47 \div 0.00058$;   56   10. $0.02574 \div 17.36$;   1485

11. Find the digits in the quotients given below as you would if you were dividing one whole number by another. Locate the decimal point as you did in the examples above.

    (a) $53.248 \div 6.4$ (b) $31.032 \div 4.31$
    (c) $2.035 \div 8.14$ (d) $0.4992 \div 1.56$
    (e) $4.5 \overline{)51.300}$ (f) $5.4 \overline{)488.700}$
    (g) $0.4 \overline{)0.575}$ (h) $2.9375 \div 0.235$
    (i) $0.2 \div 0.007$ (j) $0.127 \overline{)0.30861}$

5. CONVERTING FRACTIONS TO DECIMALS

It is important to be able to calculate decimal names for rational numbers quickly and accurately. Changing from fractions to decimals requires quite a bit of calculation. Often you can estimate well enough for practical purposes. For example, $\frac{7}{99}$ is almost the same as $\frac{7}{100}$, and thus we can write the decimal 0.07 as an approximation for $\frac{7}{99}$.

EXERCISES

Write a decimal in tenths, hundredths, or thousandths, whichever you prefer, that you think is exactly the same as, or almost the same as, the given rational number. You may do as much mental arithmetic as you please to get a "good" approximation, but *do not* do any written work.

1. $\frac{1}{9}$ 　　　　 2. $\frac{4}{5}$ 　　　　 3. $\frac{18}{100}$ 　　　　 4. $\frac{7}{50}$

5. $\frac{17}{99}$ 　　　　 6. $\frac{7}{49}$ 　　　　 7. $\frac{1}{8}$ 　　　　 8. $\frac{1}{7}$

9. $\frac{1}{3}$ 　　　　 10. $\frac{2}{3}$ 　　　　 11. $\frac{86}{1000}$ 　　　　 12. $\frac{73}{999}$

13. $\frac{63}{500}$ 　　　　 14. $\frac{63}{501}$ 　　　　 15. $\frac{614}{1001}$ 　　　　 16. $\frac{614}{1002}$

17. $\frac{64}{200}$ 　　　　 18. $\frac{64}{300}$ 　　　　 19. $\frac{64}{250}$ 　　　　 20. $\frac{5}{8}$

21. $\frac{9}{12}$ 　　　　 22. $\frac{3}{2}$ 　　　　 23. $\frac{7}{7}$ 　　　　 24. $\frac{61}{10}$

The examples below show how *accurate* decimal approximations for rational numbers may be found.

Examples

(1) $\dfrac{23}{50} = \dfrac{46}{100} = 0.46$ 　　　 (2) $\dfrac{74}{200} = \dfrac{37}{100} = 0.37$

[*Note:* 2 is a factor of both 74 and 200.]

(3) $\dfrac{56}{300} \approx \dfrac{18.7}{100} = 18.7 \times 0.01 = .187$

[*Note:* Since 3 × 100 is 300, and 3 × 18.7 is approximately 56, we can think of 3 as a factor of both the numerator and denominator and write a "reduced" fraction.]

---

* The symbol ≈ means "is approximately equal to."

(4) $\dfrac{41}{7} = \dfrac{4100}{700} \approx \dfrac{585.7}{100} = 5.857$

[*Note:* $4100 \div 7 \approx 585.7, 700 \div 7 = 100.$]

(5) $\dfrac{43}{65} = \dfrac{4300}{6500} \approx \dfrac{66.15}{100} = 0.6615$

(6) $\dfrac{11}{542} = \dfrac{11000}{542000} \approx \dfrac{20.2}{1000} = 0.0202$

EXERCISES

1. Write a decimal for each of the following numbers. Some of your answers will be approximations.

(a) $\dfrac{17}{50}$ (b) $\dfrac{3}{50}$ (c) $\dfrac{12}{200}$ (d) $\dfrac{24}{600}$

(e) $\dfrac{11}{25}$ (f) $\dfrac{12}{400}$ (g) $\dfrac{41}{200}$ (h) $\dfrac{41}{300}$

(i) $\dfrac{41}{700}$ (j) $\dfrac{11}{30}$ (k) $\dfrac{17}{90}$ (l) $\dfrac{412}{2000}$

(m) $\dfrac{131}{500}$ (n) $\dfrac{46}{250}$ (o) $\dfrac{217}{3000}$ (p) $\dfrac{4672}{6000}$

(q) $\dfrac{72}{13}$ (r) $\dfrac{1}{13}$

2. Since $7 \times 14 = 98$, $\frac{1}{7} = \frac{14}{98}$ and 0.14 is a good approximation for $\frac{1}{7}$. Use the facts that $7 \times 142 = 994$, $7 \times 1428 = 9996$, and $7 \times 14,285 = 99,995$ to express $\frac{1}{7}$ approximately in *thousandths, ten thousandths,* etc. Can you prove that each of these approximations is less than $\frac{1}{7}$?

3. Use the fact that

$$\dfrac{1}{7} = \dfrac{15}{105} = \dfrac{143}{1001} = \dfrac{1429}{10003} = \dfrac{14286}{100002}$$

to give other decimal approximations of $\frac{1}{7}$. Can you prove that each of these approximations is more than $\frac{1}{7}$?

4. Use the method of Exercise 2 to get decimal approximations to $\frac{1}{13}$ which are slightly less than $\frac{1}{13}$. [*Hint:* $13 \times 7 = 91$, $13 \times 76 = 988$, $13 \times 769 = 9997$.]

5. Use the method of Exercise 3 to get decimal approximations to $\frac{1}{13}$ that are slightly more than $\frac{1}{13}$.

6. Use the method above to get decimal approximations to $\frac{1}{17}$ that are slightly less than $\frac{1}{17}$; slightly more than $\frac{1}{17}$.

7. Use the information given in Exercises 2 through 6 to compute close decimal approximations in *hundredths* to the following rational numbers.

(a) $\frac{2}{7}$ (b) $\frac{3}{7}$ (c) $\frac{4}{7}$ (d) $\frac{5}{7}$ (e) $\frac{3}{13}$

(f) $\frac{7}{13}$ (g) $\frac{2}{17}$ (h) $\frac{5}{17}$ (i) $\frac{10}{13}$ (j) $\frac{13}{17}$

In the chapter on rational numbers we saw that we could think of the rational number a/b as the number $a \div b$. For example, since $7 \times \frac{41}{7} = 41$, it follows that

$$41 \div 7 = \tfrac{41}{7}$$

It turns out that thinking about the rational number $\frac{41}{7}$ as $41 \div 7$ is very helpful in expressing it as a decimal. This suggests a method, closely related to the one used in the six examples given before the last list of exercises, for computing a decimal for $\frac{41}{7}$. Simply divide 41 by 7:

$$
\begin{array}{r}
5.857 \\
7\overline{)41.000} \\
35 \\
\overline{60} \\
56 \\
\overline{40} \\
35 \\
\overline{50} \\
49 \\
\overline{1}
\end{array}
$$

EXERCISES

Compute decimals for the following rational numbers, using any method you wish.

1. $\frac{5}{6}$ 2. $\frac{3}{24}$ 3. $\frac{15}{13}$ 4. $\frac{27}{48}$

5. $\frac{7}{12}$ 6. $\frac{13}{90}$ 7. $\frac{17}{51}$ 8. $\frac{34}{250}$

9. $\frac{6}{19}$ 10. $\frac{17}{500}$ 11. $\frac{23}{16}$ 12. $\frac{16}{23}$

13. $\frac{57}{18}$ 14. $\frac{31}{11}$ 15. $\frac{1}{37}$ 16. $\frac{29}{43}$

6. SCIENTIFIC NOTATION

The following exercises review some of the important ideas relating to decimals and at the same time introduce a new idea.

EXERCISES

Write each of the following, using decimal notation.

1. $(6 \times 100) + (2 \times 10) + (5 \times 1) + \left(2 \times \frac{1}{10}\right)$

2. $(7 \times 10) + \left(4 \times \frac{1}{10}\right)$

3. $(8 \times 1000) + (7 \times 100) + (6 \times 1) + \left(2 \times \frac{1}{100}\right)$

4. $(8 \times 10 \times 10 \times 10) + (7 \times 10 \times 10) + (6 \times 1)$
$$+ \left(2 \times \frac{1}{10} \times \frac{1}{10}\right)$$

5. $(6 \times 10 \times 10) + (3 \times 10) + \left(2 \times \frac{1}{10} \times \frac{1}{10}\right)$

6. $(8 \times 10 \times 10 \times 10) + \left(6 \times \frac{1}{10} \times \frac{1}{10} \times \frac{1}{10} \times \frac{1}{10}\right)$

In working the above exercises, you used the following multiplication facts:

$$10 \times 10 = 100$$
$$10 \times 10 \times 10 = 1000$$
$$10 \times 10 \times 10 \times 10 = 10,000$$
$$10 \times 10 \times 10 \times 10 \times 10 = 100,000$$

We can think of 100 as the product of 2 factors ten, 1000 as the product of 3 factors ten, 10,000 as the product of 4 factors ten, etc. Let us agree to use the following abbreviation:

Instead of 10×10, we write 10^2.

Instead of $10 \times 10 \times 10$, we write 10^3.

Instead of $10 \times 10 \times 10 \times 10$, we write 10^4.

$$\overbrace{\text{Instead of } 10 \times 10 \times \cdots \times 10}^{\text{12 factors}}, \text{ we write } 10^{12}.$$

Each of the numbers 10^2, 10^3, 10^4, etc., is called a *power of ten*. We call 10^2 the *second* power of ten, 10^3 the *third* power of ten, etc. We agree that $10^1 = 10$. We also write 3^2 for 3×3, etc.

EXERCISES

1. Write the usual symbol for each number below.

   (a) 10^4 (b) 10^6 (c) 6^2

   (d) 4.321×10^3 (e) 5.236×10^2 (f) 4^3

   (g) 2^4 (h) 8×2^3 (i) 0.0042×10^4

   (j) $10^3 \times 10^2$ (k) $10^3 + 10^2$

   (l) $10^3 + 10^2 + 10^1 + 1$ (m) $10^5 \div 10^3$

   (n) $10^5 \div 10^1$ (o) $10^4 - 10^3$

2. Use our new notation to write each number below as the product of a whole number and a power of ten.

   (a) 200,000   (b) 3,000,000,000

   (c) 5,000,000   (d) 34,000,000,000,000

3. Write the usual symbol for each number below.

   (a) $10^2 \times (10^2 + 10^1 + 3)$

   (b) $10^3 \times \left[(3 \times 10^2) + (5 \times 10^1) + 7 + \left(4 \times \dfrac{1}{10} \right) \right]$

   (c) $10^5 \times \left(\dfrac{1}{10^2} + \dfrac{4}{10^3} + \dfrac{7}{10^4} \right)$

   (d) $10^6 \times \left(\dfrac{3}{10^2} + \dfrac{7}{10^4} \right)$

4. Draw a number line like the one shown in Fig. 13–3 and mark dots to show the following numbers: 3^1, 3^2, 3^3, and 3^4.

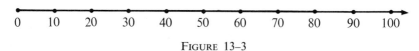

FIGURE 13–3

5. On the number line for Exercise 4, show

   (a) $3^3 + 3^1$ [Note that $3^3 + 3^1$ is *not* 3^4.]

   (b) $3^3 \times 3^1$

The weight of the earth, in pounds, is a very large number. It is approximately

$$12,000,000,000,000,000,000,000,000$$

SCIENTIFIC NOTATION   235

We may abbreviate this number as 1.2×10^{25}. This abbreviated form is called *scientific notation*. A number is written in scientific notation if it is expressed as the product of some number between 1 and 10 and a power of ten.

Example 1. Write 3420 in scientific notation.

Solution. Since 3.42 is between 1 and 10 and $3.42 \times 1000 = 3420$, we write 3420 as 3.42×10^3.

Example 2. Write 92,000,000 (the number of miles from earth to sun) in scientific notation.

Solution. Since 9.2 is between 1 and 10 and $9.2 \times 10,000,000 = 92,000,000$, we write 92,000,000 as 9.2×10^7.

Example 3. We write 10,000,000,000 as 1×10^{10} rather than as 10×10^9.

EXERCISES

1. Which of the following products are written in scientific notation?
   (a) 4.32×10^3 (b) 53×10^2 (c) 0.0034×10^5
   (d) 1.14×10^4 (e) 4.3×10^2 (f) 10×10^4
   (g) 0.01×10^4 (h) 6.537×10^6 (i) 34×10^3

2. Convert those numbers in Exercise 1 which are not in scientific notation to this notation.

3. Represent the following numbers in scientific notation. Each number is a distance measured in feet.
   (a) 555 (height of Washington Monument)
   (b) 1472 (height of Empire State Building)
   (c) 29,000 (height of Mt. Everest)
   (d) 21,000,000 (length of Missouri-Mississippi River)
   (e) 41,800,000 (diameter of earth)
   (f) 4,567,000,000 (diameter of sun)
   (g) 9,100,000,000,000 (diameter of giant star)
   (h) 31,000,000,000,000,000 (distance light travels in one year)
   (i) 132,000,000,000,000,000 (distance to nearest star beyond our sun)
   (j) 3,000,000,000,000,000,000,000 (diameter of Milky Way)
   (k) 31,000,000,000,000,000,000,000 (distance to extragalactic nebulae)
   (l) 100,000,000,000,000,000,000,000,000 (possible radius of universe, according to Einstein)

4. Represent the following numbers in scientific notation. All are weights of the given objects in pounds.
   (a)   An average man: 160
   (b)   A large elephant: 9000
   (c)   A whale: 300,000
   (d)   The atmosphere of the earth: 11,400,000,000,000,000,000
   (e)   The sun: 4,000,000,000,000,000,000,000,000,000,000,000
   (f)   The Milky Way: 6,000 . . . forty-one zeros
   (g)   The universe (according to Einstein) 400,000 . . . fifty-two zeros

5. Represent the following numbers in scientific notation. These are times, in seconds, of the given periods.
   (a)   Hour: 3600
   (b)   Day: 86,400
   (c)   Month: 2,550,000
   (d)   Solar year: 31,556,900
   (e)   Average life of man: 2,000,000,000
   (f)   Revolution of Pluto about the sun: 7,820,000,000
   (g)   Half-life of radium-226: 52,400,000,000
   (h)   One rotation of the Milky Way: 6,000,000,000,000,000
   (i)   Estimated life of the sun: 100,000,000,000,000,000
   (j)   Half-life of uranium-238: 142,000,000,000,000,000

6. Represent the following velocities (given in miles per hour) in scientific notation.
   (a)   A sprinter: 21.7
   (b)   A race horse: 42.3
   (c)   An eagle: 120
   (d)   A gas engine plane: 500
   (e)   Sound traveling through air at standard conditions: 742
   (f)   A rocket engine plane: 4000
   (g)   An artificial satellite: 18,000
   (h)   Escape velocity of rocket from earth: 25,000
   (i)   Earth in orbit around the sun: 66,600
   (j)   Hydrogen electron around its nucleus: 4,700,000
   (k)   Light: 669,600,000

Chapter 14

PERCENT
NOTATION

1. INTRODUCTION

We have studied the use of both fraction symbols and decimal symbols for rational numbers. In this chapter we shall use *percent symbols*. The word *percent* comes from the Latin phrase *per centum*, which means *by the hundred*. Of course, you are familiar with the percent sign "%." The following definition explains how this sign is used.

If a is any rational number, then

$$a\% = a \times \frac{1}{100}$$

You should think of 3% as $3 \times \frac{1}{100}$. Of course, you can write this in any of the ways shown below:

$$3\% = 3 \times \frac{1}{100} = 3 \times 0.01 = \frac{3}{100} = 0.03$$

Using the above definition, we see that

$$\tfrac{1}{2}\% = \frac{1}{2} \times \frac{1}{100} = 0.5 \times 0.01$$

$$50\% = 50 \times \frac{1}{100} = 50 \times 0.01$$

$$200\% = 200 \times \frac{1}{100} = 200 \times 0.01$$

$$0.1\% = \frac{1}{10} \times \frac{1}{100} = 0.1 \times 0.01$$

$$2.3\% = \frac{23}{10} \times \frac{1}{100} = 2.3 \times 0.01$$

You must be able to replace quickly and correctly any percent symbol by the fraction and decimal symbols which stand for the same number. Give the decimals for the five percent expressions above, as well as the fractions in lowest terms.

EXERCISES

1. Write each of the numbers (a) through (f) as a product of two numbers in *fraction* notation. Do not simplify.

(a) 7% (b) $\frac{2}{3}\%$ (c) $3\frac{1}{2}\%$ (d) 451%

(e) $\frac{1}{20}\%$ (f) 3.4%

2. Write each of the percents given below as a product of two numbers in *decimal* notation. Do not simplify.

(a) 4% (b) $\frac{2}{10}\%$ (c) 3.1% (d) $12\frac{1}{2}\%$

(e) $\frac{1}{4}\%$ (f) 321%

3. Write each of the numbers (a) through (n) as a *fraction* in lowest terms.

(a) 25% (b) 12% (c) 20% (d) 50%

(e) 100% (f) 2% (g) $\frac{1}{2}\%$ (h) 0.1%

(i) $12\frac{1}{2}\%$ (j) $6\frac{1}{4}\%$ (k) 240% (l) $33\frac{1}{3}\%$

(m) $66\frac{2}{3}\%$ (n) $16\frac{2}{3}\%$

4. Write each of the percents given below as a *decimal* in hundredths.

(a) 11% (b) 24% (c) 7% (d) 123%

(e) 150% (f) 1% (g) 426% (h) 3%

5. Write each of the numbers of Exercise 4 as a decimal in thousandths.

6. What does it mean to say that 100% of the students in the class have television sets in their homes?

2. USING PERCENT NOTATION

Percent notation is used a great deal because it is often convenient to speak of *hundredths.*

You should think of the use of decimal and percent notation as an attempt to *simplify* the use of fractions. When we use fraction notation, we consider fractions whose denominators may be 1, 2, 3, 4, 5, 6, 7, ... When we use decimal notation, we use only special fractions whose denominators are

$$1, 10, 100, 1000, \ldots$$

When we use percent notation, we think in terms of the denominator 100 *alone.*

We summarize these statements as follows.

With fraction notation, we think of halves, thirds, fourths, fifths, . . . ;

with decimal notation, we think of tenths, hundredths, thousandths, . . . ;

and with percent notation, we think of hundredths only.

Comparing fraction, decimal, and percent notations

The following examples illustrate the use of percent notation.

Example 1. *About 6% of the students were excused from classes for a field trip.*

This means that about $\frac{6}{100}$ of all the students were excused. If there are about 500 students in the college, then about $\frac{6}{100} \times 500$, or 30, went on the trip. When we hear that 6% took the trip, we think:

About six students out of each hundred made the trip.

Example 2. *Our state sales tax amounts to 3%.*

This means that for each sale, 0.03 of the price is added on as a tax. For example, if the price is $20, then since

$$0.03 \times 20 = 0.60$$

the total cost is $20.60. When we hear that a sales tax is 3%, we think:

For each dollar, an extra 3 cents will be added on as tax.

Example 3. *The salesman gets a 20% commission on his sales.*

This means that $\frac{20}{100}$ of the money collected by the salesman is paid to him as part of his wages. For example, if in one week, the salesman has sales amounting to $650, his commission is

$$\frac{20}{100} \times \$650 = \$130$$

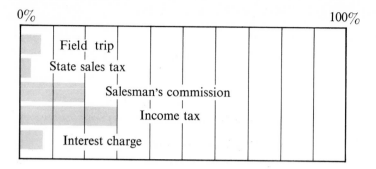

When we hear that a salesman receives a 20% commission we think:

Out of each $1 *that is received from sales, he gets* 20 *cents.*

Example 4. *Income taxes will take* 30% *of my income this year.*

When we hear this we know that for each $1 earned, 30 cents will have to be paid in taxes.

Example 5. *A bank charges* 7% *interest per year on money borrowed.*

This means that 0.07 of the money borrowed from the bank for one year must be paid as an interest charge. If the sum of $2000 is borrowed at this rate for one year, the interest is

$$0.07 \times \$2000 = \$140$$

Hence the borrower must repay $2140 at the end of the year. When we hear of a 7% interest rate we should think:

If $100 *is borrowed at this rate for one year, then at the end of the year the* $100 *plus* $7 *interest must be repaid.*

EXERCISES

1. One cent is $\frac{1}{100}$ of a dollar. What percent of a dollar is
   (a) a dime? (b) a quarter? (c) a nickel? (d) a half-dollar?

2. Use the diagram in Fig. 14–1 to answer the following questions.
   (a) What percent of the squares is marked 1? marked 2? marked 3? marked 4? marked 5?
   (b) What percent of the squares is not marked?
   (c) What percent of all the squares is in the top two rows?

1	1	1	1	1															
2	2	2	2	2	2	2													
3	3	3	3	3	3	3	3	3	3	3	3	3	3						
4																			
5	5	5	5	5	5	5	5	5	5	5	5	5	5	5	5	5	5	5	5

FIGURE 14–1

3. On a test, a student answered correctly 87 problems out of 100. What percent grade did he receive?

4. Draw a circle and shade 75% of it.

5. If a player made 46 free throws out of 100 attempts, what percent of his tries was successful?

6. On a spelling test, a student spelled correctly 46 words our of 50. What was his grade in percent?

7. A player made 24 free throws out of 50 attempts. What percent of his tries was successful?

8. What percent is a quarter of a half-dollar? a dime of a half-dollar? a nickel of a dime? a nickel of a half-dollar? a nickel of a quarter? a dime of a quarter?

9. A player made 13 free throws out of 25 attempts. What percent of his tries was successful?

10. What percent of the bar in Fig. 14–2 is shaded? unshaded?

FIGURE 14–2

11. A school has an enrollment of 483 children. About 5% were absent. How many were absent?

12. During one month, a salesman has sales of $2400. Besides his salary, he receives a 4% commission on sales. What is his commission for the month?

13. A man with an income of $44,000 in one year paid about 32% of this income in taxes. Approximately how much did he pay in taxes?

14. During a basketball game the players on one team scored on almost exactly 23% of their field-goal attempts. If they shot 74 times from the field, how many field goals did they score?

15. If the state sales tax is 2%, what tax is charged upon a $17.40 purchase? What would be the total cost of a chair priced at $76?

16. A man borrowed $7400 for one year at an interest rate of 6% per year. At the end of the year he repaid the loan of $7400, together with the interest. What total amount did he pay?

17. Using your ruler, draw a line 5 in. long. Draw a second line 60% as long as the first one.

18. The Missouri-Mississippi system is the longest river in the world; its length is about 106% of the length of the Amazon River, which is 4000 mi long. What is the length of the Missouri-Mississippi?

19. Draw a square $\frac{5}{4}$ in. on each side. Draw lines dividing it into 25 small squares. Label 16% of these squares 1; label 40% of the squares 2; label 12%, 3 and the remainder, 4.

20. The population of Florida was about 1,900,000 in 1940. By 1950 the population had increased about 46%. During the next 10 years the increase over the 1950 population was almost 80%. Compute the approximate 1950 and 1960 populations.

3. USING PERCENT IN ESTIMATING

An important skill is the ability to estimate accurately what percent one number is of another number. In doing this, we use the facts listed below.

$$1000\% = 1000 \times 0.01 = 10$$
$$100\% = 100 \times 0.01 = 1$$
$$10\% = 10 \times 0.01 = 0.1$$
$$1\% = 1 \times 0.01 = 0.01$$
$$0.1\% = 0.1 \times 0.01 = 0.001$$
$$0.01\% = 0.01 \times 0.01 = 0.0001$$

Hence

$$1000\% \text{ of } 2145 = 10 \times 2145 = 21{,}450$$
$$100\% \text{ of } 2145 = 1 \times 2145 = 2145$$
$$10\% \text{ of } 2145 = 0.1 \times 2145 = 214.5$$
$$1\% \text{ of } 2145 = 0.01 \times 2145 = 21.45$$
$$0.1\% \text{ of } 2145 = 0.001 \times 2145 = 2.145$$
$$0.01\% \text{ of } 2145 = 0.0001 \times 2145 = 0.2145$$

EXERCISES

1. If N is 4123, how much is
   (a) 1000% of N?   (b) 100% of N?
   (c) 10% of N?   (d) 1% of N?
   (e) 0.1% of N?   (f) 0.01% of N?

2. If 10% of N is 31.28, how much is
   (a) 1% of N?   (b) 100% of N?
   (c) 0.1% of N?   (d) 1000% of N?

3. If 0.1% of A is 0.034, how much is
   (a) 1% of A?   (b) 100% of A?
   (c) 0.01% of A?   (d) 1000% of A?

4. If 5% of B is 4.25, how much is
   (a) 1% of B?   (b) 10% of B?   (c) B?
   (d) 0.1% of B?   (e) 0.01% of B?   (f) 0.001% of B?

5. If 3% of C is 23.4, how much is
   (a) 30% of C?   (b) 300% of C?   (c) 0.3% of C?
   (d) 0.03% of C? (e) 1% of C?   (f) C?

6. Estimate the percent that the shaded area of each bar in Fig. 14–3 represents.

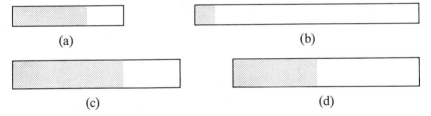

FIGURE 14–3

7. Estimate the percent represented by each shaded area in Fig. 14–4.

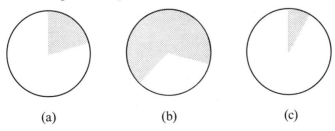

FIGURE 14–4

8. A student was asked what percent 18.5 is of 18,543. He estimated that it is about 10%. This is a very poor estimate. Which of the following estimates would you choose?

   (a) 1%   (b) 0.1%   (c) 0.01%

9. Which of the following estimates for 0.1% of 4021 do you consider the best?

   (a) 4000   (b) 40   (c) 4   (d) 0.4

10. Which is the best estimate for 200% of 1214?

   (a) 20%   (b) 2%   (c) 0.2%   (d) 0.02%

11. Assuming that $N = 514.21$, give estimates for

   (a) 200% of N (b) 20% of N (c) 2% of N (d) 0.2% of N

12. Pick the number that most nearly tells what percent 43,500 is of 141,358.

   (a) 300%   (b) 30%   (c) 3%   (d) 0.3%

13. Pick the number that is most nearly 2% of 79,534.12.

   (a) 160,000   (b) 16,000   (c) 1600   (d) 160

14. The 1960 census for a certain city showed that its population was approximately 85,400. If about 9000 people in this city are more than 65 years old, about what percent of the population is over 65?

15. If approximately 35,000 people living in the city of Exercise 14 are under 25 years old, about what percent of the population is under 25?

16. Approximately what percent of the inhabitants of the city of Exercise 14 are between the ages of 25 and 65?

17. Estimate the following percents of 40,325.46.

   (a) 10%   (b) 1%   (c) 20%   (d) 2%
   (e) 200%   (f) 0.1%   (g) 0.4%   (h) 0.01%
   (i) 0.03%   (j) 0.002%

18. Estimate what percent each of the following numbers is of 140,857.

   (a) 140,000   (b) 1400   (c) 14
   (d) 140   (e) 1.4   (f) 1,400,000

19. Show that 1% is $\frac{1}{10}$ of 10%. If 10% of a number N is 85.2, what is 1% of N?

20. Show that 1% is $10 \times 0.1\%$. If 0.1% of a number N is 4036, what is 1% of N?

4. RELATIONS BETWEEN FRACTION, DECIMAL, AND PERCENT NOTATIONS

As we saw earlier, it is easy to change from percent notation to fraction or decimal notation. For example, we may change $3\frac{2}{5}\%$ to a fraction as shown below:

$$3\tfrac{2}{5}\% = \tfrac{17}{5} \times \tfrac{1}{100} = \tfrac{17}{500}$$

and to a decimal as follows:

$$3\tfrac{2}{5}\% = 3.4 \times .01 = 0.034$$

It is easy to express decimals as percents. For example, since

(a) $0.34 = 34 \times 0.01$,   we have $0.34 = 34\%$
(b) $2.1 = 210 \times 0.01$,   we have $2.1 = 210\%$
(c) $0.015 = 1.5 \times 0.01$,   we have $0.015 = 1.5\%$
(d) $0.00043 = 0.043 \times 0.01$,   we have $0.00043 = 0.043\%$

EXERCISES

1. Express each number below in percent notation.
   (a) 0.43   (b) 0.07   (c) 0.001   (d) 1.31
   (e) 42.1   (f) 0.014   (g) 0.00056   (h) 742

2. Express each number below in fraction notation.
   (a) 21% (b) 2.1% (c) 0.21%
   (d) $13\frac{1}{3}\%$ (e) $33\frac{1}{3}\%$ (f) 7.5%

3. Express each number in Exercise 2 in decimal notation. For (d) and (e) give approximate values to the nearest hundredth and also to the nearest thousandth.

The arithmetic involved in changing from fraction notation to percent notation is sometimes difficult, but the ideas are simple. The example below shows one method of executing the change.

Example. Change $\frac{11}{17}$ to percent notation.

Solution. If we knew the number p, such that

$$\frac{11}{17} = p \times \frac{1}{100}$$

then we would know that $\frac{11}{17} = p\%$. (Why?)

But $\frac{11}{17}$ is the *product* of the two factors p and $\frac{1}{100}$; so

$$p = \tfrac{11}{17} \div \tfrac{1}{100}, \qquad p = \tfrac{11}{17} \times 100, \qquad p = 64\tfrac{12}{17}$$

and hence

$$\tfrac{11}{17} = 64\tfrac{12}{17}\%$$

A general (easy) rule for writing any number in percent notation is given below.

$$r = p\% \quad \text{if} \quad r = p \times \frac{1}{100}$$

Therefore

$$p = r \div \frac{1}{100} = r \times 100$$

To express any number r as a percent, multiply r by 100

Looking at this formula in another way, we may also say the following:

Since

$$\frac{11}{17} = \left(\frac{11}{17} \times 100\right) \times \frac{1}{100}$$

it follows that

$$\frac{11}{17} = \left(\frac{11}{17} \times 100\right)\%$$

Since

$$r = (r \times 100) \times \frac{1}{100}$$

it follows that

$$r = (r \times 100)\%$$

Examples.

$$\frac{1}{2} = \left(100 \times \frac{1}{2}\right)\% = 50\%$$

$$0.03 = (100 \times 0.03)\% = 3\%$$

$$\frac{3}{8} = \left(100 \times \frac{3}{8}\right)\% = 37\tfrac{1}{2}\%$$

$$\frac{1}{400} = \left(100 \times \frac{1}{400}\right)\% = \frac{1}{4}\%$$

EXERCISES

1. Use the equations below to express the given fractions as percents. Study each equation carefully to make sure that it is a true statement.

(a) $\dfrac{3}{4} = \left(\dfrac{3}{4} \times 100\right) \times \dfrac{1}{100} = \left(\dfrac{3}{4} \times 100\right)\%$

(b) $\dfrac{2}{3} = \left(\dfrac{2}{3} \times 100\right)\%$ (c) $\dfrac{3}{2} = \left(\dfrac{3}{2} \times 100\right)\%$

(d) $\dfrac{7}{50} = \left(\dfrac{7}{50} \times 100\right)\%$ (e) $\dfrac{12}{7} = \left(\dfrac{12}{7} \times 100\right)\%$

(f) $\dfrac{2}{1} = \left(\dfrac{2}{1} \times 100\right)\%$ (g) $\dfrac{1}{200} = \left(\dfrac{1}{200} \times 100\right)\%$

(h) $10 = (10 \times 100)\%$ (i) $\dfrac{1}{1000} = \left(\dfrac{1}{1000} \times 100\right)\%$

2. Use the equations below to express the given decimals as percents.

(a) $0.13 = (0.13 \times 100) \times 0.01 = (0.13 \times 100)\%$
(b) $0.005 = (0.005 \times 100)\%$
(c) $1.26 = (1.26 \times 100)\%$
(d) $31.4 = (31.4 \times 100)\%$

3. Determine the number p in each equation below.

(a) $\dfrac{3}{5} = p\%$ (b) $\dfrac{11}{50} = p\%$ (c) $\dfrac{7}{8} = p\%$

(d) $\dfrac{4}{3} = p\%$ (e) $\dfrac{1}{400} = p\%$ (f) $\dfrac{25}{4} = p\%$

4. Determine p in each equation below.

(a) $0.31 = p\%$ (b) $0.031 = p\%$
(c) $3.1 = p\%$ (d) $0.0031 = p\%$
(e) $0.215 = p\%$ (f) $4.02 = p\%$
(g) $0.125 = p\%$ (h) $0.2925 = p\%$

5. Use the fact that $a/100 = a\%$ to determine p in each equation.

(a) $\dfrac{41}{100} = p\%$ (b) $\dfrac{24}{200} = p\%$

(c) $\dfrac{7}{50} = p\%$ (d) $\dfrac{11}{25} = p\%$

(e) $\dfrac{11}{20} = p\%$ (f) $\dfrac{16}{10} = p\%$

(g) $\dfrac{210}{1000} = p\%$ (h) $\dfrac{63}{300} = p\%$

You will remember that each rational number is the quotient of two whole numbers:

$$4 = 4 \div 1, \qquad \frac{17}{11} = 17 \div 11, \qquad \frac{a}{b} = a \div b$$

This fact provides us with a way of changing from fraction to percent notation. We simply divide the numerator of the fraction by the denominator, getting a decimal for the fraction, and then change from the decimal to percent notation. Two examples are given below.

Example 1. Change $\frac{11}{8}$ to a percent.

$$11 \div 8 = 1.375 \qquad or \qquad 137.5\%$$

Example 2. Change $\frac{11}{37}$ to a percent.

$$
\begin{array}{r}
0.29 \\
37{\overline{\smash{\big)}\,11.00}} \\
\underline{74} \\
360 \\
\underline{333} \\
27
\end{array}
$$

$$\frac{11}{37} = 29\frac{27}{37}\% \qquad \text{or about} \qquad 30\%$$

EXERCISES

Use the method above to change the following fractions to percents.

1. $\frac{1}{4}$ 2. $\frac{1}{8}$ 3. $\frac{1}{16}$ 4. $\frac{1}{32}$ 5. $\frac{1}{3}$

6. $\frac{1}{6}$ 7. $\frac{1}{12}$ 8. $\frac{1}{24}$ 9. $\frac{3}{5}$ 10. $\frac{3}{10}$

11. $\frac{3}{20}$ 12. $\frac{3}{40}$ 13. $\frac{1}{7}$ 14. $\frac{1}{14}$ 15. $\frac{5}{9}$

16. $\frac{5}{18}$ 17. $\frac{3}{11}$ 18. $\frac{13}{12}$ 19. $\frac{23}{14}$ 20. $\frac{86}{73}$

5. PROBLEM SOLVING

Of course, problems stated in the language of percent are no different from problems stated in terms of fractions or decimals. In all such problems we are working with rational numbers. The percent symbols can always be replaced by fraction or decimal symbols if we wish. For many problems, it is helpful to write number sentences (*equations*).

Example 1. $N = 30\% \times 421$.

This is an equation you might write for the problem:

> If there are 421 students in a college and *about* 30% of them are freshmen, approximately how many students are freshmen?

Solving for N, we have

$$N = 0.3 \times 421 = 126.3$$

There are about 126 freshmen.

Example 2. $240 = 30\% \times N$.

You might write the above equation for the problem:

> There are 240 freshmen in a college. This is *exactly* 30% of the total enrollment. How many students are there in the college?

Solving for N, we have

$$240 = 0.3 \times N$$
$$N = 240 \div 0.3 = 800$$

There are *exactly* 800 students in the college.

Example 3. $836 = p\% \times 2200$.

You might write this equation for the problem:

> If there are approximately 2200 students in a college and if 836 of these are sophomores, about what percent of the total are sophomores?

Solving for p, we have

$$836 = p \times \frac{1}{100} \times 2200$$
$$836 = p \times 22$$
$$p = 836 \div 22 = 38$$

Approximately 38% of the students are sophomores.

EXERCISES

Write equations for the following problems and solve.

1. In a crowd of 513 people about 30% are men. Approximately how many men are in the group? Can you say *exactly* how many men are in the group?

2. If a person spends about 18% of his income for rent and his monthly income is $740, approximately how much does he spend each year for rent?

3. In a shipment of 35,000 light bulbs approximately 0.13% were defective. About how many were defective?

4. The ball player leading the American League in batting has made hits about 34.2% of the number of times he has been at bat (that is, his *batting average* is 0.342). If he has been 360 times at bat, how many hits has he made?

5. A taxpayer reports that last year taxes were $3560, amounting to about 20% of his income. Approximately what was his income last year?

6. There are 189 tenth-grade students in a high school. This is exactly 35% of the total enrollment in grades 10, 11, and 12. How many students are there in the school?

7. The specific gravity of a certain block of wood is approximately 0.80. This means that the weight of the wood is about 80% of the weight of the same volume of water. If a cubic foot of this wood weighs about 50 lb, what is the approximate weight of a cubic foot of water?

8. The length of a yardstick is approximately 91.44% of the length of a meter stick. Compute the approximate length of a meter stick in inches.

9. If a child spent 45¢ out of an allowance of $1.50, what percent of his allowance has he spent?

10. In a time interval of 15 min what percent of the distance around the clock is traced out by the minute hand?

11. In a group of 350 students in freshman class, 154 had a brother or sister who had not yet started college. What percent of these freshmen students had a brother or sister of pre-college age?

12. An antifreeze solution for a radiator contains 6.4 qt of alcohol and 9.6 qt of water. What percent of this mixture is alcohol?

13. Make up a verbal problem to go with each equation below:

   (a) $N = 40\% \times 850$ (b) $200 = 40\% \times N$
   (c) $1 = p\% \times 16$ (d) $440 = p\% \times 1760$

The two examples below describe rather complicated problem situations. Study these examples carefully.

Example 1. $C + (20\% \times C) = 3600$.

You might write this equation for the problem:

> An automobile dealer bought a car from a factory and sold it to a customer for $3600. If the dealer added on 20% of the factory price before selling the car, what was the factory price paid by the dealer?

Solving for C, we obtain

$$C + (0.2 \times C) = 3600$$
$$(1 \times C) + (0.2 \times C) = 3600 \qquad \text{(Using the property of 1)}$$
$$1.2 \times C = 3600 \qquad \text{(Using the distributive principle)}$$
$$C = 3600 \div 1.2 = 3000$$

The dealer paid the factory $3000.

Example 2. $P - (20\% \times P) = 38.40$.

You might write this equation for the problem:

> During a sale a merchant marked the prices of all his suits down 20%. One suit was sold for $38.40. What was the price of this suit before the sale?

Solving for P, we have

$$P - (0.2 \times P) = 38.40$$
$$(1 \times P) - (0.2 \times P) = 38.40$$
$$0.8 \times P = 38.40$$
$$P = 38.40 \div 0.8 = 48$$

The price of the suit before the sale was $48.

When working problems like Example 2 you might reason as follows.

> If 20% of the price marked on the suit is subtracted, then the new price will be 80% of the original price.

In symbols:

$$P - (20\% \text{ of } P) = (100\% \times P) - (20\% \times P) = 80\% \times P$$

EXERCISES

1. Make up a problem to correspond to each equation below. Do not solve any of the equations.
    (a) $N = 22\% \times 350$ (b) $400 = 25\% \times N$
    (c) $652 = p\% \times 2140$ (d) $A + (30\% \times A) = 60{,}432$
    (e) $B - (30\% \times B) = 43.40$

2. Write an equation for each problem below. Do not solve any of these equations.
    (a)   The area of Texas is about 270,000 square miles. This is about 48% of the area of Alaska. What is the area of Alaska?

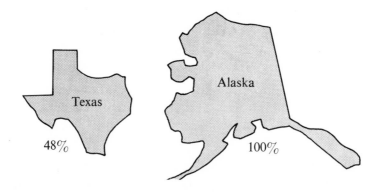

    (b)   If a child has spent 35% of his $8 monthly allowance, how much has he spent?
    (c)   A ball player has made 163 hits in 521 times at bat. What percent of his times at bat has he made hits?
    (d)   During 20 years the population of one state increased about 88%. At the end of this 20-year period the population was 3,500,000. What was the population at the beginning of the period?
    (e)   A housewife estimates that 45% of her weekly budget is spent on rent and food. Each week she has left about $65 for other living expenses. Approximate her budget.

3. Solve the following equations:
    (a) $N = 20\% \times 215$ (b) $46 = 20\% \times N$
    (c) $48 = p\% \times 160$ (d) $R + (50\% \times R) = 900$
    (e) $R - (40\% \times R) = 450$

Write equations and work the following problems.

4. In a certain city, about 32% of all people are between the ages of 20 and 40. If the city population is approximately 143,000, about how many people are between these ages?

5. One day on a trip a family drove 440 mi. The next day they drove 20% farther. How far did they drive on the second day?

6. Taxes collected in one city for the year 1960 were about $450,000. This was almost exactly 80% more than had been collected 10 years before. What was, approximately, the amount of taxes collected in 1950?

7. A basketball team had 31 free-throw attempts during a game. They scored 21 points on free throws. What percent of their free throws were made? (Round off you answer to the nearest whole percent.)

8. In one year, a large corporation had earnings after taxes of $35,200,000. These earnings are about 6.4% of the value of the corporation. Approximately what is the value of the corporation?

9. A man borrowed $2400 for one year at an interest rate of 6.5% per year. How much interest did he owe at the end of the year?

10. A businessman borrowed a sum of money from a bank at an interest rate of $5\frac{1}{2}$% per year. At the end of the year he owed $687.50 in interest. How much had he borrowed?

11. A real estate salesman received a commission of 5% on the sale of an estate.

    (a) If the estate sold for $62,400, what was his commission?
    (b) If his commission was $2174, what was the selling price of the estate?
    (c) If after deducting the commission paid to the salesman the owners of the estate received $79,800, what commission did the salesman earn?

12. The price of a suit is reduced $6 during a sale.

    (a) If this is a 10% reduction on the regular price, what is the sales price?
    (b) If the regular price is $75, express the reduction as a percent of the regular price.

Chapter 15

APPLICATIONS OF
RATIONAL NUMBERS

1. INTRODUCTION

The rational number system is the number system used by the business world. Decimal and percent notation is used more than fraction notation. In this chapter we shall study a few of the chief practical uses of rational numbers. You should remember many of the facts given in this chapter, especially those which concern relationships between different units of weight and measurement. We cannot possibly study all the ways in which rational numbers are used in the everyday world, but if you have a good understanding of decimal and percent notation, you will find that you can usually solve the problems of arithmetic that you meet in practice.

2. MEASUREMENT OF LENGTH

Measurements of length as small as 1/1,000,000,000,000 of an inch can be made by present-day methods. The distance from the earth to one of the *nearest* stars, Sirius, is about 50,000,000,000,000 miles. It is difficult to imagine how scientists measure such small and large

distances. Between the very large and the very small, there are lengths which we measure every day by more ordinary methods. To understand the use of rational numbers in all types of measurement, we first study the usual methods of measurement.

The majority of the people on our globe use a system of weights and measures known as the *metric system*. The metric system is well suited to decimal notation. In this system, relationships between different units of weight and length are very simple. In the *English system* of weights and measures used in the United States, relationships between different units are much more complicated. Compare the tables of linear measures given below.

English system	*Metric system*
12 inches = 1 foot	10 millimeters = 1 centimeter
3 feet = 1 yard	10 centimeters = 1 decimeter
16.5 feet = 1 rod	10 decimeters = 1 meter
5280 feet = 1 mile	100 centimeters = 1 meter
	1000 meters = 1 kilometer

In these two systems consider the problem of changing from smaller units to larger ones.

$$1610 \text{ millimeters} = 161.0 \text{ centimeters} = 16.1 \text{ decimeters} = 1.61 \text{ meters}$$
$$161 \text{ inches} = 13\tfrac{5}{12} \text{ feet} = 4\tfrac{17}{36} \text{ yards}$$

Explain why the metric system is easier to use than the English system.

Explain the use of the prefixes in the metric system, according to the meanings given below.

milli-	means	**one-thousandth**
centi-	means	**one-hundredth**
deci-	means	**one-tenth**
kilo-	means	**one thousand**

The units of length in the English system developed over many years. Our term *mile* owes its origin to the Romans, who ruled England for 1000 years. A Roman pace (Fig. 15–1) was a double step. The Roman phrase, *mille passum*, means *one thousand paces*. From the word "mille," which means 1000, we get our word "mile."

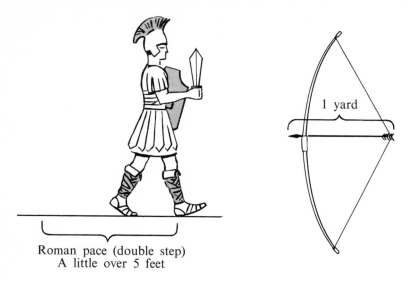

Roman pace (double step)
A little over 5 feet

FIGURE 15–1

FIGURE 15–2

It is said that one of the English kings ordered his officers to go to a certain church on Sunday and line up the feet of the first 16 men who came out of church so that the toe of each man just touched the heel of the man in front. The length of these 16 feet was divided into 16 equal parts, and one of these parts became the official English foot.

The yard is also said to owe its origin to an English king. It was the distance from the king's nose to the end of his thumb when his arm was stretched out, or the length of his arrows (Fig. 15–2).

Many old units of measure are related to parts of the body. The length of the second joint of your index finger is nearly one *inch* (Fig. 15–3). Horses are measured by *hands*. A hand is the width of the palm, roughly 4 inches. If you spread your thumb and little finger as far apart as possible, you have a unit of measure called a *span*, about 9 inches. A biblical unit of measure, the *cubit*, is the distance from the elbow to the tip of the fingers, about 18 inches. Goliath is said to have a height of "6 cubits and a span." Sailors still use a measure called a *fathom*, about 6 feet. This was originally the distance between outstretched fingertips, with the arms stretched out to the side at shoulder height.

English units of weight and measurement are of ancient origin. The metric system, however, was established in France at about the time of the French revolution, shortly before 1800. It was agreed that a

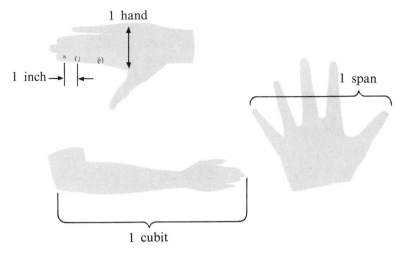

FIGURE 15–3

meter should be *one-ten millionth of the distance from the North Pole to the equator.* Of course, exact measurement of this distance was impossible; however, the length of an arc of 10 degrees on the meridian passing through Paris was carefully measured, and as a result of this measurement the length of the meter was determined (Fig. 15–4).

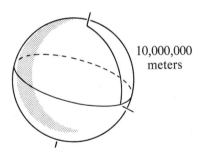

10,000,000
meters

FIGURE 15–4

A platinum bar, known as the *International Meter,* is deposited at the International Bureau of Weights and Measures in Paris. Three fine lines are engraved near each end of the bar. The meter is defined to be the distance between the middle lines of the two groups at a temperature of 0° centigrade. Today our own units of measure are actually defined in terms of this standard meter. You should know the following approximate relationships between our units and the

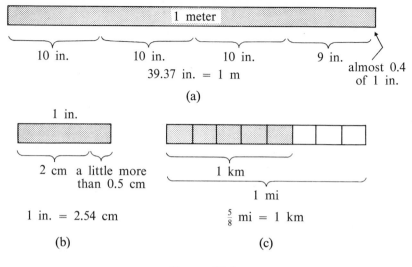

FIGURE 15-5

metric units of measurement. The scale drawings in Fig. 15–5 describe these relationships.

EXERCISES

1. Actually, 1 in. is a little more than 2.54 cm. Multiply 39.37 by 2.54, and interpret this result.

2. Show that 1 meter is a little more than 3.28 ft and a little more than 1.09 yd.

3. The Olympic Games include a 100-meter dash rather than a 100-yd dash. Would you expect the record time for 100 meters to be more or less than the record for 100 yd?

4. If a runner can run the 100-yd dash in 10 sec, about how long would you expect it would take him to run the 100-meter dash?

5. Express 742 in. as feet in decimal notation; express 742 cm in meters.

6. Express 23,735 ft in decimal notation as miles; express 23,735 meters in kilometers.

7. Express 387 yd in inches; 387 meters in centimeters.

8. How many millimeters are there in an inch? Is a millimeter less than $\frac{1}{16}$ in.? less than $\frac{1}{32}$ in.?

9. How many inches are there in a mile? centimeters in a kilometer?

10. Approximately how many centimeters are there in a foot? in a yard?

11. Assume that the circumference of the earth is 25,000 mi and that 1 km is $\frac{5}{8}$ meter. Compute the distance in meters from the North Pole to the equator.

12. Suppose that the *metric system*, with the prefixes, milli, centi, deci, kilo, were used to measure *time*.

 (a) Which would be longer, a deciday or an hour?

 (b) About how many centidays would it take to make an hour?

 (c) Which would be longer, a milliday or one minute?

 (d) What do you think would be meant by a decimilliday? a centimilliday? Find how many seconds each of these would be.

 (e) Assuming that the day starts at midnight, tell what time would be indicated by 0.375 of a day.

 (f) Draw a decimal clockface.

13. What might be meant by a kilobuck? a centibuck?

3. MEASUREMENT OF TIME

Units of time used in science are the *millisecond* and the *microsecond* (one-millionth of a second). It takes a fly about a millisecond to beat its wings once. A bullet fired from a rifle passes through the rifle barrel in about a millisecond.

A high-speed rifle bullet will travel a distance equal to the width of one of the letters printed in this book in a microsecond. An electron beam will travel from its source to the screen in a TV-tube in about one-tenth of a microsecond. The time it takes an atom to emit visible light is about one-thousandth of a microsecond. An air molecule spins around its axis once in about one-millionth of a microsecond. An electron revolves around the proton in a hydrogen atom in about one-billionth of a microsecond.

4. MEASUREMENT OF WEIGHTS AND VOLUMES

Weight can be measured so closely that even the pencil mark needed to dot the "i" in "metric" is easily weighed. In the metric system, units of weight are closely related to units of length. A cubical container 10 centimeters on an edge holds 1000 cubic centimeters of water. The weight of this volume of water at a temperature of 4° centigrade is the basic metric unit of weight, the *kilogram*. This volume of water, 1000 cubic centimeters, is referred to as a *liter*. A liter is a little larger than our United States *quart*. A quart of water weighs about 2 pounds, and so we see that a kilogram is more than 2 pounds.

The prefix "kilo-" means "one thousand," and the weight of one cubic centimeter of water is called one *gram*. The following tables describe metric and United States units of weight and volume.

UNITS OF WEIGHT

United States	*Metric*
437 grains = 1 ounce	1000 milligrams = 1 gram
16 ounces = 1 pound	1000 grams = 1 kilogram
2000 pounds = 1 ton	1000 kilograms = 1 metric ton

UNITS OF VOLUME

United States	*Metric*
2 pints = 1 quart	1000 cubic centimeters = 1 liter
4 quarts = 1 gallon	1000 milliliters = 1 liter

We now discuss relationships between the different units which you should remember. The diagrams in Fig. 15–6 and in the figures that follow may prove helpful.

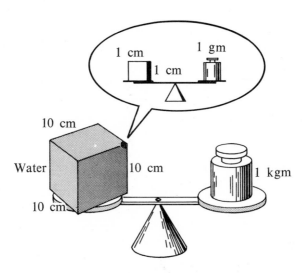

FIGURE 15–6

(a) If each dot in Fig. 15–7 represents 1 *gram*, then the complete collection of dots represents 1 *pound*.

FIGURE 15–7

(b) If each dot below represents $\frac{1}{10}$ of a pound, then the complete collection of dots represent 1 *kilogram* (1 kgm).

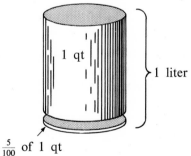

10 tenths or 1 pound

1 pound

0.2 of 1 pound

(c) Figure 15–8 illustrates the relationship between 1 quart (qt) and 1 liter.

1 qt

1 liter

$\frac{5}{100}$ of 1 qt

FIGURE 15–8

We can now summarize the following relationships.

$$1 \text{ pound} = 454 \text{ grams}$$
$$2.2 \text{ pounds} = 1 \text{ kilogram}$$
$$1.05 \text{ quarts} = 1 \text{ liter}$$

EXERCISES

1. A box of soap flakes contains 14.5 ounces (oz) of soap. Express this quantity as a part of a pound in (a) fraction notation, (b) decimal notation, (c) percent notation.

2. A box of soap flakes contains 412 grams (gm) of soap. Express this quantity as part of a kilogram (kgm) (a) in fraction notation, (b) in decimal notation, (c) in percent notation.

3. An empty bucket weighs 3 lb. It will hold 3 gallons (gal) of water. One pint of water weighs 1 pound. What is its weight when it is filled with water?

4. A bucket holds 14.2 liters. Its weight (empty) is 1.6 kgm. What is its weight when it is filled with water?

5. A quantity of 1 gal 3 qt is poured from a container holding 2 gal 2 qt and 1 pt of water. How many pints remain?

6. From a container holding 9 liters of water, a quantity of 3476 cm³ of water is poured. How many cubic centimeters (milliliters) remain?

7. How many kilograms are there in 11, 430 gm?

8. How many metric tons are there in 11,430 kgm?

9. Approximately how many pounds are there in a metric ton? How many kilograms are there in a United States ton?

10. Which is the larger unit of weight, the grain or the gram?

11. Approximately how many ounces are there in a kilogram?

12. Approximately how many grams are there in an ounce?

13. Approximately how many cubic centimeters are there in a quart? in a pint?

14. Diamonds are weighed in *carats*. A carat is $\frac{1}{5}$ gm. About how many 1-carat diamonds would it take to make up a pound?

15. A diamond crystal called the great Cullinan crystal was found in a mine in South Africa in 1905. In the rough, this crystal weighed 3106 carats. Express this weight in grams; in ounces.

16. The largest gem cut from the great Cullinan crystal is a diamond known as the *Star of South Africa*. Its weight is 530.2 carats. Express this weight in ounces.

5. MEASUREMENT OF TEMPERATURES

In the United States, temperatures are usually measured on a *fahrenheit* (F) scale. Countries using the metric system of weights and measures ordinarily use the *centigrade*, or celsius (C) scale. On the fahrenheit scale, the temperatures at which water freezes and boils are 32° and 212°, respectively. On the centigrade scale, these temperatures

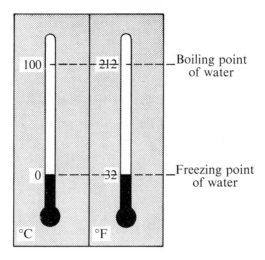

are 0° and 100°. We may write

$$0°C = 32°F$$
$$100°C = 212°F$$

to show that the centigrade temperatures given on the left are the same as the fahrenheit temperatures on the right side of the equals sign. From the relation between the two temperature scales we see that a change in temperature of 180 degrees F is the same as a change of 100 degrees C. Just as the meter is a greater unit of length than is the yard, so the centigrade degree is a greater unit than the fahrenheit degree. We see that a change of 10°C in temperature is the same as a change of 18°F. A change of 1°C is the same as a change of $1.8°(\frac{9}{5}°)$F.

EXERCISES

1. Express a temperature of 50°C in degrees fahrenheit.
2. Express temperatures of 10°, 20°, 30°, 40°C as fahrenheit temperatures.
3. Show that a temperature of 14°F is the same as a temperature of −10°C (10 below zero, centigrade).
4. Express a temperature of 40° below zero centigrade as a fahrenheit temperature.
5. In one year, in the central part of the United States, the lowest temperature was −20°F and the highest was 100°F. Express these temperatures on the centigrade scale.
6. The temperature of the surface of the sun has been estimated to be approximately 6000°C. Show that this is approximately 11,000°F.

7. Temperatures at the interior of the sun have been estimated to be as high as 20,000,000°C. Express this temperature on the fahrenheit scale.
8. Scientists believe that the lowest possible temperature is −273°C, that is, 273° below zero. Show that this is approximately −460°F.

6. INTEREST

One of the chief uses of percent notation is to describe the amount of *interest* charged for borrowed money. This amount depends upon the *principal*, the *term* of the loan, and the *interest rate* charged. For example, if a bank charges an interest rate of 6% per year, a customer who borrows $100 for 1 year would, at the end of the year, pay back to the bank the $100 principal plus an interest payment of 6% of $100, or $6:

$$0.06 \times 100 = 6$$

The total amount paid would be $106. If the money were borrowed for only 6 months at the rate of 6% per year, the interest charge would be only $3, and the borrower would repay $103.

We can make the following statement.

Amount repaid = amount borrowed plus interest

Amount = principal + interest

$$A = P + I$$

Sometimes the interest rate is described in terms of a month rather than a year. For example, if a customer borrowed $100 for one year at an interest rate of 2% per month, his interest charge would be $2 for each month. How much interest would he have to pay for the whole year? How much would the borrower pay back at the end of the year?

You should think of an interest rate of 6% per year as a charge of $6 for each $100 borrowed for one year. An interest rate of 2% per month is a charge of $2 for each $100 borrowed for one month. In other words,

---

Interest = principal × rate × time

$$I = P \times R \times T$$

EXERCISES

1. A man borrowed $100 from a bank for one year and at the end of the year repaid $108.

    (a) How much of this amount of $108 is his interest payment?

    (b) If he had repaid the loan at the end of 6 months, how much money would he have paid to the bank?

    (c) What yearly rate of interest did the bank charge him for his loan?

2. Find the interest on $500 borrowed for 6 months

    (a) at a rate of 7% per year,

    (b) at a rate of 1% per month.

3. A man borrows $3000 from a bank for 90 days (one-quarter of a year). His interest rate is 5% per year. At the end of this time he pays the bank $2000. How much does he still owe?

4. A man borrowed a certain amount of money for 1 year at a rate of 6% per year. At the end of the year he owed, besides the principal, $30 interest. How much money had he borrowed?

5. A man borrowed a certain sum of money at 2% per month. At the end of 5 months he repaid the loan and interest by paying $275. How much money had he borrowed?

6. A sum of $1200 was borrowed at an interest rate of 7% per year. At the end of a certain length of time the principal and interest were repaid by a total payment of $1228. For how long was the money borrowed?

7. One man borrowed a certain sum of money and, when he repaid it, he owed $80 interest. A second man borrowed twice as much money for twice as long a time at the same interest rate. How much interest did the second man pay?

8. One man borrowed a certain sum of money at 6% per year and, when he repaid the loan, he paid $90 interest. A second man borrowed the same amount of money for the same length of time, but his interest charge was only $75. What was the interest rate charged to the second man?

9. Two men borrowed the same amount of money, one for 9 months at 8% per year and the other for 12 months at 5% per year. Which man had to pay more interest?

10. A man loaned $10,000 for a certain length of time at a certain rate, and was repaid $12,000 in interest and principal. If he now loans the $12,000 for the same length of time and at the same rate, what is the total interest that his $10,000 will have earned him?

Gas	Tax	Total
$19\frac{9}{10}$	10	$29\frac{9}{10}$
$20\frac{9}{10}$	10	$30\frac{9}{10}$
$21\frac{9}{10}$	10	$31\frac{9}{10}$
$22\frac{9}{10}$	10	$32\frac{9}{10}$
$23\frac{9}{10}$	10	$33\frac{9}{10}$

7. TAXES

Many states raise money from sales taxes. Business firms that sell directly to the public (restaurants, gasoline stations, department stores, etc.) are required to pay a certain percent of their sales in taxes to the state. For example, if the state sales tax is 3% and a grocery store has sales of $50,000 during a year, then the amount of tax paid to the state is

$$0.03 \times \$50,000 = \$1500$$

Of course, the store collects tax on each sale it makes to a customer. If your grocery bill is $14.20 before the tax is computed, the tax is

$$0.03 \times \$14.20 = \$.426$$

You would pay $.43 in sales tax, and your total bill would be

$$\$14.20 + \$.43\,(\text{tax}) = \$14.63$$

EXERCISES

1. The retail price of a chair is $52.40. The state sales tax is 3%. What is the total cost of the chair?

2. Mr. Jones estimates that each year he buys from stores in his state items that would cost $6500 without a sales tax. If the state sales tax is 2%, how much sales tax does he pay on these purchases?

3. The state sales tax is $2\frac{1}{2}$%. A large grocery store collects $2500 in sales taxes in one month. Approximately what were the grocery sales for this month?

4. If you buy $11.87 worth of groceries (before tax) and the sales tax is 4%, what is your total bill?

The Federal government obtains most of its revenue from income taxes. Each person who receives an income of more than $600 a year must file a tax return. Taxpayers are entitled to certain deductions for medical expenses, support of dependents, state and local taxes, donations to charities, etc. For example, suppose that a taxpayer with five dependents earned $7000 in one year. If for each dependent he is entitled to a $600 exemption, then he does not have to pay any tax on

$$5 \times \$600 = \$3000$$

of his income.

Suppose that this taxpayer can also make the following deductions from his income.

Donations to church and charities	$ 250
Interest paid on borrowed money	200
Taxes on his home and personal property	190
Sales tax paid on retail purchases	200
Medical expenses	160
Total	$1000

Then his total deductions are $4000, and hence he is taxed only on the remainder of his income:

$$\$7000 - \$4000 = \$3000$$

We say that his *taxable income* is $3000. His federal tax is 20% of this amount:

$$20\% \times \$3000 = \$600$$

During the year the taxpayer's employer has deducted $584.60 from his paycheck for federal taxes; thus, when he mails in his tax return to the Collector of Internal Revenue, he sends a check only for the balance:

$$\$600 - \$584.60 = \$15.40$$

EXERCISES

1. Is it wise to deduct taxes in advance from an employee's paycheck?
2. Mr. Stevens has an income of $10,000. He is married and has two children. His deductions for taxes, interest, donations, etc., are $1800. What is his taxable income?
3. If a taxpayer's taxable income is more than $400 and less than $8000, he pays a tax of 20% on the first $4000 of taxable income and 22% on the balance. What federal income tax must Mr. Stevens pay?

4. Mr. Stevens' payroll deductions for federal income taxes amounted to $1150 during the year. How much additional tax must he pay?

5. A wealthy business man earns in one year a total taxable income of $50,000. On the first $44,000 of this $50,000 he must pay $16,760 in taxes, and on the remainder he is taxed at a rate of 59%. What is the total income tax that he must pay?

6. A lawyer has had an income of $12,000 during the year. His medical and dental expenses have been $650. Not all of this is deductible. He can only deduct medical expenses in excess of 3% of his income. What deduction can he make for these expenses?

7. If your taxable income were $1,000,000 for one year, your income taxes would be $235,480 on the first $300,000 of this income, and you would be taxed at a rate of 91% on the remaining $700,000. What would be your total income tax? What would be left from the $1,000,000 for personal expenditures?

8. ARITHMETIC IN BUSINESS

A great deal of mathematics is needed to keep business records. A business man who operates a retail store buys goods from a whole-sale firm, or perhaps directly from a factory. Let us call what he pays for these goods his *cost of goods*, or simply *cost*. To sell these goods, he must hire salesmen, pay rent on his store, etc. Let us call the money he spends for these purposes his *expenses*. If he is to be a successful businessman, the sale of his goods to customers must return him all the money (his cost and expenses) invested and, in addition, permit him to make a *profit*. If we call the money received from customers *sales*, we have the following equation:

$$\textbf{Sales} = \textbf{cost of goods sold} + \textbf{expenses} + \textbf{profit}$$
$$S = C + E + P$$

For example, suppose that a grocery store sells $800,000 worth of groceries in one year. The wholesale cost of these groceries was $520,000. The expenses of operating the store were $260,000. Then $800,000 = $520,000 + $260,000 + P$; the store's profit is $20,000.

If the store had a value of $200,000, then, since the profit, $20,000, is 10% of $200,000, we would say that the store owners made a profit of 10% on their investment.

EXERCISES

1. A clothing store buys 500 shirts for $1.60 each. Each shirt is sold for $2.50. The store owner estimates that the expenses incurred in selling the shirts amount to $.70 per shirt. What is his total profit on the 500 shirts?

2. A department store rings up sales of $70,500 during one month. The goods sold were bought for $48,700. Expenses of operating the store for the month are $20,600. What is the profit made?

3. If, for the store of Exercise 2, expenses had been $25,000, the store would have lost money. How much would this loss be?

4. A grocery chain builds a new store at a cost of $120,000. During the first year this store earns a profit of $9600. Express this profit as a percent of the cost of building the store.

5. To build the store of Exercise 4 the grocery chain borrowed $120,000 from a bank at an interest rate of 5% per year. How much interest did the chain have to pay at the end of the year? For this particular year, how much money did the grocery chain actually make by building the store?

6. A businessman sells television sets. Sets of one size cost him $125 each, and he sells them for $180. He estimates that the expenses connected with the sale of these sets are about $35 for each set. How much profit does he make on the sale of 60 of these sets?

7. A merchant has sales of $140,000 during a year. His expenses amount to 25% of sales. The wholesale cost of goods sold is $110,000. Did the merchant make a profit during the year? How much was his profit or loss?

8. An article is marked to sell for $8. Its price is reduced 15%, and it is sold at this new price. If the article cost the merchant $5.40 and if selling expenses are about $1 each, did the merchant make a profit? How much was his profit or loss?

9. INSURANCE

There are many different kinds of insurance: life insurance, fire insurance, health insurance, theft insurance, etc. Insurance plans make it possible for a group of people to *share a risk*.

Mr. Smith had bought a home for $16,000. He wished to purchase fire insurance. He found that he could insure his house for $15,000 and that the cost for this insurance would be $45 per year. The insurance agent told him that this cost is based on an *insurance rate* of 30¢ per year for each $100 of protection. Mr. Smith bought the insurance and was given an *insurance policy*, a written agreement between himself and the insurance company. The $45 that he paid for the first year's insurance is called his yearly *insurance premium*.

EXERCISES

1. What would Mr. Smith's yearly premium have been if the insurance rate had been 40¢ per year for each $100 of insurance?
2. Find the yearly premium on a fire insurance policy for $20,000, given that the insurance rate is 36¢ per $100 of insurance; the rate is $3.40 per $1000 of insurance; the insurance rate is $\frac{1}{2}\%$; $\frac{3}{8}\%$.
3. Mr. Jones had a home valued at $14,000. He could not insure it for its full value, but he did insure it against fire for 80% of its value at a yearly rate of 0.4%. What was his yearly premium for protection against fire?
4. A house valued at $22,000 was insured for 75% of its value. The contents of the house were also insured for $5000. If the rate was $3.10 per year for each $1000 of insurance, what annual premium was paid?
5. An insurance company which charged a yearly insurance rate of $3.20 per $1000 for fire insurance found that, on the average, each year two houses burned out of each thousand that the company insured. Let us assume that, on the average, each house is insured for $15,000. What profit does the insurance company make on each group of 1000 houses that it insures?

Most heads of families carry life insurance. Of course, very few people can afford to pay for enough life insurance to give their families complete protection. For example, Mr. Green works in a factory and earns $7500 per year. He has $15,000 of life insurance. He and his wife have three small children, aged 2, 5, and 9. If he should die, the insurance would provide only $7500 per year for two years. Even if he carried as much as $50,000 of life insurance, this amount would be less than what Mr. Green earns in 7 years. For his life insurance, Mr. Green pays a yearly premium of $24.17 per $1000. What total amount does he pay each year for life insurance?

Mr. Green bought this life insurance policy when he was 30 years old. He will pay the yearly premium each year as long as he lives, and upon his death, his family will receive $15,000.

In addition to his life insurance, Mr. Green's family is also protected by social security insurance. If he should die, his wife will receive social security payments of about $200 per month until the youngest child is 18 years old.

EXERCISES

1. If Mr. Green dies at age 70, he will make 40 payments on his life insurance policy. What total amount of money will he have paid to the insurance company?

2. If Mr. Green dies at age 70, will the insurance company lose money on his policy?

3. Mr. Smith bought a 30-payment life insurance policy for $20,000 at age 35. His yearly premium is $32.11 per $1000 of insurance. After making 30 payments upon this policy, he will quit paying the premiums, and then, at the time of his death, his family will receive the $20,000 life insurance. If Mr. Smith dies at age 75, how much will he have paid the company in premiums? How much will he have paid if he dies after making 15 payments? How can an insurance company afford to sell this kind of insurance?

10. APPROXIMATE MEASUREMENT

Measurements of lengths are not completely accurate. When we measure a string with a ruler and give its length as $5\frac{7}{8}$ in., it is not likely that the end of the string fell exactly upon the $\frac{7}{8}$-in. mark. When we use a ruler we usually try to measure to the "nearest mark." If our ruler were marked in eighths, then to give the length as $5\frac{7}{8}$ would imply that the end of the string fell closer to the $5\frac{7}{8}$-in. mark than to either the $5\frac{6}{8}$-in. or the 6-in. mark. We would say that we have rounded off the length to the nearest eighth of an inch.

String being measured

Even in counting we round off. If we read that the population of a city is 120,000 we can be quite sure that this is not the exact population. We would expect that the population has been rounded off, to perhaps the nearest 10,000. The count recorded by the census takers might have been 118,473.

When approximations are given it is important that we know the accuracy of these approximations. If a length is given as 31 ft *to the nearest foot*, we assume that the length is somewhere between 30 ft 6 in. and 31 ft 6 in. If the length is given as 31 ft *to the nearest inch*, we assume that the length is somewhere between 30 ft $11\frac{1}{2}$ in. and 31 ft $\frac{1}{2}$ in. If the population of a city is given as 120,000 *to the nearest* 10,000, we assume that the population is between 115,000 and 125,000. If the population is given as 120,000 *to the nearest* 1,000, we assume that the population is between 119,500 and 120,500.

EXERCISES

1. The population of a city according to a census is 57,482. Give the population rounded off to
   (a) the nearest hundred
   (b) the nearest thousand
   (c) the nearest ten thousand.

2. The length of an object is given to the nearest thousandth of an inch as 3.146 in. Give the length rounded off to the nearest
   (a) hundredth of an inch
   (b) tenth of an inch
   (c) inch
   (d) half-inch
   (e) quarter-inch
   (f) eighth-inch
   (g) sixteenth-inch.

3. The population of a city is given as 430,000 to the nearest 10,000. Between what two numbers do you assume the population lies?

4. The length of a wire is given as $7\frac{3}{8}$ in. to the nearest $\frac{1}{8}$ in. Between what two numbers do you assume the length lies?

5. If the length of a wire is given as $7\frac{3}{8}$ in. to the nearest $\frac{1}{16}$ in, between what numbers does the length probably lie?

Chapter 16

INTRODUCTION
TO GEOMETRY

1. INTRODUCTION

The first great mathematicians were the Greek geometers who lived more than 2000 years ago. The geometry that they developed is still taught in schools throughout the world. Students of geometry today study many of the same ideas that students of Greek geometry studied.

Many of the simple practical uses of geometry were known to the Egyptians and Babylonians at a time when Greek civilization was still in its early stages. These ancient people in Babylon and Egypt used their knowledge of geometry as they surveyed their fields, built the great pyramids, and studied the stars. We owe our way of measuring angles to the Babylonians.

But it was the Greeks who *organized* geometrical knowledge and showed that it is possible to build all of geometry upon a *few basic ideas*. In this chapter our main purpose is to describe how the Greek mathematicians looked upon the world of geometry.

2. IMAGINARY WORLD OF GEOMETRY

The great progress that the Greeks made was largely due to their ability to think of geometrical objects as *ideas* and not as *physical things*. To an Egyptian a geometrical fact was something to be discovered by measurement. To an Egyptian surveyor, a straight line was a rope that he and his helper had stretched tight. To a Greek geometer, however, the rope was only a crude imitation of a line. The Greek mathematicians felt that in the real world there are no lines that are exactly straight. Only in the imaginary world of geometry are there actually such things as points and lines.

How large is a point? Look at the *dot* below. The dot is a *physical object* because we can *see* and touch it. Is it a point? Doesn't it look too large to be called a point?

•

Imagine erasing half of this dot, then half of the remainder, then half

273

of the second remainder. Imagine continuing this process on and on. Will what we have left ever seem just the right size for a point? No matter how small any *physical object* may be, it is far too large for a point. *Let us just erase the dot entirely and imagine that there are points which have no size at all.* This is what the Greek mathematicians did.

How wide is a line? Look at the streak of ink below. Is it part of a straight line?

Suppose that measurement shows that this ink streak is about one-hundredth of an inch wide. Now, one-hundredth of an inch is ten-thousandths of an inch. Imagine erasing part of the streak, leaving it the same length but only one-tenth as wide. The width of the streak remaining would be one-thousandth of an inch.

Let's erase nine-tenths of this streak. Now we have left a streak one ten-thousandth of an inch wide. But this streak is still far too wide for a "line."

It is clear that no matter how often we imagine removing part of our ink streak, what we have left is too wide to be called a line. *We might as well erase the entire streak and imagine a straight line with no width at all.* This is what the Greek geometers did.

How thick is a plane? A sheet of paper makes us think of a plane. But 500 sheets of thin paper make a stack about one inch high. So each sheet is about two-thousandths of an inch thick. Imagine slicing one of these sheets into 10 sheets, each of which is one-tenth as thick as the original sheet. Then the thickness of one of these new sheets is about 2/10,000 in. This is much too thick for a plane. Slice off a thinner sheet whose thickness is only one-tenth as much. We do not seem to be making any progress. It does not seem that we are ever going to get something as thin as a plane should be. Let us copy the Greeks. *Wad up the paper and throw it away and imagine a plane that has no thickness at all.*

To play the fascinating game called geometry, we have to agree that *points, lines,* and *planes* are things that we only think about. We cannot really draw them—we can only draw *pictures* that remind us to think about them. But this is not so very strange. Did you ever see or touch a number? We look at sets of objects and invent *ideas* that we call numbers; in much the same way we look at objects in the physical world and invent *ideas* that we call *points, lines, planes, angles, circles, cubes,* etc.

The drawings that you make in this chapter will suggest many interesting properties of the imaginary world of geometry. But you should always remember that the drawings themselves do not *prove* anything. They only serve to remind us of the *ideas*, point, line, plane. Before we can prove that anything is true about our imaginary geometry world, we must agree in advance upon some of the properties of our imaginary points and lines.

EXERCISES

1. One student *marks* two chalk dots on a blackboard. A second student uses a meter stick to draw a streak of chalk connecting the two dots. We erase his "line," and a third student uses the meter stick to draw a second streak of chalk connecting these two "points." Do you think that these two students drew their streaks of chalk in *exactly* the same positions? In the physical world, how many different "straight" streaks of chalk can be drawn through two chalk "points" on the blackboard?

2. Now *think* of two points in your imaginary world of geometry. Think of a straight line connecting these two points. Is there any other straight line that connects these points?

3. One student *marks* two dots of chalk on the board. He labels them *A* and *B*. A second student marks a dot between the two dots and labels his dot 1. A third student marks a dot between dots 1 and *B* and labels his dot 2. A fourth student marks dot 3 between 2 and *B*. Can this process of marking dots between dots go on forever, without dots overlapping? In the real world, how many *different* dots of chalk can be placed between two chalk dots one inch apart?

4. *Think* of two points in your imaginary world of geometry. Call them *A* and *B*. *Think* of a point 1 between *A* and *B*; a point 2 between 1 and *B*; a point 3 between 2 and *B*. Can this process of thinking of points between points go on forever in your geometry? No matter what two points you choose in your mathematical geometry, how many points are there between them?

5. One student *marks* two dots on the blackboard. He labels one of them *A* and the other *B*. A second student goes to the board with a compass and *draws* a streak of chalk that looks like a "circle" with center at *A*. This "circle" goes through "point" *B* (Fig. 16–1). We erase his circle, and a third student draws a "circle" with center at *A* and containing *B*. Do you think that these students drew their two streaks of chalk in

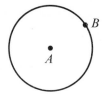

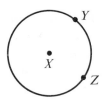

FIGURE 16–1   FIGURE 16–2

exactly the same positions? In the physical world, how many different "circles" are there with the chalk mark *A* for center and containing chalk mark *B*?

6. *Think* of two points *A* and *B* in your geometry. How many circles are there having *A* as center and containing *B*?

7. A student *marks* a spot of chalk on the blackboard and labels it *X*. He then draws a "circle" with *X* as center. He now marks two dots of chalk *Y* and *Z* on the circle (Fig. 16–2). A scientist, who can measure distances to the nearest millionth of an inch, measures the distances *XY* and *XZ*. Do you expect him to obtain the same distance for each?

8. *Think* of an imaginary circle with center *X*, and *think* of two points *Y* and *Z* on your circle. *Think* of the distances *XY* and *XZ*. Are they exactly the same? What statement can you make about all the points on a geometric circle?

These eight exercises suggest some important ideas that are used in the study of geometry. Figures 16–3 and 16–4 illustrate some of these ideas.

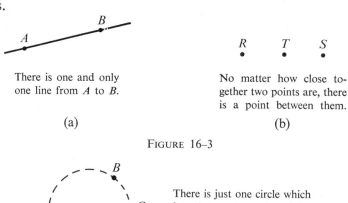

There is one and only one line from *A* to *B*.

No matter how close together two points are, there is a point between them.

(a)   (b)

FIGURE 16–3

There is just one circle which has *A* as center and contains *B*. The distances *AB* and *AC* are exactly the same.

FIGURE 16–4

By now you probably understand the purpose of this chapter. Actually, we are asking you to do, in a few days, something that was accomplished very gradually over hundreds of years by generations of mathematicians. We shall look together at things in the physical world. These physical objects will suggest to us that we invent ideas in the imaginary world of geometry. Our task is to describe these mathematical ideas clearly so that you will have a fine background for further study in geometry.

It will be helpful to make some agreements about words and pictures in geometry. We shall name *points* with capital letters, *A*, *B*, *C*, etc., and we will use *dots* to suggest that you think about our imaginary points. We shall name lines with the special small letters *l*, *m*, and *n*. If we need to name more than three lines in one problem, we shall use subscript notation and speak of lines l_1, l_2, l_3, etc. (We read these symbols as "*l* sub one," "*l* sub two," "*l* sub three," or simply as "*l* one," "*l* two," and "*l* three." We could also say, "first line," "second line," and "third line.") Since an imaginary line of geometry is really a special collection of points, we could mark a row of dots (Fig. 16–5) to suggest that a student think about a line.

FIGURE 16–5   FIGURE 16–6

Instead of drawing rows of dots, we shall picture straight lines by drawing figures such as the one shown in Fig. 16–6. The arrowheads suggest that a line is endless in both directions.

When we wish to represent just part of a line, that is, two points on a line and the points between these two points, we use a picture like the one in Fig. 16–7. Of course, there are many other points of the line between *A* and *B*. However, since we do not wish to emphasize these points, we have not marked them by dots.

FIGURE 16–7   FIGURE 16–8

Often when talking about lines in geometry, we need to single out a few special points on the lines and hence we mark these points. Do not think that just because no other dots are marked, there are no other points on the lines. Figure 16–8 shows a line and just 3 of the many points on the line.

Frequently, we speak of "line *AB*" or "line segment *AB*." Of course by *line AB* we mean the endless straight line that contains the two points *A* and *B*. By *line segment AB* we mean the set of points on line *AB* consisting of points *A* and *B* and all points between *A* and *B*. We call the points *A* and *B* the *end points* of the segment.

EXERCISES

1. Four points are shown below. Each pair of points determines a line; for example, the points *A* and *D* determine line *AD*.

    (a) Does any straight line contain 3 of these 4 points?

    (b) How many different straight lines do these points determine? That is, how many lines contain at least two of these points?

    (c) Name all the straight lines determined by these points.

2. Mark 5 points so that no line contains 3 of your points. Answer questions (b) and (c) of Exercise 1 for your set of 5 points.

3. Figure 16–9 shows three different sketches. Figure 16–9 (a) suggests that two different lines can contain the same point. We say that the two lines *intersect* in the point *A*. Do lines l_3 and l_4 intersect in a point? lines l_5 and l_6?

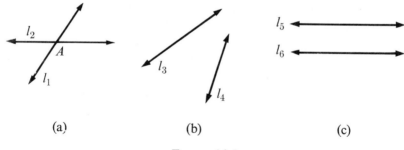

(a)   (b)   (c)

FIGURE 16–9

4. Draw a picture of two lines so that the marks you draw do not cross each other; however, draw this picture so that someone who looked at it would know that you are thinking about two lines that intersect.

5. Draw a picture to represent two lines which do not intersect in any point.

6. Look back at the figure of 4 points shown in Exercise 1.

   (a) Do lines AC and BD intersect?

   (b) Do lines AD and BC intersect?

   (c) Do lines AB and DC intersect?

   (d) Do lines AB and AD intersect? in what point?

   (e) Describe the points which are on segment AD and also on segment BC.

   (f) Is there a point that is on both line segment AD and line segment BC?

7. Figure 16–10 pictures a line l and four points A, B, C, and D on l.

FIGURE 16–10

   (a) Name all the line segments that have two of these four points for end points. How many of these segments are there?

   (b) Which is the shortest of the line segments? the longest?

   (c) Name two of these segments which have no point in common.

   (d) Name two segments which intersect in the single point C.

   (e) Describe the points which are on segment AD and also on segment BC.

   (f) How many of these segments contain the point D? the point C? the point A?

8. Figure 16–11 pictures four lines, l_1, l_2, l_3, and l_4. How many points are there that lie on two of these lines?

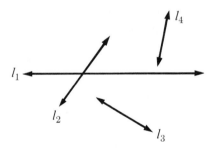

FIGURE 16–11

9. Line PQ contains the point R. Does line QR contain the point P? Draw a picture if you need to do so.

10. What can you conclude if you know that line l_1 contains points A and B and line l_2 also contains points A and B?

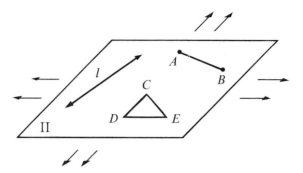

FIGURE 16–12

We live in a three-dimensional world that we call *space*, and so we imagine a world of geometry that has three dimensions also. The walls, floor, and ceiling of a room suggest the idea of *planes* in our geometrical space. We think of each plane as a boundless set of points. Figure 16–12 shows a plane, Π (Π is the symbol for the capital Greek letter pi). Of course, there are more points, lines, and triangles than we can count in plane Π. We have shown only a few of these. All the points of line *l*, line segment *AB*, and triangle *CDE* lie in plane Π. In each plane, there are many interesting special sets of points that we call lines, line segments, angles, triangles, squares, rectangles, circles, etc.

A look at an edge of a room where the floor meets a wall, or a wall meets the ceiling, or two walls come together will suggest to you that two planes can intersect in a line. Of course, the floor and ceiling suggest that two planes *can* have *no* common points. Figure 16–13 (a) and (b) shows these relationships.

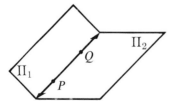

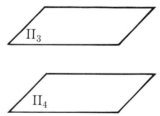

Line *PQ* lies on both Π_1 and Π_2 There is no point that is on both Π_3 and Π_4

(a)   (b)

FIGURE 16–13

EXERCISES

1. Draw a picture of a plane Π and a line *l* in plane Π.
2. Draw a picture of a line *l* and three planes Π₁, Π₂, and Π₃ each of which contains *l*.
3. Draw a picture of a plane Π and mark a point *P* on plane Π. Now draw a picture of a line *l* which contains the point *P* but does not lie in plane Π.
4. Draw a picture of a plane Π and mark 3 points *P*, *Q*, and *R* on Π. Now mark a fourth point *S not* on Π. Draw the three line segments *SP*, *SQ*, and *SR*.
5. Draw a picture of two planes Π₁, and Π₂ which do not intersect. Draw two circles of the same size, one in Π₁ and one in Π₂. Mark two points *P*₁ and *Q*₁ on the circle in Π₁. Mark two points *P*₂ and *Q*₂ on the circle in Π₂. Draw the line segments *P*₁*P*₂ and *Q*₁*Q*₂.
6. Draw two planes Π₁ and Π₂ which do not intersect. In Π₁, mark 3 points *A*₁, *B*₁, and *C*₁ which determine a triangle. In Π₂ mark 3 points *A*₂, *B*₂, and *C*₂ which determine a triangle of the same size and shape. Draw these triangles and draw line segments *A*₁*A*₂, *B*₁*B*₂, and *C*₁*C*₂.

3. PLANE FIGURES

A plane figure is a set of points all of which lie in one plane. Examples of plane figures are lines, line segments, triangles, circles, etc. To study geometry successfully, it is necessary to know the definitions for many plane figures. We shall give a few of these definitions in this section.

Although we have already given a definition of a line segment, we shall include it here again for completeness (Fig. 16–14).

It is convenient to use special symbols for lines and line segments. We agree that the symbols

$$\overleftrightarrow{AB} \quad \text{and} \quad \overline{AB}$$

stand for *line AB* and *line segment AB*, respectively.

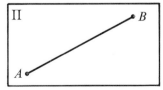

Line segment *AB* is a set of points.
The points in this set are *A* and *B*
and all points between *A* and *B*.

FIGURE 16–14

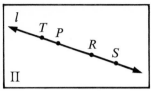

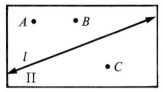

Point *P* splits *l* into two *half-lines*. Each half-line is a set of points. Points *R* and *S* are in the same half-line. Points *R* and *T* are in different half-lines. Point *P* is not in either half-line.

FIGURE 16–15

Line *l* splits Π into two *half-planes*. Each half-plane is a set of points. Points *A* and *B* are in the same *half-plane*. Points *A* and *C* are in different half-planes. Line *l* is not in either half-plane.

FIGURE 16–16

Each point *P* on a line splits the line into two *half-lines* (Fig. 16–15). Each line *l* in a plane Π splits the plane into two *half-planes* (Fig. 16–16).

Definition. *If P is a point on a line l, then the set of points consisting of P and all the points in one of the half-lines is called a* ray. *Point P is called the* end point *of the ray. If A is a point of the ray other than P, we represent ray PA by the symbol* $\overrightarrow{PA}$ *(Fig. 16–17).*

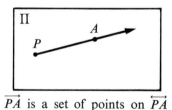

$\overrightarrow{PA}$ is a set of points on $\overleftrightarrow{PA}$

FIGURE 16–17

EXERCISES

1. Write the symbol we have agreed to use for each set of points given in Fig. 16–18 (a) through (c).

2. Use the points on the line in part (c) of Exercise 1 to name one segment and two rays.

3. What set of points is on both of the rays that you named in Exercise 2?

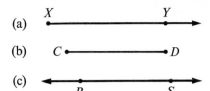

FIGURE 16–18

4. Draw a figure and label points on it to agree with each symbol given below.

(a) $\overleftrightarrow{RS}$ (b) $\overleftrightarrow{DE}$ (c) $\overline{AB}$

5. Are $\overrightarrow{PA}$ and $\overrightarrow{PB}$ shown in Fig. 16–19 the same ray or are they different rays?

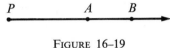

FIGURE 16–19

6. Is any segment as long as a ray?

7. Name all the rays shown in Fig. 16–20 having end point P.

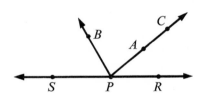

FIGURE 16–20

8. Use only the three points marked on the line in Fig. 16–21 and name as many different rays as possible.

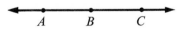

FIGURE 16–21

9. Draw a picture of two rays which
   (a) have no point in common;
   (b) have exactly one point in common;
   (c) have more than one point in common.

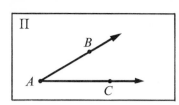

$\angle BAC$ is the set of points on
$\overrightarrow{AB}$ or $\overrightarrow{AC}$.
A is the *vertex* of $\angle BAC$.
$\overrightarrow{AB}$ and $\overrightarrow{AC}$ are sides of $\angle BAC$.

FIGURE 16–22

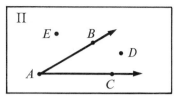

D and E are not points of $\angle BAC$.
D is in the interior of $\angle BAC$.
E is in the exterior of $\angle BAC$.

FIGURE 16–23

Definition. *Two rays that have the same end point form a figure called an* angle *(Fig. 16–22). If the rays are $\overrightarrow{AB}$ and $\overrightarrow{AC}$, we use both symbols, $\angle BAC$ and $\angle CAB$, to describe this angle. We read these symbols as "angle B, A, C" and "angle C, A, B." The common end point of the two rays is called the* vertex *of the angle. The rays are called the* sides *of the angle.   A point not on the angle is either in the interior of the angle or in the exterior of the angle (Fig. 16–23).*

EXERCISES

1. Draw an angle, $\angle RST$. Which point is the vertex of $\angle RST$? Which rays form the angle? If point A is between R and S, is A a point of the angle? If point B is between R and T, is B a point of the angle? Name a set of points to which B belongs. If point S is between points C and R, is C a point of the angle? Name a set of points to which C belongs. If point R is between S and D, is D a point of $\angle RST$?

2. Draw a picture of $\angle ABC$. Mark a point F in the interior of $\angle ABC$ and a point H in the exterior of $\angle ABC$.

3. Point C is between A and B. Is point C on ray AB? on ray BA?

4. Point B is between A and D. Is point D on ray AB? on ray BA?

5. Point A is between E and B. Is point E on ray AB? on ray BA?

6. Points A and B are on line l. They are also on line m. What conclusion can be drawn?

7. How many points has a line segment?

8. Draw a sketch of $\angle XYZ$. Draw a picture of an $\angle ABC$ so that $\overrightarrow{YX}$ and $\overrightarrow{BA}$ are the same ray but $\overrightarrow{YZ}$ and $\overrightarrow{BC}$ are different rays.

9. Draw a picture of an angle. Now draw a sketch of a second angle which contains every point of the first angle. What can you say about the two angles?

10. Points R and S are in $\overline{AB}$. Do R and S lie on $\overrightarrow{AB}$?

11. Draw a picture of two lines whose intersection is exactly one point. Mark the points you need in order to name all the angles formed by these lines, and write symbols for these angles.
12. Is it possible for two line segments to have exactly two points in common? Illustrate your answer by a sketch. Prove that your answer is correct.
13. Draw a picture illustrating that the intersection of a line and an angle can be

      (a) exactly one point   (b) two points
      (c) no point   (d) an unlimited number of points

14. Make a sketch of a line and a circle illustrating that their intersection can be

          (a) no point   (b) one point   (c) two points

Can the intersection be more than two points?

We have defined line segments, rays, and angles. We also need to define triangles.

> **Definition.** *A triangle is a special set of points consisting of three points not on any one line and the segments determined by these points. We refer to the triangle determined by three points A, B, and C as "triangle ABC" or simply as △ABC. Points A, B, and C are called* vertices *of the triangle (Fig. 16–24). A point not on the triangle is either in the interior of the triangle or in the exterior of the triangle (Fig. 16–25).*

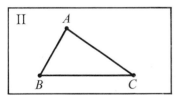

△ABC is the set of points on
$\overline{AB}$ or $\overline{BC}$ or $\overline{CA}$.
A, B, and C are the *vertices* of
△ABC.
$\overline{AB}$, $\overline{BC}$, $\overline{CA}$ are the sides of
△ABC.

FIGURE 16–24

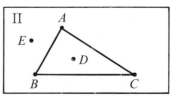

D and E are *not* points of △ABC.
D is in the *interior* of △ABC.
E is in the *exterior* of △ABC.

FIGURE 16–25

EXERCISES

1. Draw a sketch of a triangle so that
   (a) all three sides have approximately the same length;
   (b) two sides have approximately the same length and the third side is quite a bit shorter than each of these;
   (c) no two sides have equal lengths;
   (d) the length of one side is approximately the sum of the lengths of the other two sides. (Could the length of one side be the sum of the lengths of the other two sides?)

2. Can the intersection of a line and a triangle be exactly one point? exactly two points? exactly three points?

3. What can you say about a line and a triangle that have at least three points in common?

4. Draw a picture of two triangles whose intersection consists of
   (a) 1 point   (b) 2 points   (c) 3 points
   (d) 4 points   (e) 5 points   (f) 6 points
   (g) more than 6 points

5. How many triangles are shown in each part of Fig. 16–26.?

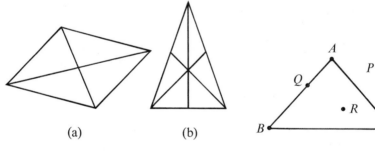

(a)   (b)

FIGURE 16–26   FIGURE 16–27

6. The following problems refer to the points shown in Fig. 16–27.
   (a) Which points are in the interior of △ABC?
   (b) Which points are in the interior of ∠C? of ∠B? of ∠A?
   (c) Which points are points of △ABC?
   (d) Which points are in the exterior of △ABC?
   (e) Which points are not in the interior of any angle of △ABC?

7. Draw a triangle and label it △RST.
   (a) Mark a point A on ∠R which is not a point of the triangle.
   (b) Mark a point B in the interior of ∠R and in the exterior of ∠S.
   (c) Mark a point C on ∠T which is in the interior of ∠S.

4. SPACE FIGURES

We can think of line segments, lines, rays, angles, and triangles as sets of points in one plane. Indeed, we can picture all these sets easily on a flat sheet of paper. However, we can imagine sets of points in space which do not lie in one plane. The pictures drawn in Fig. 16–28 suggest such sets of points. If the picture shows a closed figure (for example, a cube), only the points on the *surface* are points of the set. Other points are in the *interior* or *exterior* of the figure. Describe the sets of points pictured in Fig. 16–28.

A cube has six *faces*. Each face is a *square and the interior points of the square*. The front face of the cube shown in Fig. 16–29 is the square $ABCD$ and all points in the interior of this square. The points A, B, ... are *vertices* of the cube. The line segments AB, BC, ... are *edges*. How many vertices and edges are there in a cube?

The six faces of the cube lie in six different planes. Some pairs of these planes intersect. Other pairs do not. For example, the *planes* that contain the top and front faces intersect in the line $\overleftrightarrow{DC}$. The front and top *faces* intersect in $\overline{DC}$. The three faces, front, top, and right, intersect in the one point C. If you look in a corner of your classroom, you will see a similar intersection. The top and bottom faces do not intersect. We say that the planes that contain these two faces are *parallel* to each other. We also say that lines $\overleftrightarrow{DC}$ and $\overleftrightarrow{AB}$ are parallel to each other because they are in one plane and do not intersect. Although $\overleftrightarrow{AB}$ and $\overleftrightarrow{GF}$ do not intersect, we do not say that they are parallel to each other since they are not both in one plane. Lines AB and GF are said to be *skew* to each other.

EXERCISES

Exercises 1 through 15 refer to the cube shown in Fig. 16–29.

1. Name the two faces whose intersection is $\overline{DH}$.
2. Name two planes whose intersection is $\overleftrightarrow{DH}$. Name two parallel planes.
3. The plane of the front face contains points A, B, C, and D. Suppose that a plane contains points A, B, and C. Must it also contain D?
4. Name the three faces which intersect in F.
5. Name all lines parallel to $\overleftrightarrow{GF}$.
6. A plane contains line AE and point C, and hence it contains at least three vertices of the cube, A, E, and C. Does it contain a fourth?
7. Describe the intersection of the top face with the plane that contains $\overleftrightarrow{GF}$ and point A.

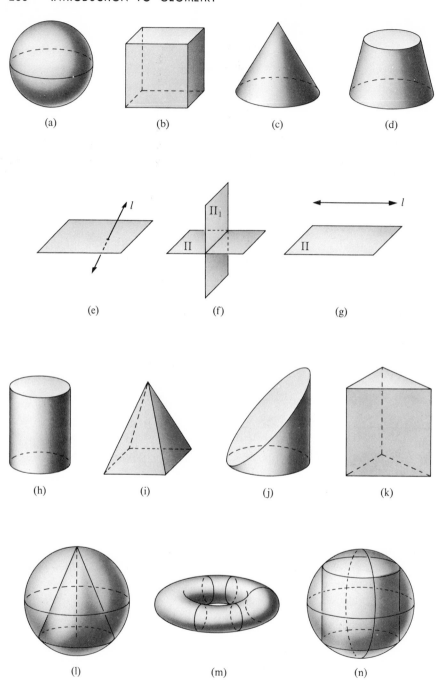

FIGURE 16–28

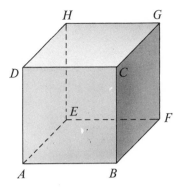

FIGURE 16–29

8. What is the intersection of the plane of Exercise 6 with the front face? with the back face? with the plane that contains the front face? with square $ABCD$? with the interior of square $ABCD$?

9. The plane that contains $\overleftrightarrow{HE}$ and $\overleftrightarrow{CB}$ intersects each of the six faces of the cube. Name each of these intersections.

10. The plane of Exercise 9 intersects all the edges of the cube except two. Name these two edges.

11. Does any one plane contain all four points H, E, D, F?

12. We know that a plane which contains points E, C, and A also contains point G. Suppose that a plane contains E, C, and a point between A and D. Does this plane contain a point of segment GF?

13. Each set of three vertices of the cube determines a triangle. For example, points A, B, C determine a triangle whose two sides AB and BC are of the same length.

    (a) Find three vertices that determine a triangle in which no two sides have the same length.

    (b) Find three vertices that determine a triangle whose three sides have the same length.

14. Which of the vertices A, B, and F is closest to G? Which is farthest from G?

15. Which of B, A, and E is closest to C? Which is farthest from C?

Each of the following space figures suggests an answer to the questions referring to it.

1. (a) If two points A and B are in a plane II (Fig. 16–30), is every point of $\overleftrightarrow{AB}$ in plane II?

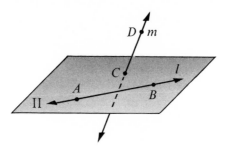

FIGURE 16–30

(b) If point C is in plane Π and D is not, how many points of $\overleftrightarrow{CD}$ are in Π?

2. (a) In Fig. 16–31, how many different planes are there that contain a given line AB?

(b) If C is a point not on line AB, how many planes are there that contain line AB and point C?

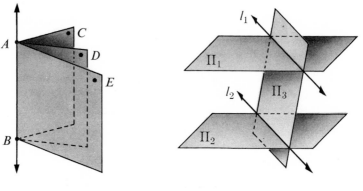

FIGURE 16–31   FIGURE 16–32

3. If planes Π_1 and Π_2 (Fig. 16–32) are parallel to each other and plane Π_3 intersects Π_1 in line l_1 and Π_2 in line l_2, what can be said about the lines l_1 and l_2? Point out an illustration of this geometric fact in your classroom.

4. If a plane intersects a sphere (Fig. 16–33), there are two possible results. What are they?

5. The *base* of the cone in Fig. 16–34 is a circle and its interior in plane Π. Point V is called the *vertex* of the cone. If a plane parallel to Π intersects the cone, there are two possible results. Describe them.

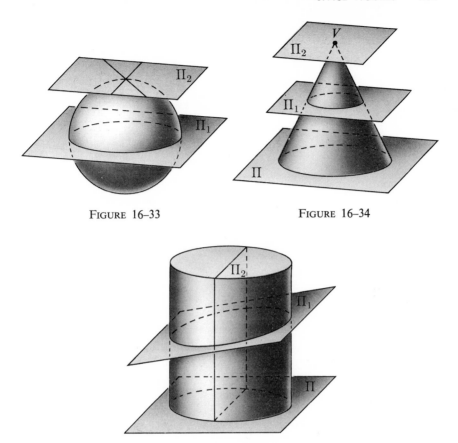

FIGURE 16–33   FIGURE 16–34

FIGURE 16–35

6. The cylinder shown in Fig. 16–35 has a circular base in plane Π.
Describe the intersections of planes Π_1 and Π_2 with the cylinder.

EXERCISES

The earth is shaped like a sphere. At any one moment light from the sun
lights up about half of the earth's surface. As the earth turns on its axis
from west to east, part of the earth's surface moves from darkness into sun-
light and part of the surface moves from light to darkness (Fig. 16–36).

1. If you are at a spot on the earth moving from darkness into light, what
   time of day is it?
2. Give the month and approximately the day when the earth is in the
   position shown in the figure.

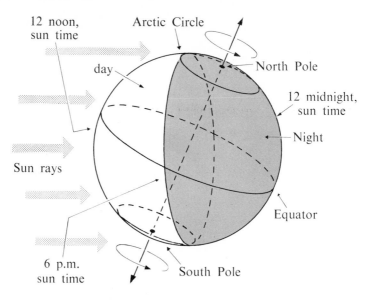

FIGURE 16–36

3. If the earth is in the position shown in the figure and you see the sun directly overhead, what time of day is it? Where are you on the earth?
4. Let us assume that when the earth is in the position shown in the figure, it is 6 p.m. in Paris. About what time is it at this moment in your home town?
5. Can a straight line be drawn on the surface of the earth?

5. RECREATIONAL MATH

The following puzzles are very old. Perhaps you have heard one of them before.

1. Use 6 sticks, all the same length, and without breaking any of them, place them in such a way that you obtain exactly four triangles having the same size and shape.
2. Consider the array of 9 dots below:

$$\begin{matrix} \bullet & \bullet & \bullet \\ \bullet & \bullet & \bullet \\ \bullet & \bullet & \bullet \end{matrix}$$

Place your pencil at one dot and, without lifting your pencil from the paper, draw four straight line segments so that each dot lies on one of the segments.

FIGURE 16–37

3. Can you begin at one of the five points and trace the figure (Fig. 16–37), without lifting your pencil from the paper or retracing any line segment?

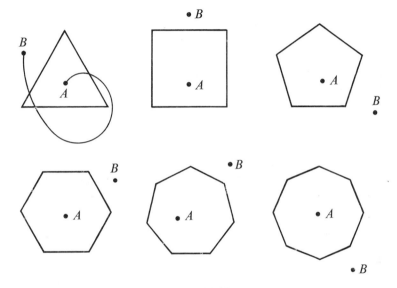

FIGURE 16–38

4. A *triangle*, a *square*, a *pentagon*, a *hexagon*, a *septagon*, and an *octagon* are pictured in Fig. 16–38. In each figure, *try* to connect the *interior* point A to the *exterior* point B with a continuous curve that crosses each side of the polygon once and only once. The first problem is completed as an example.

5. If you have played chess, try the following.

   (a) Place 8 queens on a chess board so that no queen can capture any other queen.

   (b) Place 4 queens on a 6 × 6 board so that no queen can capture any other queen, but so that if a fifth queen is placed upon any one of the 32 vacant squares, one of the queens can capture the fifth one.

6. Try to trace the figure below according to the conditions described in problem 3, beginning at one of the 8 points.

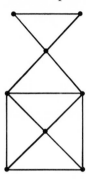

FIGURE 16–39

7. Points *x*, *y*, and *z* are the *midpoints* of the sides of a triangle. Can you figure out an accurate way of drawing the triangle?

8. There are 47 different triangles pictured in Fig. 16–40. Can you count them?

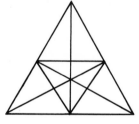

FIGURE 16–40

REVIEW EXERCISES—GROUP III

Compute as indicated. Give each answer in lowest terms.

1. $3 + \dfrac{5}{6}$

2. $\dfrac{18}{6} + \dfrac{5}{6}$

3. $\dfrac{(3 \times 6) + 5}{6}$

4. $2 + \dfrac{3}{4}$

5. $\dfrac{(4 \times 2) + 3}{4}$

6. $\left(3 + \dfrac{5}{6}\right) \div \left(2 + \dfrac{3}{4}\right)$

7. $3\frac{5}{6} \div 2\frac{3}{4}$

8. $3 - \frac{4}{3}$

9. $\frac{(3 \times 3) - 4}{3}$

10. $\frac{9}{3} - \frac{4}{3}$

11. $5 - \frac{2}{7}$

12. $\frac{(7 \times 5) - 2}{7}$

13. $\left(3 - \frac{4}{5}\right) \div \left(5 - \frac{2}{7}\right)$

14. $\frac{3}{4} \div \frac{1}{2}$

15. $\frac{1}{2} \div \frac{3}{4}$

16. $\left(\frac{2}{3} \times \frac{4}{7}\right) \div \left(\frac{3}{21} \times 2\right)$

17. $\left(\frac{4}{7} \times \frac{2}{3}\right) \div \left(2 \times \frac{3}{21}\right)$

18. $\left(2 \times \frac{3}{21}\right) \div \left(\frac{4}{7} \times \frac{2}{3}\right)$

19. $\frac{3}{8} - \frac{2}{7}$

20. $\frac{2}{7} - \frac{3}{8}$

21. $\left(\frac{5}{6} \div \frac{2}{5}\right) \times \frac{2}{5}$

22. $\left(\frac{5}{6} \times \frac{2}{5}\right) \div \frac{2}{5}$

23. $\frac{2}{3} \times \left(\frac{5}{6} - \frac{1}{6}\right)$

24. $\left(\frac{2}{3} \times \frac{5}{6}\right) - \left(\frac{2}{3} \times \frac{1}{6}\right)$

25. $\frac{2}{3} \times \left(\frac{7}{6} - \frac{1}{6}\right)$

26. $\left(\frac{2}{3} \times \frac{7}{6}\right) - \left(\frac{2}{3} \times \frac{1}{6}\right)$

27. $\left(\frac{1}{6} \times \frac{5}{8}\right) + \left(\frac{1}{6} \times \frac{3}{8}\right)$

28. $\frac{1}{6} \times \left(\frac{5}{8} + \frac{3}{8}\right)$

29. $\frac{3}{7} \times \frac{5}{13} + \frac{3}{7} \times \frac{8}{13}$

30. $\frac{3}{7} \times \left(\frac{5}{13} + \frac{8}{13}\right)$

31. $\left(\frac{7}{8} - \frac{3}{5}\right) + \frac{3}{5}$

32. $\left(\frac{7}{8} + \frac{3}{5}\right) - \frac{3}{5}$

33. $\left(\frac{7}{8} - \frac{3}{8}\right) - \frac{1}{4}$

34. $\frac{7}{8} - \left(\frac{3}{8} - \frac{1}{4}\right)$

35. $\left(\frac{7}{8} - \frac{3}{8}\right) + \frac{1}{4}$

36. $\left(\frac{7}{8} + \frac{3}{8}\right) - \frac{1}{4}$

37. $\frac{7}{8} + \left(\frac{3}{8} - \frac{1}{4}\right)$

38. $\frac{2}{3} \div \left(\frac{1}{3} \div \frac{1}{4}\right)$

39. $\frac{7}{8} - \left(\frac{3}{8} + \frac{1}{4}\right)$

40. $\left(\frac{2}{3} \div \frac{1}{3}\right) \div \frac{1}{4}$

41. $\frac{2}{3} \div \frac{5}{5}$

42. $1 \div \frac{2}{3}$

43. $1 \times \frac{3}{2}$

44. $\frac{5}{8} - 0$

45. $0 \div \dfrac{5}{8}$

46. $\dfrac{5}{8} \div \dfrac{5}{8}$

47. $\dfrac{5}{8} \div \dfrac{8}{5}$

48. $\dfrac{5}{8} \times 0$

49. $\left(\dfrac{5}{8} + \dfrac{3}{4}\right) \div \dfrac{1}{2}$

50. $\left(\dfrac{5}{8} \div \dfrac{1}{2}\right) + \left(\dfrac{3}{4} \div \dfrac{1}{2}\right)$

51. $\left(\dfrac{3}{4} \div \dfrac{1}{2}\right) + \left(\dfrac{1}{4} \div \dfrac{1}{2}\right)$

52. $\left(\dfrac{3}{4} + \dfrac{1}{4}\right) \div \dfrac{1}{2}$

53. $\left(\dfrac{5}{8} \times \dfrac{3}{4}\right) \div \dfrac{1}{2}$

54. $\left(\dfrac{5}{8} \div \dfrac{1}{2}\right) \times \dfrac{3}{4}$

55. $\left(\dfrac{3}{4} \div \dfrac{1}{2}\right) \times \dfrac{5}{8}$

56. $\left(\dfrac{5}{8} \div \dfrac{1}{2}\right) \times \left(\dfrac{3}{4} \div \dfrac{1}{2}\right)$

57. $\dfrac{4}{4} \div \dfrac{3}{3}$

58. $\dfrac{1}{4} + \dfrac{2}{7}$

59. $\dfrac{(1 \times 7) + (2 \times 4)}{4 \times 7}$

60. $\dfrac{5}{6} + \dfrac{2}{5}$

61. $\dfrac{(5 \times 5) + (6 \times 2)}{6 \times 5}$

62. $\dfrac{2}{3} - \dfrac{1}{5}$

63. $\dfrac{(2 \times 5) - (3 \times 1)}{3 \times 5}$

64. $\left(\dfrac{2}{3} \times \dfrac{5}{6}\right) \times 3 \times 6$

65. $\dfrac{3}{8} \div 2$

66. $\dfrac{3}{8} \times 2$

67. $\dfrac{1}{5} + \dfrac{1}{9}$

68. $\dfrac{5 + 9}{5 \times 9}$

69. $\dfrac{2}{6} - \dfrac{4}{18}$

70. $\dfrac{9}{11} - \dfrac{90}{121}$

71. $\dfrac{5}{40} - \dfrac{3}{16}$

72. $18\dfrac{3}{13} - 7\dfrac{6}{39}$

73. $(3 + 5) \div \left(\dfrac{1}{3} + \dfrac{1}{5}\right)$

74. $(7 + 13) \div \dfrac{1}{7} + \dfrac{1}{13}$

75. $(11 - 7) \div \left(\dfrac{1}{7} - \dfrac{1}{11}\right)$

Chapter 17

MEASUREMENT

1. INTRODUCTION

Before we can measure a distance in the real world, we must choose a unit. The measuring process then consists of laying this unit off repeatedly. We shall see that measurement in the imaginary world of our geometry is much like measurement in the real world. There is one interesting difference. In the real world, a number given for a distance, for example, is understood to be an approximation. Thus when we say that the sun is 93,000,000 miles from the earth, we are not worried if someone tells us that we are in error by more than 100,000 miles. When we learn from one person that the distance to a neighboring town is 100 miles, we are not surprised to hear someone else say it is 98 miles. When one inspector in a steel mill measures the thickness of a steel bar as 0.412 inch and another gets a measurement of 0.414 inch for the same bar, we are not concerned. We know that measurements in the physical world are approximations.

In the world of geometry we make *exact* measurements. The purpose of this chapter is to describe the approximate measurement process in the real world and the exact measurement process in the imaginary world of geometry.

2. MEASURING SEGMENTS

In the real world, we never expect to find two boards, or two sticks, or two pieces of string, or two ink streaks that are *exactly* alike. But in the imaginary world of geometry every line segment has many exact copies. To measure $\overline{AB}$ with unit segment CD, you can think of laying off copies of $\overline{CD}$ on $\overline{AB}$ (see Fig. 17-1).

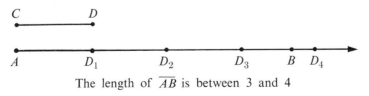

The length of $\overline{AB}$ is between 3 and 4

FIGURE 17-1

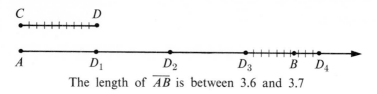

The length of $\overline{AB}$ is between 3.6 and 3.7

FIGURE 17–2

To measure $\overline{AB}$ with greater accuracy, we can think of laying off *one-tenth* of $\overline{CD}$ on $\overline{D_3B}$ (Fig. 17–2).

Now we can imagine dividing one of the tenths of $\overline{CD}$ into 10 parts and measuring $\overline{AB}$ in *hundredths*. Even though we cannot draw accurate pictures, we can *imagine* this measurement process as it continues in our geometry. One of two things must happen:

(1) One of our end points falls on B.

(2) No point ever falls on B.

For example, the process might come to an end, and we might get the *exact* length of $\overline{AB}$:

$$3.6511483001429$$

But the measuring process might go on forever. We might get the result

$$3.66666666\ldots$$

where the 6's continue indefinitely. Since we happen to know that

$$\frac{2}{3} = 0.666666\ldots$$

we would know that in this case the length of segment AB is *exactly* $3\frac{2}{3}$. Whether the measuring process comes to an end or not, *there is just one number that is the length of $\overline{AB}$.*

Of course, when we measure, we do not need to divide our unit segment into tenths. We can divide it into as many parts as we please. In the physical world, when our unit segment is a foot rule, we divide the foot unit into twelfths. Then we divide one of these small units in halves or fourths, etc.

EXERCISES

1. Make tracings of the segments shown in Fig. 17–3.

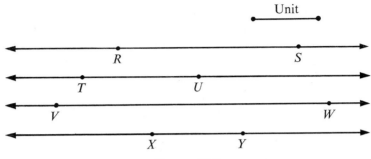

FIGURE 17–3

(a) How many times must you mark off the unit on $\overrightarrow{RS}$ to get beyond point S?

(b) Estimate the length of $\overrightarrow{RS}$ to the nearest unit; to the nearest half-unit.

(c) Estimate the lengths of $\overline{TU}$, $\overline{VW}$, and $\overline{XY}$ to the nearest unit. Check your estimates by laying off the unit segment on each.

(d) How much longer is $\overline{VW}$ than $\overline{TU}$?

2. In the physical world, suppose that our unit $\overline{CD}$ is one yard long. Figure 17–4 illustrates the measurement process.

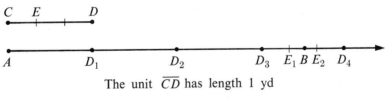

The unit $\overline{CD}$ has length 1 yd

FIGURE 17–4

(a) Because B is between D_3 and D_4, what can be said about the length of $\overline{AB}$? What is the length of $\overline{AB}$ to the nearest unit?

(b) Segment CD has been divided into three congruent parts. Three copies of $\overline{CE}$ have been laid off on $\overline{D_3 D_4}$. Point B is between E_1 and E_2. What can you say about the length of $\overline{AB}$?

(c) Suppose that $\overline{CE}$ is divided into 12 congruent parts. Copies of one of these parts are laid off on $\overline{E_1 E_2}$, giving points F_1, F_2, F_3, ... Suppose that B is between F_7 and F_8. What can be said about the length of $\overline{AB}$?

(d) Imagine that $\overline{F_7F_8}$ is divided into 16 congruent parts with points $G_1, G_2, G_3, \ldots$ Given that point B is between G_4 and G_5, describe the length of $\overline{AB}$.

3. Figure 17–5 shows how a ruler is used to measure a segment. Note that the ruler lays the unit segment off on the segment being measured. Estimate the length of $\overline{AB}$ to

(a) the nearest inch,

(b) the nearest half-inch,

(c) the nearest quarter-inch.

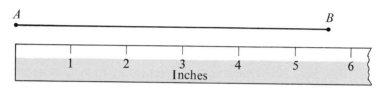

FIGURE 17–5

4. Use your ruler to measure the segment shown in Fig. 17–6. Locate its length

(a) between consecutive inches,

(b) between consecutive half-inches,

(c) between consecutive quarter-inches.

(d) Give the length to the nearest inch; the nearest half-inch; the nearest quarter-inch.

FIGURE 17–6

5. Draw a segment whose length is

(a) between 4 and 5 in.,

(b) between $4 + \dfrac{1}{2}$ and 5 in.,

(c) between $4 + \dfrac{1}{2} + \dfrac{0}{4}$ and $4 + \dfrac{1}{2} + \dfrac{1}{4}$ in.,

(d) between $4 + \dfrac{1}{2} + \dfrac{0}{4} + \dfrac{1}{8}$ and $4 + \dfrac{1}{2} + \dfrac{1}{4} + \dfrac{0}{8}$ in.,

(e) between

$4 + \dfrac{1}{2} + \dfrac{0}{4} + \dfrac{1}{8} + \dfrac{0}{16}$ and $4 + \dfrac{1}{2} + \dfrac{0}{4} + \dfrac{1}{8} + \dfrac{1}{16}$ in.

6. Using $\overline{AB}$ as the unit segment, you find that the length of $\overline{XY}$ is 4 and the length of $\overline{RS}$ is 8. Draw a figure that shows these facts. What are the lengths of $\overline{AB}$ and $\overline{RS}$ if $\overline{XY}$ is the unit? What are the lengths of $\overline{AB}$ and $\overline{XY}$ if $\overline{RS}$ is the unit?

7. When $\overline{AB}$ is the unit, the length of $\overline{CD}$ is $\frac{5}{2}$. What is the length of $\overline{AB}$ if $\overline{CD}$ is the unit? Draw a picture.

8. How do *you* express the length of a yardstick using the foot as the unit? the inch as the unit? an eighth of an inch as the unit? a mile as the unit?

9. What is the *perimeter* (distance around) of a rectangle whose length is 2 ft 3 in. and whose width is 1 ft 7 in.

10. What is the perimeter of a triangle whose sides have lengths 1 ft 4 in., 2 ft 1 in., and 1 ft 11 in.?

3.   MEASURING THE CIRCUMFERENCE

Measuring the circumference of a circle is quite different from measuring the length of a segment. We cannot lay our unit segment off on the circumference. In the real world, of course, we could measure the approximate circumference of a can by wrapping a string around it and then measuring the string (Fig. 17–7). Or we could measure the approximate circumference of a wheel by rolling it through one turn and measuring the distance it travels. Using these techniques, we can get good approximations to the circumference of a circular object.

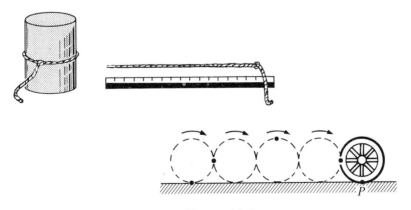

FIGURE 17–7

In the world of mathematics we measure our imaginary circles with absolute accuracy. Figures 17–8 through 17–10 describe a method for doing this.

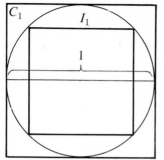

The perimeter of square C_1 is 4.
The perimeter of square I_1 is
2.828 . . .

FIGURE 17–8

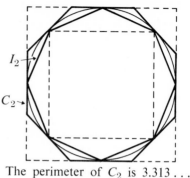

The perimeter of C_2 is 3.313 . . .
The perimeter of I_2 is 3.061 . . .

FIGURE 17–9

Consider a circle whose diameter is our unit segment (Fig. 17–8). We measure the distance around two squares, one outside the circle and touching it, the other inside the circle. We say that the square C_1 is *circumscribed* about the circle and the square I_1 is *inscribed* in the circle. The perimeter (distance around) of the first square is 4 (explain why this is so), and the perimeter of the second square is a little more than 2.8 (do not try to explain why this is so).

Now we circumscribe an eight-sided figure about the circle by "cutting off the corners" and also inscribe an eight-sided figure (Fig. 17–9).

If, in the same way, we replace the eight-sided figures by sixteen-sided figures and call these figures C_3 and I_3, we find that

the perimeter of C_3 is 3.182 . . .

the perimeter of I_3 is 3.121 . . .

For thirty-two-sided figures, these distances are

3.151 . . .   and   3.136 . . .

For sixty-four-sided figures, these distances are

3.142 . . .   and   3.141 . . .

Of course, we do not obtain these numbers by physical measurement. We compute them by the methods of geometry. We find these numbers by *thinking* and *computing*, not by using a ruler.

TABLE 17–1

Number of sides	Circumference of circumscribed figure (Column 1)	Circumference of inscribed figure (Column 2)
4	4	2.828 . . .
8	3.313 . . .	3.061 . . .
16	3.182 . . .	3.121 . . .
32	3.151 . . .	3.136 . . .
64	3.142 . . .	3.141 . . .
	:	:
	:	:
$\pi = 3.1415926535 . . .$		

Let us list the results obtained in Table 17–1.

There is *one* number that is smaller than *all* the numbers in Column 1 above and larger than *all* the numbers in Column 2. The *number* is represented by the symbol π. Its value to 10 decimal places is given above. *This is the number that is the circumference of a circle whose diameter is* 1.

If a circle has diameter 2, its circumference is $\pi \times 2$, and in general, if d is the diameter of a circle, its circumference is $\pi \times d$ (Fig. 17–10).

$$C = \pi \times d$$

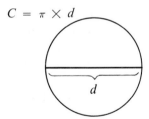

The circumference formula for circles

FIGURE 17–10

Two good approximations to π are $\frac{22}{7}$ and $\frac{355}{113}$. Two other approximations that are sometimes used are 3.14 and 3.1416. The decimal for π has been computed to 100,000 decimal places.

EXERCISES

1. Use the fact that $\pi \approx \frac{22}{7}$ to compute the approximate circumference of the circle whose diameter is

   (a) 14   (b) $\dfrac{7}{11}$ (c) $\dfrac{3}{5}$

2. Use the fact that $\pi \approx 3.14$ to find the approximate circumference for each circle in Exercise 1.

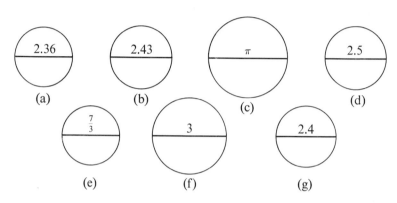

FIGURE 17–11

3. Without using pencil and paper, decide which of the circles in Fig. 17–11 has the smallest circumference. Then list the circles in order from smallest to largest circumference.
4. A wheel has a diameter of about 42 in. About how many feet will it travel if it turns 120 times? About how many times will it turn in traveling one mile? (Use the approximation $\frac{22}{7}$ for π.)
5. Find the diameter of the circle whose circumference is 33 in.

   (a) Use $\dfrac{22}{7}$ for π.   (b) Use 3.14 for π.

6. Compute to the nearest thousandth of an inch the *difference* in the two approximations that you obtained for the diameter of the circle in Exercise 5.
7. Use the fact that $\pi = 3.1415926535\ldots$ to decide which of the two numbers $\frac{22}{7}$ and 3.14 is the better approximation to π.
8. Which is the better approximation to π, 3.1416 or $\frac{355}{113}$?
9. A sheet of paper $11\frac{1}{2}$ by 8 in. is rolled up so as to form a cylinder 8 in. high. What is the circumference of a circular base of this cylinder? What is the diameter of a base?

4. MEASURING AREAS OF REGIONS

We measure the area of a region by choosing a unit area and laying it off on the region to be measured. The area is the number of units it takes to cover the region. Usually the unit area is chosen to be a square, but this is not necessary.

EXERCISES

Four possible unit areas are pictured in Fig. 17–12. Use these to work the problems that follow.

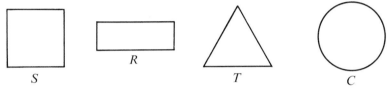

S R T C

FIGURE 17–12

1. Estimate the number of times

        (a) unit area S (b) unit area R (c) T (d) C

can be placed without overlapping in the region shown in Fig. 17–13.

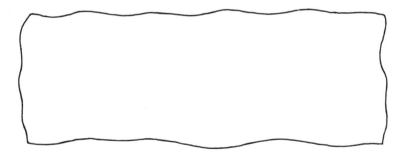

FIGURE 17–13

2. For each unit area that you used in Exercise 1, estimate how much, i.e., what fractional part, of the region to be measured was left uncovered.
3. Estimate the area of the region in Exercise 1, given that

    (a) T is the unit,   (b) S is the unit,

    (c) R is the unit,   (d) C is the unit.

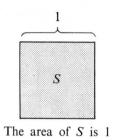

1

The area of S is 1

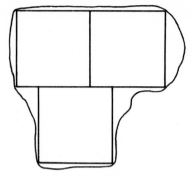

The area of R is a little more than 3

FIGURE 17–14

To measure a region R with a unit square S (see Fig. 17–14) you can think of laying off a number of copies of S on R, as shown in the figure.

To measure the area of region R with greater accuracy, we can think of laying off on the remainder of R copies of a little square S_1 that is *one-hundredth* of S, as shown in Fig. 17–15.

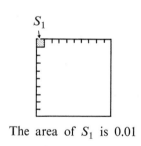

S_1

The area of S_1 is 0.01

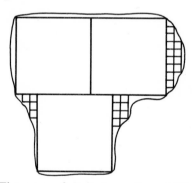

The area of R is more than 3.23

FIGURE 17–15

Now we can imagine dividing S_1 into 100 smaller squares and measuring the area of R in ten-thousandths. Even though we cannot draw accurate pictures, we can imagine that in our geometry this measurement process continues on and on. For a region such as R, the measuring process would go on forever. *There is just one number that is the area of region R in terms of unit square S.*

EXERCISES

1. Suppose that we cover a region R by laying off 3 unit areas S and 173 squares of dimensions 0.1 by 0.1. What is the area of R?

2. Suppose that we cover a region R by laying off 5 unit areas S, 124 squares of dimensions 0.1 by 0.1, and 234 squares of dimensions 0.01 by 0.01. What is the area of R?

It is quite easy to measure the area of a rectangle if its length and width are whole numbers. Thus, for the rectangle shown in Fig. 17–16, we easily find that the area is 3×5.

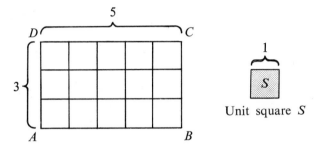

The area of rectangle $ABCD$ is 3×5

FIGURE 17–16

EXERCISES

1. What is the area of a rectangle whose length is 7 and whose width is 5?

2. The area of a rectangle is 72. Its length is 12. What is its width?

3. One rectangle whose sides have whole-number lengths has an area of 60. A second rectangle is twice as long and three times as wide as the first. What is the area of the second rectangle?

4. Using unit square S, we find that the area of a rectangle is 24 square units. Each side of square T is one-fifth as long as a side of S. What is the area of the rectangle if T is chosen for the unit square?

The length and width of a rectangle may not be whole numbers. In Fig. 17–17, the rectangle has length 3.2 and width 1.7.

We can get the area of R by counting. R is covered by 3 squares S and 244 squares S_1, where S_1 is 0.1 by 0.1. (Show that this number

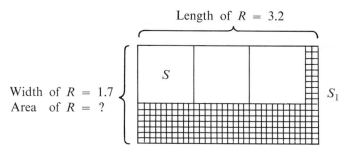

FIGURE 17–17

244 is correct.) Since each copy of S_1 has an area of 0.01, the area of R is

$$3 + 2.44 = 5.44$$

Note that

$$3.2 \times 1.7 = 5.44$$

Hence, in this case, we also get the area of R by multiplying the length and width together. Explain why this is so.

EXERCISES

In all the problems below, S, S_1, and S_2 are squares that may be used as unit squares. Each side of S_1 is one-tenth as long as a side of S. Each side of S_2 is one-tenth as long as a side of S_1. Hence, if S is chosen as unit square, the area of S_1 is 0.01, and the area of S_2 is 0.0001.

1. What are the areas of S and S_2 if S_1 is the unit square?

2. What are the areas of S and S_1 if S_2 is the unit square?

3. With S used as the unit square, a rectangle R has length 4.1 and width 2.3. Draw a figure and show by counting that the area of R is 9.43 square units. Show that this result is the product of length and width.

4. What are the length and width of the rectangle of Exercise 3 if S_1 is chosen as the unit square? What is the area if S_1 is the unit?

5. What are the length and width of R if S_2 is the unit square? What is the area of R with S_2 used as the unit?

6. The area of a rectangle with S as the unit is 7.68. What is its area with S_1 as the unit? with S_2 as the unit?

7. The area of a rectangle with S_1 as the unit is 612. What is its area if S is the unit? if S_2 is the unit?

8. The length and width of a rectangle are 34.2 and 15.4 when S_1 is the unit square.

(a)   What are the length and width if S_2 is the unit?
(b)   What is the area if S_2 is the unit?
(c)   What is the area if S_1 is the unit?
(d)   What is the area if S is the unit?
(e)   What are the length and width if S is the unit?

$$l = \tfrac{14}{3}$$

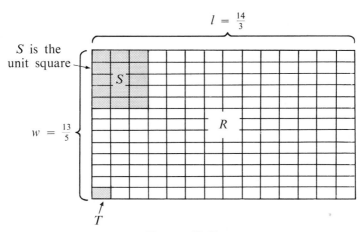

FIGURE 17–18

In Fig. 17–18, rectangle R has length $\tfrac{14}{3}$ and width $\tfrac{13}{5}$. If T is a rectangle $\tfrac{1}{3}$ by $\tfrac{1}{5}$, R can be covered by 14×13 copies of T. Since the area of $T = \tfrac{1}{15}$, or $\tfrac{1}{3} \times \tfrac{1}{5}$, the area of R is

$$(14 \times 13) \times \left(\frac{1}{3} \times \frac{1}{5}\right) = \frac{14}{3} \times \frac{13}{5}$$

EXERCISES

1. Draw a picture of a rectangle R whose length is $\tfrac{3}{2}$ in. and whose width is $\tfrac{4}{3}$ in. Cover R by rectangles $\tfrac{1}{2}$ by $\tfrac{1}{3}$. What is the area of each of these small rectangles? What is the area of R?

2. Show that the rectangle of Exercise 1 can be covered by little squares $\tfrac{1}{6}$ by $\tfrac{1}{6}$. How many of these squares are needed to cover R? What is the area of R?

3. How many rectangles $\tfrac{1}{5}$ by $\tfrac{1}{7}$ are needed to cover a rectangle R whose length is $3\tfrac{2}{5}$ and whose width is $1\tfrac{4}{7}$? What is the area of one of these small rectangles? What is the area of R? Show how to cover R by squares, all having the same size, and show that covering R in this way gives the same number for the area that you obtained by using the rectangles $\tfrac{1}{5}$ by $\tfrac{1}{7}$ given above.

4. A rectangle R has length 3.4 and width $\frac{13}{4}$. What is its area?

5. Find the width of a rectangle, given that its area is 7.75 square units and its length is 3.1.

6. The length of a rectangle is 2.1 yd and the width is 1.2 yd. What is its area in

   (a) yd² (sq yd)?   (b) ft² (sq ft)?   (c) in² (sq in.)?

7. The length of a rectangle is 2.1 m and its width is 1.2 m. What is its area in

   (a) m²?   (b) cm²?   (c) mm²?   (d) km²?

8. The length of a rectangle is 2 ft 4 in., and its width is 11 in. What is its area in

   (a) ft²?   (b) in²?   (c) yd²?

We take for granted that the area A of a rectangle R which is l units long and w units wide is $l \times w$ square units (Fig. 17–19).

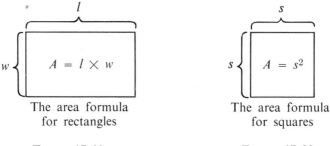

The area formula for rectangles	The area formula for squares
FIGURE 17–19	FIGURE 17–20

We can use this fact to obtain area formulas for other figures. In particular, if the rectangle is a square, then its length and width are equal. If we call the length of each side of the square s, then the area is $s \times s$ or s^2 (Fig. 17–20).

Figure 17–21 represents a *parallelogram*. Sides $\overline{AB}$ and $\overline{CD}$ are parallel to each other and have the same length. Sides $\overline{AD}$ and $\overline{BC}$ are also parallel and have the same length. We call the length of side $\overline{AB}$ the *base* of the parallelogram. The distance between sides $\overline{AB}$ and $\overline{CD}$ is called the height of the parallelogram. Imagine snipping off the right corner of the parallelogram and moving it over as shown in the figure. You can see that the area of the parallelogram is

$$\text{base} \times \text{height}$$

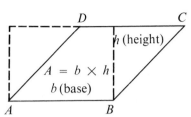

The area formula for parallelograms

FIGURE 17–21

The area formula for triangles

FIGURE 17–22

Once we know the area formula for parallelograms, it is easy to derive the area formula for triangles. Consider △RST. If, as shown in Fig. 17–22, △RVT is an exact copy of triangle RST, then $RSTV$ is a parallelogram. Since the area of the parallelogram is $b \times h$, the area of the triangle is

$$\tfrac{1}{2} \times b \times h$$

EXERCISES

1. Find the areas of the triangles with the following dimensions:
   (a) $b = 3$ ft, $h = 20$ in.,
   (b) $b = 2.4$ m, $h = 315$ cm.

2. A triangle has an area of 216 in². Its base is 1 yd long. What is its height?

3. A triangle and a parallelogram have the same base. The areas of the two figures are equal. How do their heights compare?

4. In triangle ABC (Fig. 17–23) points D and E are midpoints of sides $\overline{BC}$ and $\overline{CA}$. Show that triangles ADC and BEC have equal areas. Show that triangles BOD and AOE have equal areas. Show that the area of △AOB is equal to the area of region $CDOE$.

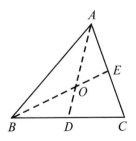

FIGURE 17–23

5. Give the areas of the triangles shown in Fig. 17–24.

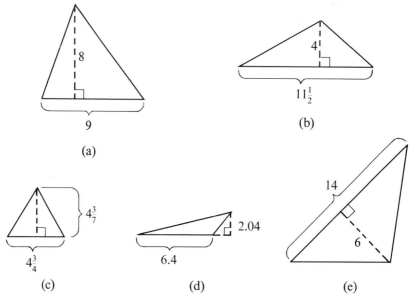

(a)

(b)

(c)   (d)   (e)

FIGURE 17–24

6. Show that if a line is drawn from any vertex of a triangle to the midpoint of the opposite side, it divides the triangle into two triangles whose areas are equal.

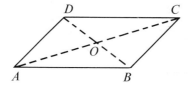

FIGURE 17–25

7. In Fig. 17–25, *ABCD* is a parallelogram. It can be proved that the diagonals $\overline{AC}$ and $\overline{DB}$ bisect each other. That is, the lengths of $\overline{AO}$ and $\overline{CO}$ are the same and the lengths of $\overline{DO}$ and $\overline{OB}$ are the same. Show that triangles *DOC* and *AOB* have equal areas; that triangles *DOA* and *COB* have equal areas.

8. Give the areas of the parallelograms shown in Fig. 17–26.

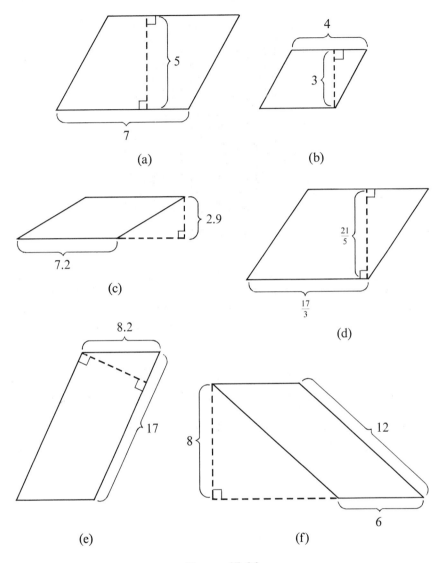

FIGURE 17–26

9. Two triangles have equal heights. The base of one triangle is twice as long as the base of the other. If the area of the smaller triangle is 42 in², what is the area of the other?

10. Two triangles have equal heights. The base of one triangle is 4 in. longer than the base of the second, and its area is 60 in² more than the area of the second. What is the height of each triangle?

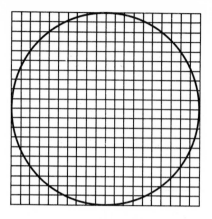

FIGURE 17–27

Figure 17–27 shows a circle of radius 1 unit drawn on paper marked off in squares one-tenth of a unit on one edge. Count the covering squares and estimate the area of the circle by counting each square that overlaps the circumference as a half square. You should get a number close to the number π!

We can explain this fact as follows. Imagine drawing a great many radii of a circle. These radii divide the circular region into many small, almost triangular regions, as shown in Fig. 17–28. Now let us magnify one of these. The enlarged region is shown in Fig. 17–29. The resulting figure resembles so much a triangle with height r and base s that it is reasonable to believe that its area is $\frac{1}{2} \times r \times s$. If we add up

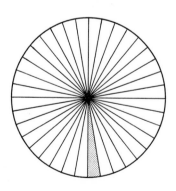

r is the radius of the circle
s is the length of the arc

FIGURE 17–28   FIGURE 17–29

the areas of all these triangular regions (Fig. 17–30), we obtain

$$\left(\frac{1}{2} \times r \times s_1\right) + \left(\frac{1}{2} \times r \times s_2\right) + \left(\frac{1}{2} \times r \times s_3\right) + \cdots$$

$$\frac{1}{2} \times r \times (s_1 + s_2 + s_3 + \cdots)$$

$$\frac{1}{2} \times r \times C$$

where C is the circumference of the circle.

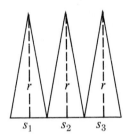

$s_1 \qquad s_2 \qquad s_3$

FIGURE 17–30

$$A = \pi \times r^2$$

The area formula
for circles

FIGURE 17–31

Since the circumference, C, is $\pi \times d$ or $\pi \times 2 \times r$, we finally get for the area of the circle (Fig. 17–31):

$$\frac{1}{2} \times r \times \pi \times 2 \times r = \pi \times r^2$$

EXERCISES

1. Use the fact that $\pi \approx \frac{22}{7}$ to find the approximate area of the circle whose radius is about

   (a) 7 in.   (b) 14 ft   (c) $\frac{7}{2}$ mi

2. Using 3.14 for π, find the approximate area of a circle whose radius is about

   (a) 25 cm   (b) 10 m   (c) 5 km

3. A circle whose diameter is 4 in. is cut out of a square piece of tin 4 in. on a side. What is the area of the piece of tin which is left over?

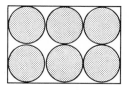

FIGURE 17–32

4. In Fig. 17–32, 6 circular disks each of whose diameter is 1 in. are placed on a rectangular region 3 in. by 2 in. What percent of the surface of the rectangle is covered by the circles?

5. If the rectangle of Exercise 4 is covered by circular disks of 0.1-in. diameter, placed in the same pattern, what percent is covered? What percent would be covered by disks whose diameter is 0.01 in.?

6. Find the area, in square feet, of a circular flower bed 20 ft 6 in. in diameter.

7. Find the surface area, in square meters, of a circular pond whose diameter is 12.4 meters.

8. A circular flower bed is surrounded by a walk 6 ft wide. The diameter of the flower bed is 60 ft. What is the surface area of this walk?

9. The cost of building the walk of Exercise 8 was $8.50 per square yard. What was the total cost of the walk?

5.   MEASURING VOLUMES OF REGIONS IN SPACE

We measure the *volume* of a region in three-dimensional space by repeatedly laying off copies of a unit region. Usually we choose our unit region to be a cube (Fig. 17–33), but this is not necessary. Let C be any cube. We choose an edge of this cube to be our unit segment. All 12 edges of C are congruent to one another. The six faces are all unit squares.

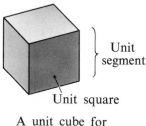

Unit
segment

Unit square

A unit cube for
measuring volumes

FIGURE 17–33

$$V = l \times w \times h$$

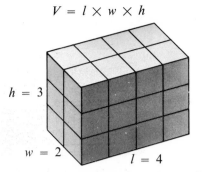

$h = 3$

$w = 2$

$l = 4$

The formula for the volume of
a rectangular solid

FIGURE 17–34

If R is any three-dimensional region (Fig. 17–34), we determine its volume in cubic units by laying off copies of C and counting. If R is a box-shaped region and the edges of R have whole-number lengths, this counting process is very simple.

If the edges of a rectangular solid do not have whole-number lengths, then, after laying off all possible copies of the unit cube C, we divide C into small cubes *one-tenth* of a unit on each edge and lay off copies of one of these small cubes. For example, for a boxlike solid of dimensions 3.2 by 4.1 by 2.3, we would first lay off 24 copies of C and then begin to use the small cubes.

EXERCISES

1. Give the volume of each region shown in Fig. 17–35.

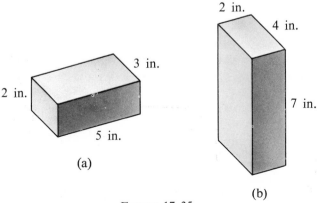

3 in.

2 in.

2 in.

5 in.

(a)

2 in.

4 in.

7 in.

(b)

FIGURE 17–35

2. A match box is 4 in. long, 2 in. wide, and $1\frac{1}{2}$ in. deep. What is its volume in cubic inches?

3. What is the volume in cubic inches of a cube of lead $\frac{1}{2}$ ft on each side?

4. A room is 16 ft long, 11 ft wide, and the ceiling is 9 ft high. How many cubic feet of air will the room hold?

5. Show that a rectangular region 3.2 by 4.1 by 2.3 can be covered exactly by $32 \times 41 \times 23$ small cubes one-tenth of a unit on an edge. Use this fact to show that the volume of the region is $3.2 \times 4.1 \times 2.3$ cubic units.

6. About how many cubic centimeters (cm^3) are there in a cubic inch?

7. A cubic centimeter of water weighs 1 gm. What is the approximate weight, in grams, of 1 cubic inch (in^3) of water?

8. A bushel of wheat occupies about 1.25 cubic feet (ft^3) of space. How many bushels can be stored in a rectangular bin 12 ft 6 in. by 10 ft by 8 ft?

9. A bushel of ear corn occupies about 2.5 ft^3 of space. How much corn can be stored in a rectangular crib 32 ft long, 8 ft wide, and 10 ft high?

10. A concrete sidewalk is 150 ft long, 4 ft wide, and 9 in. thick. How many cubic feet of concrete were used?

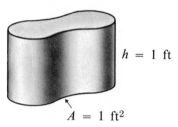

$h = 1$ ft

$A = 1$ ft^2

FIGURE 17–36

11. The area of the bottom of the container shown in Fig. 17–36 is 1 ft². The height is 1 ft. What is the volume of the region within the container? We call such a region a cylindrical region.

12. A cubic foot of air at sea-level pressure weighs about 0.0807 lb. What is the approximate weight of the air in a room 20 ft long, 12 ft wide, and 9 ft high?

13. What is the approximate weight, in tons, of a cubic mile of air at sea-level pressure?

14. At sea-level pressure, the atmosphere of the earth would have a volume of about 1,000,000,000 cubic miles. What is the approximate weight of the earth's atmosphere?

15. A cubic foot of water weighs about 62.5 lb. Lead is about 11.4 times as heavy as water. What is the weight of a cube of lead 2 ft on each edge?

16. The volume of the sun is about 4.5×10^{28} ft³. On the average, 1 ft³ of the sun weighs about 90 lb. Compute the approximate weight of the sun in pounds; in tons.

17. There is enough water in the oceans of the earth to cover the entire surface of the earth to a depth of about $1\frac{1}{2}$ mi. The surface of the earth is about 200,000,000 mi². Compute the approximate weight of all the water on earth.

18. From the exercises above you know the weight of the atmosphere of the earth. About how many times as heavy is the water of the earth?

19. The weight of the water vapor in the earth's atmosphere is about 0.3% of the weight of the air itself. About what part of the water of the earth is in the air in the form of water vapor?

20. The weight of the atmosphere is about 1/1,000,000 of the weight of the earth. What is the approximate weight of the earth? About what part of the mass of the earth is water?

6. MEASURING ANGLES

We measure an angle by choosing a unit angle and laying it off on the angle to be measured. For angle measurements, a natural unit of measure is the *right angle*. In the physical world there are many things which suggest right angles. The four angles of a square or rectangle are right angles. The angles at the corners of a book suggest right angles.

If you fold a piece of paper properly (Fig. 17–37), the crease and an edge of the paper suggest two right angles. We say that the *sum* of two right angles is a *straight angle*. Can you explain why?

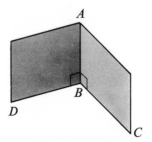

The folded sheet of paper
suggests two right angles,
$\angle ABC$ and $\angle ABD$

FIGURE 17–37

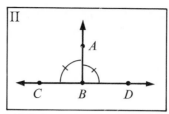

∠*ABD* is congruent to ∠*ABC*.
Both of these angles are right angles.
Lines *AB* and *CD* are perpendicular
to each other.

FIGURE 17–38

Two angles that are exact copies of each other are said to be *congruent* to each other. If a ray has its end point on a line and forms with the line two angles that are congruent to each other, we call the angles *right angles*, and we say that the ray and the line are *perpendicular* to each other (Fig. 17–38).

EXERCISES

1. How many right angles are formed by pairs of edges of a cube?
2. Draw a picture of two intersecting lines which form four right angles.
3. At a corner of a room three planes intersect. Point out the right angles that are formed. One lies in each plane.
4. Draw a triangle that has one right angle and whose other two angles are approximately congruent to each other.
5. Try to draw a triangle that has two right angles.

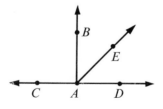

FIGURE 17–39

6. Referring to Fig. 17–39, we say that ∠*EAD* is *smaller than* right angle *BAD* and that ∠*EAC* is *larger than* right angle *BAC*. We call ∠*EAD* an *acute* angle (this means it is smaller than a right angle), and we call ∠*EAC* an *obtuse* angle (this means it is larger than a right angle).

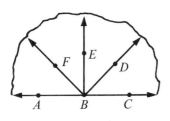

FIGURE 17–40

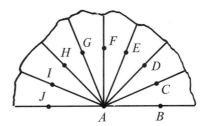

FIGURE 17–41

Fold a piece of paper twice so that when it is unfolded the creases look as shown in the sketch of Fig. 17–40. The four angles, $\angle DBC$, $\angle EBD$, $\angle FBE$, $\angle ABF$, should all be congruent to each other. Each angle should be half a right angle.

(a) In Fig. 17–40 name two acute angles.

(b) Name two obtuse angles.

(c) Is $\angle FBD$ acute? obtuse?

(d) Fold your paper a third time so that the creases from B suggest 8 angles, each of which is one-fourth of a right angle. How many right angles formed by your creases have vertex B?

7. In Fig. 17–40, let us take $\angle DBC$ as the unit angle. Then the *measure* of $\angle EBC$ is 2 and the measure of $\angle DBA$ is 3. With $\angle DBC$ as unit angle, what is the measure of

(a) $\angle FBC$?   (b) $\angle FBD$?   (c) $\angle ABC$?

8. Figure 17–41 shows a paper that has been folded three times so that 8 small angles, all congruent to one another, have been formed.

(a) What is the measure of $\angle EAB$ if $\angle DAC$ is the unit?

(b) What is the measure of $\angle CAB$ if $\angle DAB$ is the unit?

(c) What is the measure of $\angle IAC$ if $\angle IAJ$ is the unit?

(d) What is the measure of $\angle FAB$ if $\angle CAB$ is the unit? if $\angle DAB$ is the unit? if $\angle GAB$ is the unit? if $\angle HAB$ is the unit? if $\angle IAB$ is the unit? if $\angle JAB$ is the unit? if $\angle EAB$ is the unit? if $\angle FAB$ is the unit?

(e) Pick out two angles above such that when one is used as the unit, the measure of the other is $\frac{1}{2}$, 2, $\frac{1}{5}$, 5, $\frac{2}{3}$, $\frac{3}{2}$, $\frac{3}{4}$, $\frac{4}{3}$.

9. Draw an acute angle less than one-half of a right angle; more than one-half of a right angle.

10. Draw an obtuse angle less than $\frac{3}{2}$ of a right angle; more than $\frac{3}{2}$ of a right angle.

An angle whose measure is 1° (one degree)

FIGURE 17–42

The unit angle used most often is *one-ninetieth of a right angle.* Such an angle is called an angle of *one degree.* We write the symbol "1°" as an abbreviation for "one degree." You should think of the unit, *one degree,* much as you think of the unit, *one foot,* or the unit, *one square inch.* The degree is a unit used over almost the entire world for measuring angles. Babylonian astronomers measured angles in degrees many thousands of years ago. You should be able to estimate the degree measure of an angle with fair accuracy.

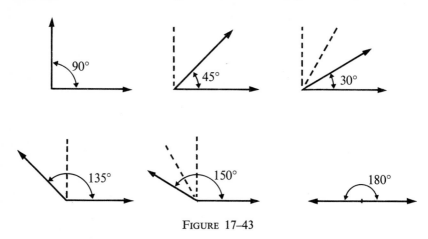

FIGURE 17–43

Since the measure of a right angle is 90°, the measure of one-half of a right angle is 45°; the measure of one-third of a right angle is $\frac{1}{3}$ of 90°, or 30°, etc.

EXERCISES

1. Estimate degree measures for the angles shown in Fig. 17–44.

2. Decide for each pair of angles shown in Fig. 17–45, how much larger (how many degrees larger) one angle is than the other.

3. Draw an angle whose measure is about

        (a) 40°   (b) 20°   (c) 100°

        (d) 170°   (e) 10°   (f) 85°

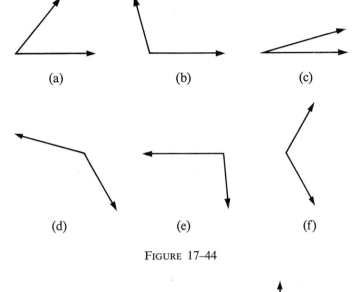

FIGURE 17–44

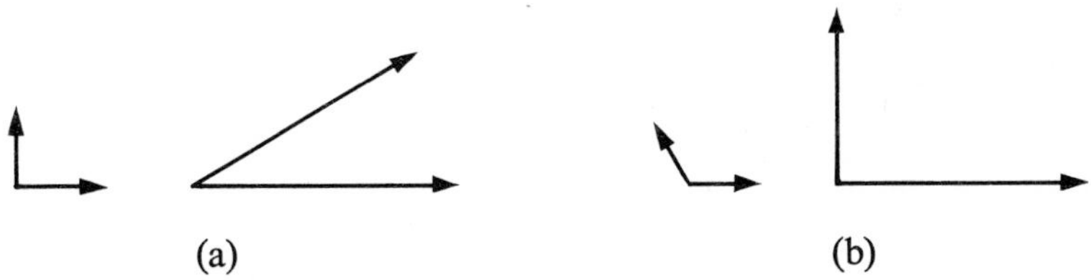

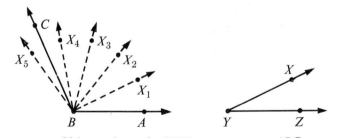

FIGURE 17–45

Using unit angle XYZ to measure $\angle ABC$

FIGURE 17–46

If $\angle ABC$ is any angle and $\angle XYZ$ is the unit angle, we lay off $\angle XYZ$ on $\angle ABC$. Figure 17–46 describes the measurement process. Angles ABX_1, X_1BX_2, etc., are copies of $\angle XYZ$. In the figure, the measure of $\angle ABC$ in terms of unit angle XYZ is more than 4 and less than 5.

EXERCISES

1. Make a tracing of each angle in Fig. 17–47 on thin paper. Lay these over unit angle $\angle XYZ$ to measure each of the angles to the nearest whole number.

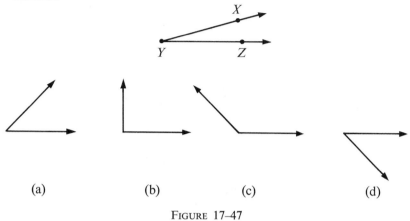

FIGURE 17–47

2. Estimate the degree measure of each angle shown in Fig. 17–47.
3. The measure of $\angle XYZ$ is 20° and it is divided into four 5°-angles. Use tracings to measure each of the angles in Fig. 17–48 to the nearest 5°.

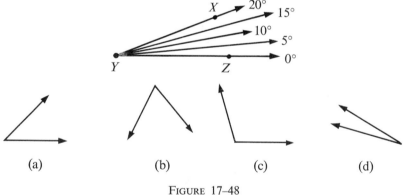

FIGURE 17–48

In Fig. 17–49 an angle one-sixth of a right angle has been laid off repeatedly. We have numbered the rays 0, 1, 2, . . . , 12.

Using this angle as unit angle, we find that the measure of a right angle is 6. A convenient way of measuring an angle is to make a tracing and lay it on the figure, which is really a device for measuring angles, called a *protractor*.

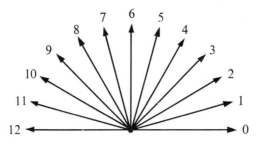

FIGURE 17–49

EXERCISES

1. Suppose that a tracing of an angle is placed on Fig. 17–49 in such a way that one ray of the angle falls on the ray marked 3 and the other falls on the ray marked 7. What is the measure of this angle?

2. What is the measure of an angle, given that the rays of a tracing of the angle fall on:

   (a) rays 0 and 5?   (b) rays 2 and 7?
   (c) rays 2 and 9?   (d) rays 4 and 11?

3. Make a copy of each of the angles in Fig. 17–50 and get the measure of each angle by laying the copy upon the protractor shown in Fig. 17–49.

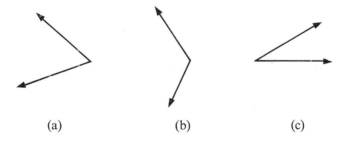

(a)   (b)   (c)

FIGURE 17–50

4. On thin paper make a tracing of the protractor shown in Fig. 17–49 and measure each angle below by laying your copy of the protractor upon them. This is the way in which protractors are ordinarily used.

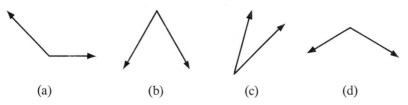

(a)   (b)   (c)   (d)

5. Use the fact that the degree measure of the unit angle used to construct our protractor is 15° and compute the approximate degree measure of each angle in Exercise 4.

A protractor for measuring angles in degrees is shown in Fig. 17–51. It is not necessary to draw in the rays from *A*.

The protractor may be laid off on an angle or the angle may be laid off on the protractor, and the degree measure can be estimated. The vertex of the angle being measured must be placed upon *A*.

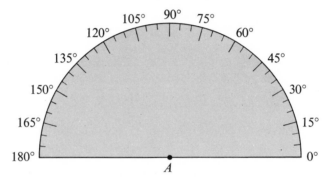

FIGURE 17–51

EXERCISES

1. Draw an angle whose measure you estimate to be about 55°. Make a tracing of this angle and lay it on the protractor in Fig. 17–51 to see how close you came to 55°.
2. Make a tracing of the protractor on thin paper and use it to measure the angles given in Fig. 17–52.

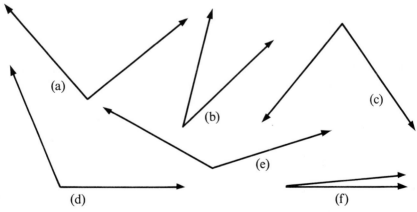

FIGURE 17–52

3. Draw pictures of four triangles of various sizes and shapes. For each triangle measure the three angles and add the degree measures of these three angles.
4. Cut out a triangular region. Mark the angles 1, 2, and 3 as shown in Fig. 17–53(a). Now tear off the corners and put the angular regions together (Fig. 17–53b).
5. The measures of two angles of a triangle are 70° and 60°. Estimate the measure of the third angle.

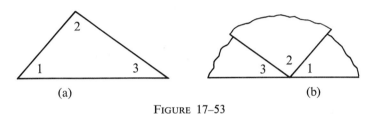

(a)   (b)

FIGURE 17–53

7. RECREATIONAL MATH

A sequence of numbers known as the Fibonacci sequence (named for a thirteenth-century Italian mathematician) can be used to construct interesting geometric paradoxes in which areas seem to disappear. This sequence is

$$1, 1, 2, 3, 5, 8, 13, 21, 34, 55, \ldots$$

Studying these numbers, you will see how they are determined. What will be the next three numbers?

Note that if you square any number in the sequence and compare this result with the product of the two numbers on either side, the difference between these two results is only 1. For example,

$$5 \times 5 = 25, \qquad 3 \times 8 = 24$$
$$8 \times 8 = 64, \qquad 5 \times 13 = 65$$
$$13 \times 13 = 169, \qquad 8 \times 21 = 168, \text{ etc.}$$

The Fibonacci sequence has many other interesting properties. Note that

$$2 \times 3 = 6, \qquad 1 \times 5 = 5$$
$$3 \times 5 = 15, \qquad 2 \times 8 = 16$$
$$5 \times 8 = 40, \qquad 3 \times 13 = 39, \text{ etc.}$$

Try to find some other properties of this sequence.

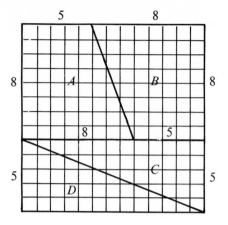

FIGURE 17–54

These number relationships lead to interesting results. Let us consider a square 13 by 13 cut along the lines indicated in Fig. 17–54. The cut-out pieces, *A*, *B*, *C*, *D*, can be fitted together as shown in Fig. 17–55.

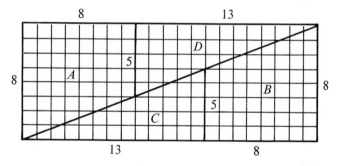

FIGURE 17–55

It seems that we have formed a rectangle 8 by 21 whose area is 168 square units. The area of the original square was 13 × 13, or 169, square units. How did the one square inch disappear?

EXERCISES

1. Cut an 8 by 8 square out of cardboard and cut it into pieces that seem to fit together to form a 5 by 13 rectangle.

2. Cut out an 8 by 13 rectangle and cut it into pieces as shown in Fig. 17–56. Reassemble the pieces to form what seems to be a rectangle 5 by 21.

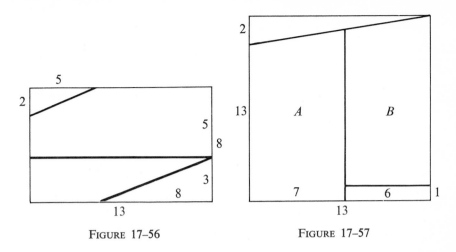

FIGURE 17–56   FIGURE 17–57

3. Cut out a square 13 by 13 and cut it into pieces as shown in Fig. 17–57. Reassemble these four pieces to form what appears to be a 13 by 13 square with one square unit missing. [*Hint:* Interchange pieces *A* and *B*.]

Chapter 18

RATIO AND PROPORTION

1. INTRODUCTION: RATIO IN GEOMETRY

The ideas of ratio and proportion that we shall study in this chapter were introduced by the Greek mathematicians more than 2000 years ago. These men were especially interested in geometry, and hence they invented ratio ideas as an aid for working problems in geometry. The Greek mathematicians wished to compare the sizes of geometric figures, and they believed that *all such comparisons could be made in terms of whole numbers alone.* This is the reason that even today, in speaking of the ratio of one object to another, we nearly always think of whole-number relationships.

A few examples below will make it clear how the Greeks used the idea of *ratio* in geometry to compare the sizes of two segments, or two angles, or two regions.

Example 1. Both segments $\overline{AB}$ and $\overline{CD}$ have been measured by the same unit segment $\overline{XY}$ (Fig. 18–1). The measures of $\overline{AB}$ and $\overline{CD}$ are 4 and 3, respectively.

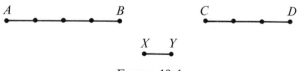

FIGURE 18–1

The ratio of the length of $\overline{AB}$ to the length of $\overline{CD}$ is 4 to 3. Instead of speaking of the ratio of the *lengths* of the segments, we usually say more simply:

The ratio of $\overline{AB}$ to $\overline{CD}$ is 4 to 3.

EXERCISES

1. What is the ratio of the length of $\overline{CD}$ to the length of $\overline{AB}$?
2. If we had measured $\overline{AB}$ and $\overline{CD}$ with a segment half as long as $\overline{XY}$, how would we have described the ratio of $\overline{AB}$ to $\overline{CD}$? the ratio of $\overline{CD}$ to $\overline{AB}$?

Example 2. Both angles A and B have been measured by the same unit angle, X (Fig. 18–2). The measures of $\angle A$ and $\angle B$ are 5 and 8, respectively.

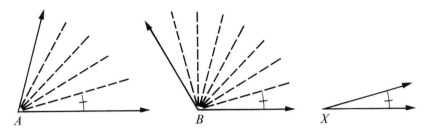

FIGURE 18–2

The ratio of the measure of $\angle A$ to the measure of $\angle B$ is 5 to 8. We often say more simply:

The ratio of $\angle A$ to $\angle B$ is 5 to 8.

EXERCISES

1. What is the ratio of the measure of $\angle B$ to the measure of $\angle A$?
2. If we had measured $\angle A$ and $\angle B$ with an $\angle Y$ only one third as large as $\angle X$, how would we have described the ratio of $\angle A$ to $\angle B$? of $\angle B$ to $\angle A$?

Example 3. Rectangles R and S have been measured by the same unit square I (Fig. 18–3). The measures of R and S are 8 and 15, respectively.

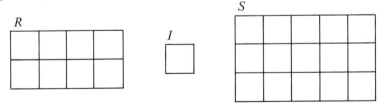

FIGURE 18–3

The ratio of the area of rectangle R to the area of rectangle S is 8 to 15. We may also say:

The ratio of region R to region S is 8 to 15.

EXERCISES

1. In Fig. 18–3, what is the ratio of the area of the rectangular region S to the area of the rectangular region R?

2. In Fig. 18–3 what is the ratio of the length of R to the length of S? of the width of S to the width of R? of the perimeter of R to the perimeter of S?

3. If, instead of using I as unit square, we had used a smaller unit square J whose side was only half as long as the side of I, how might we have described the ratio of the area of R to the area of S? the ratio of the perimeter of R to the perimeter of S?

Example 4. The triangular region ABC has been divided into four congruent regions. The four triangles have the same size and shape (Fig. 18–4).

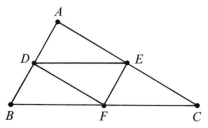

FIGURE 18–4

We might say that triangle ABC has been *measured* by the unit triangle ADE.

The ratio of triangle ADE to triangle ABC is 1 to 4.

EXERCISES

Exercises 1 through 5 refer to Fig. 18–4.

1. What is the ratio of triangle ADE to region $DBCE$? (Figure $DBCE$ is called a trapezoid.)

2. What is the ratio of triangle ADE to parallelogram $DBFE$?

3. What is the ratio of parallelogram $DBFE$ to parallelogram $DFCE$?

4. What is the ratio of segment $\overline{AD}$ to segment $\overline{DB}$? of $\overline{AC}$ to $\overline{AE}$? of $\overline{DE}$ to $\overline{BC}$? of $\overline{AC}$ to $\overline{DF}$? of $\overline{EF}$ to $\overline{AB}$?

5. From the figure, can you determine the ratio of $\overline{AD}$ to $\overline{AE}$?

When we say that the ratio of a first segment to a second is 3 to 5, we mean that if we choose a unit segment such that the measure of the first segment is 3, then the measure of the second segment is 5 (Fig. 18–5).

First segment   Second segment

FIGURE 18–5

The ratios 3 to 5 and 5 to 3 describe the relationship between the lengths of the segments. We do not really need this *ratio language* to compare the lengths. We certainly could say:

The first segment is $\frac{3}{5}$ as long as the second.

The second segment is $\frac{5}{3}$ as long as the first.

We are not introducing new mathematical ideas when we use the *ratio language*, 3 to 5 and 5 to 3. All we are doing is inventing a new way of talking about *rational numbers*. However, the ratio language is helpful in solving certain problems.

EXERCISES

1. Using Fig. 18–6, describe the ratio of $\overline{AB}$ to $\overline{CD}$ if (a) $\overline{XY}$ is chosen as the unit segment; (b) $\overline{RS}$ is the unit; (c) $\overline{TU}$ is the unit; (d) $\overline{CD}$ is the unit.

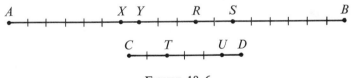

FIGURE 18–6

2. Using unit segment $\overline{XY}$, we find that the lengths of two segments $\overline{EF}$ and $\overline{GH}$ are 12 and 10, respectively.
   (a) Draw pictures of the three segments $\overline{XY}$, $\overline{EF}$, and $\overline{GH}$.
   (b) What is the ratio of $\overline{EF}$ to $\overline{GH}$?
   (c) Segment $\overline{RS}$ is $\frac{1}{3}$ of $\overline{XY}$. Using $\overline{RS}$ as unit segment, how would you describe the ratio of $\overline{EF}$ to $\overline{GH}$?
   (d) Choose a unit segment $\overline{UV}$ larger than $\overline{XY}$ so that when $\overline{EF}$ and $\overline{GH}$ are measured by $\overline{UV}$, the lengths are whole numbers. With this unit $\overline{UV}$, how do you describe the ratio of $\overline{EF}$ to $\overline{GH}$?

(e)   Is there any segment longer than $\overline{UV}$, of part (d), that measures both $\overline{EF}$ and $\overline{GH}$ in whole numbers?

3. Segment $\overline{AB}$ is $\frac{6}{5}$ as long as $\overline{CD}$.

(a)   Draw a picture of these segments.
(b)   Which segment is the longer?
(c)   What is the ratio of $\overline{CD}$ to $\overline{AB}$?
(d)   If $\overline{AB}$ is 1 ft long, how long is $\overline{CD}$?
(e)   If $\overline{CD}$ is 20 mi long, how long is $\overline{AB}$?
(f)   When $\overline{XY}$ is the unit segment, the length of $\overline{AB}$ is 24. What is the length of $\overline{CD}$, with $\overline{XY}$ as unit?
(g)   When $\overline{UV}$ is the unit segment, the length of $\overline{AB}$ is 15. What is the length of $\overline{CD}$, with $\overline{UV}$ as unit?
(h)   What is the length of $\overline{AB}$ if $\overline{CD}$ is the unit?
(i)   What is the length of $\overline{CD}$ if $\overline{AB}$ is the unit?

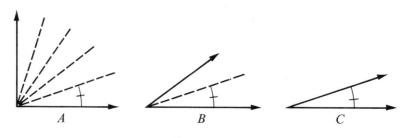

FIGURE 18–7

4. Using Fig. 18–7, answer the following questions.

(a)   What is the ratio of $\angle B$ to $\angle A$?
(b)   When $\angle D$ is the unit angle, the measure of $\angle C$ is 5. Using $\angle D$ to measure $\angle A$ and $\angle B$, how might we describe the ratio of $\angle A$ to $\angle B$?
(c)   How many angles larger than $\angle C$ are there such that with each of these angles as the unit angle the measure of $\angle A$ is a whole number?
(d)   Is there any angle larger than $\angle C$ such that with this angle as unit angle the measures of $\angle A$ and $\angle B$ are both whole numbers?
(e)   Choose a unit angle such that the measure of $\angle A$ is 40. What is the measure of $\angle B$ when this unit is used?
(f)   For what rational number a/b is the following statement true?

$$\angle A \text{ is } \frac{a}{b} \text{ of } \angle B.$$

5. In Fig. 18–8 lines parallel to the sides of triangle ABC form several congruent triangles.

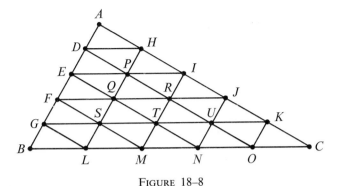

FIGURE 18–8

(a)   What is the ratio of triangle ADH to AEI? to AFJ? to AGK? to ABC?
(b)   What is the ratio of CIM to CJN?
(c)   What is the ratio of $EITG$ to $AJUD$?
(d)   Express $\overline{AB}$ as a multiple of $\overline{AE}$; $\overline{AC}$ as a multiple of $\overline{AI}$; $\overline{BC}$ as a multiple of $\overline{EI}$; $\overline{FR}$ as a multiple of $\overline{BO}$.
(e)   Express the area of AEI as a multiple of the area of CHL; the area of CHL as a multiple of the area of AEI.
(f)   What is the ratio of the *perimeter* of DEP to the perimeter of DFR?
(g)   What is the ratio of the area of $GLMRD$ to the area of $NJIPQ$?

2.   USING THE LANGUAGE OF RATIO TO COMPARE SETS

In the last section we used the language of ratio to compare sets of points with each other. In everyday life it is convenient to use this language to compare other pairs of sets.

A recipe for fruit punch might call for mixing cups of lemonade and cups of grape juice *in the ratio of* 5 *to* 2.

In a group of students the *ratio of boys to girls might be* 4 *to* 3.

On a student's test paper *the ratio of correct answers to incorrect answers might be* 8 *to* 2.

A basketball team might have *a ratio of free throws scored to free throws attempted of* 4 *to* 10.

In each of these examples we are comparing two sets. In the first example we are comparing a set of cups of lemonade with a set of cups of grape juice. With each 5 cups of lemonade we match 2 cups of grape juice. We could draw a picture such as that in Fig. 18–9.

Each cross represents a cup of lemonade and each circle, a cup of grape juice.

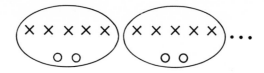

FIGURE 18–9

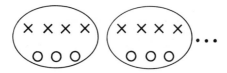

FIGURE 18–10

Figure 18–10 shows the ratio of boys to girls (second example), where crosses represent boys and circles represent girls.

The ratio of correct answers to incorrect answers as described in the third example may be pictured as shown in Fig. 18–11.

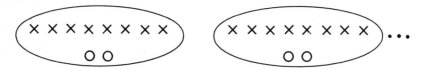

FIGURE 18–11

The language of ratio is useful because it encourages us to visualize clearly the relationships between certain sets.

For the four examples above, we can also say:

> *The ratio of cups of lemonade to cups of grape juice is the rational number $\frac{5}{2}$.*
> *The ratio of number of boys to number of girls is the number $\frac{4}{3}$.*
> *The ratio of correct answers to incorrect answers is the number 4.*
> *The ratio of free throws scored to free throws attempted is the number 0.4 (or 40%).*

Each time we compute a ratio we have the following situation.

1. *We have two sets.*
2. *We associate a number with each set.*
3. *We divide one of these numbers by the other.*
4. *We interpret this result and call it the ratio of the one number to the other.*

Example 1. At a party for 10 cub scouts, 80 cups of cider were drunk.

It is clear what our two sets are (a set of cub scouts and a set of cups of cider). The numbers we associate with these sets are 10 and 80. We obtain the two ratios:

$$80 \div 10 = 8, \qquad 10 \div 80 = \frac{1}{8}$$

The number 8 is the ratio of number of cups of cider drunk to number of scouts. The number $\frac{1}{8}$ is the ratio of number of scouts to number of cups of cider drunk.

The important thing is to be able to use these ratios. For example, we can say:

On the average each cub scout drank 8 cups of cider.
One cup of cider is only $\frac{1}{8}$ of what a thirsty boy scout is likely to drink.

EXERCISES

1. In each part of Exercise 1 two sets are described. Compute the ratio of the number of each set to the number of the other set, and then use each ratio correctly in a sentence.
   (a) The 10 cub scouts of the above example ate 60 doughnuts at their party.
   (b) A car was driven 240 mi on 16 gal of gas.
   (c) We drove 250 mi in 5 hr.
   (d) The column of air that stands above a table whose area is 1000 in² has a weight of 15,000 lb.
   (e) Ten cubic feet of water weighs about 625 lb.
   (f) During one year an insurance company collected $5,000,000 from its policy holders in premiums and paid out $4,000,000 in claims.
   (g) The sun is about 92,000,000 mi from the earth, and the moon is about 250,000 mi from the earth.
   (h) The radius of the earth is about 4000 mi, and the radius of the sun is about 400,000 mi.
   (i) One hundred families filled out questionnaires showing that they had a total of 250 children.
   (j) For working 80 hours, a laborer was paid $120.
2. In a certain class, the ratio of girls to boys was 5 to 4. If there are 80 boys in the class, how many students are there in all?
3. In a basketball game the ratio of field goals scored to field goals attempted was $\frac{2}{5}$. If 30 field goals were scored, how many shots did the team take from the field?

4. In a certain business the ratio of all money received from customers in one year to total expenses was $\frac{107}{100}$. If total expenses were $50,000, how much money was received from customers? How much profit did the business earn in the year?

5. In a certain field, the ratio of pigs to sheep is 8 to 3. If there are 165 pigs and sheep altogether in the field, how many sheep are there?

6. At a dinner party the ratio of number of people to number of pints of ice cream eaten was $\frac{5}{2}$. If we are planning a party for 240 people with about the same appetites, how much ice cream should we buy?

3. PROBLEM SOLVING BY MEANS OF THE LANGUAGE OF RATIO

In the first sections of this chapter we have studied the use of the language of ratio in geometry and in simple everyday situations. In this section we shall use these ideas to solve problems of several different types.

Example. Fifteen students drink 12 quarts of lemonade at a party. We are planning the same kind of party for 25 students. How much lemonade shall we make?

First solution. We compute the ratio $\frac{12}{15}$ or $\frac{4}{5}$. We *understand* the meaning of this ratio. *Each student drinks about $\frac{4}{5}$ of a quart of lemonade.* For our 25 students, we shall need

$$25 \times \frac{4}{5}, \quad \text{or} \quad 20 \text{ quarts}$$

Second solution. We compute the ratio $\frac{25}{15}$ or $\frac{5}{3}$. We *understand* the meaning of this ratio. *We are going to have $\frac{5}{3}$ as many students at our party as there were at the other party.* We will need $\frac{5}{3}$ times as much lemonade.

$$\frac{5}{3} \times 12 = 20$$

Third solution. Use N to stand for the number of quarts of lemonade our 25 students will drink. We reason as follows:

The ratio of *number of students* to *number of quarts of lemonade* should be the same at both parties.

Hence

$$\frac{15}{12} = \frac{25}{N}$$

We can write this equation as

$$\frac{5}{4} = 25 \div N$$

We see that 25 is the product of the factors $\frac{5}{4}$ and N; so

$$N = 25 \div \frac{5}{4} = 20$$

The method of the third solution is the one usually used in problems of this type. Our common sense helps us to write equations such as

$$\frac{15}{12} = \frac{25}{N}$$

Then, if we know enough arithmetic we can complete the problem. Equations like these, built up from four numbers, are called *proportions*. Skill in setting up these equations is important in science.

EXERCISES

1. Fifteen students eat 50 sandwiches at a party. How many sandwiches shall we prepare for 27 students? Work this problem by each of the three methods used for the above example.
2. The ratio of the weight of an adult elephant to the weight of a large sulfur bottom whale is about 1 to 30. About how many elephants would it take to balance one whale on the scales? If an adult elephant weighs about 8000 lb, how much, approximately, does a large sulfur bottom whale weigh?
3. The ratio of the speed of an artificial satellite to the speed of a rocket-engine plane is about 9 to 1. What is the ratio of the time that it takes a satellite to cross the United States to the time that it takes a rocket-engine plane to do so?
4. Given that a rocket-engine plane can travel 2100 mph, use the information in Exercise 3 to determine the approximate speed of an artificial satellite.
5. We find that we can drive 72 mi on 5 gal of gas. Our tank holds 22 gal. How far can we drive on a tankful of gas?
6. A certain city has 9000 inhabitants. 720 persons were chosen at random, and it was found that 254 of these persons were under 18 years of age. Estimate the number of persons in the city less than 18 years old.
7. For each inch in the height of the Great Pyramid there are about 2 in. in the height of the Empire State building. The Great Pyramid is about 755 ft high. Estimate the height of the Empire State building.

8. There are 880 yd in a half mile. A member of the track team ran 220 yd in 28 sec. *If* he could continue at this rate for a half mile, how long would it take him to run the half mile?

9. Explain why the equation

$$\frac{220}{28} = \frac{880}{N}$$

gives the answer to Exercise 8, and solve this equation.

10. Three cats catch 8 mice in one day. If the hunting conditions stay about the same, approximately how many mice would you expect 7 cats to catch in one day?

11. A distance of 1 in. on a map stands for 75 mi. The map distance between two cities is 7 in. How far apart are the cities?

12. In a factory, out of 500 parts produced 7 were found to be defective. About how many defective pieces would you expect to find in an output of 20,000?

13. The cost for tractor fuel used in plowing a 22-acre field was $17.25. What will be the approximate fuel cost for 100 acres?

14. The phone book for a certain large city lists 60 columns of Smiths out of a total of 8000 columns of names. If this city is typical of the rest of the United States, and the population of the United States is about 200,000,000, about how many Smiths are there in the United States?

15. Use your phone book to estimate the number of people named Jones in the United States. Estimate the number of people named Brown. Estimate the number of people with your last name.

16. Two cattlemen rent several sections of land for the summer months for $3000. The first man pastures 500 cattle on the land and the second 700. How much of the $3000 rent should the first man pay?

17. A box containing 18 oz of soap flakes sells for 39¢. About what price should be marked on a box containing 30 oz of the same brand of soap flakes? Use the equation

$$\frac{39}{18} = \frac{N}{30}$$

to solve this problem and explain why this equation gives the correct answer.

18. There are 1760 yd in a mile. There are about 100 m in 110 yd. About how many meters are there in a mile?

19. The ratio of the diameter of the earth to the diameter of the sun is about the same as the ratio of the diameter of the sun to the diameter of the largest known stars. If the diameters of the earth and sun are 8000 and 800,000 mi, respectively, what is the approximate diameter of the largest star?

20. A solution of 240 cc contains 12 cc of acid. How much acid is there in 100 cc of this solution?

21. What percent of the solution in Exercise 14 is acid?

22. In traveling a mile, a wheel turns 720 times. What is the ratio of the circumference of the wheel to one mile?

23. Twelve men can complete a job in 18 days. How many days will it take a crew of 18 men to do the job?

24. The ratio of the melting point of iron to the boiling point of iron is about the same as the ratio of the boiling point of iron to the temperature on the surface of the sun. The boiling point of iron is about 5400°F, and the temperature at the surface of the sun is about 10,000°F. What is the temperature (approximately) at which iron melts?

25. It is interesting that the ratio of the mass of a hydrogen atom to the mass of an average man is about the same as the mass of an average man to the mass of the sun. The mass of a hydrogen atom is about $37/10^{28}$ pounds. What, approximately, is the mass of the sun in pounds?

4. RATIO AND PERCENT

Ideas of ratio and percent are closely related. Suppose that we are comparing the lengths of the two line segments in Fig. 18–12 and wish to say that the length of $\overline{AB}$ is a certain percent of the length of $\overline{CD}$.

A B C D

FIGURE 18–12

If the ratio of $\overline{AB}$ to $\overline{CD}$ is $a/100$, then the length of $\overline{AB}$ is $a\%$ of the length of $\overline{CD}$. Let us choose a unit such that the measure of $\overline{CD}$ is 100. Then if the measure of $\overline{AB}$ is 63, we know that the ratio of $\overline{AB}$ to $\overline{CD}$ is 63 to 100, and the length of $\overline{AB}$ is 63% of the length of $\overline{CD}$.

You may find this way of thinking convenient when you wish to estimate what percent one number is of a second. For example, suppose we need to express 65 as a percent of 803. Think of two line segments, one 65 units long and the other 803 units long. Now choose a new unit segment whose length is 8 of the old units. With this new unit, the length of the longer segment is about 100, and the length of the other is about 8. We see that the ratio of the shorter segment to the longer is about 8 to 100. The length of the shorter segment is about 8% of the length of the longer segment.

This approach is much the same as thinking that

$$1\% \text{ of } 803 \text{ is about } 8$$
$$65 \text{ is about } 8 \times 8$$
$$65 \text{ is about } 8\% \text{ of } 803$$

EXERCISES

1. The ratio of one number to a second is 72 to 100. What percent is the first number of the second?

2. One number is 57% of a second. What is the ratio of the first number to the second?

3. The ratio of $\overline{AB}$ to $\overline{CD}$ is 39 to 100. Draw pictures of these segments. What percent is the length of $\overline{AB}$ of the length of $\overline{CD}$?

4. The length of $\overline{RS}$ is 45% of the length of $\overline{TU}$. What is the ratio of the length of $\overline{RS}$ to the length of $\overline{TU}$?

5. The ratio of boys to girls in a freshman class is about 103 to 100. Express this ratio in percent.

6. The ratio of number of students in one junior high school in a certain city to number of students in the senior high school is 527 to 1504. Express the number of students in the junior high school as a percent of the number of senior high-school students.

7. A first car has driven 184 mi and a second 200 mi on equal amounts of gasoline. What is the ratio of miles per gallon for the first car to miles per gallon for the second? Express this ratio in percent.

First segment   Second segment

FIGURE 18–13

8. In Fig. 18–13, estimate the ratio of the first segment to the second. About what percent is the length of the first segment of the length of the second?

9. Estimate what percent the length of the second segment is of the length of the first in Exercise 8.

10. Express in percent:

    (a) the ratio of 21 to 50   (b) the ratio of 195 to 300
    (c) the ratio of 450 to 1000   (d) the ratio of 54 to 75
    (e) the ratio of 1 to 200   (f) the ratio of 3 to 1000
    (g) the ratio of 43 to 25   (h) the ratio of 540 to 200

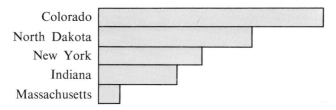

FIGURE 18–14

11. The bar graph in Fig. 18–14 compares the areas of five states. Estimate the area of each of the other states as a percent of the area of Colorado.

12. The area of Colorado is about 104,000 square miles. Estimate the areas of the other states in Exercise 11.

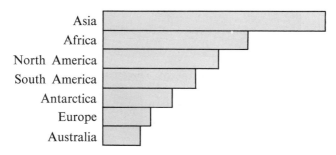

FIGURE 18–15

13. The bar graph in Fig. 18–15 compares the areas of the seven continents. Estimate the area of each of the other six continents as a percent of the area of Asia.

14. The area of Asia is about 17,000,000 square miles. Estimate the area of each other continent.

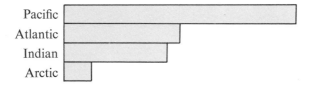

FIGURE 18–16

15. The bar graph in Fig. 18–16 compares areas of the oceans of the world. Estimate the area of each ocean as a percent of the area of the Pacific Ocean.

16. The area of the Pacific Ocean is about 64,000,000 square miles. Estimate the area of each of the other oceans.

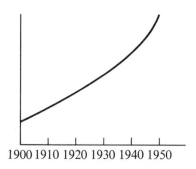

1900 1910 1920 1930 1940 1950

FIGURE 18–17

17. The chart (line graph) in Fig. 18–17 shows the relative growth in population of the state of Florida from 1900 to 1950.
    (a) Estimate the ratio of the 1910, 1920, 1930, 1940, and 1950 populations of Florida to the 1900 population.
    (b) Estimate the 1920 population as a percent of the 1940 population; the 1950 population as a percent of the 1910 population.
    (c) If the 1900 population was about 525,000, estimate the population in 1910; 1930; 1940; 1945; 1950.
    (d) Estimate from the chart the 1960 population and check your guess by looking up the actual population in some reference book.

18. Approximate 1950 populations for the inhabited continents are listed below. Draw a bar graph to compare these populations.
    Asia 1,314,000,000; Europe 533,000,000; North America 213,000,000; Africa 200,000,000; South America 108,000,000; Australia 8,200,000.

19. Heights above sea level of six mountains are given below. Compare these by means of a bar graph.
    Everest 29,141; McKinley 20,300; Popocatepetl 17,883; Matterhorn 14,705; Pikes Peak 14,110; Fuji 12,394.

20. Population figures for California at 10-year intervals are given below.
    1900: 1,500,000;   1910: 2,400,000;   1920: 3,400,000;
    1930: 5,700,000;   1940: 6,900,000;   1950: 10,600,000.

    Draw a line graph like the one in Exercise 17 to illustrate this information. Make a guess concerning the 1960 population of California and check your guess.

5.   RATIO AND PROPORTION IN SCIENCE

The ratio and proportion language is used often in scientific work. Examples are given below.

Example 1. A solution of 12 cc contains 1.5 cc of acid. How much acid is there in 100 cc of this solution.

We write the proportion

$$\frac{12}{1.5} = \frac{100}{x}$$

and solve for x, the number of cc of acid in 100 cc of the solution. Note that each rational number, 12/1.5 and 100/x, is the *number of cc of solution for each cc of* acid.

Example 2. As a body of gas is heated or cooled it expands or contracts according to a very simple law. If temperature is measured from absolute zero on the so-called *Kelvin* scale, doubling the temperature of a body of gas approximately doubles its volume. (A change of 1°K is the same as a change of 1°C, but 0°K = −273°C.) Suppose that at 300°K a body of gas has a volume of 1500 cc. We can find the volume of this same body of gas at 400°K from either of the proportions

$$\frac{1500}{300} = \frac{x}{400} \; ; \quad \frac{1500}{x} = \frac{300}{400}$$

In each of these proportions x represents the volume of the gas in cc at the 400°K temperature. In the first proportion the number 5 presents the information that for each 1°K unit of temperature there are 5 cc of gas. Expressed another way, each change in temperature of 1°K changes the volume of the gas by 5 cc, and we assume that the volume at 0°K is 0 cc. In the second proportion, the ratio $\frac{3}{4}$ presents the information that the measure of the first temperature is $\frac{3}{4}$ of the measure of the second temperature; hence the volume at the first temperature is about $\frac{3}{4}$ of the volume at the second temperature.

Example 3. As a light is moved away from an object, less light falls upon the object. We say that as the distance from a source of light to an object increases, the *illumination* decreases. When the distance from light source to object is doubled the illumination falls off to one-fourth of the original illumination. If distance is multiplied by a factor of 3, illumination is multiplied by a factor of $\frac{1}{9}$. A simple proportion describes this law. If the distances are d_1, d_2 and the corresponding illuminations are I_1, I_2, then we have the relationship

$$\frac{I_1}{I_2} = \frac{d_2^2}{d_1^2}$$

For example, if a light 3 ft from a spot on a table gives an illumination of 100 candlepower, then we find the illumination when the light is placed 6 ft from the spot by using the proportion

$$\frac{100}{I_2} = \frac{6^2}{3^2}$$

Example 4. A basic principle accepted in physics is known as Avogadro's law. This is the conjecture that equal volumes of any two gasses have; if their temperatures are approximately the same, almost the same number of molecules. There are interesting consequences of this law. Suppose we weigh a liter of oxygen and a liter of hydrogen at room temperature and find that the ratio of their weights is about 16 to 1. By Avogadro's law there is about the same number of molecules in each liter of gas. Denote this number by N; denote the weight of *one* molecule of oxygen by o and that of *one* molecule of hydrogen by h. Then, by Avogadro's law,

$$\frac{N \cdot o}{N \cdot h} = \frac{16}{1}$$

Hence, *the weight of one molecule of oxygen is about* 16 *times the weight of one molecule of hydrogen.*

Example 5. The rate of flow of current (I amperes) through a circuit when a constant electromotive force of a certain number of volts is impressed depends in very simple fashion upon the resistance (R ohms) of the circuit. If 40 amps per second flow through a circuit with a resistance of 100 ohms, then if another resistor is introduced into the circuit, changing the resistance to 200 ohms, the rate of flow is reduced to 20 amps. We have the proportion

$$\frac{I_1}{I_2} = \frac{R_2}{R_1}$$

We say that the rate of flow of current varies *inversely* with the resistance.

If we have a 120-amp current when the resistance is 80 ohms, then with a resistance of 200 ohms we determine the rate of current flow from the proportion

$$\frac{120}{I} = \frac{200}{80}$$

EXERCISES

1. At 340°K the volume of a body of gas is 80 cc. Find its volume at
   (a) 680°K,   (b) 170°K,   (c) 510°K,   (d) 100°K

2. The volume of a body of gas is 240 cc at 300°K. After being heated its volume is 300 cc. What is the new temperature?

3. The gas in a balloon occupies a volume of 3000 cubic feet at 350°K. How much will the balloon increase in size if the gas is heated to a temperature of 300°K?

4. A light 5 ft from a table gives an illumination of 200 candlepower. Describe the illumination if the light is placed
   (a)   10 ft from the table,   (b)   25 ft from the table,
   (c)   4 ft from the table,   (d)   1 ft from the table.

5. Energy from the sun falls upon the earth at a certain average rate per square yard of surface area. Compare this rate of flow of energy with that per square yard for a planet 10 times as far from the sun as is the earth.

6. The weight of a molecule of one gas to the weight of a molecule of a second gas is 20 to 3. The molecules of these two gasses combine to form a third gas. When we weigh 22 liters of the first gas it weighs about 20 gm.
   (a)   What is the weight of 22 liters of the second gas?
   (b)   If 22 liters of the third gas weigh 29 gm, how might the molecules of the two gasses have combined to form the new gas?
   (c)   If 11 liters of the third gas weigh 23 gm, how might the molecules of the two gasses have combined?
   (d)   If 22 liters of the third gas weigh 98 gm, how might the molecules of the two gasses have combined?
   (e)   In part (d) above, if you know that the 22 liters of the third gas contains 22 liters of the first gas, how have the molecules combined? How many liters of the second gas are in the 22 liters of the third gas?
   (f)   In part (d), if you know that the 22 liters of the third gas contain 88 liters of the first gas, how have the molecules combined? How many liters of the second gas are in the 22 liters of the third gas?

7. If current flows through a circuit at the rate of 60 amps against a resistance of 100 ohms, what will be the rate of flow with a resistance of

(a)   50 ohms?   (b)   200 ohms?   (c)   60 ohms?

8. In Exercise 7 what resistance is needed to cut the current flow to 20 amps? to increase the current flow to 300 amps?

6. HOW THE IDEAS OF RATIO AND PROPORTION LED TO THE INVENTION OF NEW NUMBERS

In the beginning of their study of geometry the Greek mathematicians believed that all comparisons of the sizes of geometric objects could be made using whole numbers alone. In all of our examples presented in this chapter we have made our ratio comparisons in just this way. Everything we have done, using the language of ratio, could have been done using the language of rational numbers. The ratio language has been a mere convenience.

However, as the Greeks studied geometry carefully, they discovered to their amazement that there are pairs of line segments whose ratios *cannot be described by whole numbers.* Let us see clearly what this means.

Let $\overline{AB}$ and $\overline{CD}$ be segments and $\overline{XY}$ a chosen unit segment. If the measures of $\overline{AB}$ and $\overline{CD}$ are 23 and 89, respectively, we say that the ratio of $\overline{AB}$ to $\overline{CD}$ is 23 to 89. If their measures are 14 and 31.2, the ratio is 14 to 31.2. In this latter case we have not described the ratio in whole numbers, but *by choosing a new unit segment* $\frac{1}{10}$ *as long as* $\overline{XY}$ we can describe the ratio as 140 to 312. If the measures of $\overline{AB}$ and $\overline{CD}$ in terms of $\overline{XY}$ are $\frac{51}{7}$ and $\frac{415}{13}$, respectively, then choosing a new unit segment $\frac{1}{91}$ as long as $\overline{XY}$, we can describe the ratio as 663 to 2075. It is easy to see why the Greeks first thought all ratios were capable of whole number descriptions. The Greeks believed for many years that: *For any two given segments there is a unit segment which is contained a whole number of times in each of the given segments.*

Perhaps it was by studying a figure like the following that the Greeks made the startling discovery that the italicized statement above is false. Figure $ABCD$ is a square. The circle with center at A and containing B cuts the diagonal of the square at E. Line EF is tangent to the circle and so is perpendicular to line AC. Lines CG and FG are perpendicular to AC and BC, respectively. It follows that $CEFG$ is a square. (Can you prove this?) Now a beautiful argument can be

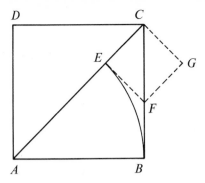

made showing that *there is no segment which is contained a whole number of times both in side $\overline{AB}$ and diagonal $\overline{AC}$.* We sketch this argument briefly:

If there were a segment $\overline{XY}$ contained a whole number of times in both $\overline{AB}$ and $\overline{AC}$, then it would be contained a whole number of times in $\overline{EC}$, hence in $\overline{EF}$, hence in $\overline{FB}$, hence in $\overline{FC}$. Therefore this segment, $\overline{XY}$, would also be contained a whole number of times in both side and diagonal of the small square *CEFG*. Now we repeat the construction and argument, getting a still smaller square such that $\overline{XY}$ is contained a whole number of times in both side and diagonal of this third square. Repeating this argument as many times as needed we come finally to a square whose side is *less than* $\overline{XY}$, and yet our argument leads to the conclusion that $\overline{XY}$ is contained a whole number of times in this side! This false conclusion establishes that we have made a false assumption. But the only possibly false assumption is the original one that $\overline{XY}$ measures $\overline{AB}$ and $\overline{AC}$ in whole numbers. Hence, there is no segment that is contained a whole number of times in both side and diagonal of a square.

Although rational numbers suffice for measurement in the real world, as this example shows they do not suffice for measurement in the imaginary world of geometry. And in many other areas of mathematics the rational number system is not powerful enough to meet our needs. The Greeks recognized that the rational number system was inadequate. However, it was not until the nineteenth century that mathematicians finally invented the number system that we call the *real numbers* and placed this number system upon a firm logical footing. The story of how this was done would lead us far from the basic objectives of this book. This is a story you can read in future years.

Chapter 19

PROBABILITY

1. INTRODUCTION

Every day we make decisions without being *sure* that we are right. Statements like the following reflect our uncertainty.

It *probably* will rain today.
The Tigers will *probably* win their game.
I *probably* won't get an A on the test.
The Yankees will *probably* win the pennant.

It is difficult to state precisely what such statements mean. Common variants of such statements are:

I'll bet you even money that the Tigers win.
I'll bet two to one that the Yankees win the pennant.
I'll bet dollars to doughnuts that I don't get an A on the test.

In this chapter we shall study carefully some ideas related to the theory of probability. This is one of the most important applications of mathematics. The theory of probability is fundamental for work in statistics. The exercises below are designed to focus attention upon everyday use of the word "probably."

EXERCISES

1. Someone brings you a box of 10,000 light bulbs. You do not know whether they are good or bad. You select 10 of these bulbs and screw each into a light socket. If a bulb lights, you write down G (for good) and if not, you write down B (for bad). Your record for the bulbs is:

   G G G G G G B G G G

   If an eleventh bulb is now selected, would you say that it is *probably* good?

2. A hat contains 3 red balls and 2 white balls. You will be blindfolded and will then draw one ball from the hat. Would you say that you *probably* will draw a red ball?

3. The situation is the same as in Exercise 2 except that you are going to draw 2 balls from the hat, one at a time without replacing the first ball you draw. Would you say that the second ball you draw will *probably* be red?

4. You have 4 pennies in a cup. You will shake these well and then pour them on a table. Do you think you will *probably* get 2 heads and 2 tails?

5. If, instead of 4 pennies as in Exercise 4, you have 10, do you think you will *probably* throw 5 heads and 5 tails? If you have 100 pennies, will you *probably* throw 50 heads and 50 tails?

6. You take a penny out of your pocket. It is an ordinary penny with a head on one side and a tail on the other. You toss it five times and record whether a head (H) or a tail (T) turns up. Your record is:

$$H\ H\ H\ H\ H$$

Do you think that on the sixth toss

(a) a head will *probably* turn up?

(b) a tail will *probably* turn up?

7. A biologist injects a vaccine into several rats and then exposes all of them to the same disease. If a rat gets the disease, the biologist records S (for sick), and if not, he records W (for well). He has the following record:

$$S\ W\ W\ W\ W\ W\ S\ S\ W\ W\ W\ W$$

If another rat is given the vaccine and exposed to the disease, do you think it will *probably* stay well?

8. The biologist of Exercise 7 exposed several rats to the disease without giving them vaccine. His record was:

$$S\ S\ W\ S\ S\ S\ S\ S\ W\ W\ W\ S$$

Do you think that the vaccine *probably* protects rats from the disease?

9. Forty persons are to be selected at random. Do you think that there are *probably* two persons in the group whose birthdays fall on the same day of the same month?

10. You know that there are five balls in a hat. A friend is blindfolded. He draws out a ball and holds it up for you to see. You record the color of the ball, and he puts it back into the hat, mixes the balls up, and draws another. You have kept the following record of draws, where B stands for black, R for red, and G for green.

$$B\ G\ B\ G\ R\ R\ R\ B\ B\ G\ B\ B\ B\ R\ B\ R\ R\ G\ B\ R$$

Can you say now how many balls of each color are *probably* in the hat?

11. Ten students have a gift exchange. The gifts are put into a box, and each student draws one. Do you think that *probably* some student will get his own gift?

2. SAMPLE SPACES

In this section we shall learn how to compute probabilities in simple situations. For example, you *probably* would agree with the following statements.

(a) If a coin is to be tossed, the chance that a head will appear is 1 out of 2.

(b) If a cubical die with the numerals 1, 2, 3, 4, 5, and 6 on its faces is to be rolled, the chance that a 4 will come up is 1 out of 6.

(c) If a ball is to be drawn from a hat containing 3 red and 2 black balls, the chance that a red ball will be drawn is 3 out of 5.

In (b) you probably reasoned as follows. Six things can happen when a die is rolled. Any number is as likely to turn up as any other number; so the chance of getting a 4 is 1 out of 6. However, you *probably* are not sure how to compute the chances that

(a) if 4 coins are tossed, two will fall heads and two tails;

(b) if two dice are rolled, the sum of the numbers that appear will be 6;

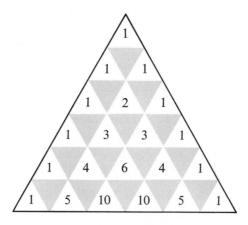

Pascal's Triangle, a number array important in probability theory.

(c) if three balls are drawn in succession from the hat above, two will be red and one black.

Instead of saying that the chances that something will happen are 1 out of 2, or 1 out of 6, or 3 out of 5, we often say that the *probability* that something will happen is $\frac{1}{2}$, or $\frac{1}{6}$, or $\frac{3}{5}$.

EXERCISES

1. The three numbers 3, 6, and 8 are written on separate slips of paper, and the slips are placed in a hat. We are going to draw out one slip.
    - (a) What is the chance that we will draw the 3?
    - (b) What is the probability that we will draw the 3?
    - (c) What is the probability that we will draw a slip with an even number on it?
    - (d) What chance do we have of drawing a number larger than 7?

2. We are going to draw two slips from the hat of Exercise 1.
    - (a) What is the chance that we will not draw the 3?
    - (b) What is the probability that we will draw the 3 and 6?
    - (c) What is the probability that one of the two numbers drawn will be the 8?

3. Toss a penny 20 times and keep a record of the number of heads that come up. Does the result of this experiment agree with your belief that the chance of getting a head on any one toss is 1 out of 2?

4. Roll a die 30 times and keep a record. You might get one of the following kind.

$$
\begin{array}{ll}
1: & \text{////} \\
2: & \text{卌} \\
3: & \text{卌} \\
4: & \text{卌 //} \\
5: & \text{///} \\
6: & \text{卌 /}
\end{array}
$$

Does your experiment convince you that any one number is more likely to turn up than any other number?

5. If you toss two pennies, you will get either 2 heads, 1 head and 1 tail, or 2 tails. Toss 2 pennies 32 times and keep a record as indicated below.

$$HH: \qquad HT: \qquad TT:$$

Does your experiment convince you that
    - (a) you are more likely to get 2 tails than 2 heads?
    - (b) you are more likely to get 1 head and 1 tail than 2 heads?

If you are in doubt about part (b), toss the pennies some more times until you have made up your mind.

When we set up an experiment such as those described in the exercises above and make a list of all the possible things that can happen, we say that we are making a *sample space* for our experiment. For example, a sample space for the experiment of tossing one coin is the set

$$\{H, T\}$$

A sample space for the experiment of rolling one die is the set

$$\{1, 2, 3, 4, 5, 6\}$$

If our experiment is asking a person the month of his birthday and recording his answer, a sample space is

$$\{Jan, Feb, Mar, Apr, May, June, July, Aug, Sept, Oct, Nov, Dec\}$$

Often, if we think carefully about a *sample space* for an experiment, we can reason out the probability that certain things will happen. If we plan to choose some student at random, what is the chance that his birthday will fall in a month whose name begins with a "J"?

For complicated experiments it may be quite difficult to set up a sample space. As an example of an experiment that is a little more complicated than any of the three above, suppose that we are planning to toss two coins, a penny and a nickel, and record what happens. We could make the sample space shown in Fig. 19–1. Each dot stands for one thing that can happen. The lower left-hand dot stands for 2 heads. The dot in the upper left-hand corner stands for the penny turning heads and the nickel tails. Our marks show that in six tosses,

1 time both coins came up tails

3 times the nickel came up heads and the penny tails

0 times both coins came up heads

2 times the nickel came up tails and the penny heads

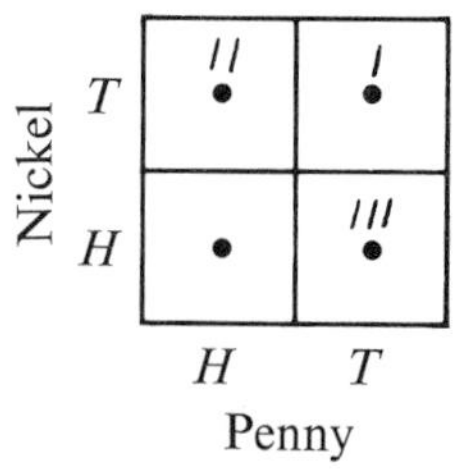

FIGURE 19–1

EXERCISES

1. Record the result of a penny-nickel tossing experiment as shown above. Toss the two coins at least 40 times.
2. Does the result of your experiment in Exercise 1 make you believe that any one of the four things is more likely to happen than any other?

3. A sample space for rolling two dice is shown in Fig. 19–2. In performing this experiment, you should have dice of different color so that you can think of one as the *first* die and of the other as the *second*.

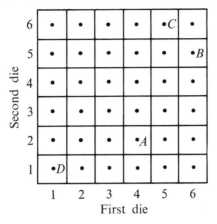

FIGURE 19–2

(a) What event is represented by dot *A*? dot *B*? dot *C*? dot *D*?
(b) According to the sample space, how many different things can happen if you roll two dice?
(c) What is the chance that the event represented by dot *A* will happen? the event represented by dot *B*? dot *C*? dot *D*?
(d) What is the probability that the sum of the numbers on the two dice will be 10 or more?
(e) What is the probability that you will roll a double?
(f) What is the probability that the sum of the numbers that turn up will be 8?

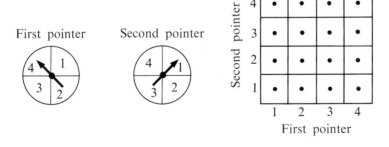

FIGURE 19–3

4. A sample space for the experiment of spinning two pointers is shown in Fig. 19–3.

(a) What is the probability that the first pointer will stop on 3 and the second on 2?

(b) What is the probability that both pointers will stop on numbers larger than 2?

(c) What is the probability that the sum of the numbers indicated by the pointers will be 6?

(d) What sum are you more likely to get than any other? What is the probability of getting this sum?

5. A sample space for tossing three coins, a penny, nickel, and dime, is shown below.

$$\{HHH, \ HHT, \ HTH, \ THH, \ HTT, \ THT, \ TTH, \ TTT\}$$

(a) Tell what event is associated with each symbol in the sample space.

(b) What is the probability that all three coins will come up tails?

(c) What is the probability that the penny will come up heads, the nickel heads, and the dime tails?

(d) What is the probability that exactly two heads will turn up?

6. From a deck of playing cards two cards are to be drawn in succession. After the first card is drawn it is to be replaced and the pack will be thoroughly shuffled before the second draw.

(a) How many elements are there in the sample space for this experiment?

(b) What is the probability that both cards drawn will be spades?

(c) What is the probability that one card will be an ace and the other a king?

(d) What is the probability that one card will be an ace and the other a king?

7. We are going to toss a coin and then roll a die.

(a) Construct a sample space for this experiment.

(b) What is the probability that the toss of the coin will produce a head and a 3 will come up on the die?

8. An experiment consists of tossing a coin, rolling a die, and drawing a card from a pack of playing cards.

(a) How many "points" are in a sample space for this experiment?

(b) What is the probability of tossing a head, rolling a 4, and drawing a diamond?

(c) What is the probability of tossing a tail, rolling an even number, and drawing a card from one of the black suits.

9. In driving to work a motorist crosses two intersections with traffic lights. At each intersection the cycle is one minute. At the first inter-

section the light shows green on the highway for 30 seconds. At the other intersection it is green for 40 seconds. If the motorist obeys the traffic laws,

(a) What is the probability that he will not be stopped by either of the lights?

(b) What is the probability that he will be stopped by both lights?

(c) What is the probability that he will be stopped by exactly one light?

10. The probability that a man of age 50 will live another year is 0.987. How large a premium should an insurance company charge him for a $10,000 term life insurance policy for one year? (Ignore extra charges for company expenses.)

11. In a history test a student matches 3 historical events with 3 dates. If he has no knowledge of the subject and guesses,

(a) What is the probability that he will miss all three?

(b) What is the probability that he will get exactly one date and event matched correctly?

12. A coin is to be tossed 4 times. What is the probability that on some 3 consecutive tosses either 3 heads of 3 tails will appear?

13. Answer the question of Exercise 12 if the coin is to be tossed 5 times.

14. A ship sails out to sea. There is one chance in three that it will encounter a storm. If it meets a storm, the probability that it will spring a leak is $\frac{1}{10}$; if it springs a leak, the chances are 4 out of 5 that the engines can pump the water out; if the engines cannot pump the water out, the chances are 9 out of 10 that the ship's air compartments will keep it afloat; if the ship sinks, each passenger has 3 chances out of 4 of being saved. What is the probability that a given passenger will be lost at sea?

15. A pair of dice is rolled. You are told that the sum of the numbers that turned up is less that 6. What is the probability that the sum is 4?

16. In a set of 4 light bulbs, 2 are good and 2 bad. You test them one by one. What is the probability that you will find the last defective bulb with the third bulb that you test?

17. In a room are two chests of drawers. There are two drawers in each chest. In each drawer in one of the chests is a silver ball. In the other chest there is a silver ball in one drawer and a gold ball in the other. You are to enter the room, choose a chest, and open a drawer. If you find a silver ball in the drawer opened, what is the probability that the other drawer in that chest will contain the gold ball?

Appendix

Appendix

THE SLIDE RULE

1. INTRODUCTION

The *slide rule* is a simple mechanical device (see Fig. A–1) used to perform certain arithmetic operations. Even though its accuracy is limited, it is extremely useful to engineers, scientists, and businessmen. Many computations do not require a high degree of accuracy, and for such computations, the slide rule, due to its small size and ease of operation, is an ideal tool.

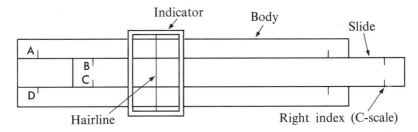

FIGURE A–1

An Englishman, William Oughtred, constructed the first slide rule in the early 1700's. Its construction is based upon some concepts from advanced mathematics that we shall not study here. *In this section we are concerned only with the mechanical operation of the rule.* You will learn about the underlying principles during your second course in algebra.

It was mentioned above that the slide rule is not a very accurate computing device. This does not mean that if we multiply 2 by 3, we will not get 6. On the other hand, it does mean that if we multiply 327 by 568, we will obtain 186,000 rather than 185,736. Of course this result, 186,000, would probably not satisfy a banker, and it certainly would not satisfy a laboratory technician who has to make a very precise measurement. However, there are many occasions when 186,000 is a satisfactory approximation to the product 327 × 568. For example, one might be computing the approximate number of square feet in a plot of land.

2. READING THE SCALE

The first thing we must master is the reading of scales C and D on the slide rule. These scales are identical and appear on all slide rules.

The left and right ends are marked with the numeral "1," and are called *left* and *right index*, respectively. The major divisions are marked from "2" through "9," and each of these divisions is further divided into tenths. Other divisions are given as space permits. Note that the section between "1" and "2" is not only divided into tenths, but each of these parts in turn is subdivided into tenths. Less detailed divisions appear as we move on toward the right index.

In reading the scale on a slide rule, one ignores the decimal point in a number. That is, the numbers 0.0157, 15.7, and 1570 are all indicated by the same mark. Of course, many other numbers have this same reading as shown in Fig. A–2.

1.57, 15.7, 1570, 0.00157, etc.

FIGURE A–2

Since we ignore the decimal point in reading the scale, we begin by examining the first nonzero digit (reading from left to right). For example, in finding a setting for the number 0.0027, we consider only the digits "2" and "7." This is also true of numbers such as 27, 2.7, 0.000027, 2,700,000, etc. In the work that follows, whenever we say "first digit," we mean "first nonzero digit, reading from left to right." For example, for the number 0.0203, the first digit is 2, the second is 0, and the third is 3.

All numbers whose first digit is "1" are indicated between the major divisions "1" and "2" and those whose first digit is "2" are indicated between the "2" and the "3." This process continues on through the digit "9." In locating the placement indicated by the second digit, we simply repeat the above process, using the smaller divisions between the larger ones (see Fig. A–3).

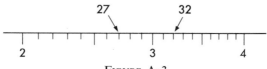

FIGURE A–3

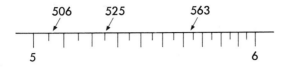

FIGURE A–4

When interpreting "three-digit" numbers on the scale, we usually can get only a rough approximation for the number represented in the third position (see Fig. A–4).

EXERCISES

1. Write three numerals to indicate each of the readings shown in Fig. A–5.

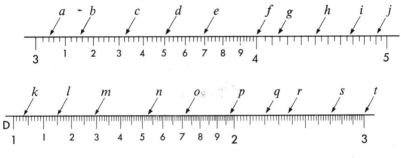

FIGURE A–5

2. Indicate the numbers below on the D-scale of your slide rule and check your setting with a classmate or your instructor. You can do this by using the hairline on the indicator.

(a) 123	(b) 645	(c) 300	(d) 856
(e) 343	(f) 179	(g) 528	(h) 950
(i) 60	(j) 600	(k) 0.006	(l) 0.0385
(m) 74.2	(n) 0.00396	(o) 0.849	(p) 2.63

3. MULTIPLICATION

If you have mastered the work in Section 2, you are ready to begin computing. We mention this because reading the scale is probably the most difficult part of learning to use the slide rule. Once you can read the scale efficiently, the rest is easy.

First we should mention that the slide rule is *not* an instrument for addition and subtraction. The main use of the C- and D-scales is to

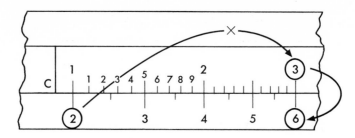

FIGURE A–6

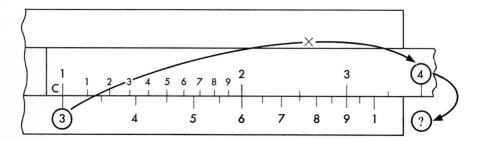

FIGURE A–7

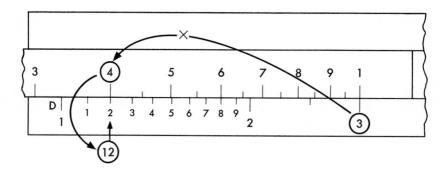

FIGURE A–8

find products and quotients. Other scales are used to find approximate square roots and cube roots. In our study here, we are principally concerned with multiplication and division.

The best way to learn to multiply on your slide rule is to work some very simple example like 2 × 3. Set the left index of the C-scale over "2" on the D-scale. Set the hairline on the indicator over "3" on the C-scale. Find the result "6" on the D-scale under the hairline (see Fig. A–6).

Note that if we attempt to follow exactly the same pattern to find the product 3 × 4, the "4" on the C-scale extends beyond the limits of the D-scale (see Fig. A–7). When this happens, we simply place the *right* index of the C-scale over the "3" (see Fig. A–8).

EXERCISES

1. Find the proper setting on your slide rule for each of the following products.

   (a) 2 × 2   (b) 5 × 3   (c) 4 × 2   (d) 6 × 3

   (e) 3 × 7   (f) 2 × 5   (g) 5 × 6   (h) 7 × 5

2. In Exercise 1, how did you decide to place the decimal point?

3. How would you indicate the product 10 × 10 on your slide rule? Explain.

4. Can the slide rule be used to multiply by zero? by one?

5. Can you multiply by $\frac{1}{2}$ on the slide rule? Explain.

For the problems in Exercise 1 it was easy to locate the decimal point correctly. For other problems it may be more difficult. We place the decimal point by mentally getting approximate answers. Consider the two products 1960 × 2.25 and 2000 × 2. Of course, we know the product 2000 × 2 is 4000, but if we examine the two problems carefully, we see that these products are "fairly close" to each other. In working the problem 1960 × 2.25 on the slide rule, we read the numeral "441." Knowing that our answer is near 4000, we conclude that (see Fig. A–9)

$$1960 \times 2.25 = 4410$$

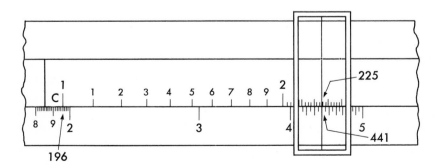

FIGURE A–9

The trick that enables you to place the decimal point lies in finding an "easy" problem which has an answer "close" to the answer of the problem you are trying to solve. With a little practice you can become quite efficient at this. Actually it is good practice to estimate the answer to many problems, whether or not you are using the slide rule. Estimates often keep you from giving absurd answers. Many times we become so involved in tedious computations that we forget to ask ourselves whether the answer that we get for a problem is reasonable.

Nearly all of our slide rule calculations are approximations. That is, we are usually limited to accuracy in the first three digits, since we cannot, in general, read more than three places on our rule. We shall refer to this accuracy as "three-place" or "slide-rule accuracy."

EXERCISES

1. Estimate the following products by finding "easy" problems which have results "close" to the actual products. (You should avoid using pencil and paper if possible.)

    (a) 958 × 3.16   (b) 2150 × 59.1
    (c) 7790 × .506   (d) 82.6 × 58.3
    (e) 3.03 × .123   (f) 659 × 176
    (g) .009 × 358   (h) .534 × 1920
    (i) 6.30 × 72.1   (j) 58.1 × 9100
    (k) .0389 × 61.4   (l) 8120 × 954
    (m) .0009 × 2100   (n) 4.26 × 7.65
    (o) 8.34 × 32.6   (p) 92.6 × 58.3
    (q) 39.0 × 603   (r) 106 × 19.2
    (s) 11.3 × .062   (t) 584 × 6.29

2. Using your slide rule and the results from Exercise 1, find the products in Exercise 1 to slide-rule accuracy.

3. If you think carefully about the relationship between multiplication and division, you may be able to discover the method for division. Try this on the problem 2 × 3 and see whether you can explain the slide-rule setting for 6 ÷ 3. If you think that you understand the problem, try your method on the following:

    (a) 6 ÷ 3   (b) 12 ÷ 3   (c) 5 ÷ 2
    (d) 15 ÷ 5   (e) 20 ÷ 4   (f) 18 ÷ 6

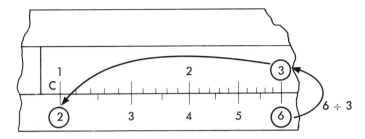

FIGURE A–10

4. DIVISION

Division on the slide rule is the reverse of multiplication. We can see this by looking carefully at an example. We know that $6 \div 2 = 3$ and $6 \div 3 = 2$ simply because we know the multiplication fact $2 \times 3 = 6$.

To understand the slide-rule setting for division, it is convenient to think of division as a multiplication problem for which we already know the answer. For example, consider the problem

$$6 \div 3$$

We should now think of the way in which multiplication is related to this problem:

$$? \times 3 = 6$$

All we need do is remember the multiplication procedure. That is, we read the product "6" on the D-scale directly under the "3" on the C-scale. Therefore by placing the "3" on the C-scale over the "6" on the D-scale, we can look under the index on the C-scale and find the number in question (see Fig. A–10). Note that the setting is identical to that for the multiplication of 2 and 3. The only difference is in the way in which we read the scales.

Here again, we locate the decimal point by considering a simple problem whose answer is close to our answer.

EXERCISES

1. The following exercises are designed to help you become familiar with the division procedure before attempting more difficult problems. Find the slide-rule setting for the following quotients.

   (a) $8 \div 2$ (b) $9 \div 3$ (c) $12 \div 3$

   (d) $18 \div 2$ (e) $20 \div 5$ (f) $24 \div 8$

2. Estimate the following quotients by finding "easy" problems which have answers "close" to the actual quotients.

(a) $589 \div 21$ (b) $871 \div 2.93$ (c) $54.8 \div 9.16$

(d) $548 \div 9.16$ (e) $548 \div 91.6$ (f) $78.0 \div 38.6$

(g) $78.0 \div 3.86$ (h) $780 \div 3.86$ (i) $780 \div .386$

(j) $780 \div .0386$ (k) $7.80 \div 3.86$ (l) $7.80 \div 38.6$

(m) $7.80 \div 386$ (n) $.780 \div 386$ (o) $.0780 \div 3860$

(p) $54.2 \div 37.6$ (q) $384 \div 1260$ (r) $9.32 \div 52.80$

(s) $.736 \div 1.05$ (t) $11.70 \div .063$

3. Using your slide rule and the results from Exercise 2, find the quotients in Exercise 2 to slide-rule accuracy.

4. Find a decimal representation, to slide-rule accuracy, for each of the following rational numbers. (Recall that $\frac{3}{8} = 3 \div 8$ or .375.)

(a) $\frac{5}{8}$ (b) $\frac{1}{7}$ (c) $\frac{3}{13}$ (d) $\frac{9}{7}$ (e) $\frac{5}{12}$

(f) $\frac{2}{9}$ (g) $\frac{17}{6}$ (h) $\frac{6}{17}$ (i) $\frac{1}{18}$ (j) $\frac{5}{53}$

5. Explain how the following calculations can be performed on your slide rule without the aid of pencil and paper.

(a) $(689 \times 107) \div 97.3$ (b) $455 \div (384 \times .462)$

6. Note that the CI-scale on your slide rule is simply a "backward" duplicate of the C-scale. Try to explain the relation between the C- and the CI-scale. [*Hint:* Note that "5" on the CI-scale is "in line" with "2" on the C-scale and "8" on the CI-scale is "in line" with "125" on the C-scale.)

7. Set the hairline over the "2" on the D-scale. Note that the hairline is over the "4" on the A-scale. Now move the hairline to "3" on the D-scale. What do you read on the A-scale? (Note that the A-scale is simply two "half-size" D-scales placed side by side.) Repeat this procedure for 4; for 8. Can you explain the relationship between numbers on the D-scale and numbers on the A-scale?

In this study we have only attempted to introduce you to the slide rule by explaining some of the simpler types of manipulation. If you have become interested enough to want to continue this study, you can find further instruction in booklets published by the manufacturer of your rule.

Index

INDEX

addends, 21
addition, basic facts of, 61
  as inverse of subtraction, 29
  key facts of, 63
  as an operation, 21
angle, 284
  acute, 320
  exterior of, 284
  interior of, 284
  measuring an, 319
  obtuse, 320
  right, 319
  sides of, 284
  straight, 319
  vertex of, 284
area, 305
  of circle, 314
  of parallelogram, 310
  of rectangle, 310
  of square, 310
  of triangle, 311
arrays, for ordered pairs, 35
  in mental multiplication, 82
  to represent distributive law, 48
  to represent factors and products, 38
associative property, of addition, 26
  of multiplication, 43
Avogadro's law, 346

Babylonians, 273
bar graphs, 343
base of numeration system, 4

centigrade scale, 209
centimeter, 208
circle, 275
  area of, 315
  circumference of, 301
common denominator, 163

commutative property, of addition, 25
  of multiplication, 42
  shown by arrays, 42
conclusion, 118
cone, 290
  base of, 290
  vertex of, 290
counting, 9
  in addition, 12
  in subtraction, 12
cube, 287
  edges of, 287
  faces of, 287
  vertices of, 287
cylinder, 291

decimal notation, 211
  in addition, 218
  changing to fractions, 214
  changing to percents, 245
  in division, 221
  expanded form of, 216
  in multiplication, 221
  reading, 215
  in subtraction, 218
deductive reasoning, 108
denominators, common, 163
diagrams in problem solving, 97
distributive property, 46
  shown by dot arrays, 47
division, of rational numbers, 180
  with a remainder, 87
  by repeated subtraction, 85

Egyptians, 273
equations in problem solving, 31
estimating, 101, 227, 242

factors of a number, 33
fahrenheit, 209

371

fathom, 256
formula for interest, 264
fraction notation, 139
  changing to decimal, 230
  changing to percent, 245
  improper, 174
  mixed, 174
  proper, 174

geometric figures, 274
geometry, 273
graphs, bar, 343
  line, 344
greatest common factor, 164
Greek geometers, 273

hexagon, 293
hypothesis, 117

"if . . . then . . ." statements, 107
income taxes, 207
inequalities, 17
insurance, 269
integers, 123
  addition of, 124
  division of, 132
  equations for, 123
  multiplication of, 132
  negative, 123
  positive, 123
  subtraction of, 127
interest, 264
international meter, 257

Kelvin scale, 345
kilometer, 255

least common denominator, 169
lines, 274
  intersection of, 278
  parallel, 287
  perpendicular, 320
  skew, 287
logic, 113
logical reasoning, 107
lowest terms, 163

magic squares, 183
measurement, 297
  of angles, 319
  approximation of, 271
  of areas of regions, 305
  of circumference, 301
  of length, 254
  of segments, 297
  of volumes of regions, 316
multiplication, associative property of, 43
  basic facts of, 75
  commutative property of, 42
  difficult facts of, 79
  key facts of, 77
  as an operation, 33
  shortcut method of, 91

Nim, 120
Nova, 1
  basic multiplication facts, 79
  key addition facts, 65
numbers, 1
  as ideas, 9
number line, for integers, 127
  picturing addition and subtraction on, 15
  picturing division of rational numbers on, 194
  picturing division and multiplication on, 52
  for rational numbers, 150
  for whole numbers, 14

octagon, 293
one, properties of, 39
  in division, 192
operations, as inverses of each other, 50

parallel lines, 287
parallelogram, 310
  area of, 310
percent notation, 237
  changing to decimal, 237
  changing to fraction, 237

perimeter, 98
pi (π), 303
place value, 4
planes, 274
  intersecting, 287
  parallel, 287
points, 273
powers of ten, 233
prime numbers, 110, 177
principal, 264
problem solving, suggestions for, 94
proofs, 111
protractor, 324

quotient, 88

rate of interest, 264
ratio, 330
  of angles, 330, 331
  of numbers, 337
  problem solving, using in, 338
  of regions, 331
  in relation to percent, 341
  in science, 345
  of segments, 330
rational numbers, 139
  addition of, 158
  decimal approximations for, 230
  division of, 181
  multiplication of, 153
  subtraction of, 181
real numbers, 349
reciprocal of a rational number, 187
"Recreational Math" sections, 19, 53,
  71, 89, 119, 137, 175, 197, 292,
  327
rectangular numbers, 53
reducing fractions, 163
remainder, in division, 88

sales tax, 266
sample spaces, 352
scientific notation, 233
septagon, 293
sets, 9
  in addition and subtraction, 22
  in division and multiplication, 35
sieve of Eratosthenes, 178
space figures, 287
  interior of, 287
  surface of, 287
  volume of, 316
statistics, 350
subtraction, by additive method, 69
  as inverse of addition, 29
  left to right, 68
  as an operation, 21
symbols, 1

taxes, 266
triangle, 285
  exterior of, 285
  interior of, 285
  vertices of, 285
triangular numbers, 55
truth table, 114

Units of measurement, 255
  for angles, 319, 322
  English system, 255, 256, 259, 260
  metric system, 255, 257, 259, 260

volume, 316

zero, 12
  in addition, 24
  in multiplication, 40
  in division, 41, 193